QUILL
of the
WILD
GOOSE

**CIVIL WAR
LETTERS and DIARIES
of
PRIVATE JOEL MOLYNEUX,** 141st. P.V.

assembled and edited by:
Kermit Molyneux Bird

Copyright © 1996 by Kermit Molyneux Bird

ALL RIGHTS RESERVED - No part of this book may be reproduced in any form without permission in writing from the publisher, except by a reviewer who wishes to quote brief passages in connection with a review.

This Burd Street Press publication
was printed by
Beidel Printing House, Inc.
63 West Burd Street
Shippensburg, PA 17257 USA

In respect for the scholarship contained herein, the acid-free paper used in this book meets the guidelines for permanence and durability of the Committee on Production Guidelines for Book Longevity of the Council on Library Resources.

For a complete list of available publications
please write
Burd Street Press
Division of White Mane Publishing Company, Inc.
P.O Box 152
Shippensburg, PA 17257 USA

Library of Congress Cataloging-in-Publication Data

Molyneux, Joel.
    Quill of the wild goose : civil war letters and diaries of Private Joel Molyneux, 141st. P.V. / assembled and edited by Kermit Molyneux Bird.
       p.   cm.
    Includes index.
    ISBN 1-57249-038-1 (alk. paper)
    1. Molyneux, Joel--Correspondence. 2. Molyneux, Joel--Diaries. 3. United States. Army. Pennsylvania Infantry Regiment, 141st (1862-1865) 4. United States--History--Civil War, 1861-1865--Personal narratives. 5. Pennsylvania--History--Civil War, 1861-1865--Personal narratives. 6. Soldiers--Pennsylvania--Correspondence. 7. Soldiers--Pennsylvania--Diaries. 8. Sullivan County (Pa.)--Biography. I. Bird, Kermit, 1919-   . II. Title.
E527.5 141st.M65 1996
973.7'448--dc20
                                              96-17600
                                                CIP

PRINTED IN THE UNITED STATES OF AMERICA

Contents

FOREWORD xiii

PREFACE 1

CHAPTER 1: INTRODUCTION 6

   INVOLVEMENT 6

   CHANGES 10

   MILITARY TERMS 16

   THE 141st REGIMENT 18

   BACKGROUND and EXPLANATION of JOEL'S WRITINGS 19

   TREATMENT and EDITING 21

CHAPTER 2: AUGUST AND SEPTEMBER 1862 24

   Letter #1 24

   Letter #2 26

   Letter #3 28

   Letter #4 31

   Letter #5A 33

   Letter #5B 35

   Letter #6A 36

Letter #6B 38

CHAPTER 3: OCTOBER 1862 40

    Letter #7A 40

    Letter #7B 40

    Letter #8 41

    Letter #9A 43

    Letter #9B 44

    Letter #9C 45

    Letter #10A 45

    Letter #10B 48

CHAPTER 4: NOVEMBER 1862 51

    Letter #11A 51

CHAPTER 5: DECEMBER 1862 53

    Letter #11B 53

    Letter #12A 53

    Letter #12B 55

    Letter #13 56

    Letter #14 58

CHAPTER 6: JANUARY 1863 61

    Letter #15 61

Letter #16A	63
Letter #16B	65
Letter #16C	66
CHAPTER 7: FEBRUARY 1863	**67**
Letter #17	67
Letter #18A	68
Letter #18B	70
Letter #19A	70
Letter #19B	71
Letter #20	72
Letter #21	73
CHAPTER 8: MARCH 1863	**75**
Letter #22	76
Letter #23A	79
Letter #23B	80
CHAPTER 9: APRIL 1863	**82**
Letter #24	82
Letter #25A	84
Letter #25B	86
Letter #25C	89

Letter #26A	91
Letter #26B	93
CHAPTER 10: MAY 1863	**95**
Letter #27	96
Letter #28A	98
Letter #28B	100
CHAPTER 11: JUNE 1863	**102**
Letter #29A	102
Letter #29B	103
Letter #30	104
CHAPTER 12: JULY 1863	**108**
Letter #31A	109
Letter #31B	110
Letter #32	112
Letter #33	114
Letter #34	114
Letter #35A	116
Letter #35B	117
CHAPTER 13: AUGUST 1863	**120**
Letter #36	120

Letter #37	121
Letter #38	124
Letter #39	126
CHAPTER 14: SEPTEMBER 1863	**128**
Letter #40	128
CHAPTER 15: OCTOBER 1863	**133**
Letter #41A	134
Letter #41B	136
CHAPTER 16: NOVEMBER 1863	**139**
CHAPTER 17: DECEMBER 1863	**143**
Letter #42	143
Letter #43	145
CHAPTER 18: JANUARY 1864	**149**
Letter #44	149
Letter #45A	151
Letter #45B	153
Letter #46A	155
Letter #46B	156
Letter #47A	158
Letter #47B	160

CHAPTER 19: FEBRUARY 1864 — 162

    Letter #48 — 162

    Letter #49 — 163

    Letter #50 — 166

    Letter #51A — 168

    Letter #51B — 170

CHAPTER 20: MARCH 1864 — 172

    Letter #52 — 172

    Letter #53 — 175

CHAPTER 21: APRIL 1864 — 178

    Letter #54 — 179

    Letter #55A — 181

    Letter #55B — 182

CHAPTER 22: MAY 1864 — 184

    Letter #56 — 187

    Letter #57 — 188

    Letter #58A — 189

    Letter #58B — 190

    Letter #58C — 191

    Letter #59 — 193

CHAPTER 23: JUNE 1864 — **195**

    Letter #60A — 198

    Letter #60B — 198

    Letter #61 — 200

    Letter #62A — 201

    Letter #62B — 202

CHAPTER 24: JULY 1864 — **204**

    Letter #63 — 204

    Letter #64A — 208

    Letter #64B — 209

    Letter #65A — 211

    Letter #65B — 212

    Letter #65C — 213

    Letter #65D — 213

CHAPTER 25: AUGUST 1864 — **214**

    Letter #65E — 214

    Letter #66 — 215

    Letter #67A — 218

    Letter #67B — 219

    Letter #67C — 220

    Letter #68 — 221

CHAPTER 26: SEPTEMBER 1864 — 224

    Letter #69A — 225

    Letter #69B — 228

    Letter #70 — 230

    Letter #71 — 232

CHAPTER 27: OCTOBER 1864 — 234

    Letter #72 — 234

    Letter #73 — 237

    Letter #74 — 240

CHAPTER 28: NOVEMBER 1864 — 242

    Letter #75A — 243

    Letter #75B — 244

    Letter #76 — 247

    Letter #77 — 249

    Letter #78 — 251

CHAPTER 29: DECEMBER 1864 — 253

    Letter #79 — 253

    Letter #80 — 256

CHAPTER 30: JANUARY 1865 — 258

    Letter #81 — 259

Letter #82A	260
Letter #82B	262

CHAPTER 31: FEBRUARY 1865 — 264

CHAPTER 32: MARCH 1865 — 267

Letter #83A	267
Letter #83B	268
Letter #84	270
Letter #85	272
Letter #86	273

CHAPTER 33: APRIL 1865 — 276

Letter #87	279
Letter #88	281
Letter #89A	284

CHAPTER 34: MAY AND JUNE 1865 — 286

Letter #89B	286
Letter #90	287
Letter #91	290
Letter #92	291

CHAPTER 35: AFTERTHOUGHTS — 295

AFTER THE WAR	295

Children of Edward and Rebecca Molyneux   312

Children of Joel L. and Elvira Molyneux   312

    BLACKS in the CIVIL WAR   313
    WOMEN in the CIVIL WAR   314
    HORSES in the CIVIL WAR   314
    PETS in the CIVIL WAR   315
    TENTS in the CIVIL WAR   316

APPENDIX: THE 141ST REGIMENT   **318**

    THE UNION ARMY, VOLUME I. (1908)   318

    MAJOR BATTLES of The 141st REGIMENT   320

ACKNOWLEDGMENTS   **321**

INDEX   **322**

FOREWORD

"I have often read of a battlefield, but to know is to witness." Joel Molyneux journal entry, 6 June, 1863. A characteristic of the successful television series, "The Civil War", was the sense of immediacy. Its authenticity was created by the inclusion of excerpts from letters, diaries, and memoirs of participants and eye-witnesses describing everyday events that, taken together, told the story of the traumatic sundering of our young nation.

This book chronicles the insights and outlooks of one such player, Joel Molyneux. He served as a private during his 34 months' service in the 141st Regiment, Pennsylvania Volunteers, in the Union Army of the Potomac. Joel's writings, from 27 August 1862 to 5 June, 1865, give us front-row seats at the dramatic events of the War between the States. In this play, he acts out the roles of himself, his family, friends, and acquaintances, as he strives to maintain a balance between Joel the Soldier and Joel the Civilian.

"My desk is an empty cigar box I picked up," Joel wrote. *"My candlestick is the bottom of a tin cup, and my chair is my blanket folded up."* With these and similar field expedients, using wild goose quills as pens and paper scrounged from any source available, Joel writes of the uncertainties of his life as a common soldier, and of his wishes for the quick end of *"this cruel war"*. On Saturday, 16 July, 1864, his journal entry read: *"The rebellion has now raged over three years and the end cannot be foreseen yet. O! The world of misery that has been endured and heaven only knows what is to come."*

His business-like handling, through his brother, David, of his back-home domestic affairs, was important early in the war. In their correspondence, they discussed disposing of some lumber, selling Joel's sheep and cattle, collecting his county-bounty, and paying his poll tax. Later, he tells of teaching a former slave, Stephe, to read and write. He records visiting sick and wounded comrades in hospitals and writing letters home for them.

Bachelor Joel discusses his hopes for the future with his beloved bride to be, Elvira McCarty. He had been her teacher in a one-room school, and was ten years older than she. Their courtship is limited to their exchange of letters, and Joel suffered the torment of not being quite sure of the depth of her commitment to him. This doubt was exacerbated by some undescribed problems they had during his furlough back home at Christmas, 1863. Nevertheless, his love for her remained constant, and inspired some beautifully graphic pastoral similes. He wrote this after discovering he had not read the final page of her latest letter: *"... in your letter, I failed to read the last page. It was only the more pleasant this morning. 'Twas like finding a ripe peach long after thinking them gone from the tree."*

Joel Molyneux creates the story of a real person, interacting with his friends and loved ones, while living through one of the grimmest realities of life -- war! His story is recreated by Kermit Molyneux Bird, who has lovingly assembled, and edited his grandfather's letters and journals. Joel's moral standards, devotion to duty, love of country, and love for his fellow man may now serve as a model to be emulated by us today.

John H. McLain
Brigadier General (Retired)
Army of the United States
Sarasota, Florida

Private Joel Molyneux, Company K, 141st Reg.

Private Samuel Molyneux, Company K, 141st Reg.

Cousin J. K. 'Doc' Bird

Private Ezra Little, Company C, 141st Reg.

Sergeant Richard McCabe, Company I, 141st Reg.

Lieutenant Colonel Guy H. Watkins, 141st Regiment

Colonel Henry J. Madill, C. O., 141st Regiment

Colonel Charles Graves, Provost Guard (1905)

Civilian Joel Molyneux, about 1865

Elvira McCarty, about 1865

Mr. and Mrs. Joel Molyneux, wedding day

Elvira and Joel Molyneux (about 1910)

Joel with grandson, Max, about 1914

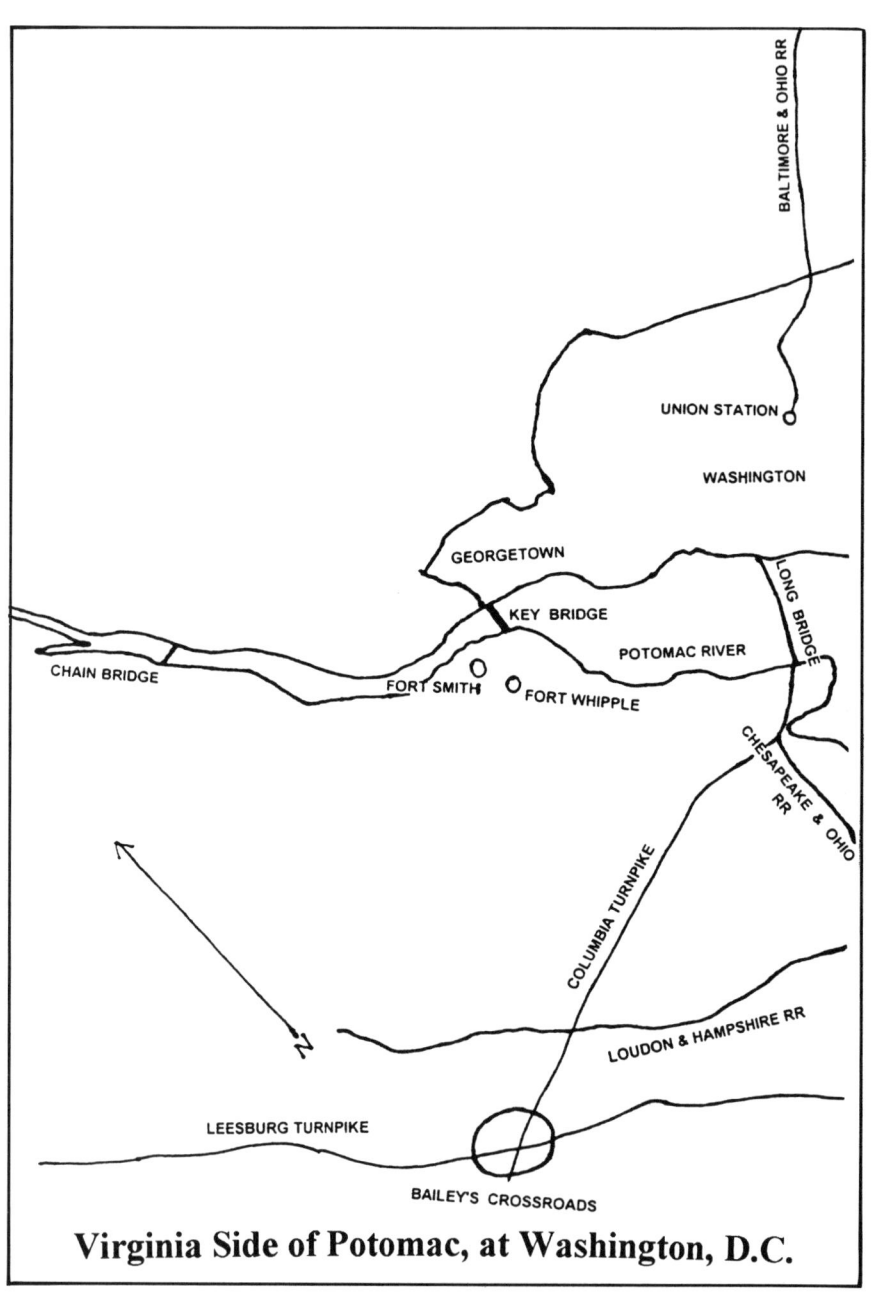

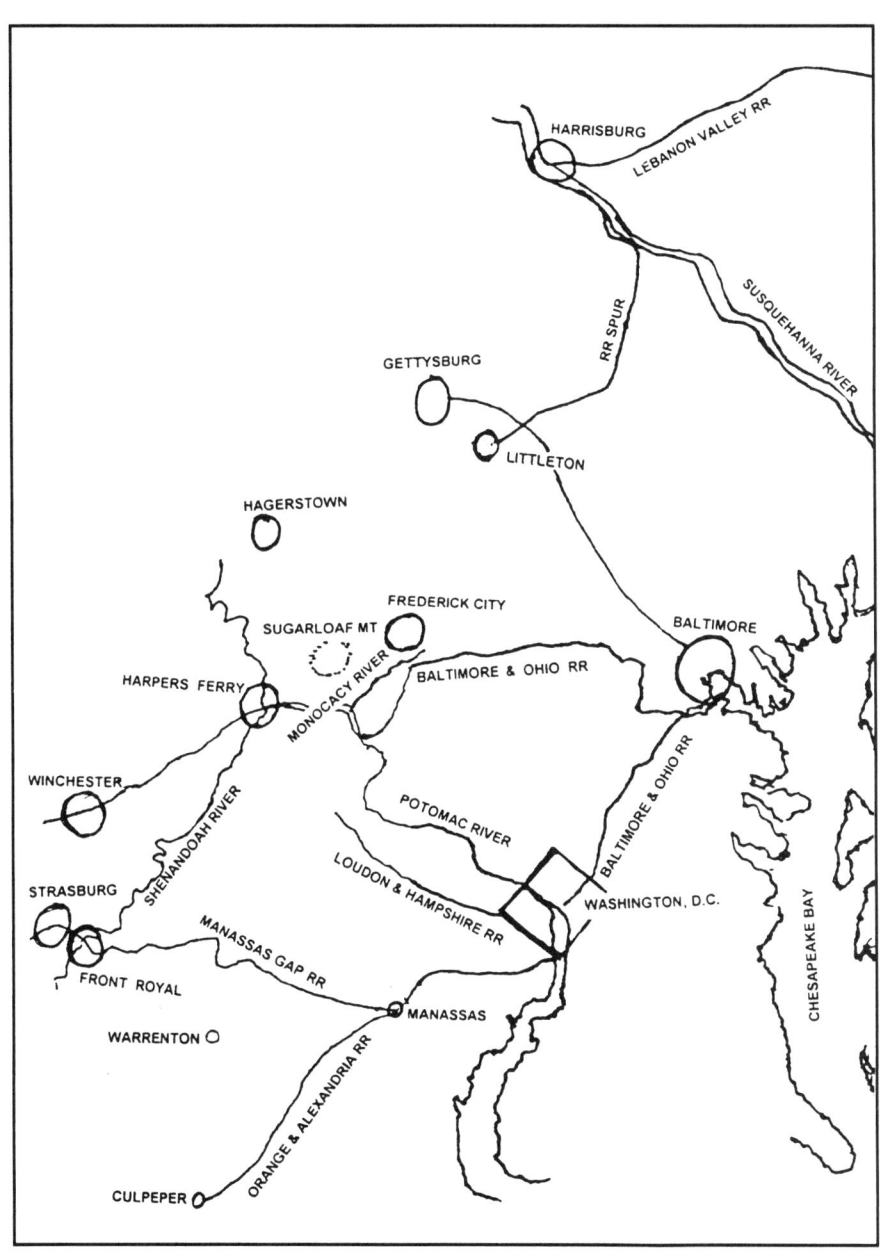

Northern Virginia, Maryland, and Pennsylvania

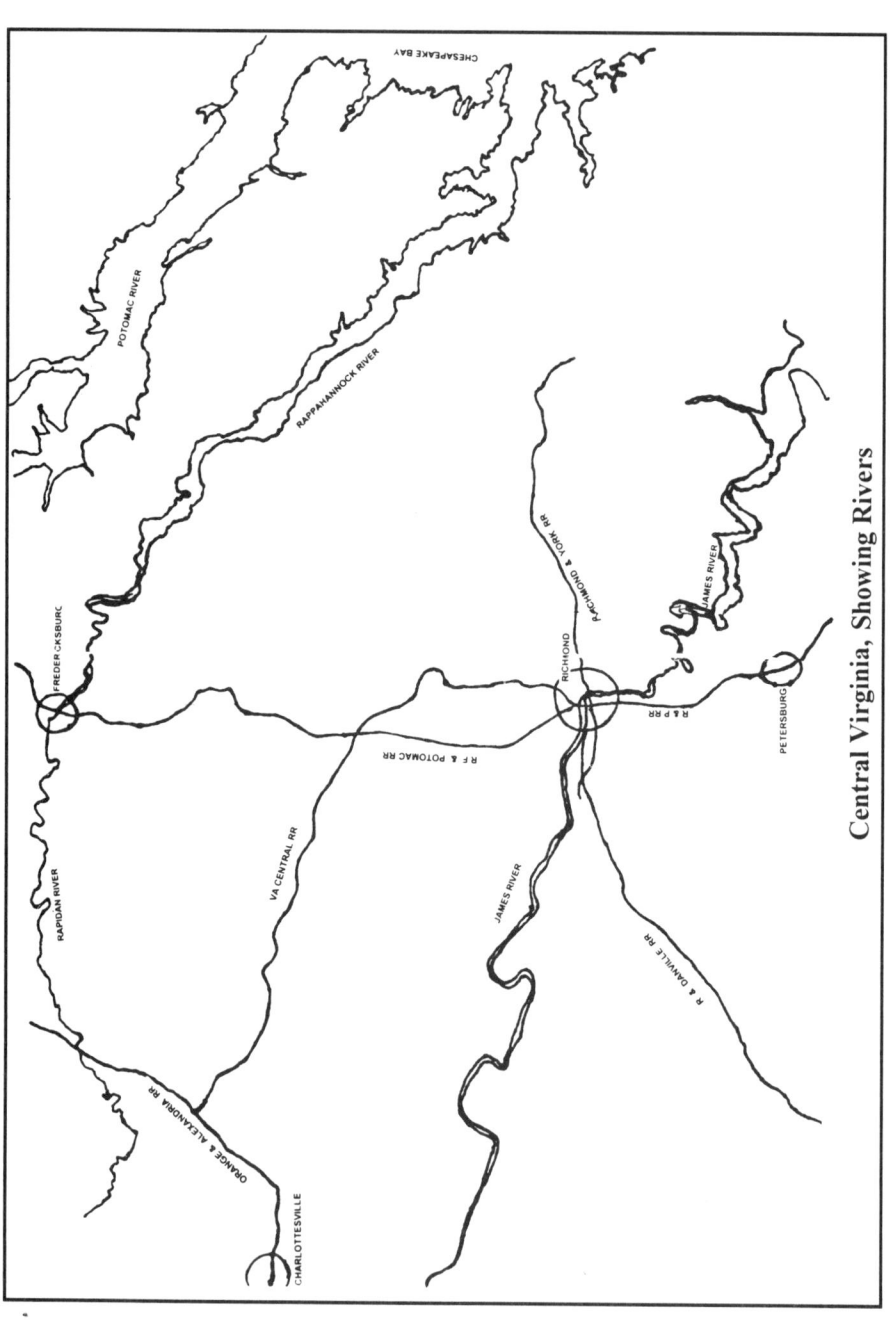

White Sulphur Springs Va Aug 11

Dear Brother

Your 2 last letters reached me the 2d was glad to get them though they had been some time upon the way my health is still very good the diarhea that troubles most people down he that have been brought up in the North I have not been effected with since last fall James Pardee arrived all safe to his Regt. I think it was the 30 ult. he seems to be in much better health & spirits than when he left us here. I saw George the 24th ult perhaps I may have written of it before, he is looking well & feeling finely W Snell & D Bryan were with him all right I did not get to see Mike although he was with his Regt— he was away after berries when I was with them he was taken prisoner at G— but paroled amediately the Gov— [ ] Regt [ ] We have now been encamped here now 2 weeks

Facsimile of Letter, as Handwritten by Joel

PREFACE

"God resists the proud, but gives grace to the humble." (James 4:6)

This book is the living story of 34 months in the life of Private Joel Molyneux, 141st Regiment, Pennsylvania Volunteers. It records his time serving with the Army of the Potomac during the Civil War. It is the true account of a soldier who discovered that what he first thought of as a romantic adventure, a skylarking affair, a picture book war, was a grim and deadly commission. With good cause, he later referred to the war:

"This cruel war! O! this war is dreadful! 'Tis horrible! If I could forget the scenes I have witnessed. O, when will wars and tumults cease? Our loss is great. A man was shot before our whole div. for desertion. It was a sad sight to see him march behind his own coffin to his grave, and then be shot. 'Twas really dreadful to behold!"

A former teacher, Joel liked to write. He wrote well! His creative outlet was to keep a daily diary and to write personal letters home, 136 of which we have assembled here. Observe through his eyes this June 19, 1864, Sunday evening camp scene at the siege of Petersburg:

"To my left hand, on a little knoll, is a battery in position with their hollow black mouths open towards the rebs. Behind them, in a hollow, caissons with ammunition. To my right is an ammunition train. A little front of this is our div. Hd Qrs. Then, a line of rifle pits, and on a little further, another line. Then a line of pickets. Now and then a cannon breaks out in its deep tones to remind us of actual war. A short distance to the rear I hear musical tones of a band as it is playing. Close by me is a grave marked with a pencil, a Sixth New Jersey Volunteer, killed June 16th.

O! There in the east is the moon! 'Tis full tonight! Surely this is at least the same as the one you see. Yes, there is the man picking his sticks. But, 'tis dark now and this is written by candle light 'Tis time for sleep. Mail goes out early in the morning. I must send this, so I close."

His September 29, 1862, letter to friend, Vi, closed:

"Good Bye, Elvira. May Heaven's choicest blessings ever be with thee is the wish and prayer of one that loves you better than he has words to express."

In January 1864 he penned this to his future bride:

"If I had no one to love me I hardly know what would become of me."

Joel joked that he would someday write a book. In January 1865 he confided to sweetheart, Elvira:

"And many other things they do, of which I will tell you when I write my book about school ma'ams. It will doubtless be a splendid book, and I think of having pictures in it, too. You will buy one, I suppose? You remember, don't you, the Molyneux Dictionary that was to be? They will both be published at the same time. This time I am writing a wild goose letter, or at least my pen is made of a wild goose quill, and it squeaks every time I make a letter."

The goose feather quill was a common writing instrument of the period. A wild goose was a free-flying bird. Thus, the title of this book seemed manifest.

As a free-flying writer, Joel was not obsessed by the closeness of sickness, imprisonment, injury or death; loneliness, strain, or misery of war. His writing freed him to maintain his health and stability at a time when others were deserting and losing their sanity. It helped ensure his returning home again. It released him to express what he saw and felt. That's the simple beauty of this book! It's not a Civil War history written later by an historian! It is simply a day-by-day account of one individual, in the center of events, expressing his feelings and telling of his daily and nightly activities, during that crucial period in our nation's history!

So, in a long-delayed, roundabout way, Joel wrote this book. My part has been to arrange his letters and diaries in chronological order, type, and present them in readable form. I edited a tiny bit here and there. I told who people were, and added some background, and explanations of the people and times.

By today's standards, Joel's language is stilted, Victorian, and liberally laced with misspelled words. Many of his sentences were incomplete. He used many passive verbs. But, I have retained his language as written, and have kept him the living person he was. He was not a professional writer nor was he a war hero. He was not given to or interested in heroics! He was just an ordinary guy caught up in the war. He spent much of his working day building or reinforcing his shanty, and spent many of his night-time hours writing letters and trying to keep warm.

Volunteering in the Union army in August 1862, Joel served with others in the 141st Regiment, Pennsylvania Volunteers. They were recruited from northern Pennsylvania. The majority of the soldiers starting with him ended up in hospitals, prison camps, and cemeteries. Many of his fellow soldiers were buried where they fell in the battlefield. Only a few regiments in the Army of the Potomac exceeded the casualty losses of the 141st.

The conflagration that swept the country during those four years of the 1860's scarred and burned indelible imprints on the lives of all concerned. The conflict lasted 1,500 days. Joel was involved for 1,018 long, hard days and an equal number of miserable, lonely nights. He had willingly volunteered for the assignment, so complained little of the hardships. Joel's writings do not mention it, but records preserved by the family include a Citation for Bravery. Private Joel Molyneux was indeed a war hero, but never thought of himself in those terms.

Joel wrote his first letter on the train going south from his home in northern Pennsylvania to Camp Curtin, a training camp in Harrisburg, Pennsylvania. A few days later, his 141st Regiment went to several training camps along the Potomac River in Alexandria and Arlington, Virginia. As the recruits of the 141st became trained, Joel wrote from Poolesville, Maryland, and from various camps along the Monocacy, Potomac, Rappahannock, Appomattox, Rapidan, and James Rivers. Their first battle was at Fredericksburg, Virginia. There, the 141st was with Franklin's Column, several miles downstream from the main action. They were being held in reserve and stood on a bluff where they watched the terrible massacre on Marye's Heights. Then later, in January of 1863, they took part in General Burnside's humiliating "Mud March" along the Rappahannock River, amid taunts from the derisive Confederates lined up across the river.

Later battles included Chancellorsville where Joel and others in the division headquarters ran for their lives. At the crucial Battle of Gettysburg his regiment fought gloriously in the Peach Orchard. There, on July 2, 1863, Joel lost his best friend and first cousin, Samuel Molyneux. They were at several locations following Lee's army in the Shenandoah Valley, at Kelly's Ford, and White Sulphur Springs, Virginia, where they wintered. Then they fought in the devastating Battles of The Wilderness, Spotsylvania Court House, North Anna River, Cold Harbor, culminating at the long, drawn-out campaign and siege of Petersburg and Richmond.

In the closing days of the war, the 141st Regiment saw action at the Battles of Sayler's Creek and High Bridge. The 141st was in southern Virginia, some miles south of Appomattox Court House, when Confederate General Robert E. Lee surrendered his Army of Northern Virginia to Union General Ulysses S. Grant's Army of the Potomac. That was on Palm Sunday, April 9, 1865. The 141st Regiment then had a long hike back to Washington, D.C. There, they marched in the victory parade, May 23, 1865, and mustered out a few days later.

During most of his 34 months' enlistment, Joel was on detached service as provost guard assigned to the First Division Headquarters of the III Corps. That division later transferred to the II Corps. Both were in the Army of the Potomac. He served under the many generals who commanded that famous army. Joel wrote of seeing Generals Birney, Sickles, Graham, Hancock, Warren, Taylor, Northregg, McDowell, McClellan, Pope, Burnside, Hooker, Meade, Sheridan, Sherman, and Grant. He also mentioned Lee, Jackson, Stuart, Hill, and many other generals.

President Abraham Lincoln and family reviewed Joel's III Corps several times. Joel told of seeing General Ulysses S. Grant ride by with his two small sons. Governor Andrew Curtin of Pennsylvania visited his corps, and camped with Joel. At war's end, President Johnson reviewed the II Corps for the last time. Booth had assassinated President Lincoln six weeks earlier.

Circumstances forced Joel to do things against his compassionate nature. Witness his diary entry, February 17, 1865:

"Hoffler of the 124th New York was executed today for desertion. A sad affair! I'd helped in carrying his coffin when marched through the div."

A diary entry April 13, 1865, just after Lee's surrender, adds a bit of wry humor:

"March in the mud, very bad game. Move slow, pass High Bridge. Stream up; have to wade, boys holler!"

Born and raised in Pennsylvania's rural Sullivan County, Joel lived on the family farm a few miles from the village of Forksville. His grandfather was Britisher William Molyneux, a weaver, who had been impressed by the British navy. William deserted by "jumping ship" and settled in Pennsylvania's uninhabited northern Pennsylvania in 1794. He was the first white settler in the area that is now Sullivan County. William bought his farm from noted scientist and writer, Joseph Priestley, who had purchased large tracts of land in that area. Joel's mother, Rebecca (nee Bird), was youngest daughter of Powell Bird and Lydia (nee Hannant), another early family that had settled in that Loyalsock Valley area. Rebecca was the first white child born in Sullivan County (January 1, 1797).

Joel's father, Edward Molyneux, had become an indentured servant at the time his father was impressed into the Royal Navy. Thus he was not free to emigrate England with the rest of the family when his father returned to retrieve them. He had to serve until he reached his majority (was 21). In a sense, both Joel's father and grandfather had been enslaved, or at least forcibly detained, and freedom may have been a sensitive issue to Joel and other descendants of William and Edward Molyneux. With that background, it is little wonder that Joel felt sympathy for slaves whom he met during his tenure in the army.

Mail call was an important time of day for all soldiers, and Joel understood that to get letters he needed to write letters. In almost every letter he wrote, he begged or ordered the recipient to write back. He corresponded regularly with 20 or more people, but the letters saved by his family and printed in this volume were to his immediate family members and Elvira McCarty. She was 16 when they started corresponding in September 1862 and 19 when he returned in June 1865. They married in December of that year. They were parents of six children who lived to maturity. My mother, Winifred, was their youngest child.

Mom related many stories about her father, Joel, and held him in high regard. To me, as a child hearing these stories, Private Joel sounded like a ten-foot tall general. It surprised me to learn, when I grew older, that he had been only a private. A photograph at the time showed a wiry young man with brown hair, light complexion, and blue eyes, weighing 160 pounds, 5 foot 8 inches tall. He stood ramrod-erect, giving the impression of being larger than he was.

The average or typical Union soldier was 5 foot 8¼ tall, weighed 143½ pounds, had brown hair, blue eyes, and light complexion. Average age at enlistment was 18 or 19. Thus, other than his age at enlistment, Private Joel Molyneux fit the description of a typical enlisted soldier in the Union army.

Elvira, of medium height, had abundant dark, glossy hair. Her face featured her deep blue eyes. She walked with a graceful gait and bearing. Joel kept that vision of her during his long marches and nights of loneliness! It sustained him! He always knew he would come home, and he even thrived under miserable living circumstances because he had a tangible goal firmly set in his mind. His October 22, 1862, letter to her clearly expressed his security dependence on her:

"When anything goes wrong, and I get despondent, it is your likeness I take out to look at and that countenance, so full of hope and cheerfulness, that I catch it immediately and look forward to the future when the wars are all over and we shall come back to the land whence we started. And then the thought of a girl and pleasant home somewhere with the one I love, and I am as cheerful as ever."

The writings presented in this book are a written kaleidoscope covering Private Joel Molyneux's service in the Civil War. Joel's last diary entry, June 5, 1865, heaves a huge sigh of relief:

"Are home at last, safe and sound, and my own man again!"

CHAPTER 1: INTRODUCTION

INVOLVEMENT

The American Civil War has been called The War Between the States, The War for Southern Independence, The War of the Rebellion, The Second Revolution, The War of Northern Aggression, or The War of Secession. Regardless of its name, a lot of fighting went on! The Union never declared war on the Southern states. Rather, the North treated the fighting as an insurrection or rebellion against the established U.S. government. The Southern states, though, formed a separate country, the Confederate States of America, that did formally declare war on the United States -- on May 3, 1861.

This four-year conflict caught the imagination and feelings of Americans more intensely than any other American war. Why? A costly war, it was devastatingly destructive in terms of lives and property. Even more, it was a personal war!

The conflict involved almost every person living in the United States during the Civil War period. This was true whether they were white, black, or Indian; slave or free; from the North, South, New England, Midwest, Southwest, or West. It involved farmers, villagers, and city-dwellers. They could have been male, female, young, old, Republican, Democrat, or Whig. They could be rich, middle class or poor; slave-owner, or abolitionist. Everyone was part of the moving events of the times. This involvement applied to people living then, and pertains to many of us living in the United States today. Some estimates show about half of present-day Americans have relatives who fought in the Civil War.

Many of us ask:

- What could the participants in that war have been thinking?
- What frame of mind caused them to kill their brothers so wantonly?
- What was it in the times that brought about such intense feelings of hatred?
- What basic fears triggered the conflict?
- Was there a curse over the nation that caused such fratricidal activities?
- Could the issue of slavery been resolved without resorting to arms?

These are complex questions, but we do gain some insights to answer them by reading Joel's thoughts as recorded here.

I'm personally connected with the conflict because Joel was my maternal grandfather. Joel had a brother-in-law, cousins, and several nephews in the conflict. We become acquainted with these as we read Joel's writings. We also get acquainted with Joel's brothers, sisters, parents, and grandparents.

Additional interest in the conflict is sparked because General JEB Stuart's cavalry, on their way from York County, Pennsylvania, to the Battle of Gettysburg marched through my home town of Wellsville, on July 1, 1863. Our neighbor, Aunt Ellie Wells, a young girl present at the incident, related this little, true story to us Wellsville children during the 1930's.

"The villagers of Wellsville, mostly women for the men were serving in the army, heard the Confederate army was approaching the village from the City of York. They wisely gathered together the horses of the locality, drove them over to Round Top, and hid them on the far side of the mountain. They also buried their family silverware in their backyards before the Confederate troopers arrived. When the Confederates did come riding into town, the women laid out a spread and served them breakfasts. The rebels were well-mannered, polite, and after they had eaten their unexpected breakfasts, paid for the food they ate. Of course, they paid for the food with Confederate money but that was the only money they had."

General JEB Stuart had instructed his troops: **"Behave like gentlemen!"** His cavalry unit had been scouting around various points in York County, and one of the places they visited was Hanover, in the southern part of the county. A shoe factory there had caught the attention of Confederate supply agents, for the South was running short on shoes. The local Hanover citizens took up arms to defend themselves, and a unit of Union cavalry engaged Stuart's vaunted troopers. General Stuart narrowly escaped pursuers by allegedly jumping his horse across a 15-foot ditch, with several feet to spare. He was riding his mare, "Virginia."

A third personal connection is that Union troops controlled our village of Annandale, Virginia. They occupied houses to the extent that the whole village was in a shambles when they left at war's end. The little white, clapboard-sided Methodist Church on Columbia Pike served as their horse stable, and soldiers partially tore it down for firewood. When Union soldiers vacated the village, they burned the remnant of the church standing. Reverend Wakefield, the former minister of the church, lit the match that did the torching. It was arson, true, but not of the malicious type. Joel related that his unit camped in Annandale, and then moved two miles farther south. That put him near my own property. There is still a remnant of a Civil War trench in our back yard, and although improbable, it is possible Joel's unit camped on our land. Connections such as these give us a personal interest in the Civil War. In May 1865, Joel mentioned marching through Burke, Virginia, crossing the

Occoquan River, and wading Accotink Creek. I attend church in Burke and our water comes from the Occoquan Reservoir. Accotink Creek is near our house.

The war's greatest impact was on the South, in part because much of the war was waged on Southern soil. This may explain why Southerners retain a depth of engrossment with the conflict rarely found among their fellow citizens in other parts of the country. Some Confederate units never surrendered at the termination of the fighting — they just disbanded and went home. Later, the government granted most of them paroles. So, to some Southerners, the war is not over yet. When you use the expression "the war," a Southerner immediately concludes you are referring to the Civil War. Some parts of the country have never completely recovered from the impoverishment of the war and the subsequent reconstruction era. Many Southerners read Civil War books and visit the Civil War battlefields with the far off hope that "maybe this time we'll win."

People now living in the Carolinas and Georgia were closely involved, for the ravaging Sherman army marched through their areas and intentionally burned their cities, villages, farm buildings, and fields. People in Mississippi had their houses and barns torn down to provide timbers for the bridges needed by the Union troops in the Battle of Vicksburg. Farmers in Virginia's Shenandoah Valley were in the uncomfortable position of providing their cows, horses, chickens, grain, hay, and wagons to armies of both sides.

Union troops sacked and burned Fredericksburg, Virginia; Atlanta and Athens, Georgia; and Charleston, South Carolina. On Dec. 13, 1864, Joel's journal reported: *Found a doz. of our men murdered for which orders were to burn every building within reach. Sussex C.H., etc. burned.*

Some cities in the North, as Chambersburg and Carlisle, Pennsylvania, were burned by Confederate troops. Some of the bitterest feelings resulted from actions that took place in Missouri, Arkansas, and Kansas. Even Indians in the Indian Territories became involved as both sides wooed them for support.

Yes! That war was real and it was close! It was not fought in far off places such as San Juan Hill, The Marne, beaches of Normandy, Korea, Viet Nam, Mogadishu, or Kuwait. Actions took place in our back yards. It was our war! Due to that closeness in geography and personal involvements, the time element of 130 years fades away.

Lastly, the Civil War was important because it cost so many human lives. Robert Meinhard, in the *Civil War Battlefield Guide,* lists Civil War casualties as follows:

Dead and Wounded in the Civil War, 1861-1865

	Dead	Wounded	Total
Federal	365,000	289,000	654,000
Confederate	260,000	194,000	454,000
Total	625,000	483,000	1,108,000

Estimates of Confederate losses may be low, for accurate figures are not available. For total losses, we must add deaths and casualties due to capture. The mortality rate of Union prisoners in Confederate prisons was about 15 percent. Of the 194,000 Union prisoners incarcerated in Confederate prisons, about 30,000 died. There are 12,912 marked graves of Union prisoners at Andersonville Prison. Of the 214,000 incarcerated Confederate prisoners, approximately 26,000 (12 percent) died in captivity in Union prisons.

Also, there was mortality due to disease, accidents, suicides, executions, murder, killed after capture, drownings, and unknown. Disease, in particular, took a heavy toll. Total losses may double the above figures. Thus, we may come up with over 2 million total casualties.

The casualty figures for the Civil War exceed the total casualties of all other American wars combined. The figures loom higher when we consider the total people. There were 22 million people living in the states that sided with the Union and 9 million people in the eleven states of the Confederacy. (This latter figure includes 3½ million slaves who were non-combatants.) About one of six American families lost a family member.

Cost in dollars? According to a report issued by the U.S. Congress in 1863, the financial cost of fighting the war was running at about $2.5 million per day. The cost to the South may have been somewhat comparable. Here again, though, accurate figures are not available. Later, during the 1864 and 1865 years, costs were higher. Dollar costs of the war continued for many years after the war. For example, Joel received a veteran's pension for fifty years, until his death at age eighty, in 1915. The state of Wisconsin didn't pay off their Civil War indebtedness until 1924.

The Civil War ended over a century ago. With that time interval we are now in a position to ask whether the war was worth one to two million young men's lives and the multi-billion dollar expenditure. Joel and Lincoln would have agreed the expenditure was necessary to preserve the Union and free the slaves. War seemed the only choice. I personally believe there were alternatives much superior to the fighting one selected by both sides. Decades earlier,

President George Washington had prayed a profound prayer for the United States:

> *Almighty God: We make our earnest prayer that Thou wilt keep the United States in Thy holy protection; that Thou wilt incline the heads of the citizens to cultivate a spirit of sub-ordination and obedience to government, and entertain a brotherly-affection and love for one another and for their fellow citizens of the United States at large.*
>
> *And finally that Thou wilt most graciously be pleased to dispose of us all to do justice, to love mercy, and to demean ourselves with that charity, humility, and pacific temper of mind which were the characteristics of the Divine Author of our blessed religion and with a humble imitation of whose example in these things we can ever hope to be a happy nation. Grant our supplication, we humbly beseech Thee.*

CHANGES

During the 34 months of Joel's involvement in the war, his attitudes changed and many basic attitudes of his fellow compatriots changed. We examine changes that took place in Joel, for they were typical of changes sweeping the country during the time of the conflict. We understand the tenor of the country as we become acquainted with him and the soldiers with whom he was associated. We also perceive specific attitudes and changes taking place back home in rural Pennsylvania during that time frame.

Personal Changes

Joel intentionally kept a part of himself emotionally detached from the war itself. His journal records daily war activities, but his letters were mostly about relations, welfare, and activities of people about him. These items seemed more pertinent to the people back home, so he dwells more on them than on the war itself. In several letters, he apologized for discussing war activities. One letter had two paragraphs discussing war events and four paragraphs talking about the advisability of raising turkeys back home and how capable he was at mending his socks. One daily diary entry tells of erecting a chimney for his shebang, and gave an equal amount of space telling he saw President Lincoln and his family in review. He mentioned his rifle only once or twice, but spoke of building and repairing shelters many times. Keeping warm was a major problem for soldiers on both sides.

Joel had willingly engaged himself in an unpleasant task that, at times, seemed hardly a part of the real world. He deliberately set his mind and discussed things he considered important. That characteristic allows us a brief biographical sketch of Joel himself. Later, we discuss some of the attitude changes that took place in the whole country. Finally, we relate some of the changes in methods of fighting and weaponry.

Joel was dedicated to the Union cause of maintaining the country's unity. This was the principal reason he enlisted in the army. However, the enlistment bounty money must have been an important incentive to him for he referred to it a number of times. Later, after Lincoln's Emancipation Proclamation, the slavery issue became important to him and to others for it gave them a "cause" to support.

Secondly, family ties were strong and were strengthened by his absence from home. He was homesick for his immediate family and his friends and buddies from northern Pennsylvania. He missed activities going on back home, particularly sleighing in the winter, and family, school, community, and church activities.

We form a picture of Joel assuming the role of older brother with the younger soldiers in the regiment. He was older than many, for most were in their late teens or early twenties. He lent them money and wrote letters for them. He also provided comrades in arms with news from home, and interceded for them where possible. He was instrumental in keeping several of his relatives from the guard house. He was genuinely concerned about the young soldiers from his area, and almost every letter home related personal stories and accounts of his companions.

Joel's letters, to and from the home area, were an important conduit of information between the war front and the home folk. News of promotions, deaths, sicknesses, injuries, imprisonments, desertions, and furloughs of his companions were of first priority in his correspondence. Joel's family letters were read publicly at family, social, and church gatherings. It is easy to envision the Molyneux family and neighbors gathered about the kitchen table, listening to a "Joel letter" being read aloud. During the Civil War many soldiers on both sides wrote long letters back home. Unfortunately, too few of them have been saved.

Joel matured spiritually during his tenure in the army. He spoke with great interest of the tent meetings of the Christian Alliance organization, and told friends in camp and back home of what he had learned from those meetings. During this same time period, there was a spiritual revival going on back home in the Millview area, and in a second hand way he became a part of that, too. Brother David and cousin "Doc", for example, accepted, as Joel expressed it, **"the Better Way"**.

As the Joel-Elvira romance developed during his first six months in service, Joel changed from a carefree young bachelor to a young man "promised" to his true love, Vi. By way of his letters, Joel actively pursued his romantic interest in Elvira. In the first letters, Joel told of corresponding with various old girlfriends. Later, he wrote Elvira he is informing former sweethearts he is "spoken for", and is now cutting off those other romantic attachments and devoting his attentions to her alone.

Private Joel Molyneux changed from a young man charged up and ready to kill rebels to a mature man greatly concerned about the welfare of those about him. He expressed sincere interest in the wounded, deserters who had been caught and were executed by the firing squads of which he was a part, Negroes who had been slaves, and particularly families back home who had lost loved ones to the "cause". One can almost see his tears of agony on the sheets of stationery as he discussed deaths, wounds, imprisonments, and sicknesses of boys he knew and loved.

Joel's provost guard experiences brought about change in his attitude towards Union army deserters. At the beginning of his tenure he thought of deserters as traitors. Later, as some of his relatives and friends deserted, he recognized most were reacting to the poor living conditions, fear of death, fear of injuries, and, even worse, fear of being taken prisoner. When living conditions were at their worst, Joel himself briefly considered deserting.

His attitudes toward the rebels changed. At the beginning of the war he was anti-reb. He was ready to exterminate them or at the very least punish them. Through his guard duties, however, he became acquainted with some of the Confederate prisoners (both those captured and those who had deserted), and found they were just ordinary young men like himself. He came to recognize the real enemies were not the "Johnnies", but rather loneliness, homesickness, disease, and mud.

While in the service Joel developed a strong opinion concerning the slavery issue. Before enlistment, Joel had never talked with a black person and probably had never seen one. As he talked with some freed slaves, however, his attitude became one of strong support for the anti-slavery stance. This attitude change was particularly noticeable after he became acquainted with one slave who had been "owned" for 101 years.

Although Joel didn't mention abolition, his basic attitude on the slavery issue agreed with that of the Abolitionists. Joel's church, The Wesleyan Methodist, had splintered off from the mainline Methodists in 1843 over that and several other issues.

He also agreed with his church in their attitude towards drinking alcohol. He was a teetotaler and decried overuse of alcohol by Union soldiers. Swearing and cursing bothered him. So far as we know he didn't use tobacco.

National Changes

At the beginning of the war, a prevalent view in the North was that the whole issue of secession was not to be taken seriously -- that when the hot heads of the South cooled off, the rebellion would collapse. After the fall of Fort Sumter and the disastrous First Battle of Manassas, however, the United States realized they had a full-scale rebellion on their hands, and unless it was curbed, the concept of the "united states" would perish -- there would be no more country as had been envisioned by the founding fathers. This alteration in thinking took place about the time Joel enlisted and arrived in Washington during the late summer, 1862. The Union army's poor showing at the Second Battle of Manassas solidified that new attitude.

Southern attitudes towards the war also changed. At the beginning of the conflict, there was confidence that the secession from the Union would be won quickly. The feeling was bolstered by the ease with which the Confederate States of America (C.S.A.) won the first battles, i.e. the capture of Fort Sumter, the two Battles of Manassas, and the Battles of Fredericksburg and Chancellorsville. The 1863 Battles of Gettysburg and Vicksburg were turning points in the war. Southern confidence dwindled, and from then on, permanent establishment of the Confederacy appeared to many Southerners to be a hopeless cause.

At the beginning of the conflict, the slavery issue seemed relatively unimportant. It was in the background, however, for it was one of the fundamental causes of the war. Years earlier, Lincoln had said that a nation could not exist half slave and half free. Thus, South Carolina seceded from the Union when Lincoln was first elected president. Slavery really did not become a fighting issue, though, until Lincoln released the Emancipation Proclamation, in 1863. That proclamation stated all slaves under the Confederacy were from then on "forever free". In itself, the proclamation statement did not free any slaves, because it applied only to rebellious areas the Federal government did not then control.

Nevertheless, The Emancipation Proclamation put President Lincoln and the Federal government in the camp of the Abolitionists who were in favor of freeing the slaves without compensation to their owners. The Proclamation did something more important for the North. It gave Northern soldiers a "cause". One reason the Southern soldiers did well in fighting, in the early years of the war, was that they had a "cause" — a new government and a new country of their own separate from the dominant Northern states. In some ways, their "cause" was similar to the one that had united the 13 colonies during the War of the Revolution, against the overbearing, non-responsive, British monarchy.

Three postwar constitutional amendments 13, 14, and 15 (1865 to 1870) put the force of law into the slavery, citizenship, and voting rights issues.

A chivalrous attitude, prevalent at the beginning of the war, diminished as the fighting became serious. Early in the war, pickets on duty refused to shoot each other, even though they were within rifle range. (Note Joel's letters written shortly after the Battle of Fredericksburg.) Later in the war, sharpshooters climbed trees and became adept at picking off enemy officers in their own camps 100 to 200 yards away. Romantic and daring dashes, as practiced so successfully by General JEB Stuart and John Mosby's Rangers (43rd Battalion of Virginia Cavalry), were slowed and some discontinued as it became more difficult to maintain a cavalry unit due to a shortage of horses and forage.

A major change took place in both Northern and Southern armies in their recruitment policies. At the start of the conflict, both sides depended on the volunteer system, but in the middle of the conflict both sides changed to a draft system. Joel reflects some of the problems of the draft system, such as the recognition of religious pacifists. Girlfriend Elvira McCarty was of a Quaker family who were pacifists. When Quakers were drafted, the question arose as to what should be done with those draftees who refused to kill another human being for any reason. Joel felt they should be required to serve, but be able to spend their service time working in hospitals, supply depots, etc. Towards the end of the war the Confederacy was drafting 15- and 16-year-old boys. In one letter, Joel mentioned some 15-year-old Confederate deserters who had been drafted at their local churches a week earlier.

At the beginning of the war, prisoners were exchanged on a man for man basis. However, towards the end of the war the North discontinued trading prisoners. They recognized that the practice helped the South more than the North, for the North had more reserves to draw upon. Also, the policy of releasing a prisoner to allow him to go home and not return to the army (parole) was discontinued by both sides during the conflict.

Military Changes

Methods of waging war changed and in those few short years much of the older style of fighting became outdated as newer weapons and techniques replaced the old. Fighting techniques and implements of war changed. As an example, infantry firearms changed from smooth bore to rifled bore. Ammunition changed from round balls to oblong bullets that were hollow at their base (Minies, or Minie balls, named after the French officer who had invented them in 1859). They expanded during their firing and provided a tighter fit in the muzzle-loading rifle barrel which gave greater accuracy, range, and velocity.

Due to the greater range of small arms, the old Napoleonic War concept of lining up troops abreast and openly charging the enemy position with wave advances became out-dated. When wave advances were used during the Civil War, the results were generally disastrous. Witness the Union losses at Marye's Hill at the Battle of Fredericksburg and the Confederate losses at the Peach Orchard in the Battle of Gettysburg.

Trenches, redoubts, and other defensive techniques became common. Both sides became aware that a defensive army had an advantage over offensive troops.

Improvements in hand-held firearms made obsolete the bayonet and sword that had been used since the Middle Ages. During this time period the paper cartridge was developed and used by both sides in the war. It was invented by King Adolphus of Sweden. The percussion cap, a small metal cap containing an explosive element, was used to fire rifles and pistols. It was the invention of Alexander Forsyth, a Scottish minister. Flame throwers came into use.

Other examples include the development of iron clad vessels such as the *Merrimac* (renamed *Virginia* by the Confederates) and *Monitor*, and the first submarines. Other inventions and developments included snorkels, periscopes, watercap time fuses, and screw propellers.

On land, there were improvements in artillery, land mines, use of railroads to transport troops and supplies, and cannons mounted on railway cars. The most famous rail car cannon was a 13-inch mortar nicknamed the "Dictator". There were improvements in artillery rifles. Rifled cannon were first used in siege warfare during the attack against Fort Pulaski. The capture of that Southern fort is the story of the elimination of Savannah, Georgia as a Confederate seaport. In April 1862, three of those formidable new weapons were advantageously used to breach Fort Pulaski's walls within 36 hours, forcing the garrison to surrender, and closing the important Savannah port.

Five different machine guns were used during the war. The most successful were the Union's Ager Repeating Gun and the Confederate Williams Rapid-fire Gun. The Gatling rapid fire gun came along late in the war, but its use was limited.

Then, there was the use of the telegraph for strategic military communications, wire entanglements, development of photography, and use of manned balloons for observation and for directing artillery fire. Rail transportation of both troops and supplies became common.

Aerial reconnaissance, from balloons, was used by both sides. An anti-aircraft gun was developed by the Union to shoot down Confederate balloons during the Peninsula campaign, but was unsuccessful in hitting any of them.

Although not a technological development, the Federal income tax came into use during the Civil War.

There may have been more technological developments initiated during that four-year conflict than during any previous war.

MILITARY TERMS

Command structure of the Union army during the early years of Joel's service, showing Joel's position.

Army of the Potomac (of the several Union armies). At Gettysburg, the Army of the Potomac was comprised of seven corps: 1, 2, 3, 5, 6, 11, and 12.

III Corps (two to twelve corps to an army.) At Gettysburg, the **III Corps** had 10,675 men.

First Division (two to five divisions to a corps).

First Brigade (two to six brigades to a division).

141st Regiment (two to ten regiments to a brigade). A full regiment had 1,000 men, commanded by a colonel. At Gettysburg, the **141st Regiment** went into battle with 200 men and nine officers.

Company K (ten companies to a regiment). A full company had 100 men, and was commanded by a captain. At Gettysburg, Joel's **Company K** went into battle with 25 men, and 18 of them were killed or wounded.

In terms of actual body-count, there was always a shortage of men. Few regiments had the 1,000 men needed for full strength. Because of battle casualties and losses through sickness, captures, and desertions, many regiments operated at 25 to 50 percent strength. For example, the 141st Regiment began with 955 men in August 1862. It lost 235 men at Chancellorsville and 136 at Gettysburg. At one point during the Battle of Gettysburg, the 141st had only 50 effectives. During that battle, at one roll call, when they called Company K, one man jumped up and hollered, "I'm Company

K!" Others however, who had been separated from the regiment, turned up later.

Forage, as a noun, meant hay or grain for horses or mules. The verb forage meant to search for food or feed.

A **parole** was a gentleman's promise, made by a captured soldier, that if his captors let him go home, he would not bear arms against them again.

Mortars and **howitzers** were artillery guns with short barrels and large bore, used to lob shells a short distance over obstacles. **Unlimber** meant to detach a cannon or artillery piece from the **limber** (two-wheeled cart to haul the gun). A **caisson** was a two- or four-wheeled cart used to haul ammunition. Of course, caissons went along with their artillery pieces, and necessarily stayed close to them. Sometimes limbers and caissons were hooked together and pulled by one team.

The principal rifle of the war was the U.S. rifle musket, commonly called the **Springfield Rifle**. It was used on both sides. Over 1.5 million Models 1861 and 1863 Springfields were manufactured during the war. It was a muzzle-loader of .58 caliber, had a range of about 450 yards, and weighed 9.75 pounds.

Works was a general term to describe defensive fortifications of all kinds. A **redoubt** was a small enclosed defensive position to hide behind.

A **corduroy** (noun) was a road that had split logs laid crosswise to provide footing and support in wet areas. To **corduroy** (verb) meant to build such a road surface of split logs. A **double corduroy** meant a double-width roadway, for two-way traffic.

A **shebang** (shanty) was a make-shift, temporary shack made of tree branches, fence rails, or any other convenient material to keep out the wind and rain. It was about three feet high, and had pup tents draped over the top and sides. Soldiers spread their combined blankets under and over themselves, rather than each individual wrapping up in his own blanket. Soldiers slept in their shebangs, side by side, spoon-style, and if one turned over, they all had to turn. (Shebang comes from the Irish "shebeen" -- an illegal or unlicensed drinking place. The word shebang has changed meaning since the Civil War. It is now used to mean a contrivance, concern, or affair.)

A **sharpshooter** was a rifle marksman many of whom climbed trees and picked off enemy officers across the lines. Many generals on both sides were killed in that manner. A **picket** was one or more sentries assigned to the perimeter of an army position to give warning or protection from enemy movements. Sometimes a whole regiment or brigade would be on picket.

A **trooper** was a cavalry man. His horse gave him speed, surprise, and elusiveness.

Horses: Infantry horses were ridden by officers, orderlies, and messengers. They were comparable to our present-day jeeps. Horses, plus oxen and mules, pulled artillery limbers, ammunition caissons, supply wagons, pontoon bridges on wheels, mail and delivery carts, and ambulances. Those vehicles were comparable to our present-day trucks. No one knows how many horses served in the armies or were killed during the Civil War, but it must have been in the hundreds of thousands. There was no way to keep an accurate tally for when a horse was lost, one was stolen to replace it. Horses ate a lot, and it was difficult maintaining feed for them.

Gear: Union troops, when out on a march, stripped down to the bare essentials, but even then they carried about 60 pounds of gear. Of course, they had a haversack and knapsack. Knapsacks were worn on the back, and haversacks were slung over one shoulder. Haversacks were used to carry rations and supplies and the knapsacks held extra clothing. Also, the marching troops had a blanket roll (gray, regulation), overcoat, canteen, gun, cartridge belt with box holding 40 rounds, and of course the half tent. In addition, soldiers on the march would carry their own personal possessions. Joel's included extra clothes, chess set, writing gear, photographs, little bags of salt, pepper, sugar, and his carving tools.

The Civil War foot soldiers also carried their eating utensils (tin fork, knife, spoon, cup, and plate). No provision was made for washing these utensils, and sometimes their cutlery would go for weeks without a cleaning --- other than wiping off with leaves or grass. If the scum got too thick on the eating tools that could be taken care of by jabbing them down in the earth a few times. Is there any wonder that stomach and intestinal diseases were so prevalent? Little clothes washing was done. Clothes once taken off were parted with forever.

Confederate soldiers had similar equipment, although not so much nor so good. For example, most of their canteens were made of wood rather than tin. Much of their equipment, including many of their rifles, was similar to Union issue, obtained from dead, wounded, or captured Union soldiers.

THE 141st REGIMENT

Officially, Private Joel Molyneux was in the 141st Regiment during the whole period of his enlistment. Physically, though, he was on detached service from the regiment and was assigned to the provost guard of the headquarters of his division. In that position he kept in close contact with his regiment. He seldom marched with them, though, and did not participate in the actual battle fighting in which they were involved.

Several historical books describe the battles and activities of the 141st: *The History of the Hundred Forty First Regiment,* David Craft, 1885; *The History of Bradford County, Pennsylvania,* Samuel P. Bates, and *Personal Reminiscences of the War* by J. D. Bloodgood, Late Sergeant, Co. I, Hunt and Eaton, New York, 1893. There is also an interesting unpublished account of Sergeant McCabe's memories of his nine months in the 141st Regiment. Colonel Henry J. Madill kept a diary during his tenure during the war. All five are on file at the Archives Library, Army War College, Carlisle, Pennsylvania.

While casualty figures are not necessarily proof of fighting quality, it is one way to measure the ability or involvement of fighting units. Among Union infantry regiments, the 141st had the second greatest percentage casualty loss in a single battle: Gettysburg. There, the 141st had 75.7 percent casualties. Considering that the 141st was in the battle only two days, July 2 and 3, that's a high percentage. Highest percent casualties in a single battle was the 1st Minnesota, 82 percent casualties, also at Gettysburg. Among Union infantry regiments, the 141st had the third greatest percentage deaths in a single action. Twenty-four percent of their number were killed at the Battle of Gettysburg. Regiments with higher percent deaths in a single action were: 1st Minnesota (28 percent at Gettysburg), and 15th New Jersey (26 percent at Spotsylvania).

Some Confederate units, fighting against heavy odds and at a disadvantage with regard to arms and ammunition, suffered greater percentage losses. As examples, the 3rd North Carolina lost 90 percent of their troops (deaths, wounded, and missing) at the Battle of Antietam. The 26th North Carolina lost 87 percent at the Battle of Gettysburg. One company, Captain Tuttle's, of the famous 26th, went into the battle with three officers and 84 men. All three officers and 83 of the 84 men were killed, missing, or wounded. In that same 26th Regiment, Company F went into action with a total of 91 men: three officers and 88 men. Every man of the rank and file was killed or wounded. The 1st Texas Regiment lost 82.3 percent at the Battle of Antietam.

BACKGROUND and EXPLANATION of JOEL'S WRITINGS

One of the chief contributors to a good morale in both the Northern and Southern armies was regularity in getting letters from home. Both veterans and recruits alike responded to letters from home. Mail calls played a great part in a soldier's life -- in the field or in camp. The mail brought not only personal letters, but newspapers, magazines, food, clothing, and other desirable items from home. Usually recipients shared contents with tent mates.

So far as letter writing was concerned, many soldiers indulged in extensive letter writing for the first time in their lives. Never in our nation's history have so many letters been written as occurred during the war. Many of the letters written were penned by soldiers in the field. Some soldiers were illiterate, but even they had letters written for them by their team mates. Incoming letters were read aloud to the illiterate soldiers.

On August 2, 1861, the Federal government passed an order that allowed all letters written by soldiers to be sent through the mails without payment. The soldier merely wrote on the envelope "Soldier's Letter". Postage had to be paid by the recipient.

Joel wrote his letters and diaries in various army camps, in the field, and some under battle conditions. As we read, we get into the mood by visualizing a row of white, army-issue, canvas tents. It's night, and we see him hunched in his tent with an open fire by the tent flap, sitting on his haversack, using a candle for a light and writing with a quill pen. Thus, his handwriting is hard to read.

Joel wrote at least one letter every day when he was able, or four or five letters a week. Since he was in the army 145 weeks, this totals about 600 to 700 letters that he wrote on his own account. In addition, he wrote letters for other enlistees (perhaps two a month). Many soldiers were unable to write because they were illiterate, wounded, or sick. The Bible tells us we each have a ministry. Joel's ministry was writing letters!

Although Joel corresponded with many people besides his immediate family, we don't have those letters. The letters we do have and presented here are letters he wrote mainly to his family and future wife, Elvira. We have letters that Joel wrote to two of his brothers, David and Jesse. We also have letters he wrote to David's bride, Hannah, and Jesse's wife, Phide. He wrote to his sister, Sallie, and Sallie's husband, John Pardoe McCarty. He wrote often to cousin, Angie. One of Joel's letters was to cousin, "Doc" Bird. Several of Joel's letters to the Molyneux household contained paragraphs directed to his mother, Rebecca. All of Joel's letters preserved in this book were written to the above-mentioned nine persons.

Five letters in this collection were written to Joel. One was from his back home minister, Reverend Sniffin; two were from his cousin, Angie Summers; one was from his cousin, Martha Molyneux; and one was from his former teacher, Professor C. R. Coburn. We've also included one letter from Joel's cousin, Samuel Molyneux, to his two brothers, William and Thomas. Samuel was Joel's cousin and best friend, and an important part of his life. Samuel was killed at the Battle of Gettysburg, and the loss was great to Joel.

Joel carried on a correspondence with many other people besides his immediate family, and, although we don't have those letters, Joel mentioned writing them. He corresponded with the Bedford, Grange, Vough, Samuel Molyneux, and Snell families. He wrote to cousin Eliza Molyneux, his older brothers George and James Molyneux, his cousin George Copeland Bird (Doc's brother), Eliza Snell, and Jennie and Lottie Dennison of Clyde, N.Y.

He wrote to J. P. McCarty, Jennie and Kate Plotts, H. Norton, A. D. Pratt, K. B. Taylor, Kate Bull, W. H. Brame, T. W. S. Little, cousin John N. Summers, Theodocie Stackpole, Mike Farrell, Jonathan Webster, M. J. Black, Kate Tirncrook, Seddie Locke, William B. Bryan, and Ellen Woodhead. He corresponded with buddy and nephew George Pardoe, brothers Edmund and Will, and Henry Bedford, Charley Grange, William Rogers, Ezra Little and the other Little boys, and his close friend and commanding officer, Charles Graves. Most of Joel's correspondents were from the northern Pennsylvania counties.

TREATMENT and EDITING

I have arranged Joel's Civil War letters and diary entries sequentially, and assigned each letter a number. If Joel sent two or more letters in the same envelope, I added a letter to distinguish them. For example, on October 18, 1862, Joel wrote **Letter #9A** to his sister, Sallie. The next day, October 19, he wrote another letter to Sallie, **Letter #9B**. The following day, October 20, he wrote a third letter to her, **Letter #9C**. All three complete letters were mailed on October 20, in the same envelope. Postage money was important to army privates who were getting paid their $.50 per day wages. First class postage was one cent.

I copied Joel's letters and diaries entries verbatim, except I added what I thought were appropriate punctuation marks. The original writings were so old that many of the punctuation marks didn't show clearly. Also, I did some paragraphing, for Joel didn't waste valuable paper space with paragraphs and margins. I retained Joel's original language and grammar, although incorrect in many cases, for it adds authenticity. He sometimes wrote in haste and made careless errors.

In some letters, Joel wrote final messages across the top or sides. I included these afterthoughts at the end of the letter text, as P. S.'s.

In Joel's daily journal many statements were sentence fragments, and didn't have subjects. Where it was not obvious what or whom he was talking about, I added the sentence subject in brackets. In some instances, Joel left out words or didn't complete words and omitted suffixes. I left a space if I could not determine the word or suffix. In several letters there were holes in the paper itself -- presumably work of silverfish.

Original spellings, even when incorrect, were kept intact to show the stress and strain under which the letters were written. Joel didn't carry a dictionary. Like most soldiers, he seldom saw the names of people or places in print. He heard words spoken, and repeated in writing as he heard them spoken, phonetically. All soldiers in all wars have done the same. For example, Joel's Rapid Ann or Repidan was the Rapidan River. He spelled the Monocacy River several ways. The town of Manassas was spelled various ways, occasionally correct. With regard to places back home Joel quite often mentioned townships, without using the word township. As examples, "Forks" generally meant Forks Township, although if he said "The Forks", he meant the village of Forksville. "Albany" referred to Albany Township, the next township west, in Bradford County. "Elks" meant the general area of Elks Township. Townships, as a political sub-division, played a more important role than now, especially with regard to schools, taxes, and voting.

He frequently spelled paid as "payed" and accept as "except". Oh was "O", for that was common spelling a century ago. Joel's misspelling is not a reflection on his literacy. His later life showed him to be widely-read and well-educated. We are fortunate to have these writings from such a literate person.

> My editorial comments and explanations are in italics and brackets, as: *[comment]*.

Joel used many word contractions not in current use. Examples are "shan't", "s'pose", "canst", "hain't" "'taint", "'twill", "'ticular", "'twas", "'twasn't", and "'tis". "'Ere" was the poetic form of "before". "Aught" meant only. I have retained these words exactly the way they were written, for their meanings are self-evident and their inclusion adds quaintness to the writing.

"Reg't" and "REG" are regiment. "Co" is company. "CoK" is Company K; "Div" is division, "Lt" and "Lieu" are lieutenant; "Col" is colonel, "Gen" is General, and "PV" is Pennsylvania Volunteers. "W" and "Wash." refer to Washington, D.C. "St." is station. "HdQrs" is headquarters. "Dep" is deploy or deployment. "HA" and "HARTY" are heavy artillery. "HAM" is heavy artillery mortar. "Minies" or "Minie balls" are rifle bullets. "Lbers" are pounders (artillery guns).

"Rec'd" is received, and "Rec" is receive. "Couz" and "coz" are cousin; and "ans" is answer. "Inst." is instance. "hosp." is hospital, "respts" is respects, and "ad't" is adjutant (staff officer). "Johnnys", "Jonnys", "Johns", "rebs" are

Confederate soldiers. A Confederate civilian was a "Cesesh" or a "Sesesh" (Secessionist). "F" is furlough. "FL" is French Leave (AWOL). "Posish" meant position.

"Chizely" meant chilly drizzle, and "lowery" weather was overcast or gloomy. "Middlin' warm" and "middly" meant average or usual weather. "A" was for activity, "P" was for placements. "Agoin" was going. "Bestest" was best. "Recon" was reckon or sometimes reconnaissance or reconnoiter. To march "smartley" meant to march briskly. A "Copperhead" was a Northerner with anti-abolition sympathies, in short, a snake in the grass to the Northerners who didn't like them. Some called them "Confederate fellow-travelers."

Joel used the expressions: "nigger", "niger", "nig", and "darkey" for Negro, and did not mean those words to be demeaning or degrading of individuals or the Negro race. Like many other Union soldiers, Joel was willing to give his life to elevate them.

"E", "EMc", "V", "Vi", "Vil", "Vile", "Vilie", "Villie", "Friend", and "True Friend" are affectionate names for girlfriend, Elvira.

So much for explanations. Let's listen to Private Joel Molyneux relate his day-by-day account of the Civil War.

CHAPTER 2: AUGUST and SEPTEMBER 1862

Letter #1

[Joel, in his first letter home, asks his brother, Jesse, to look after his business affairs. Jesse was the eighth child in the Edward-Rebecca Molyneux family of thirteen children. Born in 1829, Jesse was 33 when he received this 1862 letter from Joel. Ten years earlier, in 1852, Jesse had married Philena (nee Roberts), born 1834, and they had two children, Lloyd and Laura. Jesse died in 1910, Philena in 1902.]

Aug. 28th, [1862]
Harrisburgh, or rather Camp Curtin [Pennsylvania]

Dear Brother:

We left Laporte on Monday about noon. Took dinner at Sonestown and saw Uncle Joel and Aunt Sarah. They're well.

[Laporte was Sullivan County's county seat. Sonestown was a rail terminal where the line from Laporte joined the narrow gauge line from Eagles Mere. "Uncle Joel and Aunt Sarah" were Uncle Joel and Sarah Bennett. Sarah (nee Bird) Bennett was Joel's mother's elder sister. She was the second child in the family of ten children of Powell Bird and Lydia (nee Hannant) Bird, early settlers of Sullivan County. Joel Bennett, a contractor, built many houses in the Sullivan County area — some of which are still in use today.]

We arrived at Muncy where we stayed all night. Took the cars *[railroad train]* about nine o'clock to arrive at camp *[Camp Curtin]* about two. There is about 14,000, perhaps 20 *[20,000]* soldiers, in camp as near as I can tell. They come in and go out some 2,000 or so every day filling up old reg. etc. We all passed inspection yesterday and were sworn in and expect to receive our uniforms today. We are to go into a new reg., the 143rd I guess, but not sure. It is from Bradford County.

[Camp Curtin was the largest training camp in the North. Strategically located at Harrisburg, Pennsylvania, it was almost on the front in late June 1863 when General Lee's Army of Northern Virginia nearly reached Harrisburg prior to the Battle of Gettysburg.]

We join a company from Smithfield under Capt. Wright. Dunham is our first lieutenant, and Difenbach, second. The rest of our officers are not elected yet. We will have perhaps a corporal from outside of the mountain. I do not know how it is agoing to be about getting a furlough. I am afraid I can't get one as few are granted. My county bounty: I have sent orders to Ingham to enter up against the county.

[In volunteer regiments, at the beginning of the war, it was common for enlistees to elect their officers. Bounties were an incentive to attract volunteers. This county bounty was $25.00, and "enter up against the county" meant to charge the county for their debt to him. The Pennsylvania state bounty was $2.00.]

There are quite a number of boys here from Hollon Hill: Bish Horton, Charley Scott, E. Little, E. Harris and brother, and some others that I know all in the same reg., but not the same co.

[Hollon Hill was a village south of Towanda, county seat of neighboring Bradford County. Joel's first cousin, once removed, whom he called "Sister Angie", lived there, and Joel seemed well acquainted with that neighborhood. Joel mentioned Ezra S. Little in several letters. One diary entry (May 7, 1863) concerned a letter Joel had received from Ezra's cousin, George Little. Later, George was wounded in the Battle of Gettysburg, and died July 5, 1863, on the way home. Myron T. Little, brother of George, was captured by the Confederates and died July 1864 at Andersonville Prison, Georgia. Another brother, John Benson Little, died in a field hospital July 28, 1864. Imagine the shock to the Little family of losing three sons in the conflict within 13 months. These latter three Little brothers lived in Picture Rocks, a picturesque village in Lycoming County.]

There was a man, a soldier, drowned here yesterday and about a dozen poisoned a day or two before we came here with eating pies brought by the peddlers. Dispatches came here last night that Seigel had shot Bredswell and then shot himself because McDowell had called him a liar. It is not credited, though.

Some say the smallpox is downtown *[downtown Harrisburg]*, but I don't know as it is so. There is some talk of our reg. staying to guard the drafted men when they come in to drill, but there is know *[no]* telling. We may go in two days or we may stay two months. I should like first rate to see them come in, but this is an awful filthy camp and when it comes wet it will be anything but pleasant.

The nine months men seem to be the ones that are hurried off. Some went from here a week ago, and have been in a fight already. Since I commenced writing I hear that two reg. leave this afternoon and that they have been doing so at the rate of two reg. a day for a long while. They are just now training a new company as they come in. Four have come in already today, not noon yet.

Last Saturday it was estimated there was 25,000 here, so we shall at least have company to say nothing of the conscripts.

I saw Harry at the capitol as we came past, but only spoke to him. Ed Lion was in camp today, but did not see him. G. Jackson came down with us from Muncy fairly backed out at Laporte, but I understood he said he would go if they, we, would go in for him to be captain. I knew he would not go when he started. *[G. Jackson had not yet been sworn in, otherwise his "backed out" would be desertion.]*

The boys seem to be all in fine spirits. Two or three are complaining of disentary *[dysentery]*, but few escape it for the first few days. I have not bought a cent's worth of trash yet, nor do not intend to as long as I can yet get along without it.

If I don't come home in the course of a week or until you hear from me again, you will have to straiten my affairs, but I will see soon what can be done and write again or come up. Letters directed *[to me]* in the care of Camp Curtain *[Curtin]* will reach us as long as we stay here, but if we leave we will let you know in due time. Your brother, Joel.

P. S. Our respects to all who may inquire.

*****

Letter #2

[This letter is from Joel's cousin, Samuel Molyneux, to his two brothers, William and Thomas. Samuel and Joel were close friends, as well as cousins. Samuel's father, John, and Joel's father, Edward, were brothers. Both had been born in England and were brought to this country by their father, William. Their mother had died in childbirth some years earlier, when they were still living in England. Samuel's mother was Martha (nee Sadler). Sam's wife, Elizabeth, was cousin and close friend of Elvira McCarty.]

Near Chain Bridge
[In Virginia, across Potomac River from Washington]
Sep. 1, 1862

Dear Brothers:

I wrote a few lines to the girls while we were yet at Camp Curtin, and by the eding *[? heading]* you will see that we are now in Virginia, getting along pretty fair for one week. As I know not how much time I may have to write I will first tell you what arrangements I made with Hickok at Harrisburg. I call on him on Thursday, engaged *[line indecipherable because of a crease in the letter]* the cherry to be $22.00, the aple $12.00 per thousand, and he agreed to take one sider mill *[cider press]* at $30.00. You will ship it *[the lumber]* to him as soon as you can, and he will ship the sider mill to Muncy Station.

I had little time to look *[at]* Harrisburg. Called on Willsons & Co. They sayed they did not want any lumber. As to the hemlock, I lernt nothing.

We are, most of us, well and in good spirits as we was when we left home though some of the boys have been unusual complaining of the dire *[diarrhea]*. They say we all have to pass through it, but I have not felt it yet. We left Harrisburg on Friday 5 ----*[text obliterated]* very slow. Got to Baltimore Saturday morning, day brake. Got breakfast at the expense of the sitizens of Baltimore. Left at 8 A.M. Arrived at Washington 3 P.M. We soon lernt they was fighting at Bull Run & could hear the firing. Marched through Washington 2 miles to the Long Bridge. Stopped their *[there]* for the ambulances to pass that were going out to bring in the wounded. These were a very long train hundreds of them going out.

We started from the Long Bridge a little after dark for Arlington Heights & marched pretty fast arrived their 9 or 10 o'clock. We had had not much more than got our napsax of *[knapsacks off]* and some of us lain down when our Regt. was ordered to march to Chain Bridge. We commenced packing when the order was given that Co. K should remain to guard the bagage. This was no unwelcome order to me, at last, as I was some tired. We remained there till probable afternoon on Sunday when we were ordered to march to join our Regt. near the Chain Bridge of some 9 miles tedious march having rained some made it quite muddy. Arrived about dark.

It is nearly noon Monday. We know not wether *[whether]* we will stay here or not, but I supose that we will remain at some point to drill for a few weeks, at least. As to the results of the fighting, we have no trustworthy information. There are so many rumors. It has been reported several times in camp that Jackson had surrendered, but I think it is very uncertain yet but I think one thing is sertain that there has been a very hard battle of 2 or 3 days of fighting, and if there is any thing to believed in wat we have here the rebels are getting the worst of it.

We are encamped on a small stream near the Potomac, but not in a city. *[The stream may have been Rock Run or Spout Run.]* There is pretty good water there. The country is rather bluffy. When you write, direct: Co K, 141 Regt., P.V., Wash., D.C. Remember me to all, as I remain your Br., Samuel Molyneux.

P. S. I have received no bounty as yet.

*****

Letter #3

[This is Joel's first letter to Elvira. It was written when Joel was 27. Born in 1835, he had been teaching school since he left Towanda Academy. By all accounts he was a good teacher. Elvira McCarty, 16 at the time she received this letter from Joel, had been a student of his at a one-room school. An engaging romance develops in the several months these first letters to her were written. Later, they became "spoken for".]

Sept. 2nd, 1862,
Near Chain Bridge, [Virginia]

Dearest Elvira:

Everything that happened since I left seems like a dream to me. I can hardly realize that in one short week I should be transferred far from the midst of those I hold most dear right in another midst of war and rebellion. Of course you know of our starting away on Sunday *[August 24, 1862]*. We arrived at Harrisburg on Tuesday afternoon and were immediately placed into a regt., the 141st. It is from Bradford County. Among them are quite a number of close acquaintances from both Bradford and Sullivan Co.

There is 100 men in a company and 1,000 in a regt. or average about this. Upon Friday, we received our uniforms and rifles and at five PM started for Washington. We rode all night; passed through Baltimore just at daybreak, ate breakfast, and proceeded to W. where we arrived Saturday *[August 30]* at three P.M. Just at dark we started from there; crossed the Long Bridge into Virginia.

[In 1862, three bridges crossed the Potomac River connecting Washington, D.C. with Virginia. The two wagon bridges were the Chain Bridge, up the river, and the Long Bridge at the center of town. The Long Bridge, situated just down river from the present 14th St. Bridge, also served as a railroad bridge for two years (1863-64). This was the bridge where the 141st Regiment got caught and almost run over by the horse-drawn ambulances dispatched to pick up wounded at the Second Battle of Manassas.

[The third bridge spanning the Potomac River in 1862 was the Aqueduct Bridge. Constructed in 1843, it carried canal boats of the Alexandria-Georgetown Canal to connect that short feeder-canal with the important C & O Canal. That water-filled bridge was located about 100 yards up river from where the present Key Bridge crosses the Potomac River, from Rosslyn to Georgetown. Above the wooden canal conduit a narrow roadway was for use of vehicles and pedestrians. During the Civil War, the canal portion of the

Aqueduct Bridge was drained so the whole bridge could be used for military purposes.

[After the Civil War, the Alexandria-Georgetown Canal was reactivated and the water-filled bridge was again used for canal boat passage. The canal was discontinued in use in the late 1880's. The bridge was rebuilt several times, and used as a toll bridge for wagon and pedestrian traffic for some years. In 1923, the Key Bridge replaced it and it was demolished in 1933. On the Georgetown side of the river, far-sighted bridge demolishers left a gray stone pier and arch that may be seen as the last remnant of the retired Aqueduct Canal Bridge.

[During the Civil War, Union army engineers built a temporary pontoon bridge across the Potomac. Joel mentioned marching across it on May 23, 1865, when he crossed the river into Washington to participate in the grand parade.]

Some seven miles *[we]* were ordered to halt for the night. Our company stayed here but the rest *[of the 141st Regiment]* moved on to Chain Bridge nine miles further on, where we joined them the next day, Sunday. It seems by some mistake we have been sent forward as a regt. of well-drilled nine months men instead of a new one of three-year men.

[The three-year men were volunteers who had signed up for three years, and like himself were new recruits. At the beginning of the war, there were three-month volunteers, for most experts expected the rebellion to last only that long. A little later they had the nine-month volunteers. The three-year volunteers were followed by the draft.

[Sergeant McCabe, in an unpublished account of the 141st Regiment, told of the fiasco of those of the 141st Regiment who went to Chain Bridge that night. They went sent there to protect the bridge from the Confederates, but didn't have bullets for their guns. Finally, their ammunition wagon arrived, but it contained the wrong size bullets for their guns. See McCabe's full account at Archives Library, Carlisle War College, Carlisle, Pennsylvania.]

I do not know yet whether they will send us back to be drilled or what they will do yet. One thing I know is that we have been put through pretty hard. I have had quite good health since I left home. Sometimes I thought my ankle would give out but I guess it will stand. Will Rogers is not feeling very good today -- very bad cold, I guess, as we have lain out two or three nights without tents.

We have all kinds of rumors here about the war. Upon Saturday, the day we were in Washington, there was a very heavy fight at Manassas.

[The Second Campaign of Manassas had been going on for several days and involved several battles: Cedar Mountain, Groveton, and Chantilly. The main battle took place along Bull Run, August 29-30, 1862. It, like the First Battle of Manassas, was a sore defeat for the Union Army of the Potomac. General Robert E. Lee was the commander of the Army of Northern Virginia and General John Pope was commanding officer of the Union forces. Casualties: 25,251 (16,054 Union and 9,197 Confederate).]

I could hear the cannon very distinctly as many as 40 or 50, and sometimes a 100 to the minute. Then came the news that our army had captured the rebel Jackson *[General Thomas J. (Stonewall) Jackson]* and his whole army; then that our army was awfully cut up and the rebels were within a few miles of us. An hour ago, word came that we were to go directly to reinforce our army and right into battle, but it turns out incorrect.

[General John Pope, in command of the Union forces, mistakenly thought he had the Confederate troops on the run and sent a message back to Washington saying he had a victory. A short time later his own troops were retreating.]

I tell you, E., the army is a dreadful place to be, in respect to language. It makes me shudder to hear; yet one is forced to *[hear]* it, but you need not be afraid upon my account. I have made up my mind to do nothing that I would be ashamed to know my friends knew or that I would not do if I were at home. I think a soldier of all others are the ones that should be prepared to die.

I suppose this will find you at your studys going to school. I know you will think of me often. I have no fear if I should be spared to come back, but that I should find you if you should also be spared, the same confiding, affectionate girl you were when I left. I think of you often and you must excuse me for reminding you of the promise concerning your ambrotype the first opportunity if you please do.

[Invented in 1855, the ambrotype was an early kind of photograph in which the positive was made of a photographic negative on glass backed by a dark surface.]

I have not yet heard a word from home, but expect letters next week. I want you should write directly and tell me all the news; it will be welcome. Do not be afraid to write. My table is a tin plate turned over upon my knee. Excuse me for using a pencil for I have no ink, and this paper I borrowed and the pencil I begged, and if this is uninteresting excuse also, for everything is so different I can scarcely collect my thoughts to anything.

My directions *[mailing address]* will be after this: Washington, D.C., 141st Regt., Pa. V., Co. K. Now I am nearly done I will go out and see if I can find anything to enclose for you from old Va. Hoping you will ever remember the one that ever remembers you is the wish of your true and affectionate friend – Joel.

P. S. I will direct this to Eldredsville. *[The wee village of Eldredsville in Sullivan County has long since disappeared, although there is yet the crossroads location with a tiny country store still in operation, a camp ground, a seldom-used church building, a cemetery, and a house or two.]* If you have left, it can be forwarded to you. If so, please state your post office address. If you are at home, give sister, Sallie, my directions and tell her not to wait for me to write first, JLM. Is that dog upon the watch yet?

*****

Letter #4

[Sister Sarah, nicknamed "Sallie" by Joel, was born in 1837 and died in 1914. She was two years younger than Joel. In 1859 she had married John Pardoe McCarty who died in 1885. Her second husband was Daniel Waters. No record of children from either marriage. It is obvious Sallie and Joel were close, for Joel stayed with her when on leave.]

Virginia sacred soil
[Near Alexandria, September 8, 1862]

Dear Sister:

Supposing that you would be looking for a letter by this time from me. I have just begged and bought a sheet for the purpose. Our regt. is now laying opposite Alexandria across the Potomac from Washington. We moved from the Chain Bridge yesterday, Sunday. Saturday, James Pardoe and I went and hunted up George *[Pardoe]* for you doubtless have heard that our whole army of Virginia has been driven back to their fortifications near Washington. I found George about five miles from Chain Bridge. He is well and hearty, though some tanned. I found Mike and Wally Snell, Dave and Sam Bryan, Jim Corkins, Jonathan Bryan and a number of others that I have been acquainted with. They are well and were in the battle of Bull Run No. Two, and the Saturday after we left home they all escaped unhurt.

I was then at Washington and distinctly heard the firing. Ez Little and En Harris Charley Scott, Bish Horton and nearly a dozen others that I am acquainted with from Hollon Hill are in the same regt. with us. I have not yet heard anything from home since we started, excepting a letter that David wrote to George Pardoe.

I have been unusually well since we started. Some of the rest have not fared quite as well. Will Rogers is quite sick now and has been for several days. A number of others have been down but are in a better fashion now. I have got so I can sleep pretty good without a bed. Last night Will Bedford, Sam M., *[Samuel Molyneux]* and I slept under a horse chestnut *[tree]* in a Virginia gentleman's door yard. Tonight, I expect will be no better as our tents have not yet reached us from Chain Bridge. *[Their tents were issued to them a week later.]*

[Historian Bates, in his book The History of Bradford County, Pennsylvania, *explains why so many men of the 141st got sick. "The biggest killer in the war was not combat, but disease. It is estimated that 62 percent of those who died, died by disease. The leading disease cause of death on both sides was diarrhea, followed by typhoid, typhus and malarial fevers, pneumonia, small pox, and measles." A little known fact about Civil War diseases is that venereal diseases were fairly common. In 1861 the Army Medical Department reported one out of 12 Union soldiers had venereal disease. Some units reported 25 to 30 percent of their soldiers had the sexually transmitted disease.]*

The prospect of the war's closing soon seems rather dull as Jackson is reported to have crossed over into Maryland with a heavy force and McDowel *[General Irwin McDowell had been in command of the Army of the Potomac when it was formed but was replaced by General McClellan after he was charged with losing the First Battle of Bull Run.]* is believed to be a traitor by almost the whole army. I thought, when I came, the rebellion soon would be crushed, but now I begin to think it is scarcely commencing. I think somehow or other I shall yet get home safe. At least I hope to see my friends again.

I never used to think that I should ever write with a pencil, but we can't help it here. It is hard work to keep things by one for writing, and you have to pay about three times what they are worth. I shall have to ask those that wish to hear from me to enclose an extra sheet with wrapper and directed ready for mailing if they can do so without causing double postage as I am half of the time out of material for writing. If it can be done so, I will pay for expenses on my part.

We have a very fine view from our camp. We can see nearly all of the city of Washington and Alexandria with the Potomac River stretching out nearly as far as the eye can reach, with schooners, sloops, gunboats, etc. To look at them in the distance they resemble a lot of dead trees in an old swamp. *[He was probably at Camp Whipple.]*

The weather is middling warm today about the same as our average is in August, but as a general thing it has not been very warm since we came down here, and the nights are quite cool. I have not seen a rebel yet, but don't know how soon I may. One night I thought they were coming for sure, but they didn't.

E. Little *[Cousin Ezra S. Little]* received a letter from Angie Pratt. He says they were coming out to get blackberries last week. Did they come? You must write soon and tell those who wish to hear from me to do the same. There is no such thing as getting furlough here, and unless I get discharged for lameness I shall not be able to come up in January, but will make it up when I do come. Write the news, etc., the talk, etc., and if the draft has taken place all about that. For my part, I have no desire to see any of my acquaintances drafted. Goodbye from your brother, Joel.

P. S. Give my love to John, Georgia, and all who may inquire for Joel. Direct: Washington, D.C., Co. K, 141st Regt. Pa.V., care of Capt. Wright.

*****

Letter #5A

[The following letter is to Jesse. He was six years older than Joel.]

September 12, 1862
Arlington Heights *[Virginia]*

Dear Brother:

I take my pencil tonight to write a few lines. We have just made another move of some six miles and are encamped on or near Arlington Heights. Some think we are on the way for Harpers Ferry. This camp has a splendid view of Washington city some two miles off. We can see the Capitol, the Potomac River shipping, etc. All sorts of rumors are afloat here. We don't know what to believe. Today's papers state that Governor Curtin *[Andrew G. Curtin of Pennsylvania]* has ordered out all able-bodied men for the defense of state. This war must surely turn one way or the other very soon.

Our regiment numbers 955 men. Our Captain is J. K. Wright of Smithfield. *[Jason K. Wright was discharged on surgeon's certificate, December 2, 1862.]* Our Colonel is Madil from Bradford

[Joel is referring to Bradford County, not the city of Bradford, in McKean County, Pennsylvania. Colonel Henry J. Madill became brevet brigadier general on December 2, 1862, brevet major general on March 13, 1865, was wounded at Petersburg, Virginia, April 2, 1865, and discharged from the army June 11, 1869. Madill had been a lawyer in Towanda before entering the army. Prior to being commanding officer of the 141st Regiment, Colonel Madill had been a major in the 35th Pennsylvania Regiment. After

discharge, Colonel Madill returned to Towanda, and became active in community affairs. He bought and lived in the building that had first housed Towanda Academy, his former school. That tiny private school, formed in 1836, closed its doors in 1929. Joel had attended school there, starting in 1856. Towanda Academy's only famous student was Stephen Foster, popular folk song writer, who attended there one year in 1840. Stephen's brother, an engineer helping build the Pennsylvania Canal, lived in Towanda while that section of the canal was being built.]

Our second in command is Lieu. Colonel Watkins. Our physician is Dr. Allen, the one that formerly lived at Dushore of Travis memory. We are in Robison's Brigade and Hentrelmans Div. and McClellan's Army. *[Watkins was killed at Petersburg, June 18, 1864. Dr. Ezra P. Allen was promoted to surgeon, 83rd Pennsylvania Volunteers, December 13, 1862. Major General George McClellan was later removed by President Lincoln from his post as commander of the Army of the Potomac later that month for lack of aggressiveness.]*

There are any number of forts almost across the river about Washington. I have seen 15 or 20. There are perhaps as many more. The defenses upon this side *[Virginia side of the Potomac River]* are considered impregnable. *[Maps of the period show the U.S. army had 23 forts in the Arlington/Alexandria area. There were also forts in Maryland and in D.C. itself. In total, there were 68 forts and batteries ringing the nation's capital.]*

We have not received any of our pay or bounty money yet, nor do not know when we will nor drawn our full suit of clothes yet being minus of shirts, haversacks for carrying our rations in. If you are exempted *[by]* the army you can arrange my affairs the best you can. You can either keep a book account of my work this summer; put it in a note. My full time, if I recollect, was 40 days and if you allow 75 cts, it will be 30 dollars. Get a note of Samuel Wright if he has not payed up yet. He borrowed 14 and has payed 7 I think, but I am not certain. What he payed he will remember. You can get a note to *[too]* of *[from]* Addison for the 7 dollars for the plow. You can settle with John Warren, and if it suits you to make the turn, can put it with yours or do as you think best.

The sheep Sam and George agreed to keep another year except a few George was a going to let Addison have. He agreed to attend to that. The cattle I want you to sell and do the best you can by them. If the 4 two year olds sell for $57.00 you may give Allen Little his note. But if they don't bring that much he is to pay what is back on the note. There will be a $2.00 a head owing to Dick for pasturing which you will pay when the cattle are sold, excepting $300 which is already payed leaving 13 dollars due Dick yet. Get what is back from Jake Snyder as soon as you can. The rest of the notes won't matter as long as they are in safe position. You will attend to the Town *[township]* order with yours. My county bounty I left it to Ingham to enter up against the County. When you see him inquire if it is all rightly attended to.

[The bounty-volunteer system worked poorly. A state would offer a cash bounty for enlistments; cities and townships and counties would add their own contribution, and the Federal government would make a further offer. In 1862 the U.S. government increased its bounty to $300.00. By 1864, there were some areas in which a man could receive more than a thousand dollars by simply joining the army. Bounty jumpers enlisted to get the bounty, deserted, went to another area and enlisted again under an assumed name, deserted again, etc. Even when they did not desert, most bounty soldiers were poor fighters because their motive for enlisting in the army was purely money and not patriotism.]

I do not think of anything else now, but when you write if there is anything more, why mention it. This paper looks like anything but fit for a letter, but it is all I have and as we were hurried off I did not get anything to carry so it was in my pocket.

*****

Letter #5B

[This short continuation letter to brother, Jesse, written the next day, was scribbled on the same sheet of paper as the previous letter.]

Saturday morning, September 13 *[1862]*

It is expected that we march again today, but don't know where to. I believe there is an attack expected very soon. We were ordered to lay upon our arms *[keep their guns and marching gear close at hand]* last night, and it may be, before you hear from me again, that we have been in an engagement. Write me soon again and give all particulars respecting the draft and all that is transpiring up in Sullivan, but I must close by sending my love to father, mother, and all the rest of the folks. Good bye from your ever affectionate brother, Joel. Address: Washington, D.C., Co. K, 141st Regt., Pa. V.

*****

[On September 17, 1862, the Battle of Antietam was fought. There were 51,844 Confederates against 75,316 Union. General Lee commanded the Southern army and General McClellan the Federal. Casualties: 26,134 (12,410 Union and 13,724 Confederate), making it the costliest single day of the war, and the fifth costliest battle.

*[On September 22, 1862, President Abraham Lincoln signed the Emancipation Proclamation. Prior, in April 1862, Lincoln had signed a bill which outlawed slavery in the District of Columbia. The 1860 U.S. census showed the District of Columbia to have 75,076 total inhabitants, including 3,181 black slaves and 11,107 free blacks. Lincoln's famous proclamation read: "**As of January 1, 1863, all persons held as slaves, within any state, or designated part of a state, the people whereof, shall then be in rebellion against the United States, shall be then, thenceforward, and forever free.**"*

[It sounds as though the Proclamation freed only slaves in the 11 Confederate states. There were still slaves in the four border states: Delaware, Maryland, Kentucky, and Missouri. Therefore, Lincoln's Proclamation attempted to free slaves where he had no authority and did not free slaves where he did have jurisdiction.

*[President Lincoln chose a time to present the Proclamation after the Union success at the Battle of Antietam, which he hoped would prove favorable. In response, in the Confederate capital of Richmond, the newspaper, <u>Whig</u>, voiced, "**It is a dash of the pen to destroy four thousand millions of our property, and is a bid for insurrection.**"*

[Interestingly, there were 11 Confederate states, but their flag had 13 stars. The two extra stars signified the two border states, Missouri and Kentucky, that the Confederacy hoped would join them in their secession attempt. At the beginning of the war they had hoped Maryland would join them, but there was little interest there. The other border state, Delaware, showed no interest in joining the Confederacy.

[On September 24, 1862, President Abraham Lincoln suspended the Writ of Habeas Corpus for persons discouraging enlistments, resisting the draft, or other disloyal acts.]

Letter #6A

Out upon Picket *[Bailey's Cross Roads, Virginia]*
Sept. 28 *[1862]*

Dearest E *[Elvira]*

Your most welcome letter I received just three days after it was mailed and for once I was not a disappointed youth and as certain as that I read it once I have read it ½ a dozen times over. The present date finds me enjoying good health and myself as far as might be expected in our present circumstances.

I have almost forgotten where we were when I last wrote to you, for the last two weeks we have been at Camp Whipple in Va. three miles from

Washington, near Arlington Heights. *[Later, Whipple had its name changed to Fort Myer, and the base is still active today.]* Friday we moved one mile south to another camp, but have not yet learned the name. I was almost sorry to leave our old camp, for we had such a splendid view of Washington, the capitol, Potomac River, and a large scope of country almost covered with encampments. I often wished you were there with me just long enough to take one look around.

This morning, Sunday, our regt. was ordered out upon picket duty some five miles from our camp. You have often heard of Bailey's Cross Roads? You can find it upon any of the war maps. Well, today we are three miles south of there. The rebs are not supposed to be very near us, consequently our situation is not thought to be dangerous. Pickets stay out 24 hours, so we expect to go back to camp in the morning.

I said that I was well. I wish I could say so of the rest of the boys. Will Rogers, C. Grange, and James Pardoe are quite sick. George and Rogers are now in the regimental hospital, poor fellows! I can stand soldiering as long as I keep my health, but do not want to be sick in any army.

So, my letter was opened before it reached you. Was it by mistake? Or how did it happen? I do not know what you thought at my sending the envelope I did, but it was the only one I could get at that time so I thought it wouldn't matter. Wasn't I glad when I saw that likeness? And you call it homely? Well, I don't care when I know that no one else calls it so. So, you are going to school and like your teacher? I am glad of that. Isn't that what they said of you last winter? I am not at all afraid of your liking that fellow, you spoke of, too much. I will trust you for three years, but I think of seeing you before half of that time.

I had such a good letter from Cousin Angie Summers last night. *[Cousin Angie Summers was actually Joel's first cousin, once removed. Her father, Job Summers, was Joel's first cousin. Job's mother, Elizabeth (nee Bird) Rowe, and Joel's mother, Rebecca, were sisters.]* She has just been out to Sallie's picking berries and says that she was sorry she did not get to see her intended cousin. Oh! Kate writes that there is a certain girl, at the Forks, very much disappointed at hearing of someone getting a watch. It's too bad, ain't it? It doesn't make any difference where we are, news flys.

["The Forks", Joel mentions, is the village of Forksville which received its name from its location at the forks of the Little Loyalsock and Big Loyalsock Rivers. In Civil War times, Forksville was a thriving little village with a woolen mill, grist mill, saw mill, dye works, several country stores, two hotels, post office, high school, etc. A small knoll-type mountain, in the center of the town, is the situs of the town cemetery. A still-used covered bridge in the town was built in 1850 by Sadler Rogers, a 17-year-old relative of Joel's.

[Forksville's one famous inhabitant was Harold Grange, of University of Illinois and Chicago Bears football fame. The Grange family moved from Forksville, when "Red" was young, and he grew up in Wheaton, Illinois. Charles Grange, who died of disease in 1863, was a great uncle of "Red". Forksville had several hundred inhabitants then, but now has only 100 or so.]

I had a letter from George Pardoe yesterday. He has just been in another battle, but escaped without being much hurt himself, though nearly a dozen were killed of my old acquaintances. Dave Bryan's brother, Sam, was badly wounded, and Ben had two of his fingers shot off. Bill, their cousin, was killed; so was Mason Rogers, a cousin of Ike's. He was with G. Pardoe, I believe.

While I was writing this our col. came along and he ordered us into a fresh place about three miles from where I commenced writing this, and have just got settled in our new position and find myself scribbling away to you again. This is a poor part of Va.! One of the boys has just remarked that the crows would have to carry haversacks with them if they flew over here, but I shall have to close for tonight as it is getting dark. So good bye for tonight. I must look out for a place to sleep, which will be at the foot of an oak tree, I guess.

*****

Letter #6B

Monday morning, *[September 29, 1862, Arlington Heights, Virginia]*

Well, how is E this morning? I have had a good night's sleep; have not slept in bed but once since I saw you. We have just had our breakfast of bread, crackers, and meat. Our daily bread here does not have any butter upon it. The red spot on the corner of this sheet is not blood, but merely grape juice. Ed. Bedford and I have been picking some for we have some sweet with the bitter. Grapes are quite plenty, and some of them are very good and then there is a lot of chestnuts. They call *[them]* chickapins. They grow upon little bushes from two to four feet high in little burrs like chestnuts, and they taste much the same. There's plenty of them. I saw yesterday for the first time persimmons — with its fruit which are about the size of Siberian crabs *[crab apples, about the size of a marble]* and taste worse while green than anything you ever thought of. You have read of them, have you not? But for fear a description letter is not interesting I will try and change the subject.

Elvira, what pleased me most in your letter was that you were trying to be a good girl, etc. We will both try and be good together now. Sometimes, I think it is no use for me to try. There is so much cursing and swearing here — nearly three out of two swears. Seems if they were trying to see who can swear the worst, but there are some good men here. Our captain is a good, praying man. I think we have a good chaplain. We have preaching twice on Sunday when it is so we can and there is meeting somewhere in the regt. every evening, but only about 100 out of 1,000 men which compose our regt., go near them. Don't think, E., that I have learned to swear. I despise it, but the constant hearing of it seems to harden one's feelings. I, for one, hope this most dreadful war will soon close. I shall not get back to camp in time to send this letter out today. Our mail goes out every morning and back in the afternoon. You will get this about Thursday. You will write again Saturday, won't you?

Goodie! Here comes our Col. Madill! We all like him, and will do anything for him. Some of the rest of our officers are cross, ugly fellows, and nobody likes them. Our col. says: "Get ready, guys, to go back to camp," so I must stop writing and get ready to go and finish this at the camp. Then, I will see how our sick boys are and perhaps there may be other news that I might wish to put in but my paper is so near done. I shall have to take a fresh sheet. If you could see me writing this you would excuse the crooked lines and letters I have made, as well as the mistakes and general appearance of this poor letter. Now for camp.

Here I am back again in camp but very tired. So, you will have to excuse me for not writing much more. I have been to see the sick boys. They are little or no better. It's hard to see strong men unable to walk without assistance. I found a letter waiting me in camp from sister, Ellen. It would do you good if you could only see how anxious the soldiers look for letters when the mail comes in. Everything stops with the soldier unless he be on duty, until he gets his letter, if any. There is some talk in camp of this war being settled soon. I only hope it will. I have yet only seen the bright side of soldiering, but I think I could enjoy home sweet home with those I love. I dreamed of being there last night, and guess it was because I had been writing to you, and when I lay down and looked up through the trees, and saw the same moon and stars I used to see at night. I wondered if you were looking at the sky, but I must stop or you will not get this back in time to write to me Saturday, and I wouldn't miss getting a letter for considerable.

Good bye Elvira. May Heaven's choicest blessings ever be with thee is the wish and prayer of one that loves you better than he has words to express. Yours as heretofore, Joel.

*****

CHAPTER 3: OCTOBER 1862

Letter #7A

[The following two letters were to David. Nine years older than Joel, David was still a bachelor at 36. These letters were written from Fort Prescott Smith — one of the several dozen forts surrounding Washington on the Virginia side of the Potomac. Fort Smith was on a bluff, near the present Arlington Cemetery, overlooking the Potomac River and Washington.]

Oct. 1st, 1862
Camp Prescott, [Virginia]

Dear Brother David:

As I was writing to Jesse I thought that I would enclose a few lines to you and send back the cheque that I took with me as I could not stop at Milton and did not have the opportunity to get it exchanged while at Harrisburg. You will send it down the first opportunity or get it exchanged for me. My county bounty, I understand, is ready to be paid now in money. I sent word to Ingham to have it entered up, but get the money if you can and let him have it. The Elkland school order — get that and do the best you can with the rest. Have you sold the cattle yet? Did Silas McCarty take what he talked of? I have not received any of my bounty yet, but expect it before a great while and will forward it on to you.

I understand you talk some of coming down to see us this fall. Do you? If you do, we would like to know it so as to send up for a few notions. I think citizens could get over *[across the Potomac River]* without much trouble. I can easily enquire and see. I do not know how long we will stay about here. We are about five miles from Washington. We moved about one miles last week; the word is now that the army is being moved forward to Richmond again, but our camp rumors are not to be relied upon. But I must close for tonight as the drum is beating for roll call and then the lights are all blown out for the night.

*****

Letter #7B

Thursday morning, 2nd of October, [1862]
[Camp Prescott Smith, Virginia]

There is nothing new to write of this morning and as the mail goes out early I shall have to close. I have written to Jesse and told him all the news. I am well and hope these lines will find you all the same. Tell Kate I will ans.

hers soon. Good bye. Write soon to your brother, J. L. Molyneux, Co. K, 141st Reg., Pa.V.

*****

Letter #8

[Although addressed to brother, David, this letter was also to his mother, Rebecca. Born January 1, 1797, she was 65 at the time this letter was written. She died in 1882. She was the first white child born in Sullivan County. It was she who brought the blood disorder, hemophilia, into the Molyneux family. She had inherited it from her mother, Lydia (nee Hannant) Bird, wife of Powell Bird. That unusual blood disease has been passed along through the genes by the females and is still a problem to some males of the Molyneux family. It's carried by the females and affects the males. Their blood won't clot.]

Dixie, Oct. 9, 1862
[Camp Prescott Smith, Virginia]

Dear Brother:

Your letter I received in due time and will endeavor to answer this evening. I am still enjoying good health. James is getting quite smart again and I think *[he]* will do duty in a few days. Will. Rogers and C. Graves still remain in the hospital and no better. Our 2nd lieu., Diefenbach, is very sick and considered doubtful if he can recover. He is very low. *[Lt. John Dieffenbach died of typhoid fever two days later, October 11, 1862.]*

We are still at Camp Prescott Smith so here we have been for the past two weeks. This morning we received orders to be ready for marching with two days cooked rations prepared. We may move tomorrow, and we may not for a week. In what direction when we do go is not certain, but likely toward Harpers Ferry.

As the rest of the boys are sending for things that they want this winter I will do the same so they can be ready if any one comes down or they can be boxed up and sent to us if we stay in the vicinity of Washington. In the first place, I want a pair of boots, cowhide that is good and not too heavy, with the soles well nailed as there is no chance for tapping here. I enclose my measure that Crawford took for me, as it is the exact measure. Be careful they are not made too small; perhaps my other boot may be some guide as they fit well. If you have leather, or can get it, get Addison to make them as he is oweing me.

Mother, I want you to make me a woolen vest. Make it full of pockets, two large ones and two smaller ones above. Pockets are handy here and you may send two pair of my best woolen socks and Kate, I want a pair of woolen gloves. I guess this ends my wants for the present unless it is a wool hat. One, like the one Thomas Pardoe had, would suit. Our caps will not turn rain, I don't think, when it comes rainy weather.

I sent that cheque back in a letter to Jesse. Have you received it? Has our clothes got home yet? We expect to get our bounty with two months pay the last of this month that being the regular pay day in the army. If you or any one else come down can *[you]* be here the first of Nov.? It would suit me first rate to send back our money. As I did not bring but two or three dollars, besides the cheque, when you write enclose $5.00. I had to lend a little to some of our boys and am about out.

Has McCarty taken that money yet? Did you say Job did not want to hire any? If any one else take it be sure they are safe. You need not let the hard money out at present. I suppose you have the county bounty before this?

Charles Snell was to see us last Sunday. We were all very glad to see him. He had no trouble in getting over from Washington; he got a recommend at Harrisburg. I saw Sam Bryan on Sunday also. His health is quite poor. I have not heard from George P. *[nephew, George Pardoe]* very lately. Had one letter just after the fight in Md. I suppose they are, the reserves, near Harpers Ferry. When you see any of Wrights ask them the address of Silas Bunzan. I have forgotten.

The weather continues very fine and warm here with now and then a night quite cool. One night it froze ice. I visited the old Arlington House a few days ago, some of Washington's family once lived there -- the Custisses. It is now headquarters for the generals. I saw old McDowel *[General Irwin McDowell]* and staff going in that direction soon after I came away. He was riding his gray horse. The soldiers are very much set against him. *[General McDowell was in command of Union troops at the First Battle of Bull Run, and was in command of the III Corps at 2nd Bull Run. He was criticized for performance in both battles and relieved of command. After retirement, in 1882, he became Park Commissioner in San Francisco.]*

But I must close as it is nearly nine. Roll calls are then and no lights are permitted to burn after that. *[The lights were kerosene lanterns and candles.]* My love to all our folks and to all theirs, that may enquire. Say to Kate that I will try and write soon. Good-bye, your brother, Joel.

P. S. My pens *[quills]* are all so sharp that I can scarcely write with them.

*****

[On October 10, 1862, Confederate President Davis proposed drafting 4,500 blacks. Their function was not to fight, but to construct forts in and around Richmond.]

Letter #9A

[Joel wrote the following three letters to his younger sister, Sallie, from three locations along the Potomac.]

Army of the Potomac
Saturday morning, Oct. 18, *[1862]*

Dear Sister:

As the mail has not yet gone out and I have been writing to Joseph Pardoes, I will this morning enclose a few lines to you. We are still upon picket on the river *[Potomac]* as mentioned their letter, but expect to be relieved today. Our mail has not come to us yet; we expected it last night as our chaplain had gone to Washington. He returned without it. It has been back now a week. There was so much he could not bring it -- 2½ bushels for the regt. I look for a peck *[as]* my share.

The cannons we heard, of which I spoke, I learn this morning were at Charles Town, Va. A heavy fight has taken place at that point. The news is that our boys completely routed Jackson with 150,000 men under him, that he fell back to Winchester and another fight was expected today. We only about half believe any thing we hear down here, unless we see for ourselves. What I wrote about white flags upon the capitol proved to be nothing more than signals. Any little thing serves to start great stories.

This morning I hear that we are likely to be sent to Hilton Head, South Carolina, but do not know it to be a fact. Yet it may be so. We had just heard that we were likely to stay in the place we are or vicinity for the winter, and that our Brigade was detailed especially for picketing purposes. So, you see we hardly know. In fact, don't know where we will be or what we will be at tomorrow.

We bought a fish line yesterday, and last night we took turns watching for rebs on the other side, and fished. When it was my turn, I caught a nice eel, one fine bullhead, and a chub. There are five of us at one post: Sam M. *[Samuel, cousin]*, myself, Sperry and Gower from Davidson, and N. Brown (Lyman's brother). Altogether, we had in the morning one eel, four bullheads, and the chub which made a good meal for the whole of us. We get but little besides hard crackers hard tack when on picket or on a march.

This morning was very cold and frosty so fire felt quite comfortable at day light. I will tell you what you may send me if you have a mind to. That is, half a dozen little sacks for carrying sugar, coffee, tea, salt, and rice, etc., with draw strings to them. They should hold nearly a pint. One for salt and one for pepper make smaller, make them out of light stuff, if colored stuff, they would look better, but that wouldn't make much difference. Those for sugar and salt, if they could be out of some thing that would not waste through, they would be better (a small bladder would be just the thing, now). We ain't 'ticular about the looks of anything now. Put them into a small newspaper or send them at twice *[at twice the normal postage rate]*. Newspapers will come in good and the postage won't be so much.

I have not heard from George very lately. Do not know where he is. I will not write anymore at present as this makes the third time since I heard from you. Did you get the likeness all right, or had it eat out and gone. *[In old photographs, sometimes the chemicals kept on working and faded out the image.]* If, when the mail comes in, or I get any other news before our mail leaves, I will pencil it in. If not, this is all, from your ever affectionate brother Joel.

*****

Letter #9B

Sunday, Oct. 19, *[1862]*
[Camp in Virginia]

Our regt. was relieved last night by another and we are now in camp with the rest of our brigade some five miles back from the river *[they are on the northeast side of the Potomac, in Maryland]* and two miles from Poolsville. It is a very pleasant Sabbath morning, but the sound of fife and drum take away serenity. A funeral sermon is to be preached this afternoon on the occasion of the death of our 2nd Lieut. Diefenbach.

Our mail has not yet come in, but expect it every hour. I heard last night from a man that came from the direction of Fort Lyon that Will Rogers had been discharged and sent home. I hope it is true, but do not think it probable. I don't think Will can ever stand camp life. If I should be so unfortunate as to lose my health, I want to be home.

Tell John *[Sallie's husband]* to run and look out of the window for there goes old Gen. Robison on a dark bay horse with heavy black beard coming down nearly to his belt. *[The "heavy black beard" was on the general.]* His staff and a troop of colonels riding at his heels. He is a rough fellow and I don't fancy him much but our Colonel *[Madill]* is a noble fellow, a warrior, and a man to boot. He is down against drinking, swearing, card playing and spending money at the suttlers. Our boys all like him, though 2/3 of them are guilty of the above-named vices.

*****

[There were several Union General Robinsons in the Civil War, but the one Joel was referring to was General John Cleveland Robinson. He had been a cadet at the Point (Class of 1839) and had fought in the Mexican, Seminole, and Mormon engagements. At the time Joel saw him, he was commander of the 1st Brigade, 1st Division, III Corps, Army of the Potomac. He was severely wounded at Spotsylvania, given the medal of honor for Laurel Hill, and a statue was dedicated to him at Gettysburg where his two brigades held five Confederate brigades at bay for four hours.]

Letter #9C

[Camp Prescott, Virginia]
Oct. 20, *[1862]*

We are all right this morning save near froze to death. Very cold morning. We got part of our mail last night. I had two letters from Mrs. Pardoe and one from ---*[text obliterated]*. James has not yet joined us, but I expect him every day. Our mail goes out this morning.

Good-bye Sally, John, and Georgia. Except my love and write soon. Your bro. Joel

P. S. Word now is that we go to Texas soon, merely rumor I guess. Tell JOB *[brother-in-law, Jonas Bedford]* if he will write to me I will promise not to tease him any more. My very best respect to Helen and Lillie with the rest of the family.

*****

Letter #10A

[The following letter is Joel's first out-and-out love letter to Vi.]

Oct. 22nd, *[1862]*
Camp near Poolsville, Md.

Dearest Friend:

Yours of the ninth found me enjoying good health. I received it Monday evening, the 20th. I was very, very glad to hear from you again and that you were enjoying good health as well as yourself. If I mistake not, I mailed my last letter to you from Camp Prescott Smith, Arlington, Va.

*[We]*Left that place two weeks ago last Saturday. We crossed the Potomac River and marched four miles to Poolsville in the state of Maryland. We were marched that distance in one and ½ days and carried with us our knapsacks and equipage which would weigh 60 lbs. We were sent to cut off the retreat of some rebel cavalry that had crossed into Md. but were too late to be of any service.

We were within hearing of the cannon at the battle of Charleston, *[Charles Town, West Virginia]* Va. that took place a few days ago. We have not been into any *[battles or skirmishes]* ourselves yet but do not know how soon our turn may come. *[Charles Town was now in West Virginia. On June 20, 1863, 40 counties in the western part of Virginia seceded from Virginia, Confederate States of America, and became the 35th state in the United States of America. At that time the population of the new state, West Virginia, was about 440,000.]*

Will Rogers and Charley Graves have been taken to the hospital. They are at Washington, I believe. They are no better. James Pardoe was left back at Camp Prescott. He was getting much better when we left; have not heard of him since, but expect that he will join the regt. in a few days. I have enjoyed myself very well since I came into the army. I feel just as though I had done my duty, conscious of this and having been blessed with the best of health for which I feel myself both thankful and fortunate.

Do you study my wishes? Or how came you to fulfill them by sending that lock of hair? I came near making the request when I wrote but feared to, lest you might think me foolish. I had such a nice visit with you in dreamland not long since it seemed so much like a reality, I thought at last I gave you my hand to say good bye and leave to join my companions in arms again; then I thought you entreated me to stay and not leave you again; I thought that I consented this time but morning came and I awoke to realities. It was a dream!

Thursday morning! I have been now just two mo. in the service since I left home. Two only of the 36 *[months]* gone. Time passes faster than I had any idea it would, with me soldiering.

Cousin Charles Snell was to see us three weeks ago Sunday. He came to Washington for Wallon who was wounded at the battle of Sharpsburg. We had a very pleasant time visiting with him. We went over to Arlington House. Don't you recollect looking at the picture of it in that geography one of those we marked, I think? It looks just like that picture, with eight large pillars in front. It has been a splendid mansion once. It used to be the residence of some of the Washington family, the Custisses, his wife's folks. I saw where they were buried just back of the mansion in a grove of oaks, but their graves were erected large marble monuments with their names engraved plainly: George Washington Parke Custis, and Mary L. Custis, his wife, with the date, etc. and a verse of scripture commencing "Blessed are the dead that die in the Lord."

["Arlington House" is now called the Custis-Lee Mansion. George Washington married the widow, Martha Custis. They had no natural children. Martha's son by her first marriage, John Parke Custis, was adopted by George. He grew up at Mount Vernon with George and Martha. When adult,

John served in the Continental army under General Washington, married Eleanor Calvert, and died of camp fever during the Revolutionary War, in 1781. Two of the four fatherless John Parke Custis children, George and Eleanor, were then adopted by the George Washingtons and taken to Mount Vernon to be raised. George Washington Parke Custis was 18 when his adopted father, ex-President George Washington, died in 1799. Martha died in 1802.

[George Washington Parke Custis moved from Mount Vernon to his 1,100 acre estate, on a hill overlooking the city of Washington. There, he built Arlington House. Completed in 1817, it was considered one of the handsomest houses in the United States. The George Washington Parke Custis couple had only one child, Mary, surviving infancy. She and Robert E. Lee, married in 1831. Professional soldier, Lee, was stationed at various military bases around the country, but when in Washington, Arlington House was their home. When the Custis parents died, the Lees inherited the estate.

*[Virginia seceded from the Union in April 1861. At that time General Lee resigned his commission in the U.S. army and became part of the Confederate cause. Shortly, General Lee and his wife left Arlington House, never to return to it. It was said that no place on earth was more loved by Lee than Arlington House. He wrote: "**my affections and attachments are more strongly placed there than at any other place in the world.**" Throughout the entire Civil War, Arlington House was used as headquarters by Union officers.*

[Lee's home was seized by the Federal government in 1864 for non-payment of property taxes, the result of a wartime law requiring property owners to appear in person when paying their taxes. Two hundred acres of the estate were set aside for a military cemetery. Now the site of our famous Arlington National Cemetery, it is the final resting place of many notables, including President John F. Kennedy and his wife "Jackie" Kennedy. Burials at the Arlington National Cemetery now average about 110 per week.]

What do you think, Vile? I have found another of my friends last night one I went to school with at Towanda *[Towanda Academy]* by the name of James Coburn. He is in our regt. and next co. but one by us. I have seen him dozens of times but did not know him. He is a first rate fellow and I am so glad to find him. *[James Coburn was the nephew of inquiry in teacher Coburn's, March 20, 1865, letter. Also, see diary June 3, 1865.]*

We begin to think that we will stay near where we are this winter but cannot tell for sure as we can believe but very little of what we hear in camp. A few days ago we heard that our brigade was to go to Texas. For a while we thought it might be so. It just seems as though I was far enough away now.

You wished to know who that lady was that felt so disappointed. It was Amelia. Did you think such a thought of her? I did not till just before I left. When you see Sallie she can tell you about it for it was her that told me the most about it. She made me promise to write to her but I have not yet. If I do, I will let you know.

I have written to quite a number of my female friends, but I can write none but friendship letters now, excepting to you. I do not wish to, for they have no place in my affections now. You ask, does distance make any difference in my feelings towards you? You said it does not to yourself, well it do to me for the farther I go away and the longer the absence, the more I love to think of thee. I burn my letters when I get them ans. but somehow I don't yours and whenever anything goes wrong and I get despondent it is your likeness I take out to look at, and that countenance, so full of hope and cheerfulness, that I catch it immediately and look forward to the future when the wars are all over and we shall come back to the land whence we started, and then the thought of a girl and pleasant home somewhere with the one I love, and I am as cheerful again as ever. But I must close.

Perhaps next time I will give you a description of the house I now live in and who lives with me, etc. and who cooks and how, etc. *[Union soldiers lived in private houses in northern Virginia, with the simple expedient of moving in.]* Let me know, when you write again, how soon your school closes, so I may know where to direct my next letter. Please excuse the soiled appearance of this letter as I write without either desk or table. May heaven's choicest blessing be ever meted out to thee is the wish, the prayer, of your true friend, Joel.

The 2nd lieutenant of our company died of typhoid fever two weeks ago Sunday –– John Diefenbach, of Dushore. Please write soon. Write soon to Joel.

'Tis said that absence conquers love,
But oh! Believe it not.
In what so ever land I rove,
Thou art not, canst not, be forgot!

*****

Letter #10B

Friday morning the 24th, *[October 1862]*
[Upperville, Virginia]

Good Morning Dear:

Well, who do you suppose my letter was from? I will tell you if you will keep it a secret. It was from a young lady at Canton going to school there ––

one that I think much of. You can guess her name. It is lucky it came, for I had your letter all ready directed to Canton, and it would have gone this morning. I am sorry you have to leave school. It is really too bad. So, your folks, can't keep house without you. I don't wonder at it. I came to just such a conclusion myself a good while ago that I couldn't either.

So, you received a letter from Mr.____ *[indecipherable text]*. If he is a respectable fellow, answer it of course. As to a future correspondence with him that should be (according to my judgment) decided by the motives that induce him to ask you to write. If it is purely friendship on his part, and he is a good letter writer, I have no objections at all, and would say write, for I owe nearly all of the little that I possess of the art, to my corresponding with those that were my superiors.

I received eight letters only last night, with yours. Yours was one, one from Sally, one from little Georgia makes three. Then one from Brother David makes four, one from Kate makes five. One from Charles Grange at the hospital in Washington. He states that he is getting some better, but Will Rogers who is with him is getting worse every day. If Charley's folks ask about him, tell them his address is: St. Aloysius Hospital, Washington, D.C. Let me see, that makes six. One from James Pardoe. We left him behind with a number of others at Camp Prescott Smith, 215 miles back. *[The number of miles he gives from Arlington to Upperville seems high. There may have been an error in deciphering the handwriting. Actual distance is about 65 miles.]* He is getting nearly well again. That's seven, and one from Lucy Bothwell, eight. But there was no love in it. It was an answer to the one that I told you I wrote before I came away. She is an excellent letter writer. If you wish to, and will promise to burn, I will exchange you the one you spoke of. This is at your pleasure, but I must certainly stop writing or you will think me crazy.

I cannot accommodate you with the soldier's picture at present as we are out of reach of any artist of that kind, at this place.

I am going to get a friend to direct this letter to you, so the good people of your vicinity will bother themselves about where it came from. Let me know what they say about it. It was very cold here this morning with frost thick enough for sleighing. The reason why you did not get a letter as you expected, when we were marching and for a week afterward, we did not have any mail. But, good bye again and write soon to JOEL.

*****

[On October 25, 1862, President Lincoln communicated with General McClellan over the Army of the Potomac. The chief executive had become increasingly annoyed with the lack of aggression on "Mac's" part and sent this telegram, **"Will you pardon me for asking what the horses of your army have**

done since the battle of Antietam that fatigues anything?" That was President Lincoln's message in response to McClellan's message about his **"sore tongued and fatigued horses."** *The next day General McClellan marched his troops and horses across the Potomac River into Virginia.]*

CHAPTER 4: NOVEMBER 1862

Letter #11A

[At the Battle of Fredericksburg, the Confederate Army of Northern Virginia, under General Lee, was well entrenched in the city, on the south side of the Rappahannock River. The problem of the Union Army of the Potomac was getting across the river and dislodging the Confederates from their toehold at Marye's Heights in Fredericksburg. From this time on, Joel was detached from his 141st Regiment and became a provost guard, at Division Headquarters. Officially, though, he remained in the 141st Regiment, until it was mustered out in Washington, May 28, 1865.]

Sunday, Nov. 30th, 1862
[Fredericksburg, Virginia]

My Dear Friend:

The long looked for *[letter from Elvira]* has come at last, so at least me thinks I hear you say, 'tis not that I did not wish to write ere this, but every day here has not the conveniences for doing so. It has been nothing but march, march, march! Until the last week we are having a little rest. We are now before Frederickburg. It is in possession of the rebs and is upon the other side of the River Rappahannac from us. Here I saw the first rebs that were not prisoners. I was down to the river and they were on picket close upon the other side. I could easily have hurt that one. I promised to for you, but we are not allowed to hurt those on picket.

Since I wrote before, I have been detached from my company as a provost guard at our division headquarters, General Birney's. There is some 50 or so of the provost. Our duty is to guard around headquarters and I like it much better than in the company, only I am separated from my mess mates. I see them every day so it don't matter so much. I don't know how long I shall stay in my present position, perhaps only for a few weeks. Maybe as long as I stay in the army. You won't care if I do, only I shan't have any chance of hurting those rebs.

I saw Sam Black, Laws, and Sam Bryan yesterday. George Pardoe is four or five miles from here, but I have not seen him very lately. Will Rogers I have not heard from since Isaac came down. James Pardoe, I think, will get a discharge soon but I guess that I have written war enough so now for a paragraph.

[James Pardoe, younger brother of George, mentioned above, was 20. He had been in the hospital, and Joel surmised a medical discharge was in order.]

So you think Ellen and Libbie act strange? Just so I thought before I came away in regard to myself they didn't used to act so, did they? I once thought they wouldn't mind fooling a little themselves, but certainly I do not think they can lay anything up against me on that score for I never wished or tried to pass for more than a friend.

I have received no letters telling how saucy you had been. If I had, I would have understood it all. My not writing the address rather fools some of them, does it not? I guess I'll keep on doing so if that is the case. I am ever so much obliged for the paper sent, for as the old soldiers here say, my paper was about played out but since then I have had the good luck to get a package or one of those stationary envelopes.

Your ans. *[to]* D.B.'s letter is perfectly right! My disposition, I trust at least, is not a jealous one. I had a letter from that Miss Locke, the schoolteacher, I spoke of at Welsboro *[Wellsboro]*. She wrote a very good letter, but closed by asking me to send her my ambrotype. Would you think she thought aught but friendship? Assuredly, I did not. Cannot I have any friends where friendship is all I ask?

But I must close for tonight. O, had I wings of a dove, how soon would I revisit home, friends, enjoyments most dear, and leave war with its desolation in my speeding behind. Good night.

*****

[In the first week of November 1863, President Lincoln finally reached the end of his abundant patience with the dilatory General McClellan, and relieved him of command of the Army of the Potomac. Lincoln replaced "Little Mac" with Major General Burnside. At the same time, he relieved General FitzJohn Porter, close friend of General McClellan, of his corps command. General Porter was replaced by General Joseph Hooker. Lincoln also replaced General Butler, then in New Orleans. Lincoln was finally cleaning house of his incompetent generals.

[The Confederacy also had its problems with incompetent and "political" generals. During the same week, the Confederate Army of Northern Virginia saw some significant "general shuffling". Generals James Longstreet and Thomas Jackson were promoted from major generals to lieutenant generals, and were to command the First and Second Army Corps, respectively. These moves were of great importance in the battles to come.]

CHAPTER 5: DECEMBER 1862

Letter #11B

Dec. 2nd, *[1862]*
[Fredericksburg, Virginia]

Still my letter is unfinished. My ink has given out so please excuse pencil. Nothing worthy of note has occurred since writing the first part of this letter. I suppose school has commenced before this. Are you attending? If so, I hope you have a good teacher to make amends for last winter. *[Joel was Elvira's teacher the previous year, so he's making a little self-demeaning joke.]* How I would like to just step in at recess!

Have you snow now, away up there in Sullivan? We have none here. You spoke of a furlough. 'Tis doubtful about getting one, besides I should freeze to come into such a cold climate in winter. 'Tis impossible to get a picture taken here, but I will send you a small one of Jeff. Davis in the shape of a reb. postage stamp. I got it of *["off of" or "from"]* a reb. prisoner at Leesburg. We have no mail now for more than a week. It seems long to wait for letters but what shall I say next? I do say my thoughts do --- *[word missing because paper was torn]* turn out. I am on guard today by the gen. tent, Birney's -- on two and off four hours, so on through the 24. Gen. Birney is a good looking man but has very light colored whiskers and mustache. Now don't laugh at me any more. *[Is Joel now sporting whiskers and/or a mustache? Many Civil War soldiers did have facial hair -- not so much because of style, but because they didn't have facilities to shave.]* But I must say good bye once more. Dearest, write soon to me again. Joel.

P. S. The wind blew smoke and ashes over my paper, so please excuse. Except my love and best wishes, Joel.

*****

Letter #12A

[This letter to brother, Jesse, reveals Joel depressed and discouraged. It is Christmas Eve, and he is away from his family. It's probably his first Christmas away from home. During this time, morale in the Union Army of the

Potomac was at an extremely low level. Also, the Army of the Potomac has just lost a disastrous battle in Fredericksburg with a great loss of life.

[Much of the responsibility for the Fredericksburg Battle disaster accrued to General Ambrose Burnside, for he may have been the most completely incompetent general commanding the Army of the Potomac. At this time, too, food and other supplies were short. The desertion rate was high, and Joel mentioned in his last paragraph that if things get worse he, too, will take French furlough. Joel suspects George Pardoe, his nephew, may have deserted. Pardoe later turned up at home in civilian clothes.]

Christmas Eve, Dec. 24, *[1862]*
[Across river from Fredericksburg, Virginia]

Dear Brother:

After so long a time, I take pen to ans. your most welcome letter. I have been writing to over 20 different persons, which occupies nearly all my spare hours. I am still enjoying good health. The rest of the boys are, I believe, usually well. James Pardoe is with the company yet. He does no duty. We are doing what we can to get a discharge for him and think perhaps he will get one soon. We have not received our box yet, not got an ans. from the man it was left with. If anyone comes down I want they should stop and see if it can be found. We are now where we were a month ago opposite Fredericksburg. I think there would be no trouble for a person to get a pass through the lines Dec. 25th.

While writing I was called out to help unload quartermaster goods which took us till nearly midnight. Some 40 wagon loads of clothing, etc. for our div. Was on guard today, and could not write till evening. I am still at Hd Qrs as provost guard. Have now been some weeks in so doing.

I missed having a part in the slaughter at Fredericksburg, but was a witness to a part of it on Saturday from heights this side of the river where I could see some five miles of our line of battle. 'Twas dreadful beyond description! On Sunday I went over the river with the rest of the guards patrolling for stragglers, and came away in the masterly retreat of Monday night with the rest of the army. Our regt. was not engaged, more than supporting a battery, being under fire a part of the time. Had one killed and four wounded. George Pardoe, you will have heard from my other letters, was missing. We have heard no news of him yet. The Reserves were so dreadfully cut up I am afraid George has not escaped as a prisoner, though we hope soon to hear from him.

I need not write of the battle, as you got that by the papers. The army is getting disheartened, in fact completely discouraged. I can hardly find three *[fellow soldiers]* that have confidence in any one man, unless it be the old soldiers in McClellan. I don't know how it appears to you up away out of reach of this terrible rebellion, but here at this time I must confess everything wears a dark, gloomy aspect.

Camp is full of rumors, but we can credit scarcely anything. If some change is not brought about soon, a bad state of affairs will indeed be ours. I have heard many brave soldiers say that they have done their last fighting for it's no use. But don't think I'm down at the heel after writing as I have. As long as my health is good I can pick along as good as most any of them. If it comes so I can't, I'll take french furlough and form new acquaintances. But I must close and write a few lines to your wife. Your brother, Joel.

*****

Letter #12B

[The 40 wagon loads of goods Joel had helped unload the previous day, December 24, contained food for the officers. The enlisted men had coffee and hard tack for their Christmas dinner. Unfair treatment such as this typified conditions that brought about the swelling unrest in the Army of the Potomac Desertion was the answer to many.]

Dec. 25th, *[1862]*
[Across the river from Fredericksburg, Virginia]

[To Philena, Jesse's wife]

I wish you a merry Christmas, Phidie. What do you think I had for dinner? Roast turkey, chicken, mutton, potatoes, green cellery, all kinds of wines, etc.? I saw Gen. Birney and staff at 'em, and had hard work to keep from making a charge upon the whole pile of officers and all, but at last made a masterly retreat and dined upon coffee and hard tac. Why, Fide, I'm getting fat as a little f--- *[fox?]* down here on such high living.

Say, how do the school ma'ams get along without me this winter? Is there any snow up there? Freezes here at night though some. Haven't had any letter from home dated later than the seventh. It is getting late. Please excuse this miserable show for a letter, but I want to mail it early in the morning. In fact, I have hardly any time to write half the letters that I should. This I wrote in such a hurry I am ashamed to look. I put two stamps inside. I can't separate them very well without spoiling them.

Direct your letters, as before, to the regt. as I see some of them nearly every day, and can get them nearly as well. I separated the stamps I spoke of this morning by boiling them, but I guess I spoilt one. Your affectionate brother, Joel. Write soon.

Letter #13

[Across river from Fredericksburg, Virginia]
Dixie Land, Dec. 26, *[1862]*

My Dear Friend:

Your most welcome letter I received last mail, or rather today. Tonight, I seat myself to ans. it. Still, I am enjoying the blessings of health. Have we not great reason to be thankful that while others have sickness and died or are suffering from disease, we are spared? Have our health with the hope of enjoying each other's society and that of our friends? Yesterday, only, I received the letter you referred to in your previous letter. It was dated Nov. second, and I think it must have played on the way.

Jabe *[Bird, Cousin J. K.]* and my sister Abel will begin to think I am getting very distant in both meanings of the word. Tell Abe the reason I have not written his letter *[is that]* it was so lazy. It was nearly two months coming. As the people who live here say, I want him to write me a 'right smart one' next time. *["my sister Abel", mentioned above, is one of several mystery correspondents to whom Joel wrote. "Sister Abel" was a man, for Joel sometimes referred to him in the masculine gender as "Abe". He was Elvira's cousin.]*

So, you were afraid I would be offended for telling Jabe to tell me to be a good boy and mind my own business!. Why! My sweet one you must not think that in the time I have known you I have not become acquainted. Yes, I did look for a letter last week every day. 'Twas no letter. No letter! Then, I thought that I would write again, but thinks I to myself, "It will be along tomorrow". They say tomorrow never comes, but I don't care if it don't. The letter has, and I am no longer a disappointed youth.

That was a bad, bad affair the battle of the 13th!

[At Fredericksburg, General Ambrose E. Burnside's Army of the Potomac had approximately 12,650 casualties. Lee's Army of Northern Virginia lost 5,300 men. The Confederate army had won an overwhelming victory, but the Union army had not been destroyed. Combat strength of the two armies in that battle was 120,000 Union and 78,000 Confederate.]

You will have learned all about it by the paper 'ere this, as I told you I thought that I should not. I did not take any part in it. Our regt. had but one killed and four wounded. It was near but *[our regiment]* was not engaged.

'Twas dreadful to listen to the cannon and musketry. Though *[I]* was out of danger I thought I would not look upon the dreadful scene. But, in the afternoon I couldn't resist the excitement, and soon found myself with hundreds of others upon the heights this side of the river and about a mile from the scene of carnage. I will not pain you by giving a description of what I saw. I came away sick of war and thinking of that rude rhyme commencing, "If I was King of France", etc.

[The nursery rhyme went: "The King of France went up the hill, with twenty thousand men; The King of France came down the hill, and ne'er went up again." From: Pigges Corantoe. Joel's analogy with the Union Army of the Potomac was appropriate. The disastrous hill for the Union troops was Marye's Heights. Prior to the battle, Edward Alexander, Confederate General Longstreet's artillery commander, described his control of Marye's Heights as follows: "A chicken could not live on that hill when we open fire on it." He was right!]

Sunday night we went over the river on to a part of the battlefield, and recrossed on Monday night with the rest when our army fell back to its old position. So, we are now just where we were more than a month ago and not near as well off, but this is enough of war.

The weather is very moderate here now. There has been no frost for several days. Tonight it looks somewhat like rain; then look out for mud. I wished you a Merry Christmas yesterday; did you have one? I will also wish you a Happy New Year, though I shall not be there to take a sleigh ride to Millview with you this time. Only wish that I was. Would risk the freezing rain. But never mind. I often think of those lines in Wells Grammar,

> Hope, the sweet vird,
> While this the air can fill,
> Let earth be ice,
> The soul hath summer still.

How miserable I should be if it was not for hope. Would you?

Vile, how many different ones do you think I have to write to? Say 20, and you will have nearly guessed it, but I ain't like the miller in ans. I have nearly a dozen to answer now. Tell Sally hers came today. Say, Vilie, please tell her that I say "yes" to those questions she asks, for fear she may wish to know before I can write to her. Perhaps she will laugh some, but then you know we don't care.

How do you like this new style of paper? It is some a cousin sent me from Clyde, N.Y., Lottie Dennison. The writing shows through so plain I have turned the sheet every page so the lines will not come so nearly opposite. Why will you not go sleigh riding when you have so many good offers? 'Twill not offend me in the least. I know you would give me the preference if I were there, that is all anyone should ask. Pray do not think me to be disposed to jealousy. Go with them, if it will be any pleasure to you. I know that I shall not be forgotten even though you be by the side of laughing Tom or witty Dan.

'Tis getting late and I must close. Good bye, good night. Except one, two, three kisses and true love of your ever faithful friend, Joel. I am still with the provost guards, but 'tis uncertain about remaining. Direct as before: Co. K, 141st Pa. V.

*****

Letter #14

Dec. 26th, *[1862]*
[Across from Fredericksburg, Virginia]

To David:

This morning, thinking my letter had so far to go, I thought that I would put in an extra sheet. "All is quiet", as newspapers say, "along the lines of the Army of the Potomac" though nearly all last night I heard cannon at a distance down the river.

There was lots of drunken fellows about yesterday and last night. Just as I was finishing my letter we were called out to dispose of some of them, and the rest of the night I had to sleep with my equipments on so as to be ready if any row might occur. There is 50 of us in the guard. I stand guard four hours in the day and four at night. The next day I am free. We do our washing, fix our tents or huts (shebangs, they are called here), get our wood, etc., and on the next day we are on police or fatigue list. That day we have to cut and haul wood for headquarters, build fires and do most all kinds of work and generally next day come on guard again, etc.

As yet, I have managed to get along without body guards, in fact have not seen one since I have been down here, though about one in every five have them here or even more. There is only two in the guard that I ever saw before I came into it.

[The "body guards" Joel was referring to were chest protectors made of pieces of metal attached to a cloth and tied on to the chest neck to waist with leather straps. They were called body armor. Although the Federal Government never issued body armor of any sort, sutlers and dealers sold iron vests to many new recruits. Most of these ended up at the bottom of the Potomac River where they sank out of sight. The vests were so heavy they were

soon thrown away; and even in battle failed to live up to expectations. Bullets of the day would go right through them, taking pieces of the vest with them. The standard infantry vest weighed 3½ pounds, while a heavier model (weighing 6 pounds) was used by artillery men and cavalry troopers. Used early on in the war, they never attained much popularity and passed out of use by late 1862, leaving only the many jokes behind. "The man in the iron stove" was standard fare.]

Charles Webster -- he and I tent together. We have a very comfortable shebang, as good as any on the street, with a fireplace at one end of it built of sods. Call and see us some afternoon, can't you?

One fellow here offered 50 cts. a week to board with us, but we thought room was better than company. John Farrel is here, Mike's brother, and a young man from Franklin, the one that used to come in and tease Norton's boys so when Caroline Porter taught school there. His name is Gregory. So Hannah Norton is teaching where I did last winter? *[Hannah Norton was of interest to Joel because his brother, David, was courting her. Later, they married.]*

How does Mary Jane W. succeed at Shrimps? *["Shrimps" was a one-room eight grade rural school east of Millview.]* 'Tis quite different learning the young ideas how to shoot and being here with the idea of learning how to shoot or be shot. Four have died out of Comp. K from Bradford and Diefenbach and Gower from Sullivan.

The capt. *[Wright]* has resigned, and now Lieu. Dunham has. He is a perfect fiddlesticks, a quick tempered, swearing fellow and Ben is the greatest calf I ever saw. Our lieu. had his heart on being capt. after Wright resigned. Some 50 of the co. signed for another man which hurt his pride so he resigned himself. I suppose he will want to be sent to the legislature or congress, but he won't get there before his co. gets back. He is now at the hospital sick. *[Dunham was discharged in December 1862, with a surgeon's certificate.]*

I should try to get a furlough to come home this winter, if it was not for losing my position here in the braves *[guard]*. I don't know, but I might get one by making believe I could get 15 or 20 recruits. If I get back in my regt. soon, I shall try it. *[During the early years of the war, when the volunteer program was in use, some soldiers were given leave to go home and recruit.]*

Our regiment has been out on picket for the last two days. I don't know where five or six miles somewhere. Sam Molyneux and Will Bedford have not gone, as they were unwell. Billy Luke and George were to see us the day before yesterday. Are well, but tired of war. Billy says he has fought his last fight.

We have four months pay now due us. We received our $25 bounty and $2 State premium two weeks ago. Some of the boys have sent their money home. I have not yet. Some of the boys have spent nearly all theirs. I have managed to live on my rations so far, and had my health. Everything I have bought since I left home has not exceeded $5.00. Every letter here costs as much as a six pence. Suttlers here sell butter for 60 cts. a lb., cheese for 30, a loaf of bread like one of mother's big biscuits is 15 cents or two shillings. I'll stick to my hard bread, meat, and coffee before I'll patronize such thieves.

[The Articles of War prescribed that civilians should be permitted to "sutle" to soldiers. ("Sutle" means to sell. It's a word that has since passed out of our English language.) Sutlers were allowed to be on posts and in camps, set up little stores there, and supply soldiers with goods and wholesome provisions, at reasonable prices. Soldiers bought food and sundries from civilian sutlers, for in many locations that was their only choice, but thought of them as legalized thieves.]

I want you to send me a coarse/fine comb in your next letter as I have lost mine, and I want Jesse to get me a small three square *[triangular]* file, smaller the better, and put it in a Sullivan Democrat *[local weekly newspaper from Dushore, Pennsylvania]* and send it to me. I'll send you 25 cents to pay for them with. If it *[the Confederate money he plans to send]* ain't good, send it back, it's good here. I got it at Leesburg of *["off of" or "from"]* a reb. Good-bye, write soon to your brother, Joel.

*****

CHAPTER 6: JANUARY 1863

Letter #15

[Most letters in this Civil War collection were from Joel to various friends and family members back home. Although Joel carried on regular correspondence with 20 or more people, he saved few incoming letters. Joel considered this one important enough to save and he probably sent it home in one of his own letters. It's from his pastor, Rev. B. D. G. S. Sniffin, minister of the Wesleyan Methodist Church in Millview, Pennsylvania. At that time, the church was meeting in the Millview school house.]

Millview, [Pennsylvania]
Jan. 12th, 1863

Mr. Joel Molyneux:

Dear Sir:

  As your brother David expects to start for Washington tomorrow morning, my wife insists upon my writing a few lines to Joel, but as David can, and will cheerfully tell you all that has transpired in this place since you left us, and all that is likely to take place in this neighborhood or vicinity, that you would care to know. I am very much cramped for the materials to make an interesting letter to a young man far away; but although for the reason above rendered, there is a famine in the news department.

  I will just say that the mercy of God is yet extended to us, and we are trying to prepare for the close of life and prevale on all we have intercors *[social intercourse]* with, to engag in the same work, but we have not succeeded as we could desire. How long we shall continue on this T. we cannot tell although it is generally believed that we shall stay another year. The last qt. co. *[quarterly conference]* invited us to remain; we have not given an answer but perhaps the question will be determined at our next qt. *[quarterly]* meeting which occurs on the 14 and 15 of Feb. at Millview.

[Millview, a pleasant settlement along the Little Loyalsock, is several miles northeast of the village of Forksville, on present State Route 87. In Joel's time, Millview was a busy community center with a grist mill, saw mill, shingle mill, two blacksmith shops, post office, school, and several dozen houses. Since then, Millview has dwindled, to about ten houses, a store, a motel, church, and parsonage. Even in Joel's time, the village was starting to decline for in a later letter he mentioned discontinuance of the post office.]

It occurs to me that I might state what may not occur to David, that in every house where we visit in our regular round of the Ct., *[circuit of churches in that locality]* we here *[hear]* the name of Joel mentioned. All apear anxious to hear from him, and at a little gathering of the young people at our house a few evenings since, it was quite common to hear, "If Joel was here it would seem like old times." Or, "If Joel was with us, as he was a year ago, we should enjoy the visit much better," and such like remarks.

My young friend, permit me to say that we felt great solicitud for you when the news reached us that the union troops had crossed to Fredericksburg, and as additional inteligence arrived disclosing the heartsickening news that the Union army had been defeted with a fearfull slawter, the inquiry pased in many anxious groups, "Is Joel among the slain? Or has he, in answer to prayer, been shielded in the time of battle? Or has he like some of his brave companions in arms fell at his post fighting in his country's cause?"

You will not be surprised at our great concern for you when you remember that you have been a child of many prayers. *[You are]* one that has been blessed with religious privileges from your erlyest moments; a father and mother to teach you the Christian religion by precept and example and loving brothers and sisters, to shed the light of example upon the path of duty, and the way to heaven. You have been taught to respect and receive the gospell that offers life to all, but as we were not quite sure that the child of such rare privilege, the young man of an amiable character has he improved his gracious opportunity? Has he found the Savior of Sinners? Has he given his heart to God, as he has given his body to his country?

An offer: a mature answer to the above query would very much relieve our anxiety, and that you may have satisfactory evidence permit us to join you in constant prayer. B.D.G.S. Sniffin.

[A question: How was Joel able to withstand 34 months of hardship without being killed, wounded, captured, or even sick (except for several colds)? That question is appropriate since about 805 of the original 955 men in the 141st Regiment were casualties (killed, died of disease, wounded, or captured). Reverend Sniffin's letter is significant, for in it we learn Joel was the object of prayers of many folks back home, not only among the Millview Christians, but also among neighbors, family, and friends. Did the united prayers of those dedicated Christians protect and bring Joel back from the war unscathed?]

*****

Letter #16A

Dixie Land, Jan. 25, *[1863]*

My Dear E:

Your ever welcome letter was duly rec. and today with pleasure I take my pen to ans. The present date finds me still enjoying good health and spirits as anyone can conveniently be expected to, all things considered. I am still in the Guard the same as when writing to you before and we are still in the same old camp we occupied then.

Doubtless 'ere this you will have heard of another grand movement made by the Army of the Potomac and also of another complete failure. Though not attended this time by a wholesale slaughter, as before, on Tuesday the 20th *[of January 1863]* our div. with the principal part of the army moved up the river some nine mile, intending there to throw pontoon bridges across the Rappannoc and attack the enemy upon the right, but rain setting in the same evening before the artillery and even the bridges had arrived at the point for crossing the roads soon became so utterly impassable and delays so unavoidable and the rebs getting wind of our intended attack, etc. that the whole expedition was given up and the troops have returned to their old quarters. Luckily for me headquarters were not moved; they were ordered to remain until a crossing had effected. So I escaped at least one hard muddy tramp and don't feel the least mite sorry, either.

I have just heard some good news and that is that George Pardoe is all safe. He has been a prisoner; was taken to Richmond and has been paroled and sent to the parole camp at Annapolis, Md. I presume 'ere this he has written home and with all the particulars, etc. I am so glad to get news of his being safe that I hardly know how to express it for I very much feared he had fallen, much more than feared to express when I have written to his folks.

Before this reaches you, you will have learned that my brother David failed in getting through the lines to see us, having just come down at exactly the wrong time if it had been the week before or even a week later I presume he would not have met with the least trouble. You can readily suppose that I again was a disappointed youth for I had heard that he was coming and I had thought of having such a pleasant time, but I have almost learned to take disappointments cheerfully. Sally wrote to me by David; he sent the letter on from Washington. She wrote upon the evening of your intended spelling school and was prevented by the snowstorm.

Day before yesterday I received some letters from the little girls that attended school last winter. Wasn't I pleased some? I have not rec. one since being in the service that I read with greater pleasure. I shall write to them soon.

Bachee wished to know if I remembered the last night of school, the little minx! How I'd like to pull her ear; but don't say anything to her about it.

I wrote to Jabe *[cousin J. K. Bird]* a few days since. Do you remember what you told him to say to me? I let on to him as if I was offended, just to tease him somehow. I can't help teasing Jab -- first I made believe being dreadfully put out for his breaking the match between Amelia and I and then told him to say to you that I was much obliged for the advice, etc. Did he tell you?

I have not heard of Amelia since I left, only by others, and I am sorry to say much what I have heard is quite unfavorable. I hear occasionally from Miss Bothwell, but only as a friend. If it was not that I knew you don't care, I would discontinue it.

Miss Locke, my Wellsboro friend, still continues to ans. and to write. She is so patriotic and writes such offhand letters. She has a style of writing all her own I can not help being amused with it. I do not think she has an idea of anything more than friendship and I am very certain that I have not. If I once thought my doing so was in the least objectionable by you, I would not even think of her again.

I think that I spoke of a Miss Taylor to you once as I came by where she lived as I came away. I called to say good-bye, etc., and as she retains my respect for very kind treatment from them, her and her parents and family, when I was teaching in their vicinity a few years since. On leaving, she asked me to write after I got to Dixie. I told her I would, then supposing her to be engaged to a young man at Dushore, Zyaner. I wrote some two months after coming down. 'Twas ans. promptly, but did not see anything out of the way only wishing me to write again soon but it was perhaps a month or more when I wrote again, and another ans. came immediately which I thought expressed rather strong sympathy. I hardly know what to do? I do not blame myself in the least for certainly I never encouraged *[her]* and just now comes another letter from her two since I have written. This one is worse than all before. I hardly know what I shall do in reference to this case. What would you do? Shall I return her letters and say nothing? Or shall I write and say I am spoke for, etc., etc.? Sister Kate writes me and says that her fellow, i.e. Miss Taylor's, was married New Years. This explains the whole of it. She don't mean to die.

Now, Vile, if you will lay by *[set aside]* your books or work as it may happen, I will chat a while with you this morning as I did not quite finish last evening. Upon looking over *[what I have already written]* I see that I nearly have complied with your request, to write all I could think of. You, in your last, wished to know if I had thought you infered in one of your letters previous that I would be jealous if you went riding, etc., with others. Not in the least! The idea that I wished to convey was that I did not wish you to debar yourself of any such innocent and pleasant recreations for fear you might offend me; this was all. I am sure you have more reason for jealousy if you were so disposed. Perhaps you intended me to profit by your example, but never fear my dear one. Your slightest wish is more to me than anything that can be bestowed upon me by others.

So, you were puzzled to know what I meant by asking you to say "yes" to Sally. Strange, she did not know what I referred to. She had just written to me and asked me if I would let John *[her husband]* have the use of a suit of my clothes, providing they should go upon a visit to Lewisburg. I just thought it be so novel for you to say "yes" for me, I thought she might wish to know before I could write her. I did not intend to put you in suspense supposing she would explain of course. When she wrote to me, your cousin Libbie *[Samuel Molyneux's wife]* put in nearly ½ a sheet. She commenced: "Dear Coz upon Sam's account" I presume so I shall tell when I ans. which I do soon. I wrote to my sister Abel a few days ago.

Enclosed I send you a ring, the first one that I ever attempted to make. I made it expressly for you. 'Tis not near so pretty as I could wish and I am afraid some to large; let me know if so and I will try again. Good Bye.

Affectionately, Joel.

*****

<u>Letter #16B</u>

January 27th, *[1863]*
[Fredericksburg, Virginia]

Before putting the letter in the mail I will write one line. 'Tis raining again today. I'm thinking that we shall have rainy muddy weather now. I hear this morning we are to move camp some eight or ten miles to where wood is more plenty. Being upon guard today, the 26th, my letter does not get finished in time to go out in today's mail. But now 'tis ready for tomorrow.

I have just learned that young Thomas Mariott died of diptheria in a hospital; I think at Philadelphia. What will poor Ester Norton do?

*****

Letter #16C

January 27th, *[1863]*
[Fredericksburg, Virginia]

We learned yesterday that Gen. Burnside has resigned and that Gen. Hooker takes command now of the Army of the Potomac. I wonder whose turn will be next? Burnside could not stand the thought of so many failures, I suppose. The rebs had hand boards up with great large letters so we could read them across the river BURNSIDE STUCK IN THE MUD, etc. 'Tis mortifying, the saucy scamps!! Such chaps had ought to be hurt some, hadn't they? Good Bye, Good Bye Joel.

P. S. Could I read your letter? You wished to know. Yes, just as easy as easy. Can you read this? Now I am going to look for that great, long letter that is to take me so long to read it.

*****

CHAPTER 7: FEBRUARY 1863

Letter #17

February 5th, 1863

Dear Brother: *[David]*

Today I take my pen to write a few lines hoping they may find you all as well at home as they leave me. At present, we are having very cold and wintry weather. Last week there was a fall of snow nearly a foot deep, but did not lay long. The last two days has been very cold, so much so they would pass for very good winter with you. Today, 'tis snowing again. 'Tis some 2 or 3 inches already, and very cold also.

We were very sorry you and Will came down just the time you did thus failing to get through the lines. If it had been a week sooner or one later you would not have had any trouble. Your letters and the receipt for those things came through all right. I have sent to Falmouth Station and have also gone to the new one that is close by us, generally called Stoneman's Switch where all our Division express boxes now stop, but can find nothing of them. The agent here says they will not leave Washington upon the account of not being directed properly, for I see by the receipt 'tis only Falmouth when they should have been directed to our company and regt. or else to me at headquarters, 1st Division, 3rd Corps, in care of the provost marshall, Captain Markle. I have just written to Wallace Snell to look them up, if he could, and redirect and send them on. I wrote to him some time ago about the box left in his care, but have not yet heard from it. I wrote to him that if he had not yet got it expressed to open it and send us a pair of boots each to us by mail.

Day before yesterday near 200 boxes came to this division. They came right in to where I am. The marshall has the charge of them, and notifies the regt. that such boxes are here, and the men come and get them. He has them all opened and searched for liquor. If it is found, it is taken. Those that were opened the other day, nearly 2/3rds of the eatables was spoiled upon account of delays, and so I would sooner pay a little more postage, and have the things I need come by mail.

I heard you had arrived home safe. We are now where we were before the move that was made when you was down. You have heard what it amounted to. We expect to move to another camping place in a few days upon account of the scarcity of wood. Here it is all cut away for miles arround, not perhaps over 5 miles or so.

You will have heard 'ere this that George Pardoe is all right, he having been a prisoner and paroled. I understand he expects to get home on a visit.

Some of our boys are getting furloughs now, one to every company, I hear, for ten days. I have not yet heard who goes from our company; when he comes back maybe then one can go. You spoke of letting money to Lipencot. If you can make it safe, you may do so such what paper money I may have (but I have not received money of our month's pay yet only my $25 bounty and $2 St.*[state]* premium.) I have not sent any home yet as I thought perhaps it might come in play sometime, but as the mail will go out soon, and this sheet is nearly full, I will close by sending my love to all & hoping to hear from you soon, I remain your affectionate brother, Joel.

P. S. Tell Kate I believe her turn comes now for a letter. Have just heard the rebs have retaken Fort Donalson. I guess the war will be over soon. I am still in the guard, and you will direct Joel L. Molyneux, Provost Guard, Head Q, Birney's Div., Washington.

*****

Letter #18A

[Joel, and other soldiers in the Army of the Potomac, carried about 60 pounds, and when marching 20 to 23 miles a day, each ounce made a difference. Thus, he did not save many incoming letters, but read them several times to remember them, or perhaps took diary notes about them — from whom, arrival date, whether or not answered, etc. A few of them he sent home with his own letters. Here are two family letters from his cousin, Angie Summers, that he sent home with his own letter.]

Liberty Corners *[Pennsylvania]*
Feb. 15, 1863

My Own Dear Brother: *[Cousin Angie and Joel were about the same age and had so intimate a familial relationship that they considered themselves brother and sister.]*

Your letter of the first was duly received; was perused with pleasure. Was glad to hear from you once more to know you was well. Was glad to hear from George. Had almost given up ever hearing from him again. Had thought he had fallen.

I was much obliged to you for the ring you sent me, but it was too small and would not go on my little finger. You know my fingers are very large, but I can keep it to remember an absent brother.

We had a letter from brother, John, last Saturday. He is well, but has not clothes to make him warm. I wish we could send him some. He thinks perhaps there will be some prospect of his getting home to spend a few days soon. He thinks he ought to spend a few days at home, as well as all the other boys. All *[ought]* to come home. *[Angie's brother, John, was a captain in Company B, 7th Pennsylvania Cavalry. Joel carried on a steady correspondence with him.]*

Mary Jane told me to tell you she thought there were no promises between her and Charley to be broken (she thought). I told her she knew, but she wouldn't say whether there was or not. Mary Jane looks as though she had lost every friend she ever had since Charley went away. *["Charley" was Charles Grange whom Joel visited many times in the hospital. He died in June 1863. Charley's death from disease illustrates the hardship on the "Mary Janes" back home.]*

Our folks have been out to your home in Sullivan last week. The folks were all well, as usual, out there. Mr. Biddel lost two of his children. There is a good many sick with the diphtheria. Aunt Sally is no better. She has not the use of her right side at all. They were looking for Will Rogers home when they were out there. The young folks were all gone up to Sallie's *[Joel's younger sister, Sallie McCarty]* when they got out there.

Our sleighing *[weather]* is fast leaving us today. The sun shines very warm and the snow melts like everything. I am fearful that our sleigh-riding is done for this winter, but we do not enjoy our sleigh much. Last Friday evening we went. There was seven of us and only one gent. Just enough for a driver; that is all we can have. Only once in a while there is two or three, but it is a rare thing unless we get some of the old widowers. They appear to take the load now. I had an invitation to go a sleigh-riding with one last week (but was not able to go) was very sorry to disappoint and have another tomorrow evening, but fear the snow will disappoint this time, but shame such nonsense. I ought to be ashamed to write such trash to a soldier. Please do not let anyone see this not tell any one what silly trash I have written. *[Angie's subject was not "nonsense or trash", but one quite likely to pick up the spirits of war-tired Joel. Sleighing was his favorite winter outdoor activity. The very mention of sleigh-riding refocused his thoughts on the real world.]*

Angie and Ella have written to you. I presume you have received their letter long before this time. I will stop for this time. Perhaps before this time you have seen some of the men from here that has told you all the news -- they are down that way somewhere. But I will leave some room for I may have something to write of more interest than I have written before mail day.

Hannah Robbins is married. I do not know whether I have written to you since or not. Moses Coolbaugh is at home; was out to church today; looks pretty thin and feeble. Your sister, Angie.

*****

Letter #18B

Feb. 20, *[1863]*

I intended to send this last Wednesday, but went away to Burlington *[another village in Bradford County]* and forgot it. The boys are all home again. I have not seen them to know whether they saw you or not, but presume they did. We are all well as usual here. Had a letter from brother, *[John, in the 7th Pennsylvania Cavalry]* Wednesday. He is still well near Murfreesboro yet. J. D. Johnson is at Vicksburg; is well. But I will stop. Please write soon. Your sister, Angie.

*****

Letter #19A

February 20, 1863

Dearest Friend:

Your long looked for letter I received this morning. I began to think something must have happened to you. I did not know before that I should feel just as I did from not getting an ans. from you just as soon as I expected it. Now Elvira, I want to make a bargain with you, you will agree, please? That is, I will write as often as once in two weeks and you do the same, even if our letter fails being received before writing.

I should have written today if yours had not come. I have been very busy for the past two weeks. We have been moving headquarters to a new spot and it made a great deal of work as we had all of us new shantys to build, etc. besides being on guard every day. I was on guard last night, two nights before was my turn. We stand sentry but one during the night and then four hours, the rest of the time we have to sleep, that night I dreamed of being with you, it seemed so real. I thought the rest of the family had all retired. I thought you were sitting close by me and telling me all that had transpired and I was feeling so glad I was free and with you again when the corporal of the guard call out, "Third relief fall in." I was so disappointed, almost vexed at the corporal!

I have not written to one of those misses I spoke of since writing to you before, just because I did not want to. Please don't never say again, "If you find one that suits you better do not let me be in the way" not unless you really wish me to do so and I never wish to live to see the day that I think I do. I understand as much that Ike was maneuvering his best from a letter that Cousin Samuel received but I did not feel at all concerned about that because I felt you would be constant. You say, "What shall I do when Ike comes?" Vile, if your feelings are unchanged from what they were, be frank with him. Ike, in my estimation, is a good fellow and not inclined to deceive anyone. Say to him your affections are elsewhere and you can be to him only a friend! There! Have I not done for once as you requested?

I have been away now more than six months, and I do not really think I shall have to stay the three years. *[Joel's enlistment period was for three years. Actually, he served a little less than the full three years for the 141st Regiment was officially mustered out May 28, 1865.]* Today's papers state there will be another draft soon. Our government seems determined to still continue to prosecute the war, but I do indeed think that I shall see the loved object of my night and day dreams before one half of that time has elapsed.

I had almost forgotten to say I was enjoying good health on the 12th. The day you wrote I received some boxes from home with all sorts of good things to eat: apples, butter, cheese, and all sorts of dried fruit. So, I am as far as living is concerned, doing famously. I wrote to Cousin Lib some ten days ago. If I had only eight letters to ans. I should think I was well off. Yes, I do wish I was with you helping you to ans. some of yours and then you know you could help me too.

Did you receive any valentines yet? I have not. I did not even think of one upon the 14th. The tenth, you know, I was so old that day, but you did not get an opportunity this time of washing my face did you? But my paper is ended, and so must I. As ever, your friend and admirer Joel. *[February 10th was Joel's 28th birthday. From the face washing comment, it sounds as though Elvira had washed his face the previous year when they were in school together. Face washings and playful spankings were common birthday pranks among rural Pennsylvanians.]*

*****

Letter #19B

[The following letter was scribbled, upside down, between lines of the previous letter. Joel called this paper-saving technique "interlining".]

Cousin Samuel has been quite unwell but say to Cousin Lib *["Lib", Vi's cousin, was Sam's wife]*: "He is better again" if she teases you about this letter. We had a fall of snow here nearly six inches deep a few days ago and then rain for some two days. Mud is very plentyfull now.

A number of furloughs are being given to different ones recently for 15 days. Would you be pleased or not just to see me for two or three days, or would you not like such a visit? I do not think I shall be able though to get one. Your picture looks very nearly as good as ever, but if you get some photographs, send me one. We expect an artist here at Hd Qrs. in a day or two. If I can get one fit to send I'll get one for you.

Please write as soon as you receive this. Do not be afraid that I am not interested in what you may write, or that it will tire my patience to read. If I could only talk my letter, I should have one for you that would take you all night to listen to. Hoping that such may soon be the case, I will again say goodbye, dearest friend. I do not know but I have given a different form to address your letters every time, but I get them sooner when direct *[directed]* to headquarters, than to my regt. Please direct *[your letters to:]* Joel L. Molyneux, Hd Qrs, Birney's Div., Washington, D.C.

*****

Letter #20

[The following letter with no address, date, nor salutation was written to his cousin Angie Summers, about February 28, 1863 — after he had received her February 15, 1863, letter, complaining about the ring he had made for her being too small. Probably the ring had been carved from a ham bone.]

I will send you another ring made in my leisure moments and when I did *[do]* not feel like writing letters. If you like this *[ring]* better than the other, and choose to, you can let Sallie *[Joel's sister]* take the first one but just as you like as to that. Keep this to represent the star of hope between us, though 'tis not very nice having no tools to use not even a good knife.

I did not by any means intend you to think I thought you wished me to give someone else the preference to you. Please excuse if my words implied as much. Sometimes I can't make my words say what I wish them to. 'Tis funny, ain't it, when I have written so much and to be so old, too?

You say that you told them you thought, I might write to you once in a while and ask how often that is. 'Tis every two weeks, ain't it? O! Did G.P. come to see his Auntie as he is pleased to term it? If he didn't, I will come and see her myself when I return and stay long enough to make up. How will that do? I have not yet had a likeness taken and have not yet had a good opportunity. *[G. P. (George Pardoe) had been wounded, captured by Confederates, and then released on parole to go home and fight no more. This was a fairly common practice at the beginning of the war, but later the practice was discontinued, initially by the Union, since they recognized that the South had more to gain by the practice than the North.]*

Our gen. has ordered his guards to be dressed in Zoo Zoo-Zouave uniform. Wouldn't you like to see me then with red pants, blue jacket trimmed with red, red cap with a large yellow turband around it, white gloves, etc.? *[It was common practice on both sides, at the beginning of the conflict, for soldiers to wear non-prescribed uniforms.]* I'll get my likeness then, but I must say good bye.

Heaven bless and protect you is the prayer of your Joel.

*****

Letter #21

[The following letter with no date, return address, nor salutation was written to Elvira. It fits in with the other letters of late February 1863.]

I was just about saying I would get a fresh sheet of paper, and war should not be put upon it, but this does not look so overly fresh, do it? My paper has all got mussed and I can't help it dust and rain make mud not clean white paper by any means.

You say that you think just "Vile" is the best name for you. Now, be quiet while I tell you that I never did just like it. I'll tell you why. Every time I see it the proper definition comes to my mind of "vile", and I could never think you as such. Now, if you will let me change it just a little (if you have no objections to my changing your name) then I'll like it. Just so it won't be "Vile". Now I'll tell you how I would have it to suit me. Once you told me 'twas I you loved better than anyone else. Well, I didn't care if you did and now if you will only have I, right as I want you should, I shall love to have you Vilie. You know it can be pronounced as before or sound the "e" slightly as your papa used to do. What say you?

I do believe Dave and Hannah Norton will make a match yet, do you think? I had a letter from her the other day. She spoke of being at the Friends Meeting and calling to see you, but does not mention who brought her. She says, "Elvira is as --- as ever." I leave the word out for 'tis not best to flatter, you know. And if I can see straight being so far off, Kate and her brother Will will follow suit. Cousin Jennie wrote me since her visit to Elkland. She writes a cheerful letter for a girl past 30.

Does Abel really mean to kill the big turkey? If I am so fortunate as to get a furlough in the fall and is it Jennie that is to help him eat it? I really wish they would! Jennie writes me she has 30 turkeys. Have you any?

You must not think it as a certainty my coming, but I will if there is any possible means of doing so and can stay long enough to make a visit. So, you don't like teaching? If it affects your throat I would not say 'twas a very good plan to teach, but of course you are supposed to do as you please.

O! I was teaching the other day. You have often heard of the poor darkies that want to learn how to read when they get free. The Lieut. *[Charles Graves]* had one named Stephe. He has gone with him to Phila. Now, almost every officer has one hired to wait upon them, etc. They do want to learn, and this Stephe carries a spelling book with him almost every day. He would come and want me to show him about his lesson. They talk very broken; one can hardly help laughing at them.

When the lieut. was wounded I got some men to help carry him from the field hospital to a house where he could be better taken care of and then hunted Stephe up to take care of him. You had ought to have seen the poor fellow take on. He seized him by the hand, and then cried like a child for half a hour. The lieut. would say, "Never mind Stephen, I ain't killed. I'll soon get well." Poor Stephe only cried the more and said, "I node you'd be hit dis time."

[Joel mentioned Lieutenant Charles Graves, his commanding officer in the provost guard, numerous times. Graves moved up through the ranks during the conflict and became a colonel. For a while he was assistant adjutant general. After the war, he was in government service. From 1905-14 he served as U.S. ambassador to Norway and Sweden. Later, he lived in Santa Barbara, California and became mayor of that city. He and Joel maintained a lifelong friendship and visited Joel on the Molyneux home farm in Sullivan County. Mother knew him there and spoke favorably of him.]

Well, I'd say I am writing about war again. I can hardly take the time to think. Shouldn't wonder if when you read this you will think me getting very careless or foolish of late. How is it? 'Tis now about the middle of the afternoon and we have not moved as I expected, and it has also quit raining for the present and I must close my letter. I had ought to mend a pair of socks, but I don't just feel like so doing and I wish you had them to mend and I was by you to bother you. Then maybe you would say, "Mend them yourself." If so I would do it just to show you how nice I can darn. You will direct letters nearly as before, direct: Headquarters, 1st Div., 3rd Corps, Washington, D.C. Except with love and write soon to Joel. Good-bye.

*****

CHAPTER 8: MARCH 1863

[After Joel had been in the army six months, he bought a diary journal. Starting his entries March 5, 1863, he continued them until June 5, 1865. He used his journal to keep a running account of his own activities, and never expected anyone else to read it — not because it contained anything personal or confidential, but simply because it dealt only with his own operations and activities. In contrast, he anticipated his letters would be read aloud to family members, church meetings, and neighborhood groups back home.

[In his journal Joel kept a daily tally of letters received and his replies. He recorded work activities such as guarding prisoners, getting a horse shod, burying the dead (both men and horses) and participating in firing squads. He mentioned various marches, battles, and skirmishes in which he participated, and visits to hospitals. Joel recorded money he was paid and owed, as well as amounts he sent back home for banking. He entered visits to other regiments and, of course, visits to his own 141st Regiment.

[I have omitted most journal weather references, unless the weather he mentioned was unusual.

[From here on, diary entries and letters are chronologically interspersed, as written.]

Thu. 5 March. Bought this book today of Gregory, our division suttler, for 50 cts. Gen. Joe Hooker visited our Hd Qrs at Bellair residence. The weather is very fine today. Wrote one letter to V. Splendid evening, full moon.

[Sutlers, unofficial civilian provisioners at army posts, generally stocked writing supplies such as pens, paper, and candles; and quite often whiskey, to soldiers. The most popular food item, molasses cookies, sold six for a quarter.

[General Joseph Hooker relieved General Ambrose Burnside as commander of the Army of the Potomac, on January 25, 1863, after the poor performance of that army at the Battle of Fredericksburg. General Burnside had been appointed commander of the army on November 9, 1862, and relieved General McClellan. General McClellan had relieved General McDowell after the debacle at the First Battle of Bull Run. So, in his first six months, Joel served under five commanding generals: McDowell, Pope, McClellan, Burnside, and Hooker. These were some of the poorest generals in the Union army. Later, Joel served under Meade and Grant.]

Letter #22

Bellair, *[in Virginia]*
March the 5th 1863

Loved Friend:

Hoping 'ere this you have received my last, and according to what I proposed, that is writing oftener, I seat myself to have a social time with you. I sincerely wish this may find you enjoying health for nearly every letter from Sullivan bears tidings of disease and death. Truly it seems that dangers stand thick through all the ground to pack us to the tomb. I am still usually well. So are the boys from our place. Today is very pleasant with the sun shining brightly, no snow is to be seen though ten days ago we had a shower of it nearly a foot in depth and was cold and windy at the same time. How you would have laughed if you could have peeped into my cabin the next morning (as it fell in the night). 'Twas all over the floor and upon the bed all white and a drift 18 inches deep upon our feet.

Did I ever tell you about the man that I tented with? His name is George Holt, from Maine, 22 years old, good looking, full of fun. He does not swear nor drink, nor play cards, or nor use tobacco. He left a young wife at home, having been married only about five months when he enlisted which was about the same time I did. We have very good times, considering circumstances. Almost every night we get into a fracas and upset the table and break some of the chairs or dishes. But enough of this. *[See diary March 19, 1863, for what happened to tent-mate Holt.]*

I had a letter the other day from your teacher, H. Norton, in ans. to a note I sent to my scholars. *["H. Norton" was Hannah, future bride of brother David.]* Did they get them before school closed? She spoke of you as one of her near friends. I told her to set a ribond *[ribbon]* for Abe but she thinks it useless as he is eyeing someone else. Does she mean Julia?

Well, V., I suppose Ike's two weeks have elapsed and he has called for an ans. I am not fearing what that ans. has been, but I could scarcely blame you if it should be contrary to my interests and wishes considering the uncertainty of soldiering and then you know Ike is spoken of a being one of the bestest of boys in that vicinity, but how foolish I talk.

Our regt. has moved five or six miles yesterday to where wood is plenty; we expected to go today and was all ready but this morning were ordered to stay where we are. It looks some like as if we were to make an advance move soon. I saw our Commander-in-chief of this army, Joe Hooker. He is a fine looking man, but not ficil *[fickle ?]* a bit --- *[paper torn]* you might see him.

Abe wrote to me that George Pardoe was back but was dressed in citizen's clothes. I suppose that means he could not get a furlough so he took a French one *[AWOL]*. I would have done the same for I think he deserves a visit home if any one does. I hope he will not get in trouble by it; there are a great many getting furloughs now. I have not thought much about it yet.

At present, I am taking care of the horses belonging to one of the officers of the gen. staff while his man is gone home to Maine on a 15 day furlough. I don't have to stand guard so will have a chance to catch up with my sleep. I have heard it said 'twas a bad practice sitting up at nights. For the past three months I have had to stay up three nights out of the week, ½ of the night, but I have to keep my own company.

But here I am at the end of my paper, and my candle is just going out. Good bye, as ever. Write soon, your Joel. I did not get one valentine. Did you? Write long letters. Direct them to Hd Qrs., Birney's Div., Washington, D.C.

P. S. I have written this in a hurry. Please excuse where it's necessary.

*****

Fri. 6 March. Rain and sleety but ending fine. Hard feelings in the tent. Received a letter from W. Snell at W returning $5.00 I had sent to him. Henry Bedford, a prisoner, was brought to Hd Qrs. *[Joel's letters indicate he surmised Henry may have deserted.]*

Sat. 7 March. Drizzly and cloudy all day. Nothing special occurred during the day. In the evening, I got the sergeant of the guard to let H. Bedford come to my tent as it looked for a rainy night. Rained hard most of the night.

Sun. 8 March. Wrote a letter to J. K. Bird, also one to L *[probably Elvira]*. C. Brown, from Monroe *[Monroeton]* called at our tent, hunting for the 141st. Today is the Sabbath, but it seems unlike.

[J. K. Bird and George Copeland Bird were sons of George Bird, brother of Joel's mother, Rebecca (nee Bird) Molyneux. Thus, J. K. and Joel were first cousins of Joel. J. K. was single at the time of these entries. J. K. married Carolyn Younkin, June 1, 1865.]

Mon. 9 March. The 141st went by. There *[they're]* to go out on picket. Wrote a letter to Mrs. Jesse Molyneux. Rec'd one from George P. *[Pardoe]* who is at home on a F. *[furlough. Actually, George Pardoe had been captured by the Confederates, paroled, and was now out of the army. Jesse and Philena were faithful correspondents of Joel during this trying period of his life.]*

Tue. 10 March. Came near being sent back to my regt. for being called from the guard to take care of horses, but 'twas winked over for certain reasons.

Wed. 11 March. Wrote a letter to M. Farrell for Johnny. How great are the advantages even of a common school education; the value is inestimable.

Thu. 12 March. A cold windy day and squall. The 141st returned from picket. Received a letter from V, also one from sister, Sallie, mailed March the 9th. Edmund and Will B. *[Bedford]* called to see Henry B.

Fri. 13 March. I rode down to the new camp of the 141st to get the tooth extractors for Lieut. Graves. S'pose he's got the tooth ache, got it bad. Samuel has a very bad cold.

Sat. 14 March. Growing warmer now. Today Warren Travis of the 154th N.Y. Regt., Co. C, came to see me and got the things Georges sent him. Stayed all night with me; had not seen him for eight years.

Sun. 15 March. Squally, thunder, sleet and rain. Wrote a letter to Martha M. *[Molyneux, Samuel's sister].* Received one from Eliza M. *[another of Samuel's sisters].* Went to meeting in the afternoon listened to the first sermon for this year. It seemed like being in a Christian land again.

Mon. 16 March. Berry's whole brigade was drilling near Hd Qrs. Went to meeting this evening and heard a short but very good sermon. Meeting again tomorrow night. *[General Hiram Berry was given a division to command just before Chancellorsville where he was killed May 3, 1863.]*

Tue. 17 March. Went down to my regt. *[on]* horseback; had a pleasant visit. Came back and heard cannons roaring freely. The rebs are supposed to be crossing at Waterloo.

Wed. 18 March. Lieu. Graves went to Washington. Good news: 26 reb transports taken on the Yazoo. *[On the western front, Generals Grant and Porter were maneuvering past Vicksburg via the Yazoo River.]* Wrote a letter to Sister Anna Vough *[and to Warren]* Travis. Received one from Warren. Went to church in the evening.

Thu. 19 March. Hd Qrs in hot water getting ready for a horse race but can't see the point where it is to help put down the rebellion. Marshall threatens to tie Holt to a tree. *[George Holt, 22, from Maine, was Joel's tent mate. Sounds as though George was suffering an emotional breakdown. See letter March 5, 1863.]*

Fri. 20 March   Sleety, squally, cold day. 'Tis sister Sallie's birthday. In the evening I went to meeting at the Christian Commission. The meetings are increasing in interest. Saw one officer what he should be.

Sat. 21 March.   The lieu. *[Graves]* came back from W. Wrote a letter to V. Went to meeting *[Christian Commission]* in the evening, and heard a good discourse. Also, *[heard]* that S. M. *[Samuel Molyneux]* was sick.

Letter #23A

March the 21st, 1863
[In camp in Virginia]

My own dearest friend:

Your letter of the sixth and mailed the ninth was received on the 12th. 'Tis needless for me to say how pleased to get it, and how glad to learn that you were well, and hope this also may find you as it leaves me enjoying perfect health.

You mentioned of having been unwell and sore throat V. won't you please please me by being very careful of yourself. The throat is a dangerous part to be affected, and yours I have noticed as being subject to colds, etc., settling there, and 'tis much easier to keep one's health than to regain it after once lost.

I am still situated as when last I wrote two weeks ago. I looked for a letter last night, but I guess it came tonight. We are having quite stormy winter weather now; sleeted and snowed all day yesterday and the same again today. 'Twill be good sugar-making weather, I think, when it turns fine, but there is no hard maple trees here. Have not seen one in Va. or yet a hemlock. 'Tis mostly oak, pine, gum, and cedar. Yes, I wish that I could be there to help to make and eat sugar. Wouldn't we have a sweet time? Yes, I guess. I do not think of trying for a furlough at present, the thought of again bidding good-bye to home and friends would spoil my visit, and the few days I could remain the pleasure of which would hardly repay the pain of another separation.

You are right in respect to my other correspondents. It is due you and also them and perhaps an explanation also, the case of Seddie L. *[Locke]* of whom I believe I told you is sufficient proof that you are correct and if letters should be rec. in the future and I deem an explanation necessary I will do so and relate to you the facts. That will do, won't it?

I had a short time since a letter *[from]* Cousin Jabe *[J. K. Bird]*, as he is pleased to style himself. I s'pose he is like Libie cousined herself 'tis upon my Cousin Jenny's account. Libie has not ans. Was Ike a boy of his word in visiting as he proposed? If so, I may at least conjecture from the assurances you gave me, that he returned a disappointed youth or is he like myself too old for that?

I have been to church four times since writing before. There are some real good men, I think, come here from the eastern states as missionarys, and have erected large tents nearby us, and are having meetings every evening and distributing testaments, tracts, religious papers, and soldiers' hymn books. I think they are doing much good. There is a great many very good men here in the army as well as some very bad ones, and I think the army is growing better, if anything.

The papers give better news for our cause of late, and even some talk of a peace soon. I really think that the coming summer will end the fighting myself. 'Tis good to be hoped, so at least how happy I should be to know the wars were all o'er and we turned back to the land from whence we started.

*****

Sun. 22 March.   Meetings three times today, but could not attend. Rec'd letter from E.W. Snell *[Cousin Eliza W. Snell]* also one from D. and E. Pardoe. Ans. the one to E. W. S.

Letter #23B

[Continuation to Vi.]

March 22nd, *[1863]*
[In camp in Virginia]

No letters came last evening. I went to evening meeting. Tent was very full. The mail starts in a few moments. Tent fellow is getting the breakfast ready. Has quit snowing and raining. Is very muddy again. Good bye, write soon and much as before my love to you. Joel.

*****

Mon. 23 March.   Wrote a letter to H. Norton *[Hannah, Dave's girlfriend]*. Rode to corps H-D Qrs. Went to church in the evening. No letters.

Tue. 24 March.   Rainy. Blue. Drew N. Y. jackets. Went to church in the evening.

Wed. 25 March.   Gov. Curtion *[Andrew G. Curtin of Pennsylvania]* and a number of other citizens visit Hd Qrs. Rec. a letter from Angie D. Pratt.

Thu. 26 March.   Rainy but ends fine. An inspection, or rather a ground review, today in honor of Curtin. S'pose *[he]* did not go to see it.

Fri. 27 March. Witnessed a grand army horse race and ending up in a drunken debauch and niger show, a disgrace to our army. Rec. a letter from C. and F.

Sun. 29 March. Went to church at ½ past ten. Spent the evening with Capt. Bryan of the 84th, the mission tent being so crowded that no more could get in.

Mon. 30 March. Had a likeness taken for to send to my cousin. Expect to move soon. Heard Richmond being evacuated. Clouding up for a storm.

Tue. 31 March. Storming. Snow. Ground white. Received a letter from Kate Bull, date 26. Wrote one to A. *[Angie]* D. Pratt, also one to K. B. Taylor. Caught a bad cold.

CHAPTER 9: APRIL 1863

Wed. 1 April   High winds. Vane struck *[one]* of the generals. Lieu. lets one of his horses go. Stuart reported as a traitor-deserter. Commence moving to moving to join the brigade. Attended church in the evening.

[Stuart was Lieutenant Graves' orderly. At this time in the war, desertions in the Union armies reached alarming proportions. On March 10, 1863, Lincoln proclaimed an amnesty for Union deserters to stem the tide of men going absent. Men who returned to duty by April 1 would not be punished. Those who did not return by then would be reported as deserters and executed. Joel's April 24, 1863, diary entry reported Stuart had returned to the ranks, but received no punishment.]

Thu. 2 April   All is bustle today; moving camp. Arrived all safe; pitched our tent, and wrote this by light of a lantern. Feel first rate.

Fri. 3 April   Fine but coolish. Lieu. sold Dick one and ¼. *[Dick was a horse which Lieutenant Graves sold for $1.25.]* Preparing to build hut. Coleman returned from furlough. Very lonesome without a cabin with a fire.

Sat. 4 April   Cloudy, preparing for storm. Busy building shanty. Moved into shanty. Rec. a letter from Kate Bull.

Sun. 5 April   Ground covered with snow four inches deep and continues to snow. Wrote a letter to V., also one to Kate H. T. *[Tirncrook]* Snow all slush, and mud a plenty.

Letter #24

[April 5, 1863, Sunday]

My Own Dearest Friend:

'Tis just two weeks yesterday since writing to you before, date 21 and more than three weeks since receiving one from you, the last bearing the date of March sixth now one whole month ago. I am enjoying good health hoping you are doing the same though fears will arise that you are not, from my not hearing from you.

We have just made a short move of some four miles upon the account of the scarcity of wood around our old camp. We have new huts to build and every thing to fix up new. Our house yet has no chimney as we built *[it]* but yesterday and 'tis quite chilly without fire. You can judge as much from the appearance of my writing for 'tis not all sunshine here yet.

This morning I awakened to find nearly four inches of snow had fallen during the night which makes it very uncomfortable today as it remains stormy and chilly. The weather has been changeable for the past month with scarcely two fine days together. From appearances now I think we shall remain here for some time, perhaps for several months, so at least appears to be the impression around Hd Qrs. I hope so for we are in a very pleasant situation. Our regt. is camped about a mile off; the boys are well. I am not doing guard duty now but have taken the place of a man *[Orderly Stuart]* that went on furlough and has not returned. 'Tis to take care of the horses belonging to one of the officers of Gen. Birney's staff. 'Tis much easier than being up so much at night, and then I will have a horse to ride upon a march. Lieu. Graves is a very nice man. I like him much!

Last evening I received a letter from cous. Angie Summers, date April 1st. George Pardoe had just been to make them a visit. I suppose he has started back 'ere this to join his regt. Did he make you the promised visit? I had a likeness taken a few days since but *[it]* has to sober a look; it does not suit me exactly. I promised Cousin Martha M. one so I will send this to her and endeavor to get you a better one.

I spoke of having a Zouave suit, but we shall not. We have in this place New York jackets which I think looks much better. Since writing before, Gov. Curtin of Pa. visited our Hd Qrs. I like his looks well. He came to see how his troops were from Pa.

I saw Gen. Hooker's daughter the other day, but I could select many better looking girls in Elkland. Is Lib afraid you may be jealous, as she does not ans. the letter I sent? I owe one to Abe, Jabe and one to sister Sallie, one to sister Angie, David Pardoe, brother George, George Pardoe, George Little, Eliza and Martha Molyneux, and one to sister Kate B. *[sister, Lydia Bedford]*. Quite ameny, isn't it?

Kate wrote March 24th. She says every one nearly believe Ike has taken my place for a fact, says she, he did not get home last Sunday night 'til nearly daylight. She pities me, I guess, for she said she told Ike, he was real mean to try to take you away from me when I was away fighting for my country. (But enough such as this).

Today is Easter Sunday, I believe. I would not mind if I could take supper with you tonight, and then *[we could]* spend the evening with each other. There is so much I should like to tell you and you cannot think how I should like just to look into eyes once more. I pray heaven may spare us both to meet again soon. You ever loving, trusting Joel.

P. S. Excuse my short letter this time, also the yellow envelope.

*****

     Mon. 6 April   Built our chimney. The president visits our army, and a grand review of the cavalry takes place some four miles distant.

     Tue. 7 April   All is bustle here for 'tis announced that Abraham Lincoln is to honor Hd Qrs with his presence, but *[he]* did not come. A letter from E.W. and J.M.

     Wed. 8 April   The Army of the Potomac is reviewed today. President Lincoln and lady, daughter, and young son and myself were among the spectators. *[Tad was ten at the time. The Lincolns had three older sons, Robert, Edward and William, but no daughter. Thus, the young lady Joel thought was a daughter was probably an attendant. The elder son, Robert, went into politics after maturity, and was Secretary of War under President Garfield.]* Wrote to Kate B. *[Bull]*. Rec. a letter from W. H. Braime.

     Thu. 9 April   Heard cannon nearly all day at a distance. Ans. W. H. Braime's letter. Received one from S. Locke.

Letter #25A

April 9th, 1863
Dixie Station, Near Fredericksburg, *[Virginia]*

My Dear Sister: *[Sallie]*

     Again I seat myself to pen a few wandering thoughts to thee hoping they may find you in as good health as the present date leaves me. The last letters from home bear date of March 28th. Items of news were Mary Jane Black's due, protracted meeting at Bethel, Norman's moving to Forksville, and success in superceding, etc., etc. At present, we are enjoying very pleasant weather though Sunday last there was snow in the morning to the depth of nearly four inches, but it soon disappeared and now the mud is fast drying away.

     We did not move Hd Qrs as we expected to until last week, and now only have we just got comfortably fixed up in our new camp. We are now only about one mile from our regt. I called to see the boys yesterday and found our Brigade had gone out upon picket but are expected back today. I found Jesse Pardoe and C. Webster and Henry Bedford in camp being sick so they could not go out with the rest. James is quite sick again; entirely unfit for duty. I do wish the boy was only at home where he ought to be. Henry Bedford was sent back to his regt. by the Gen. as no charges were put in against him by the officers of his regt. I am glad he is back safe for I was afraid it would take all his back pay off if nothing worse was done to him.

[Apparently Henry Bedford had deserted and gone home to Sullivan County. Earlier in the year, desertions in the Army of the Potomac were running at over 200 per day, and an estimate made in January 1863 revealed that about 85,000 Union soldiers were absent from their posts. With the reorganization of the Army of the Potomac the problem of desertion was taken into hand. The living conditions of the army itself improved with comfortable huts being built, and a regular issue of fresh vegetables and fresh bread was instituted. This letter makes several favorable references to the change in the food being provisioned. As a result, many deserters returned, and that may have been the situation with Henry Bedford.]

Yesterday I witnessed a grand review of our whole army depicting the brigades during picket duty. There were, I think, near 150,000 present. The President, Lincoln, and lady, his youngest son and daughter *[attendant, not daughter]* were present. As a matter of course I fell in love with the daughter. She is truly very homely indeed, and looked much care worn. A few days before, Gov. Curtin visited us. He is noble looking, but this is enough about the notables for this time.

It seems now to be the impression here at Hd Qrs that we are to remain for some time at this point. I suppose for the purpose of guarding the rail road from Aquia Creek to Falmouth (i.e.) our div. is thought will remain. I see by the papers that the siege of Charleston has begun and operations at many points are under way. All day today I have heard heavy cannonading a long distance off supposed by some to be at Williamsburg or Yorktown. Perhaps the rebs. are attacking our forces stationed there.

I am not doing guard duty now as I took the place of a man that went home on a furlough and he has not yet returned. 'Tis to see to the horses, etc., of one of the staff officers, a Lieu. Graves a very nice man in my estimation, at least he does not drink like some of the rest. If I keep this position I shall not want for anything. I know at present I will have a horse to ride upon marches. This will be quite different to walking and carrying a one-horse load.

Ellen W. writes that 'tis reported that Mike Farrel has deserted and had been taken and sentenced to be shot. I have heard nothing of the kind before and doubt its truth.

[Several days later, on April 13, 1863, General Burnside issued General Order 38 — threatening the death penalty for treasonable behavior, which included army desertion.]

So, George Pardoe has at last started back I suppose he has had a good visit at least. There has been quite a number *[of furloughs being given]* from Hd Qrs, and nearly all of what have returned say they do not advise others to go home on furloughs. They don't feel so contented since being in civilized society again, but if I thought I could get one I would risk it, I think.

O, I must tell you about Warren Travis. In one of those boxes sent down, George's folks sent in it some things for him just marking his name on them and the 156th Regt. I did not know before he was in the army so I wrote to the 156th Pa., but got no answer. Then I wrote to the 156th, New York. *[Some northern Pennsylvania volunteers entered regiments formed in New York State.]* About three weeks after, he came after them, but I had eaten half of them up as I thought we should march soon, and began to think his regt. was in some other army besides the Potomac. He is Warren yet, all over and over, and for bigness about the same as Will Bedford. He belongs to Liesel's Corps, and then was about six miles from us if they have not since moved, and now we have *[so]* he must be within two or three *[miles]* of us. He stayed all night with me, but he is quite a hard case.

*****

Fri. 10 April   Went to the corduroy *[road]* to see the president go by. Afterward went to my regt. with the boys. Got a letter from Wm. Rogers. Wrote one to sister, Sallie.

Letter #25B

April 10, *[1863]*

[Continuation to Sallie]

Did not get my letter done yesterday so now I will endeavor to do so.

Well, I declare, instead of writing I have been to sleep. 'Tis real warm today and had just come in tired. My head is aching some. I sat down on our cot bed, took up my letter, wrote a line and the half as you see, a friend, Corporal Patterson stepped in to talk a minute. I lay down and he going out soon the first thing I knew found myself waking up some two hours after relieved of my headache.

I spoke of being out. I had been down to the main road going from Sickel's Hd Qrs to Staffor *[Stafford]* Courthouse and Aquia Creek. 'Tis a double track corduroy. I suppose you know what that is. *[A corduroy was a road made of split logs, laid crossways.]* Well, the President and family was to pass down that way this morning to review the 128th. Army Corps laying down in the vicinity of Stafford. I found our whole div. out waiting for him to pass along. They stood in double rank one on each side of the road. It strung the road nearly as far as I could see each way. Just as he came to our Division an arch of evergreens was fixed *[and]* under it the word **Welcome**. As he came to each regt. they gave nine cheers three for Lincoln, three for Gen. Hooker who rode near him, three for Mrs. Lincoln, and a tiger for his little boy, eight or nine years old, riding on a little pony in front of the carriage containing the others. *[Lincoln's youngest son, Thomas (Tad), born in 1853, was ten at the time of this letter. Tad died in 1871, at 18.]* I found my company there, and went back to their camp with them.

The boys are all better that were sick, except James. He is quite sick. He has a heavy cold, and is very miserable. He is up part of the time. He got a letter from his folks last night. C. Grange is complaining some today. Sam *[Molyneux]* is getting quite rugged again. Ezra Little has been in the hospital for some past, is now back to his company but not very stout yet. Is hardly fit for duty. He belongs to Co. C.

I got a letter this day from Wm. Rogers of Philadelphia dated April 4th. He is getting much better. He thinks by the time it gets warm weather he will be able to join his regt. He says that he has been in to seven different hospitals since he was sick, and is getting sick of them. Won't I be glad if he does come again to his regt. if he can only stand to be with us.

I heard rumor tonight that we were to move Tuesday, next. Do not know where to or if there be any truth in the story. Let me see what else I shall write. O, this sheet of paper you will wonder what is coming as you will notice 'tis a blank report I picked up so I thought that I would fill it out and send it in, but I guess I shall find more than my match to do it. I wish you had one just like it and make John *[Sallie's husband]* write it clear full, wouldn't he curl, I'll bet. Just to think he thought he could lay me on my back why I'm a fighting fellow, weigh, I 'spec, about 160. Tell him to think of that. Tell him he's got to be right on his rhubarb or I'll jerk him when I come back.

You didn't know I had a new jacket, did you? I have though. 'Tis what they call the New York jacket. All the guard had to draw them. They are neat and I like the style. We did expect to have the trousers, but they changed their notion and I was glad of it.

Mrs. Birney, the lady that offered me those mittens, went home near a month ago. I did not take them for I have a pair. *[Mrs. Birney was wife of General David Bell Birney, Division Commanding Officer.]* I must close as it has got to be bed time, the drums have beat tattoo some time since. *[Tattoo, a rhythmic rapping call on the drum before bugle, was notice to go to quarters and put out the lights. The lights were candles and kerosene lanterns.]*

I will mail this in the morning. O, I had a letter from William B. Bryan yesterday saying he had been over to Elkland and that he took dinner with you. Also, one from Ellen Woodhead and one from Jesse the day before. I had one from Cousin Angie since George and Eliza were out there. I wish that I could help you to make sugar *[maple sugar]* one day this spring. O, did Easter Sunday come this time up there? I did not see it here, but the other day I went to the suttler's and bought just half a dozen eggs. How much did I pay do you think? Only 5 cents apiece!

We are expecting to get payed again soon. On the first of next month six months pay will be due, $78. I sent home $50 with Jonas. I have spent five or six since I came into the show. When Jonas was down he left 17 stamps. They are all gone but two. I believe stamps are hard to get here so I will send this without one as you will not have to pay any more than the three cts. there. You know, I must save one for special occasions.

My berries are not quite all gone yet. I have nearly four qts. yet in all. The rest of the things are played out. My tentmate, Holt, is with me yet. We eat and drink together. What he has I have apart *[a share of]*, and what I have we both use alike.

So Dave is getting a notion for *[feeling romantic about]* Hannah N.? *[Norton]* I suppose Mrs. Sniffin *[wife of the minister at the Millview Wesleyan Methodist Church]* and some others are figuring it out. Well, as the boy said, "I have nothing to say!"

I'm sorry Dock B *[cousin J. K. Bird]* did not select better company for himself in that sleigh ride to your place. He might have known what the consequences would be. I presume it spoiled the pleasure of the whole party. Yes, I wish Thomas and Elizabeth would hurry there *[their]* cakes. (O, what a cake). Our bill of fare now is soft bread, generally with fresh beef and salt pork, coffee and sugar occasionally, beans, rice, potatoes, and molasses. I hear prices are going up your way for many things, pretty high 'tis likely; 'twill be higher before they fall. Now, I will lay this by, and go to bed.

*****

Sat. 11 April   Cannons firing again today westward. Wrote a letter to Wm. Rogers. He is at Chestnut Hill, Phila., U.S. General Hosp.

[Sickness was a constant problem among soldiers of the Civil War. This was true for the armies of the Confederacy, as well as the Union. Half the deaths from disease were caused by intestinal ailments: typhoid, diarrhea, and dysentery. Of the remainder, half died from lung problems as tuberculosis, pneumonia, and influenza. This meant that in every regiment there was a constant process of attrition that began the first day in training camp. There was little screening of physical misfits in the first place, and no adequate arrangement for replacing men who got sick. Medical science and sanitation

were at a low level. See January 2, 1864, entry for discussion of sanitation conditions of the army.

[Some soldier sickness was related to lack of planning. As an example, when the 141st Regiment arrived in the Washington area, in late August of 1862, the command had no tents. They were issued a week later. Rations were scarce and irregularly provided. These privations and exposures told upon the health of the men, nearly 300 being carried to the hospital and 500 reported unfit for duty in their first week in the Washington area. Joel contracted a lung ailment that caused incapacitation in his later life.]

Sun. 12 April   Rain set in at dark. Charles Scott called over today. Had a pleasant walk over to the bay. Wrote a short letter to Martha M. *[Sam Molyneux's youngest sister],* and sent my likeness to her. Rec. a letter from L. B. *[Lucy Baines],* also one from V. M. *[Vi McCarty]*

Letter #25C

[Second continuation to Sallie]

April 12, *[1863]* Saturday

Slept soundly and did not wake this morning until reveille beat, which is soon after daylight. Have been and fed horses, washed the saddle, have just pounded my fresh beef, and fryed it, ate breakfast, soft bread, coffee, and the beef. So far, so good.

I hear the president started for the capitol last night, that his visitors made a deal of trouble for us, don't they?

O! It is a splendid morning just cool enough to make one feel cheerful. The sun has just risen all so bright. Birds are singing merrily for robins and meadow larks are here all the winter. All is harmony, save rebel man.

I suppose the draft begins to attract attention up there by this time. Is there any what is called the copperheads about you? *["Copperhead" was a derogatory name for a Northerner who was an anti-abolition sympathizer.]* Well, they will have to come to it now, and the sooner they fall into the traces and help to put down the rebellion the better, for rebs have to be wiped out any how. The army is getting confidence in *[General]* Hooker, and the expression of the soldiers is quite different from what it was a few months ago, and from what the copperheads think it is. I would not like to see my friends brought in as conscripts, but the fault-finding ones or sympathizers of Jeff *[Jefferson Davis, President of the Confederacy]* as they really are, can't be sent on too soon. We'll make work to pay for what they are doing and have done, but the mail is about going out, and I must stop.

Good bye dearest sister, John, and Georgia. *[I believe Georgia was a neighbor girl who lived with sister Sallie and John.]* Love to all and those who may wish to hear from me by inquiring for your brother Joel.

P. S. Please write very soon, and excuse my carelessly written letter.

*****

Mon. 13 April   Preparations for moving. Saw peach blossoms yesterday. Rec. a letter from David, also one from Martha Molyneux. Visited my reg. today. Sick ones getting better.

Tue. 14 April   Appearances of rain. Orders to pack up for marching, the bustle commencing. Drew me a horse to ride. The guard have prayer meeting, but *[I]* could not attend.

Wed. 15 April   A rain storm set in last night continuing through the day; a freshet in Potomac Creek. Received a red patch to wear on our cap. Wrote a letter to T. W. S. Little.

[The red cloth patch was originally used in the Union armies as an identification marker. Later, a red patch was issued to each soldier in the Army of the Potomac as part of a general endeavor to lift morale of the dispirited troops in that army. It, along with the other efforts, such as more and better food, clothing, and housing, was successful, for the soldiers began taking pride in their army thereafter. Of course, morale was boosted by combat victories.]

Thu. 16 April   Contemplated move is postponed. Soft bread plays out. Attended prayer meeting in the evening. No letters.

Fri. 17 April   Loafed nearly all day. Went to meeting in the evening. Received no letters and was too indolent to write any.

Sat. 18 April   Went with the lieu. to Bellplain Landing. The First N.Y. have a jolification, in view of going home. Hd Qrs serenaded by a band.

[Jollification is an old-fashioned term for festivity or celebration. See entries April 22 and 23, 1863, for what happened as a result of the above-mentioned "jollification".]

Sun. 19 April   Preaching in the guard. *[General]* Sickels reviews the Corps. Lieutenant *[Graves]* sells Nelle *[horse]*. Wrote letter to V. Rec. one *[letter]* from Sister Ann. Was at prayer meeting.

[Although Union armies had one chaplain for each regiment, they seemed to have little impact on the day-to-day life of the average soldier. Joel mentioned chaplains only a few times, and then generally in the context of picking up or posting the mail. Chaplains of the day seemed unqualified or

perhaps unconcerned about the spiritual well-being of the soldiers. Joel received spiritual support from organizations such as the non-denominational Christian Commission and from informal meetings such as the two mentioned above, "preaching in the guard" and "prayer meeting". Chaplains may have participated in those informal meetings, but Joel didn't mention their involvement.]

Letter #26A

[In the following letter, Joel expresses concern that a boy back home, Ike, has been courting Vi. He tries to be broad-minded about the situation but fears losing her. She's a rare jewel and he knows it.]

Virginia, April 19, 1863

Dearest V:

Yours of April 5th was duly rec. and I notice my last was written the same day. I wonder if whilst I am writing this you are similar engaged. 'Tis very pleasant today here, just warm enough for comfort. We are still at the same camp as when I last wrote. Upon the first of the past week we were all packed up and ready for a move forward but a heavy rainstorm setting in prevented. To all appearance we shall try it again in a day or two. In what direction I cannot say, but 'twill be an advance.

I am still at div. Hd Qrs situated as I told you before. My health remains as usual, very good. Was you, as you said, "Quite well" when last writing? Do not conceal it from me if you are not, for I will imagine you are sick when perhaps you are not. Write me just as you are, won't you? Please! Now, you will!

The boys in the co. are mostly well. Cousin L. Molyneux is well again and James Pardoe is mending slowly, though he is far from rugged yet. *["Cousin L. Molyneux" was probably Joel's first cousin, Lucinda. She was a year younger than Joel, born 1835. She was married to Stephen D. Goff, and the couple had four children who reached maturity.]*

In one of your letters you said you had reason to think certain persons at Millview were interested in favor of our friend, Ike. I know 'tis so. I could not say for sure, but their brother Sam (for we know who we mean) tried to persuade me to give up all claims to him *(Ike)*, and not interfere. I asked him how I could be in his way and if I had not given him all the chance in the world by coming down here; but he reckoned that I could write, etc. As I said before, I do not know but I think it likely they may have written him to get me to relinquish in his favor. Perhaps I will, but I can't see myself doing it, unless you order it, and you won't, will you? I wish him well but not enough to wish him the bestest girl.

Oh! You mentioned my nephew Geo. Pardoe not paying you the promised visit, and that you didn't care, if I would come and stay long enough to make up. I was just going to say I would, but I will tell you what would suit me better, that will be to have you come and stay with me long enough to make up. How long would that be? Would it suit you? How I wish I was where I could hear you speak and take your hand in mine and you would say that little word. Yes, always.

You say the first ring *[Joel had carved a wooden ring for her several months earlier]* was too large a great deal. Then the last one is also, for it was near the bigness of the first one. I was thinking when I made them that I had once tried one of yours, and that one that fitted you would nearly fit my little finger, but I never once thought of my being so much more fleshy now than when I was way off up there in that cold country. Ain't I thoughtless?

You say do I remember being at your house Easter Sunday, Yes, I guess. I bought ½ dozen eggs for my Easter, only had to pay five cts apiece, that isn't much, is it? I believe I told you in my last we should not have the zoo uniform, and that we have the N.Y. jacket instead. I have not yet got the likeness to send you. I sent the one I had taken to Martha Mx. *["Mx" was Joel's abbreviation for Molyneux]* I looked so fierce in that one and you always s -- *[sass?]* me for looking cros.

So Tache thought those were reb rings. I 'spose she thinks, since we kill'em, we eat'em, and then make rings, etc. of what is left. Tell her no, by all means, **no**! As I hope to return home safe and escape rebel lead, so I trust I may not have harm befall the poor Johny Rebs by my hand, let alone make rings from the bone of one of them. But too much of this already.

You need not say you cannot write letters any more for you can and good long ones too, if you try. But I can scarcely think of anything more that will interest you, for there is an old owl only a little way off in the edge of our camp hooting just like they used to around Sallie's last winter, for 'tis now getting quite late in the evening after nine o'clock, the owl will hoot then I think of the woods between Sallie's and your house. Then, need I tell where my thoughts go next seeing they are so close to where resides the object of my affections.

I was at a meeting this evening. There is prayer meeting every evening in the guard of late. There was preaching today, but I could not attend. Would you not like to see the church? 'Tis seats arranged nicely in a pretty spot, with pine, cedar, and laurel bushes stood up around. The meetings are held just before dark.

O, we have such a fine view of the bay from near our camp. We can see Bellplain landing with vessels sailing about with their (as it appears) white wings. I nearly forgot to say anything about Sister Abe. Of course, if he wants a woman he must try, "Faint heart never won fair lady." Sometimes mittens don't fit good, but don't often kill. Let me see! How many chances does that make you have had to keep house?

I rec. a letter tonight from sister Ann V. *[Joel's sister, Ann, was three years older than Joel. She had married Abram Vough in 1853.]* I looked for one from another V. but was disappointed. I get so used to writing V. to you, I am getting most to the last of the alphabet. First 'twas 'V' you know. Now, 'tis 'U'. How soon may I commence with 'W' *[wife]* when addressing you? Won't it be funny to get a letter headed: "Dear W."? But I must bid you good bye once more. My best wishes are for your hapiness, with much love from Joel.

*****

Letter #26B

Monday, April 20, *[1863]*

'Tis morning now. Nothing of importance has yet taken place. The mail starts out soon, and I must fold this up and get it to the box. Please write often and excuse the appearance of carelessness in this as I have written in a hurry. Again, good bye and send more. Love from your Joel. Address as before: Hd Qrs., Birney's Div., Washington, D.C.

*****

Mon. 20 April   Riot at the sutlers. The riot edict issued. Eldes made a sergeant. Too rainy for meeting. No letters. Dott Sperry called.

Tue. 21 April   Nothing of importance done. Wrote letter to S.M.L.

Wed. 22 April   Disturbance with the First N.Y. as their time is out. They go in for being discharge; for some reason they are not. Wrote to L. B. *[Lucy Baines].*

Thu. 23 April   Holt gets a letter stating his brother is dead. Court martialing the First N.Y. Hear that A. J. Noble is our suttler.

Fri. 24 April   Rec'd four months pay today, $52.00. Stuart, lieu's old orderly, returns today and goes into the train. Rec'd two letters: John N. Summers and David Molyneux. *[Graves' orderly had been absent and declared a deserter. A "train" was a group of animal-drawn wagons.]*

Sat. 25 April   Went with some of the boys to get a mistletoe that was growing in an oak tree, a curiosity to me. C. Scott and E. Connel call in the evening.

Sun. 26 April   Preaching at 11, prayer meeting in the evening. Wrote a letter to Mrs. Jesse Molyneux. Was over to my regt.

Mon. 27 April   Expressed $50 home. Mrs. Graham wins *[on]* Captain Bliss' horse, Kearney by Effleiny *[race horses]*. Orders to be ready for marching in the morning. *[Mrs. Graham was wife of General C. Graham, commander of First Brigade, 1st Division, III Corps.]*

Tue. 28 April   Orders to march at four p.m. Got underway and went near six mile to near the Repper three mile or so below Fred *[Fredericksburg]*. 'Tis march again and fight.

Wed. 29 April   Preparing to cross. Commence to rain toward noon, continuing all night. Crossing here is given up.

Thu. 30 April   The army about face and march back some 15 miles. Went in to camp at 12 at night. Some four miles of the U.S. Ford, six below the junction of the R. *[Rapidan and Rappahannock Rivers]*.

CHAPTER 10: MAY 1863

Fri. 1 May. Cross the Rappahannac at the U.S. Ford without opposition. Pushed forward four mile to Chanceyville *[Chancellorsville]* on the plank road. The rebels do not show themselves much. *[This was the first day of the four-day battle of Chancellorsville.]*

Sat. 2 May. Our div. push forward two mile and 11th A. *[Army]* Corps break and we are out-flanked. Terrible fighting. Berry and Howard are killed. Hd Qrs skedaddle. I am over the river.

[Union General Hiram G. Berry was killed. However, Union General Oliver Otis Howard was not killed, as Joel had heard. He was there at Chancellorsville, as commander of the XI Corps. After the war, General Howard headed the Freedman's Bureau, and did much to help the Negro cause. Later, General Howard founded Howard University, and served as its first president, 1869-74.]

Sun. 3 May. Fighting nearly all night, and a dreadful battle in the morning. We fall back to the white house and build defenses. Rec'd a letter from Sallie.

Mon. 4 May. General Whipple is shot by reb sharpshooters. Skirmishing all day and shelling. Move Hd Qrs to the left out of range. Carried Colonel Noble of the 17th Conn *[Connecticut]* off of the field on a mule.

[Colonel Noble recovered from his wound. He was later brevetted brigadier general, and commanded the Second Brigade, 3rd Division, XI Corps. General Amiel Weeks Whipple was commander of the 3rd Division, III Corps, at Chancellorsville where he was wounded. He was taken to Washington, D.C. where he died May 6, 1863.]

[In the Chancellorsville Battle, Federals numbered 133,868 and Confederates 60,892. It was a victory for the South. Union General Hooker and Confederate General R. E. Lee were the commanders. The Union had 17,278 casualties and the Confederacy 12,821, including incomparable General "Stonewall" Jackson. Total casualties, 30,099, made this the third costliest battle of the Civil War. First and second were Gettysburg (51,112), and Chickamauga (34,624).]

Tue. 5 May. Very hot A.M., but a tremendous thunder shower in the afternoon. Got a horse that was picked up. Ordered to fall back over the river. I was sent to get the pack train ready.

[On May 5, 1863, General Burnside arrested Ohio congressman Vallandigham, unofficial leader of the Copperhead section of the Democratic Party. He was granted presidential pardon, and sent to the Confederates, but they didn't want him either.]

Wed. 6 May. Our forces crossed during the night. Train was over the river. Ammunition destroyed. Sat up all night to watch Dandy *[Graves' horse]*. Came back with the Lieu. *[Graves]* to our old quarters.

Thu. 7 May. The troops, what are left of them, are back fixing up their old deserted huts. Wrote a letter to David. Rec'd one from G.W.S. Little. Oh! when will wars and tumults cease?

Letter #27

[In camp at Chancellorsville]
May 7th, *[1863]*

Dearest:

I write just a line to let you know I am alive and well. This army, you will have heard 'ere this, has been engaged in another battle. It has been my fortune to escape unharmed, though with many, very many, it has been otherwise. I have not time to give the particulars.

Our company went into battle with 45 men. Twenty-one are left: four killed, fifteen wounded, and five missing. Samuel M. *[Molyneux]* and E. Bedford came out safe. Also C. Webster, Will and Hank Bedford were wounded and taken prisoners. 'Tis thought C. Grange, Till Bedford, and J. Pardoe were left back and were not with the company, being sick. James is at Washington, I believe.

One of your letters I rec'd Monday when we were near the battlefield, and the rebs close by. The other, of May first, came tonight. Now, we are back over the river again at our old camp. We are expecting to move again in a few days, the talk is toward Washington. I am still at Hd Qrs, and not in the guard now, of which I think I told you.

I like my position very well as Lieu. G *[Graves]* is a very nice man. I have to be out at nights but very little now, and have a horse to ride when we march. 'Tis much better than walking, I think. *[Joel had a weak ankle.]*

I have had some of the wedding cake that came from the table of the blacksmith Warren and the widow. May they live happily!

Yes, I guess I will come and take supper with you, for the Johny Rebs got my frying pan and haversack with my rations in it, but if that was all I should not care much.

O, this war is dreadful! 'Tis horrible! If I could only forget the scenes I have witnessed! But enough. I can write no more at this time. I have also written home. If we should not move I will write again soon. Tell sister, Sallie, I am safe and with much love. I remain your ever true friend, Joel L. Molyneux.

P. S. Write!

*****

Fri. 8 May. Went with the lieu. to Falmouth Station by Hooker's Hd Qrs. Nice ride. Rec'd a letter from V. Ans. it. Also, one from S.M.L.

Sat. 9 May. Busy fixing up for another march. Eight more days rations given out. Staff went over to the station to meet some gov. Went to bed early, all alone. *[The "some gov." was Governor Andrew G. Curtin of Pennsylvania.]*

Sun. 10 May. Gov. Curtin visits me again. *[He]* is staying here tonight. Fed on greens today. I am keeping Bachelors' Hall, and don't like it pretty well.

[Probably more than any other Union wartime governor, Andrew G. Curtin of Pennsylvania was a tremendous help in the war effort. He and Joel developed a friendship at this time that continued after the war. His repeated visits and overnight stays showed his interest in the common soldiers.

[General Thomas J. Jackson died May 10, 1863. On the night of May 4, at the Battle of Chancellorsville, Stonewall had been out on a reconnoiter and was accidentally shot by a volley from North Carolina's 18th Regiment. Taken to a nearby field hospital, his left arm was amputated. He was then transported 27 miles by wagon ambulance to a Confederate camp, Fairfield Farm. His wife, Mary Anna, and infant daughter, Julia, had been staying in Fredericksburg. They came to the Fairfield Farm camp to visit him while he was convalescing. Six days after he was shot, Jackson died from pneumonia. His final words: "No, no! Let us pass over the river and rest in the shade of the trees." His funeral and burial place were at Virginia Military Institute, Lexington, Virginia. "Stonewall" had been riding his favorite horse, Sorrel, when he was shot. That horse lived on until it was 36, and died in 1886. It was stuffed and taken to the Virginia Military Institute site where his former master lay buried.]

Mon. 11 May. Gov. Curtin came to Hd Qrs last evening. Also, Ed of Phil. *[Editor of a newspaper, probably <u>The Philadelphia Inquirer</u>.]* Our corps was reviewed today, did not go out. Wrote a letter to S.M.L.

[Newspapers were widely read by soldiers in the field. Most major daily newspapers, and many hometown weeklies, mailed papers to soldiers for

subscriptions. Some daily papers were sold to soldiers in the field by sutlers or vendors. A common price was ten cents — an inflated price causing troops to chip in and read shared copies.]

Tue. 12 May. Heard Richmond was taken and old Stonewall was dead. Lots of rumors. Samuel M. came over today. Rec'd a letter from G.M.P. *[Geo. Pardoe]* Ans. it in the evening.

Wed. 13 May. No news or nothing. Wrote a letter to cousin Angie Summers. C. Scott came over in the evening and stopped all night and lay with me. *[Spent the night in Joel's shebang.]*

Thu. 14 May. Sad news from the late battle field. Wrote a letter to cousin Eliza M. *[Eliza Ann Molyneux was Sam Molyneux's third younger sister. She was born in 1838, married Joseph Pardoe in 1871, and died in 1882.]* Rec'd one from K.H.T. *[Kate Tirncrook]*

Fri. 15 May. Nothing worthy of note transpires. Visited the regt. Lieu. gave me a V *[Letter from Vi]*.

Sat. 16 May. Wrote a letter to sister, Sallie.

Letter #28A

[Thus far, Joel's letters have been mostly informative ones dealing with business matters, camp gossip, welfare of fellow soldiers, and romantic ones to Vi. Few contained much detailed information about the war. Written just after the Battle of Chancellorsville, this letter is almost all about fighting and devastation of April 29 through May 5.]

Saturday 16, *[May]* 1863

Dear Sister: *[Sallie]*

I will try and pencil a few lines today hoping they will find you all enjoying health as the present date leaves me. We are having fine weather now. The roads are in good shape. We, those that are left of us, are at our old camp where we were previous to the move. I was at our regt. yesterday, in the late engagement.

It *[the 141st Regiment]* lost 154. Our company: 24 killed, wounded, and missing. Five of our co. killed, and all from our county C. King, H. Epler, D. Simmons, J. Huffmaster, G. Baumgardner. Will Bedford and Henry are both missing. Will was wounded, we knew, but nothing positive is known about them. Samuel, Edmund, Till, and Charley Webster are in the co., *[and are]* well. C. Grange is at the hospital and quite sick. I had a letter from George Pardoe, written on the ninth. He then was at Washington with James who was getting much better. George was not exchanged, yet was going back to Anapolis soon. In writing, he says direct to his regt. here. Heard John Warren is married. Also, that Jonathan Rogers house burned down, and Uncle Henry's death.

Am at Hd Qrs yet and in the same situation as when I last wrote you. Our wounded are, by a flag of truce, being all brought away that fell into rebel hands. Our Lieutenant, Colonel Watkins, supposed to have been killed, has been paroled and returned. Is only severely wounded. Quite a number of the missing are now being heard from. Our regt. is thought to have suffered the most of any. Also, our div. and corps the same. Have heard yet no correct estimate of our loss. That of our corps is put at 1,700. Should think this was nearly a fourth of the whole loss.

[Historian Bates reported: "Out of 419 men in the 141st who entered the battle at Chancellorsville, 234 were killed or wounded." Historian Bloodgood reported: "going into the battle the 141st had 417 men, and 220 were lost."]

Generals Berry and Whipple belonged to our corps., the Third. Berry in the fight of Lundy ___ *[faint and hard to read]*. Whipple was shot by a reb. sharpshooter Monday morning. He was but a few rods from our gen. and staff. I heard the ball pass close over me that struck him. I have now seen how cannon balls and shell look flying in the air. Look ugly. Had both the little and big ones quite as close as I want them, during the hardest of the fight.

Sunday morning I was back over the river getting a fresh horse for my lieutenant. From accounts this has been by far the bloodiest battle of the war, and to heaven I hope such sights as I have seen I may never be called to witness again. Ez Little is slightly wounded but not a prisoner.

Reb "Stonewall" Jackson is acknowledged killed. Their loss is thought to be two or three to our one. Papers today say G. B. McClellan takes command of the army again, but I don't believe it. How soon we move again I don't know, but think not very soon from appearances now.

[General Thomas Jackson was such a key figure in the Confederate Army of Northern Virginia, and in the mind of General Robert E. Lee, that some historians feel General Jackson's death marked a downward turning point in the war for the Confederacy.]

The paper you spoke of from Clyde came all right long ago. Let'em all get married, if they want to, I don't care.

*****

Sun. 17 May.   Rec'd a letter from Wm. Roger. Ans. same.

Letter #28B

[This continuation, to Sallie, tells how Joel and the division headquarters left the battle scene in a hurry. They skedaddled in such haste that Joel left without his haversack containing his cooking utensils, food, and writing supplies (bottle of ink, quill pens, writing paper, candles, file, etc.).]

Sunday morning, 17th, *[May 1863]*

The mail leaves here every morning. I will put in one more line, and then deliver this over to Uncle Sam. I have no news to give more than I have written. Tell Ellen I shall endeavor to answer those few lines as soon as I can command the time; feel grateful for those few. I write this with pencil for the Jonny Rebs got my ink, my little file.

So my ringmaking is done and my haversack with 50 rounds of hard tac and that B *[? box]* you sent me full of sugar, and my frying pan. That's what they got from me, but I'll try and make right with them come time. Good bye. Write soon. Except much love and remember me to my friends. As ever, your affectionate brother, Joel.

*****

Tue. 19 May.   Three rebs and one nig are brought to our Hd Qrs -- having given themselves up to our pickets.

Wed. 20 May.   Rec'd a letter from Wm. H. Braime who is going to school at Poughkeepsie, N.Y.

Thu. 21 May.   Over to my regt. and heard Wm. and Henry Bedford are at parole camp safe. Wrote a letter to Kate. Two more rebs brought in.

Fri. 22 May.   A wild turkey was chased through our camp and caught. Wrote a letter to V. *[Elvira]*

[Joel's attempts at living off the land included picking blueberries, cherries, chickapins, tree nuts, wild grapes, and greens. He caught rabbits, fish, eels, crayfish, and wild turkeys.

[Bruce Catton, in The Army of the Potomac: Mr. Lincoln's Army*, describes army food: "Out away from camp, regiments would be separated from their wagon trains for days at a time. In those cases, the men were given 'marching rations': three days' supply of hardtack, coffee, salt pork, sugar, and salt. These food supplies, and a cooking pot or frying pan, tin plate, and a canteen of water, would be carried in haversacks."*

[Catton explains, "Hardtack was the great food staple of the Civil War. It was a wheat cracker, three inches square and a half inch thick. It was solid,

hard, and nourishing. Nine or ten of these slabs constituted a day's ration. If moldy, it was thrown out. If weevily, it was issued anyway. Toasting it over the fire drove the weevils out, or you could just chomp your 'tack' in the dark so you wouldn't see the little rascals."

[Historian Catton continues "... on the march the issue of salt pork was frequently eaten raw, on the hardtack, for there was little opportunity to cook it while on the move. A favorite food was the army bean, but they were eaten primarily in camps, for beans took too long to cook while on a march."

[Hardtack pudding was made by mashing hardtack into a meal, mixing the meal with water, and kneading it into a dough. Then it was filled with apples or any other ingredient handy, folded over the top, tied in a piece of cloth, and boiled for an hour or so. Hell-fire stew: Boil the hardtack biscuits in a mixture of water and bacon grease. Lobscouse: Stew hardtack with vegetables and salt pork. Skillygalee: Soften the biscuits in water, and then fry them in bacon grease or salt pork.]

Sat. 23 May. Went in the forenoon over to Gen. Patrick's Hd Qrs., near Hooker's. In the evening went to carry some things for the lieu to the div. hospital. A letter from S.M.L. [Seddie Locke]

Sun. 24 May. Wrote a letter to Miss Theodocie Stackpole.

Mon. 25 May. Went to Potomac Cr. Sta. [Creek Station] Also visited our hospital and the regt. Rec'd a letter from David, also one from Phide.

Tue. 26 May. Spent most of the day pitching quoits. Exciting news from Vicksburg. [Quoits, old-fashioned pitching game, similar to horse shoes.]

[At this time, in another theater of the war, General Grant was laying siege to Vicksburg, Mississippi. The battle had started May 18, 1863, and the fort surrendered on Independence Day 1863. General John C. Pemberton was the commanding Confederate general. The fall of Vicksburg effectively reopened the Mississippi River to Northern trade and split the South.]

Wed. 27 May. The gen. returns from Washington; also a number of citizens from Phila. with him. Wrote a letter to cousin Jennie [Molyneux].

Thu. 28 May. Citizens [Visitors from Philadelphia] go home. Went to the station with them. Rec'd a letter from V.

Fri. 29 May. Our regt. moved down near by Hd Qrs. In the evening the battery boys have a mock theater.

Sat. 30 May. Went with Edmun. [nephew, Edmund Bedford] over to div. hospital. C. Grange very sick.

CHAPTER 11: JUNE 1863

Letter #29A

[Virginia], 1st of June, 1863

Dearest Friend:

Today health still visits me, and *[I am]* feeling like having a talk with you. I take pen, paper, etc. and seat myself for to do so. So, I am writing to a school ma'am, be I? No, I had never thought of such an event, but why not you as well as any one else? But don't I wish that it was so I could go to school. Let me see! First, I would make you laugh. Then, I wonder if I would learn to love my teacher? Would you give me the lesson? If you did I should tell you I was ready to recite for I learned that last winter a year when I was teaching odd spells and noonings, you know!

Your letter was rec'd in due time, but it was so short. Did you write a short one because I did? I thought you would rather have a short one than to have a longer and did not get it near as soon. I wrote again to you a few days afterward. I suppose you rec'd it by this time. The latest news I have from home is May 20th – yours being a little later, the 23rd.

We are having very warm days here now, and 'tis awful dusty when the wind blows. 'Tis most enough to smother us. I was to the hospital on Saturday to see Charley Grange. He is very sick; too weak to sit up. Is all wasted and worn to almost nothing, poor boy! I fear home and friends he'll see no more. Samuel is well and *[so is]* Edmund Bedford. The last we heard of Wm. and Henry Bedford they had left parole camp, and started for home, but have not heard if they had arrived.

The mail has just come in, but brought no letter for me. Well, I suppose I should write more. Did you mean that you could not write to me in the future as often as once in two weeks? I think it was two letters back that you mentioned about it. Are your parents opposed to you write *[your writing]* to me in the future as often as once in two weeks? Perhaps they were only afraid their 'Dear Girl' was sitting up writing when she should be sleeping.

Now, be honest. How do you like being a "school ma'am"? Do you board around? How would you fancy teaching winter and summer 'til you were 30, as many do? I'm getting the blues just thinking of it myself, so I'll just think that you won't teach after I have returned for fear I may come and make the scholars laugh or something else. Now what do you think?

*****

Tue. 2 June. Went to see Charley Grange and wrote a letter for him. Wrote a letter to V.

Letter #29B

[Joel put this partial letter to Elvira in the envelope with a letter already written. He dated it May 2, but its content coordinates it with diary entries written June 1, 2, 1863.]

May 2nd, evening.
[Actually written June 2, 1863]

I thought this would not reach you until next Tuesday mail, so I did not finnish yesterday. Was over to the hospital to see Grange today again. Poor boy! He is no better. He thinks he shall never get well again. I have just written a letter to his father for him and as it is not very late I will finnish yours.

Oh V. – there is close by a band of music serenading our gen. Now they are playing "The Star Spangled Banner." I can't think of what I am writing, but I don't wish you was here to listen unless you would fly away again as soon as they are done and take me with you, but you will if I keep on. I am getting silly, so I will close this short letter to you by repeating that my friendship and affection for thee are still unchanged. Yours affectionately – Joel.

P. S. Accept much love. Good-bye.

*****

Thu. 4 June. Went to Potomac Creek Station with the lieu. Visited the hospitals.

Fri. 5 June. Orders to be ready for marching. Lieu. *[Graves]* is at Washington. Very heavy cannonading toward evening, shelling the woods.

Sat. 6 June. Graves came back. Visited the hospitals. A thunder shower toward night. The army is all aquiver.

Sun. 7 June. Reviews and inspections. Williams from the 63rd is detailed for lieu.'s private orderly. Wrote a letter to the McCartys.

Mon. 8 June. Rec'd two months pay, $26. Then went to Falmouth Station to get Dandy *[Lt. Graves' horse]* shod.

Tue. 9 June.   Cleared away around the stable. Rec'd a letter from J.K. Bird.

Wed. 10 June.   Rec'd letter from L. Wrote to David. Went to div. hospital and found Charley *[Grange]* worse.

Letter #30

Wednesday, June 10, *[1863]*
[Camp at Potomac Creek Bridge]

Dear Brother: *[David]*

Again I take my pen to write to you a few lines hoping they may find you all enjoying good health. My health is still very good. Samuel and the boys in the company are well. C. Grange, who has been in the hospital for some time past, is very low indeed. I think it doubtful he recovers. He has had chronic diarhea for a long time and he is wasted away to almost nothing. The Drs. now say the consumption has sett in with it. Poor fellow. I wish that he could have been sent home before he had got so low, but now 'tis too late.

We were paid $26.00 on Monday, last 2 months pay and have had it expressed home again. I sent $30.00 (thirty dollars). Samuel had it sent in his name to the credit of William Molyneux and Bro. *[Samuel's brothers were named William and Thomas.]* Five of the thirty is yours to make up the ballance of what is coming to you for the butter and cheese & and the postage stamps sent me. The remaining 25 you can get into a 6 percent bond or put it in some place where it will draw interest if you can do so as it will be safe.

Samuel said that William Molyneux had wrote to him about wanting to buy that lumber of mine. He said they give five for the hemlock and twelve for the ash. If you think that is all it is worth where it is you can sell it to them. I would just as soon the lumber was sold, and you know how lumber has been going and you can do what you think best with it. If it is sold it will be out of the way at least. *[From the description, this was the lumber Samuel had been attempting to sell in Harrisburg, mentioned in his September 1, 1862, letter to his two brothers.]*

Sheep shearing is done by this time, I suppose. If mine has not been divided and the lambs marked, will you see that it is done? You can stack my wool up and store it away somewhere till it will pay best to sell it.

We are yet at old camp near Potomac Creek Bridge. Both the enemy and we have been making feints. One or two corps crossed below the city. The 6th, or Sedgwick's, is still over. How soon we may be into another muss nobody knows. Favorable news continues to reach here from Vicksburg. I think perhaps nothing of importance will be attempted untill affairs their *[there]* are straightened up. Had a letter last night from J. K. Bird—mailed the 4th inst. *[instance]*. William and Henry Bedford had just reached home. George Duke was at our regt. on Monday, but failed of seeing him. Arrived safe. The weather continues warm and the roads very dusty. Cherries and strawberries are ripe.

Had a letter from William Rogers a few days ago. He is yet at Phil. *[Philadelphia]* — is doing duty there, but says the drs. will not consent to his coming to his regt. I have just been over to division hospital to see Charley and find him failing fast. I am afraid he is beyond all hope of recovery. Brewster from Laporte, and Simmons from Sonestown that were badly wounded, are doing well. Such of them as can be moved are getting furloughs of 20 to 30 days.

So forth, but I must close for 'tis getting late in the evening, and mail goes out in the morning. Did the 15 dollars I sent you come to you all right? I think you never mentioned getting it. 'Twas for the proceeds of the butter and cheese. Write soon again. Love to father, mother, to all. As ever, your affectionate brother, Joel.

*****

Thu. 11 June.   Orders to march. Start at two P.M., and go by way of Stonemans I. *[Island]*, and bivouac for the night one mile beyond Harwood Church. Rec'd a letter from V.

[Official war records show that Charles Grange died on June 11, 1863, near Falmouth, Virginia.]

[For the Army of the Potomac, III Corps, of which the 141st Regiment was a part, this northward march marked the beginning of their involvement in the Gettysburg Campaign.]

Fri. 12 June.   Was upon the march by eight o'clock and move in direction of Warrenton. Halted for the night near Bealton Station. Miserable water!

Sat. 13 June.   Moved up the Warrenton road a mile and went in to camp. Army falling back or something. Bad water.

Sun. 14 June.   Lay encamped till four o'clock then marched to Catlet Station, some 15 mile. Arrived there about midnight. Water scarce and bad.

Mon. 15 June.   Was upon the road by eight. Halted at Bristo St. *[Bristoe Station]*. Very bad marching; dusty and hot. Reached Mannesa *[Manassas]* Junction and went into camp. Good water.

Tue. 16 June. Moved on to Bull Run about three mile and encamped a short distance from the old battle ground. Hear the rebs are up in Penn.

[On Tuesday, June 16, 1863, the Confederate Army of Northern Virginia forded the Potomac River near Williamsport, Maryland, on their way to the famed Battle of Gettysburg which would occur two weeks later.]

Wed. 17 June. Moved to Cenerville *[Centreville]*. Excellent water. Wrote a letter to sister, Sallie. Wish I wasn't in Dixie!

Thu. 18 June. Still at Centreville. Rec'd a letter from George Pardoe. Edmund *[Bedford]* came over to see me.

Fri. 19 June. Left Centerville for Leesburg. Marched to Gum Springs, and went into camp. A heavy shower at dark. Got wet through.

Sat. 20 June. Encamped all day. Rec'd a paper from S.M.L. Guerrillas very thick. All sorts of rumors.

Sun. 21 June. Heavy cannonading in direction of Snickers Gap. Moved camp ½ mile just by the village of Gum Springs, into a nice grove. Rumors.

Mon. 22 June. Learned yesterday's firing was a cavalry fight -- that Birney had a skirmish with some guerrillas taking seven -- after they had destroyed three or four wagons.

Tue. 23 June. Tryed to write a letter, but did not get it done in time for the mail as it went out early.

Wed. 24 June. Still encamped.

Thu. 25 June. Broke camp at Gum Springs early in the morning. Marched to Edwards Ferry. Crossed the Potomac into Md., thence to near the mouth of the --- *[indecipherable, probably Monocacy River]* March 25 *[marched 25 miles]*.

Fri. 26 June. Upon the road again. Crossed the Monnontie *[Monocacy River]* to the X *[Railroad]*. Went into camp near Point of Rocks and Sugar Loaf Mountain.

Sat. 27 June. Lieu. *[Graves]* has been appointed Adj. Gen. at First Brig. Hd Qrs. This is Frederic County. Move again. Pass through Jeffersonville and camp near a woolen factory.

Sun. 28 June. Rec'd a letter from V. and one from Angie S., and one from sister, Sallie. March again. Cross the Monontie *[Monocacy River]* after having passed through Middleton and Frederic City and Jerusalem. Camp at Walkerville.

Mon. 29 June. Upon the road. Pass through Woodborough *[Woodsboro]*, Ladysburg *[Ladiesburg]*, and Storrytown. Then went into camp three mile *[south]* of Pa. line. Rec'd letter from David, and one from H. M. and Joseph Grange. *["H. M. and Joseph" were family members of Charles Grange.]*

Tue. 30 June. Mailed a letter to Jesse and one to Joseph Grange. Broke camp. Repassed Storrytown. Marched to near Emanetsburg *[Emmitsburg]* and bivouac at a gristmill. Here live a nice family!

[Joel's letter to Joseph Grange, probably reported the death of son, Charles, who had died earlier that month.]

CHAPTER 12: JULY 1863

[Written during and following the Battle of Gettysburg, Joel's diary and letters show the severity of the fighting, in terms of men killed and wounded.]

Wed. 1 July. Marched at noon. Passed by Emmetsburg. Saw St. Joseph's convent. Crossed the Pa. line into Adams Co., and on to near Gettysburg where we met the rebs. Some fighting had been done already. A letter from Jennie and Kate Plotts.

Thu. 2 July. The battle is renewed today. The rebs desperately try to break our lines, but are repulsed. Our loss is great. Graves is wounded, and 13 of our co. *[wounded]* and five killed. Searched for Lieu G. *[Graves]* in vain. Only seven of our company left.

[The previous August there had been 95 men in Company K. The Battles of Chancellorsville and Gettysburg decimated the effectives. Company K went into the Gettysburg Battle with 25 men and had 18 casualties.]

[Colonel Madill's diary reflects the severity of the fighting in the Battle of Gettysburg. One quote, "I took 200 men and 9 officers into the fight and lost 145 men and 6 commissioned officers killed and wounded."]

Fri. 3 July. Searched for and found the lieut. *[Graves]*. Got him to the hospital, and his leave of absence fixed. Fighting and very heavy cannonading before night. Stayed at the train.

[Joel's days and nights have been busy. He has been out searching for and helping the wounded, and has also been out in the countryside scrounging for food for his living comrades.]

[Gettysburg, a great battle of the Civil War, was one of the most crucial events in the history of the United States. More than 170,000 men fought there and 51,102 became casualties. Prior to the battle, Lee's army of 75,000 soldiers was spread from Chambersburg to the edge of Lancaster County. In the battle, General Robert E. Lee lost 28,063 men. The Union army of 95,000, under General George G. Meade, lost about 23,049 men.]

[Although the battle was a Northern victory, the Army of the Potomac was too exhausted to follow up and engage Lee and his Army of Northern Virginia as they retreated back across Maryland into Virginia. Thus, Lee's Army of Northern Virginia troops successfully returned to Virginia with hundreds of wagonloads of pillage they had confiscated in their foray into southern Pennsylvania. They took along wagons, horses, mules, cattle, hogs, clothing, and shoes. The much-needed shoes came from Pennsylvania shoe factories.]

Lee's army even captured free blacks in Pennsylvania, and took them along back to Virginia to be sold as slaves. They took few of their own wounded with them.

[There were over 51,000 casualties in that three-day battle of Gettysburg. An observer, Professor Jacobs visited the battle field shortly after the battle and in his book, <u>Later Rambles</u>, related: "For several days after the battle the field everywhere bore the fresh marks of the terrible struggle. The soil was red with the blood of the wounded and slain and large number of the dead of both armies were to be seen lying in the place where the fatal missile had struck them. The work of interring 9,000 dead and removing about 20,000 wounded to comfortable quarters was a herculean task. The rebel army had left most of their dead lying unburied on the field as also large numbers of their badly wounded, and had fled to safety. There was considerable delay in properly interring the corpses that lay on the field of battle. It was only after rebel prisoners, who had been taken in battle, were impressed into the service that the work was finally completed. The (dead) men were everywhere. The whole ground around Gettysburg was one vast cemetery. When they could be conveniently brought together, bodies were buried in clusters of 10, 20, 50 or more. One grave had 400 dead men. So great was their number and such the advanced stages of decomposition of those that had lain on the field for several days during the hot weather of July, they could not be removed. The strain of digging that many graves must have been stupendous."

[In addition to human casualties, many horses lost their lives in the battle. For example, the 141st Regiment lost all of their horses. One estimate was that there were at least 5,000 horses killed in that three-day battle. It took weeks to get all dead horses burned or buried. Burying dead humans had a higher priority.]

Sat. 4 July. Went with ambulance with the lieu. to Littlestown. Expected to go to Westminister but found train at the former place. Rec'd letter from H. Norton *[Hannah]*. O, glorious Fourth! *[Littlestown is a little town about ten miles southeast of Gettysburg.]*

<u>Letter #31A</u>

Gettysburg *[Pennsylvania]*
July 4th *[1863]*

Ever dear Friend V:

My life is yet spared me so that I can at least enjoy the privilege of writing to you. We have been upon the march ever since the 10th of last month. The first of July we came into Pa. You can scarcely imagine my feelings upon entering my native state again. I had hoped when I was once more there it would be for the rest of my life and many, very many, of our poor boys will never again go hence.

Our corps engaged the enemy the second *[of July]* and have lost very many men. I have yet found *[all]* but two of the boys that came from our neighborhood. They are C. Webster and H. Hunsinger. I am in hopes they may only have lost the regt. and will be heard from soon. 'Tis awful to witness the quantity of wounded. My Lieut. Graves was very badly wounded. I have today assisted in helping to send him to Phila. I am hopeful that he may recover for he has been a good friend to me. He has always treated me as though I was a man; and a great many officers don't know how to do that.

*****

Sun. 5 July   The wounded come in by scores. I ran over the country to get a few things fit to eat. Can learn nothing of Samuel. Fighting seems to have ceased. Sent a letter off to David yesterday.

[See letters of July 13, July 21, and August 11, 1863, for details of what Joel thought happened to Samuel. Also, see letter to Joel from Samuel's sister, Martha, December 2, 1863.]

Letter #31B

July 5th, 1863
[Gettysburg, Pennsylvania]

I resume my pencil to finish my letter. Since yesterday, a number of our boys have been brought in. Edmund Bedford is wounded, but not dangerous -- just below the knee, a flesh wound. Samuel Molyneux is missing! I cannot ascertain anything positive about him. Tillman Bedford was not hurt. Our co. *[K]* now numbers seven that have got together again unhurt. Poor Charles Grange, I have learned, is dead. He died the day we left as far as I can find out. He died before the hospitals were removed. This was in our old encampment near Bell Plain. *[Charles Grange died June 11, 1863.]*

I do not know yet the correct result of this battle. 'Tis said we have gained a big victory; but 'tis said we have gained a big victory at a monstrous cost. We have taken a great many prisoners. Among the number is their noted Gen. Longstreet. *[An unfounded rumor. General Longstreet was not captured.]* The rebs are said to be retreating, perhaps the fighting is ended for this place, but we may, 'tis likely, pursue them and bring on another. You say, "Don't write so sober!" If I should tell you one tenth of what I have had to witness and listen to for the past four days you would think it no easy task, I assure you.

I cannot write long letters now. I have so many of my poor comrades to see to. I am going out in the country to try and buy some bread and things they can eat. Those brought in this morning many of them have not eaten anything for two days. Good bye. Heaven bless you is the sincere prayer of your true and loving friend – Joel.

P. S. Direct as before: HD.Qrs., First Div., Third Corps, or HD.Qrs., Birney's Div., Washington, D.C.

*****

Mon. 6 July. Brought the boys some milk. Orders to move. Rebs are retreating. Move up to the battlefield, and then went into camp. I have often read of a battlefield, but to know is to witness.

Tue. 7 July. Repass Emmitsburg and close by St. Josephs Convent and went into camp just by Mechanicsburg. Makes out to be rainy. Whew! *[At the time of the Civil War, St. Joseph's, in Emmitsburg, Maryland, was a Catholic convent and school for girls. Many wounded soldiers from both sides were housed there after the three-day battle. In the 1970's, the federal government bought part of the campus and currently operates it as the National Emergency Training Center.]*

Wed. 8 July. Broke camp and in a heavy rain storm pass Donesville *[probably Downsville]*, an iron foundry, and Frederic City. I had word Vicksburg is taken at last. Went in to camp just out of town. Supperless! *[Vicksburg had surrendered to General Grant's army, July 4, 1863.]*

Thu. 9 July. Marched through the mud to Middletown. Camped in a clover field. Wrote to Jennie Molyneux and mailed it the tenth.

Fri. 10 July. Broke camp and reached the battle field of 14 Sept., 1862. South Mountain was the spot where Gen. Reno fell. Strike Sharpsburg Pike at Keedersville *[probably Keedysville]*. Camped nearby.

Sat. 11 July. Repass Keedersville and down the Sharpsburg Pike to Boonsboro. Go into camp early in the day, one mile out of town. Some fighting at this place yesterday.

Sun. 12 July. Wrote to H. M. Grange and K. H. T. *[Probably K. B. Taylor]* Also to Kate Tirncrook. Did not march today. Are awaiting army movements. Fighting momentarily expected. "When will wars and tumult cease?"

Mon. 13 July. Little or no fighting today. Near 200 reb prisoners are taken part. Orders to move, but did not get started. Wrote a letter to V. All sorts of rumors.

Letter #32

[The Army of Potomac's III Corps was busy. They had been in the thick of the fighting at the Battle of Gettysburg. Now, they were following Lee's Army of Northern Virginia as it retreated south across Maryland and into Virginia. Joel had little time to write letters.]

Boonsboro *[Maryland]*
July 13, 1863

Dear Vilie:

I do not know as I shall have time to write three lines before orders will come "pack up and move," but I thought this morning I would at least commence one more letter to you. As you see by this, I am still alive, also am in the enjoyment of good health. I know I should be truly thankful for such great blessing. It must be in ans. to the prayers of praying ones at home, whilst with many, very many, of my poor comrades circumstances are very different. But, here is one of those sober letters again, but Vilie I can't help it without being deceitful and you would not wish me to be so, would you?

Well, I shall say just as little as I can of the War, just the particulars. When last I wrote, I mentioned C. *[Charles]* Grange's death at the Hospital near Bellplain, Va. Say, just while I think of it, I had a letter from H. M. Grange not long since asking about Charles. I ans. it yesterday. You are not alarmed of our corresponding, are you? *["H. M. Grange" may have been a sister of Charles. The letter probably was to report the death of Charles.]*

Nothing yet can I learn of Samuel Molyneux since the battle of Gettysburg. 'Tis dreadful to think of it, but I am afraid he was among the unrecognized slain. I wrote to his sister, Jennie. 'Twas the hardest letter I ever attempted to write. I dare not say to her all probabilities he is killed, yet I have some hope he may not be.

Tilliman Bedford is without doubt slain. We found a grave with a letter of his upon a ramrod beside it. Edmond B. *[Bedford]* was severely wounded, but not dangerous. C. Webster and I are now all that are left of the 12 that went from our neighborhood.

I told you in my last of my Lieut. G. being wounded and gone to Phil. leaving me alone to take care of myself, all his things, his fancy horse, Dandy, as he calls him, and one I have for my own use. I do not look for him to come back short of three months.

You heard how we whipped the Johnnys at Gettysburg; how they retreated and we after them. I felt sorry to leave old Pa. again without calling even to see folks, but upon the sixth *[of July]* we were into M. *[Maryland]* -- went back through Frederic City and Mechanicksburg, Middletown, crossed the South Mountain where the battle of last Sept. 14th was fought; thence to Antietam and turned up the Sharpsburg Pike to Boonsboro. 'Tis a town some larger than Troy *[village in nearby Bradford County, Pennsylvania]*. We are now some two mile out of town. The rebs are but a few miles in advance of us -- said to be in large force. Skirmishing commenced yesterday.

A great fight is looked for. I expect the cannon to open every moment. 'Tis said they must whip us here or surrender. How anxiously the result of this campaign is awaited by everyone if we are but successful. 'Tis hoped the war will be nearly terminated. 'Tis very rainy today. Last night we had a tremendous shower and an order has just come for the men to harness up and be ready for moving.

Since the lieut. went away I have been with the ammunition train. How would you like to see a train of army wagons? Generally have six mules to them. The wagon covered with white canvas. Some of the trains are nearly ten mile long. There are nearly 500 wagons with this corps, and there are seven different corps in this Army. *[If each of the seven corps had a similar train of 500 wagons, this adds up to 3,500 wagons pulled by 21,000 horses and mules. Trains carried ammunition, food, equipment, etc. They tagged along behind and stayed close to the army, but not so close as to be in danger of being captured by the enemy.]*

I have not yet seen George Pardoe. If he is with his regt. he was in this last battle, and *[we]* must have been within speaking distance at one time, if I had known it. He is in the Fifth Army Corps, and I am in the Third. The 1st, 2nd, 3rd, 5th, 6th, 11th, and 12th *[Corps]* are in this army, but enough on this sheet.

*****

Tue. 14 July. Marching orders get under way. Cross Antietam Creek and on to the front, but the rebs are all safely over the river. Went into camp near a line of fortifications.

Wed. 15 July. Lieu. Palmer of the wagon guard is relieved this morning. Broke camp and marched by Antietam bloody field. Pass Sharpsburg, and go into park three mile out of town upon a hillside.

Thu. 16 July. Again upon the road. Mail my letter to V. Got one from sister Kate B. Pass through Shoarsbury and Brownsville. Go into camp in view of the Maryland Heights opposite Harpers Ferry. *["Kate B." was sister, Lydia, who was married to Jonas Bedford.]*

Letter #33

July 16 *[1863]*
Near Harpers Ferry *[West Virginia]*

Dear Vilie:

I have not yet had an opportunity of mailing this letter, but perhaps will today. Am still enjoying health -- have had no letter since I was in Penn., and here nothing new to write. The rebs are all across the river *[Potomac]*. They are too smart for us. We expect to cross into Va. at Harpers Ferry. With much love I remain, Yours – Joel.

*****

Fri. 17 July. Lay in camp till nearly night, then hitch up and get on the road by near nine o'clock. On the road all night, but do not get over three miles. Sleep by the fire, darkey style. This is pleasant valley.

Sat. 18 July. Move quite early. Pass Sandy Hook and cross on pontoons the Potomac to Harpers Ferry, the noted town of John Brown. Crossed the Shenandoah. Light body *[?]* or Corts *[?]* and Rowe are missing. Camp in Secesia *[Secession Land]*.

Sun. 19 July. Blackberries are plenty here, but not withstanding we move on about six mile and camp. Reb. cavalry are seen upon the hills. Strict orders out and heavy guards accompany the train.

Mon. 20 July. Upon the road by sunrise. Pass Snickersville and Gap, a little to the left. This is Loudon Co. *[Loudon County, Virginia]*, and a beautiful country. March near 15 miles and go into camp at Tiperville.

Tue. 21 July. O pleasant day. Wrote a letter to J. P. McCarty. Was to follow Div. Hd Qrs by the villa. Did not march today. Had baked beans for dinner and flour dumplings with fresh beef for supper. *[They stayed in camp and had a chance to prepare warm meals.]*

Letter #34

[Letter to Sallie and her husband, John.]

Upperville, Va.,
July 21 *[1863]*

Dear Sister and Brother:

Doubtless you have about given up ever hearing from your Southern brother again, but at the date of this letter he was alive and in good health. He has written letters at every opportunity to different ones at home and thereabouts, but possibly all may not have arrived as they mostly were mailed at the villages and towns through which we passed in and back from our trip to Pa.

The rebs, as you will have 'ere this learned, got away from us, and on the 18th of July we recrossed the Potomac at Harpers Ferry into Va. again. Yesterday we marched 15 mile. Today, we are in camp and some 25 miles from Harpers Ferry, Loudon County.

I rec'd Sallie's letter with the enclosed one from Cousin Kate. Have written to her, since the only letter I have had this month was the one from Sister Kate Bull. She had just started for home and then was at Muncy. She hinted as though David was near getting married. I do wonder if 'tis so? So James Pardoe is at home on a 30 day furlough. I wish 'twas 300 instead. I saw the Pa. Reserves but once since George was home. They were just then going into the fight at Gettysburg. I did not get to see him nor have I heard from him since. I have heard nothing from Edmund since we left. He then was at a temporary hospital near Gettysburg. We have no news of Samuel yet. I have fears he was among those that fell.

I do not know how far the rebs are ahead of us -- that is their main force. Scouting parties are often seen and stragglers are being constantly picked up. Another battle may take place soon and it may not. We hear Vicksburg, Port Hudson, and some say Charleston is taken. If so, the Johnnys must certainly begin to think their time is nearly come to hunt their holes. This reminds me of what one of our boys said -- "that we had been chasing a grayback". He said their holes were fixed so they drawed them in after them. (don't let Sallie see this.)

So you have sold Charley *[probably a horse or bull]* and the oxen and built a shed to your barn and got a boy, and bought a colt. The war cannot have had a very bad effect in Elkland I think yet. What think you? I wish I was there to see for myself a few days. I know what you are thinking of, of course! I would call and see the neighbors! Please give my respect, will you?

Lieutenant Graves, the man I was with as orderly, was wounded at Gettysburg. He is now at Phila. in a hospital. The ball passed through his thigh, but did not break any bones. I do not look for him back in less time than three months. I am now with the ammunition train with his one horse and mine. One of his was shot in the battle. If nothing occurs to change the order of things, I shall have easy times, at least until he returns.

You may send my letters as before to Hd Qrs, First Div., Third Corps, Washington, D.C. I have an opportunity of giving this to the mail man and so I will close. Resp'ts to all enquirers. Love for those who prefer it. The same for you and sister. Joel.

*****

Wed. 22 July.   Wrote to V. Done the washing up. Start on the march again about sundown, and are on the road till after midnight, five miles, and camp near Piedmont.

Letter #35A

Uperville, [Virginia]
July 22nd, 1863

Dearest Vilie:

Please forgive my sending so soiled and crumpled a sheet of paper. 'Tis the best I have. Hoping to pick up some verses that were quite new to me, so I have copied them and thinking they may also be new to you, I enclose them to you. I mailed a letter for you the 16th. Have you rec'd it? We are now encamped by a small town called Uperville *[Upperville]*. 'Tis in Va., 25 miles from Harpers Ferry. We came here two days ago.

I wrote to John and Sallie yesterday. Have not rec'd a letter from home written this month. Today is very warm here — quite warm enough for me. Sure, blackberries are very thick in this part of Va. — the sort you know that grow up on little, low bushes. Crawlers or dewberries, some call them, but would prefer picking those that grow in Elkland if, well if "this cruel war was over", and there were plenty of them.

I have just been wondering if you were teaching today. Perhaps, though, by this time your school has closed. But what will Abel do for a housekeeper then? Seriously, he will have to get him a wife, will he not? So, Lizzie's fellow, Corn, has returned the worse for being in the army. What does one think? Does she scorn him or will she do as you said you would by me, "Try first to get me to be a better boy." I often think of that. Perhaps it has had some influence in restraining me from following bad example. I cannot tell you what a wicked place an army is; neither can I tell you how much more I thought of you when you told me you would first try and get me to be a better man if I should return as you say he has. I trust I may not. *[Here, Joel is referring to the foul and obscene language used by many soldiers. His September 2, 1862, letter to Vi devoted a paragraph to that subject.]* 'Tis now near three o'clock in Wednesday afternoon. Orders have just come to pack up and march so I must close with another short letter. My health is good and hope this will find you in better health than when you wrote before. Take care of your health, Vilie, for my sake won't you please? Good-bye. Love to you and please write soon to Joel.

*****

Thu. 23 July. Are on the road early. Do not go very far before going into park a few miles of Manassas Gap. Our forces here found the rebs upon the other side. Cannons are heard and skirmishing commenced.

Letter #35B

[Continuation of July 22 letter to V.]

Dixie, *[Upperville, Virginia]*
Thursday morning, *[July 23, 1863]*

After finishing the other sheet and getting it ready for mailing tomorrow morning, excepting the sealing, our officers came around and told us to brush up and be ready for receiving visitors. Of course, we dusted our clothes and combed our hair, etc.

At four o'clock P.M. our regt. was marched into an open field. Also, the 68th Pa. and the 114th. The 114th is a regt. of Zouaves. I think that I spoke of it in a former letter. Their uniform is red pants, blue round about red cap with a white woolen scarf wrapped around forming a sort of a turband *[turban]*, and a large yellow tassel attached to the cap to top it off with.

It seems Governor Curtin had sent us our flags by the hand of Adjutant Gen. Thomas. He presented one to each of the colonels of the regiments; with a short and very appropriate address. He said he entrusted us with the flag which he hoped would lead us to victory; that we should protect it and never desert it, and when this wicked rebellion was wiped out we should return it to the archives of the state to be preserved as a memento of our patriotism, bravery, and suffering.

He said the people of our state had not forgotten us, that the hands of many were busy in every hamlet and village to aid in our comfort and that scores of hearts were then throbbing for us (As he spoke that, I wondered if yours was one). When the colonels started toward their regiments with the flags, the bands of music struck up playing the tune "O, the Star Spangled Banner, long may it wave." It sounded so appropriate and inspiring that a person could hardly help saying to himself the often-repeated words, "Who wouldn't be a soldier?"

We have two brass bands in our brigade. One belongs to the 68th Regt. The other to the 114th Zouave Regt. Ours have not any -- only drums and fife.

But what is up now? Someone to the campfire is calling out for "Joel Molyneux", "J. L. Molyneux". Excuse me for a few minutes if you please, while I run out and see what they want of him. "A letter, letter," I hear them say!

Good! The mail has come so there be no more written tonight. Good evening, Vile.

*****

Fri. 24 July. Fifth Army Corps pass us going to the front. Saw George Pardoe and Wallace Snell and David Bryan. Did not move today. Wagons are ordered be ready to move in another direction.

Sat. 25 July. Pick berries etc. till two o'clock P.M., then move off to Salem and beyond a few mile. *[The village of Salem, Virginia, had its name changed after the war. It is now Marshall, Virginia. It was renamed after Chief Justice John Marshall who lived in that community many years.]* Go in camp. My horse, Bony, dies tonight from eating wheat. Got him at Chancellorsville *[see diary May 5, 1863].*

Sun. 26 July. On the road again. Pass through Warrenton, and park a mile out of town. The troops are very destitute for shoes and clothes. Expect to stop here and get fitted up.

Mon. 27 July. Remain in camp. Wrote to Kate B. *[Bull]* and Angie P. *[Pratt]* E. Bedford's address, U.S. General Hosp., Sec. 1st Ward, 11 M-D, Annappolis. Wm. Rogers: Chestnut Hill Hosp., Co. C, Phila., Pa.

[Nephew Edmund Bedford was wounded several times in the war. The last time was a leg wound received in the Peach Orchard engagement at the Battle of Gettysburg, July 2, 1863. Hospitalized until December 29, 1863, he returned to active duty. In March 1866, after his discharge, Edmund married Anna Merrick, went to college, became a dentist, and spent most of his life practicing in Sioux City, Iowa, and later in California. He died in Pasadena, California in 1928 at age 82.]

Tue. 28 July. Went to Hd Qrs and the regt. Rec'd two letters from David; one from Sister Sallie; one from E. Bedford; one from Wm. Rogers; one from Kate Tirncrook; one from V.; and one from Ed and Sam.

Wed. 29 July. Still encamped. Wrote to Martha M. and Wm. Rogers, also to E. Bedford.

Thu. 30 July. Went through the brigade with receipts of ordinance stores. Holt and others that were left at Frederic City came up. Wrote to Lieut. Graves.*[Holt was the tent mate mentioned March 5, March 13, April 10, and April 23, 1863.]*

Fri. 31 July. Visited Hd Qrs and the brigades. Find James Pardoe at the regt., and Sperry. Our div. move four mile to Sulphur Springs. 20 Ind. *[Indiana 20th Regiment.]* leave the div. for S. Carolina, it is supposed.

[That resort spa, Sulphur Springs, is now named Faquier Springs or Faquier Sulphur Springs, or just The Springs. It is not the famous White Sulphur Spring in West Virginia. It is west of Warrenton near the Rapidan River that Joel crossed and recrossed so often. Prior to the Civil War, the place was the site of a resort hotel, and people came there for the healing effect of the water. In one letter, Joel mentioned staying there, and sleeping under the marquee. He mentioned that the water smelled like the bottom of a well. The old hotel was destroyed during the war, and a subsequent one burned a few years ago. Now the site is a beautiful country club golf course. The hydrogen sulfide water still smells strong, as it did in 1863 when Joel was there.]

CHAPTER 13: AUGUST 1863

Sat. 1 Aug. Are in camp all day. Visit the springs. Has been a very pretty resort, but are now a pile of ruins. Wrote to E. Bedford, also to Dr. J. K. Bird.

Sun. 2 Aug. Took a walk round the ruins again and drank at the spring. I think this day is as warm as any we have had this summer. Sweat freely in the shade. No letters.

Mon. 3 Aug. Still laying in camp with nothing to do, but pick blackberries. 'Tis too warm to write letters. Feelings of ennui. *[Boredom and weariness have been problems in all armies when the troops were not in battle.]*

Tue. 4 Aug. Was at Hd Qrs and also to the regt. Wrote a letter to Norton, also one to Geo. Molyneux. Slept in a markee.

[The "markee" was probably the front door roof at the entrance of the hotel at White Sulphur Springs. The old gazebo enclosing the spring is still there, although the resort hotel is long gone.]

Wed. 5 Aug. Rec'd a letter from Edmund. *[Bedford]* Had my horse at Hd Qrs., and Lieut. Moore rode out with him.

Thu. 6 Aug. Was out haymaking today -- cutting grass for the mules.

Fri. 7 Aug. Took dinner at my old mess. Wrote one letter to V. D. Simmons is at regt. again.

Sat. 8 Aug. Wrote to L. *[Elvira]* You are a stern old fact; I'm getting indolent.

[On August 8, 1863, following his defeat at the Battle of Gettysburg, General Robert E. Lee offered his resignation to C.S.A. president, Jefferson Davis, who refused to accept it.]

Letter #36

Saturday morning,
Aug. 8th, 1863

My Friend, Good Morning.

Well, I hope. Suppose I guess what you are doing but you have heard the song of the farmer's girl so I need not repeat it: "washing the breakfast dishes", etc., etc., and today if I remember, biscuit and pies are made for the morning and the windows washed, floors cleaned, etc. And then you will no *[know]* you will not have time to write today -- tomorrow after you *[your]* parents are gone to the meeting. *[Elvira's family were Friends (Quakers), and called their church service "the meeting".]* You will think of me, and beneath some shady tree will write a long, very long letter, all to me. Now, have I guessed anything right? If I have, I'll guess again that is if I was there with you we would spill the ink, lose the pen, and tear the paper all into bits, but my love good bye. Good bye – Joel.

*****

Mon. 10 Aug.   Wrote a letter to David, and one to Mary P. *[Joel's eldest sister, Mary, had married Joseph Pardoe in 1840. Their sixth and last child was named Mary. She, therefore, was Joel's niece, and was thirteen at this time Joel wrote her, mentioned above.]*

Letter #37

[In this letter to David, Joel mentioned "diarrhea". Intestinal diseases, from poor sanitation, were probably responsible for more Civil War soldiers' deaths than bullets. Union troops coined the nickname "Virginia Quickstep" to refer to diarrhea — the most common ailment in the Civil War army.]

White Sulphur Springs, Va.
August 11, *[1863]*

Dear Brother:

Your two last letters reached me the 28th. Was glad to get them though they had been some time upon the way. My health is still very good. The diarhea that troubles most people down here, that have been brought up in the North, I have not been affected with since last fall.

James Pardoe arrived all safe to his regt. I think it was the 30th. He seems to be in much better health and spirits than when he left us here. I saw George the 24th -- perhaps I may have written of it before. He is looking well and feeling finely. W. Snell and D. Bryan were with him all night. I did not get to see Mike although he was with his regt. He was away after berries when I was with them. He was taken prisoner at G. *[Gettysburg]* but paroled immediately. The gov. will not recognize it and sent him to his regt. again.

We have now been encamped here two weeks with a probability of staying longer though 'tis not likely that we stay longer than to get the Reg'ts. filled with the drafted men that are now being sent in. I heard the enrollment papers of our county had been lost or stolen so the draft there will not take place as soon as was intended. You will have all your work, I suppose, to do over again. *[Apparently David was on the county draft board.]*

I had a letter from Eddie Bedford a few days ago. I will enclose it with this as it will not make it over weight.

W. Rogers wrote me the sixth. He is at Phil. *[Philadelphia]* still and doing well. I learn from his letter that Thomas Molyneux had been down to Gettysburg to see if anything could be ascertained about Samuel. *[Thomas was Samuel's next older brother. Born in 1827, Thomas was married to Elizabeth Huckell. They had five children.]* I suppose t'would be some satisfaction but quite a small chance of getting any trace of him. I wrote to them a short time ago, after I thought all possibility of hearing any thing more was in vain.

Very few prisoners were taken by the rebs. in that part of the field were *[where]* our regt. was so badly cut up. Only those that were wounded and could not get to the rear, and these were left when they retreated.

One of our co., T. Phillips of Davidson, was in their hands in this manner for a while and his story in regards to Sam, I fear, is correct. Phillips was shot through the arm and also through his right lung. He states that Sam in the action was right behind him and when our boys were falling the thickest he noticed some one fell nearby where Sam had stood but only just had one glance at him and at the time he thought it was Sam that fell as though he was shot dead as he was not positive it was he. I did not write this to his folks the first time I wrote for I had some hopes I should hear of him through some source, but now think Phillips' account is only too true. I think P.'s wound would prove mortal but have not heard of him since we left Gettysburg. If he has, 'twill make eight of the 24 that went into the fight of our co. that were killed and since died of their wounds.

We are expecting to get our pay for two more mos. today or tomorrow, up to the first of July. James has some eight months due him -- do not know about sending it home yet.

If I really knew anything about the war or how things were working I would tell you all I know 'tis a big thing and know as little what really has been done as what is to be done.

I have just seen the president's reply and Gov. Seymour's letter. I think that old Abe is about right and that Seymour Fernando Wood, with some others, are a devilish sight worse than Jeff Davis ever dared to be.

[Troops in the field read daily papers. Thus, they kept up with politics, fighting, and progress of the war. Joel mentions an exchange between President Lincoln and Governor Wood of New York State. Governor Wood was

in favor of preserving the unity of the country, but not in freeing slaves — anti-abolitionist. In New York City the feeling, particularly among Irish, was that freed blacks would take jobs away from whites. Wood had proposed New York City secede from the Union and become a free city. He helped organize the Peace Democrats or "Copperheads" as they were derisively called by their opponents. Small wonder idealist Joel felt strongly about Governor Wood's anti-abolition views.]

The Springs here are not a very nice place. The sulphur springs are so strong of the stuff one at first can hardly drink it. The property was, I learn, sold just before the rebellion broke out for 60 thousand dollars. Now 'tis nearly all destroyed. The finest hotel is burned and every thing is fast going to destruction. I should think, when the thing was in running order, it would accommodate four or five hundred visitors. *[The resort hotel Joel refers to had been used by soldiers of both armies. One version of the hotel's destruction was that 12 Confederate soldiers were holed up in the hotel, and artillery gunners of Union General Pope shelled the hotel from across the Rapidan River. The hotel was destroyed. It was later rebuilt, but then burned.]*

The weather has been very warm here for some days past with heavy showers occasionally. I presume that haying goes rather slow this season as hands probably cannot be had. I should like to come up and help but, of course, cannot.

I am now with the ammunition train belonging to our div., as the lieut. I was with has not returned from the hospital. He was wounded at Gettysburg. Whether I shall remain here untill he returns or go into the provost guard again I do not know. You will direct letters as before to me: (Hd. Qtrs. Birney's Div., Washington, D.C.).

Give my love to all our folks, father and mother, not forgetting yourself and write soon to your brother, Joel.

*****

Wed. 12 Aug.   Hot! Was at my regt. and signed the payrolls. Rec'd a letter from Jennie.

Thu. 13 Aug.   Rec'd two months pay, $26.00. Went to Warrenton after hay Gov. West sent to this regt. Rec'd a letter from David. *[? There was no "Gov. West" in the United States at the time Joel wrote this entry. I think the typist made a mistake in reading Joel's writing and the entry may have been Gov. Lewis of Wisconsin or Gov. Yates of Illinois.]*

Fri. 14 Aug.   Went to corps Hd Qrs on business for C. Churchill and Sergeant Young.

Sat. 15 Aug. to cousin Jennie.	Third Mich. left our div. for W.*[Washington]* Wrote
Sun. 16 Aug. leave for W.	Rec'd a letter from Jessie and Phide. The Fifth Mich.
Mon. 17 Aug. these days!	Wrote to Angie S. *[cousin Angie Summers]* One of

Letter #38

Aug. 17th, *[1863]*, White Sulphur Springs, Va.

Dear sister: *[cousin Angie Summers]*

You have begun to think I was not going to write again, but when this reaches you perhaps you may change your mind. Only think me a little negligent. I ans. John's letter nearly a month ago; he, I presume, rec'd it. Your last came up on the 28th. My health is good yet unless laziness is a disease but that you know was an old complaint of mine but now I begin to think it is taking a different form and will improve incurable. The latest news I have from home is the death of George Little and Josiah and little Jennie Mullen, Poor George; I can hardly realize he is also of the number whose life has been sacrificed by this unholy war. I rec'd a letter from Jennie M. a few days ago. Their hearts ache for G. *[George Little].* I wish I could think he was yet alive, but I cannot think there is any room for hope.

We have been encamped here now since the first of this mo., but have been under orders to be ready to march at a minute's notice for several days. Camp is full of rumors as to where we are likely to go, etc., so I will not even presume to guess.

The springs here has been quite a favorable watering place. Once *[it]* was so as to accommodate six *[600]* or 800 at a time, but everything is now in ruins. The sulphur spring is so strong of the stuff I can smell it three rod and tastes like going down into our well when we was blasting out the rock. For my part, I have some doubts about the earth being very thick through right about here.

James Pardoe seems to get along very well since coming back to his regt. He rec'd a letter from George *[Pardoe]* the other day. He then was at Rappahannac Station eight mile from us, was well. We rec'd two months pay last week, 26 dollars, but James failed to get his for want of having something to show that he had not been paid while away at the hospital. He will soon have ten months due him. We will try to have it so he can get it next pay day.

I wrote cousin Kate Jones a letter and have had an answer. I will send it to you with this. A letter has just come for me from Kate dated the 11th. I guess she enjoys herself. Well, do you think there is any danger of Will N *[Norton]* and her making a match? I wish Abe would take a fancy instead, but I guess he has no notion there.

David, I suppose, is about the same as married at last. He has had a serious time finding the one. When do you think it will come off? I would like to be present, especially at dinner time. I wonder if I would have strong black coffee, fhinzz *[?]* pork, and hardtac, but I recon *[reckon]* I shall have more of that than anything else for sometime yet.

[David and Hannah Norton married November 25, 1863. Their marriage lasted 13 years. Hannah died March 9, 1877, after the birth of their fifth child. David remarried. His second wife was Elizabeth Webster and that marriage lasted until 1894 when she also died. David married a third time, to Susan Wickham. David died in 1920, age 94. David had eight children. Many of David's descendants live in Sullivan County.]

The weather here is some warmer, I think, than up in old Sullivan. Now and then we have a very *[cold]* day, though. From what I hear from home, crops, etc., are not much earlier here than there. The corn is not yet good roasting ears. From the little I have seen, but there is scarcely anything planted here any more, and the little there is does not stand much right with the soldiers whenever they come around.

I hear the draft has been put off, for some reason, in our county a few weeks. But, like Christmas, 'tis a coming and dreaded rather worse. Are the Quakers exempt this time or not? If they are, I suppose it is by their paying the exemption fee. There are those I should be sorry to hear were among the conscripts, but I think there are some if they were drafted I would like to come and help to bring them down here myself.

I have cut out a piece from a newspaper for John to read, but I don't no *[know]* how he *[would]* like it. But I cannot write more this time. The flys are so bad there is nearly a dozen on my hands and face all the time – the regular house fly *[is]* saucy and impudent as can be, and gray backs too.

Will and Henry Bedford have not yet come up from parole camp. I got a letter David sent by them and mailed at Alexandria. I hope to see them soon. I have had quite easy times since the battles as Lieutenant G. was wounded and not returned yet. I have the care of his horse and private things he left, but look for him back now in about three weeks.

Direct to me as before when you write: H-d Qrs. Birney's Div., Washington, D.C. My best wishes to all inquiring friends and much love to John and sister Sallie, from your brother, Joel.

P. S. Write soon. Kate write *[wrote]* me that Uncle Daniel Little is dead. I have heard nothing of John Summers for a long time.

*****

Sun. 23 Aug.	Wrote to V. Rec'd a letter from Kate B. *[Bull]* One of these days!
Mon. 24 Aug.	Have just been one year away from home.
Thu. 27 Aug.	Rec'd a letter from V.

Letter #39

Sulphur Springs, Va.
Aug. 27, *[1863]*

Dear Brother: *[David]*

I rec'd your letter and also one from Kate not long since. Was glad to hear from you that you were all well too. I had written to you, also to Kate just previous to my getting yours. I suppose you have read them. I am usually well with the exception of a bad cold. 'Tis the first nearly I have been troubled with since leaving home, but am in hopes it will run itself clear so as my nose seems to be doing pretty well at it at present.

Our army is still laying encamped here. The Rappahannoc *[River]* forms our line to the front. There has been nothing of interest going on near this place of late, although we are said to be under orders to march at a minute's notice. The probabilities are that we may remain here for some time unless attackted

We have had some warm weather along back, but yesterday brought us quite a change. Very heavy winds and cool this morning. Was cold enough for frost. Some of the boys say there was.

James Pardoe appears to get along very well since joining the regt. again. We were paid two more months a short time ago, but owing to his not having something to show that he had not been paid while away to the hospital, he did not get his pay. His pay is due him since the first of November. Everything is filed now so there will be no trouble next time.

The reserves are some 10 mile from us at Rappahannoc Station or near there. I have not seen George *[Pardoe]* since now a month ago. Wm. and Henry Bedford I hear are not yet exchanged and will not be for 9 months. They forwarded the letter sent by you. Katie speaks of sending some paper & envelopes. I have not got them. It is not necessary to send such now, as I can get them here quite reasonable. Stamps is the only difficulty. Those you sent was rec'd.

The news from Charleston seems quite hopeful that that vipers' nest soon be reduced. Yesterday's papers have it that Sumpter has caved in. Hope it may prove correct. We have not rec'd any conscripts yet in our div. They seem to be slow about coming. The draft in your district must by this time be beginning to take form again for going ahead. I am anxious to hear who draw the prizes. Hope some of those good Secesh brothers, sometimes called Copperheads, will be so lucky.

I was sorry to hear of George Little's death. Fleshy persons do not seem to have much chance when taken with the fever.

I hear from Edmund occasionally. He is so that he walks about now with a cane. The wound is not yet healed; the bullet is still in his leg. He writes that he could get a 15 day furlough, but I believe does no *[not]* think of taking one.

I have not sent my last payment yet, 26 dollars. Did not have a chance to express it, and I thought it would not be safe to risk it in a letter right off after pay day.

I do not think of any thing more to write this time. I wrote to Uncle John's folks all I knew of the circumstances about Samuel. Pennington knows nothing concerning him but what I had found out and told him. He is almost beyond doubt among the slain. Hoping these lines may find all of you well. I will close with the best wishes from your brother, Joel. Direct: Hd Qrs, Birney's Div., Washington, D.C.

*****

 Fri. 28 Aug. Wrote to Edie Bedford. Was at the regt. today. Dr. Leyman gave me some medicine for my cold.

 Sat. 29 Aug. Rec'd letter from Doc J. K. Bird. *[We don't have any of J. K.'s letters to Joel, and only one from Joel to J. K.]*

 Sun. 30 Aug. Wrote to George Pardoe. Visited H. Green. A letter from Angie Summers.

 Mon. 31 Aug. Rec'd a letter from Martha Molyneux. *[First cousin, and sister of the deceased Samuel.]* Wrote a letter to Kate Tirncrook.

CHAPTER 14: SEPTEMBER 1863

Tue. 1 Sept.   Wrote to Wm. Rogers. About half dead with a cold.

Wed. 2 Sept.   Rode over to the regt. Have blowed myself nearly away. Cook for myself.

Thu. 3 Sept.   Think my cold is some better. Wrote no letters nor rec'd any. The weather remains cool. Hot weather seems to have been broke.

Fri. 4 Sept.   No news. Wrote to Sister Anna. George Pardoe and James were here. Had a pleasant visit.

Sat. 5 Sept.   Lieut. Moore lost his two horses on Thursday. He has had Dandy since. Hope Lieut. Graves comes soon.

Mon. 7 Sept.   Wrote to Jesse and Phide. The army is reviewed today by General Meade.

[Major General George Meade had replaced General Hooker as commander of the Army of the Potomac. General Hooker had resigned in protest, on June 27, 1863, just a few days before the Battle of Gettysburg.]

Tue. 8 Sept.   Hear cannonading, but it proves to be target practice.

Letter #40

[Joel had recently written Sallie. He remembered it in the middle of his letter.]

White Sulphur Springs, [Virginia]
Sept. 8, [1863]

Dear Sister:

I have just been looking over my diary and find that I have been owing you a letter for some time. I was really surprised for I had thought your last answered. Please forgive me if I really have not written, for you must by this time have thought me quite neglectful.

I have had a very bad cold for more than two weeks which has made me feel like everything else than myself. I have blowed me nearly all away with it. The last few days I have felt some better, and shall hope to be clear of it entirely, soon.

We are still here at the Springs where we stopped in the pursuit of Lee, the last of July. Nothing of importance is being done in this vicinity, and how long we are to remain here is quite uncertain.

George Pardoe paid us a visit last Friday. His regt. is at Rappahannoc Station, nine mile from here. I was really glad to see him, the next pay day he will have 10 months due him or some $130. I get a letter from Edmund now and then. He was going around with a cane. He wrote his wound was not healed but it had not bled, as we were afraid it might. He did not think of trying to get home upon a furlough. Wm. and Henry Bedford are yet unexchanged and at parole camp.

I hear of quite a number of deaths in Elkland and Forks: Little Jennie Mullen and Olive Dobson, Mrs. Wilkinson, and George Little. Death seems not alone with us upon the battlefield. The latest date of letters I have from home is Aug. 27th. By the way, in my last to you I sent a letter of Coz Kate Tirncrook. This reminds me that I have ans. your last, but we will never mind about that now.

The weather is much cooler now for the past ten days, one morning we had quite a smart frost. The ground is very dry and the roads dusty for want of rain; we have had but little for a long time.

I have not seen any conscripts yet; they are coming to the other corps. I suppose those for ours will be along soon. I hear 12 is the number for Elkland to furnish and 16 for Forks. I am quite curious to know who they may be, but perhaps do not feel quite the urge about it as those whose names are liable to be picked out by the blind man.

It has been a year, the 24th of August, since I started down here. The past one does not seem long, but the other two seem to stick out a very long way into the future.

This letter would be hardly complete if I should say nothing about the girls. I have heard Cornelia was at her brothers, and that is all George P. *[Pardoe]* spoke of calling at Greens. He seemed to think they were perfectly ——*[indecipherable, probably "matched"]* regardless even of their personal appearance. It hardly seems possible.

Do you think David will marry this fall if the match, as planned by Mrs. Sniffin, should it take place. There will be two Hannah Molyneuxes, won't they? Two of them by name at least. Kate and Abe seems "no go!" Maybe he can do better, but I remain unconvinced as to that yet. Does Ellen keep house for him yet?

O, what has become of the girl that was there awhile before Ellen? I have not heard her name for some time in my letters. Had a letter from cousin Angie *[Summers]* recently. She will not marry the preacher, I think. She, I guess, will wait for the soldier. He is a lieut. now. George Pardoe has got to corporal and is color guard. The end.

Good bye. Give my love to John and Georgia, and except the same from your ever affectionate brother Joel. Address as before: J. L. Molyneux, Headquarters, Birney's Division, Washington, D.C.

P. S. Cannon have just commenced firing down near Reppanannac Station, below us, but do not know what it is for. The rebs have either showed themselves or we are shelling the woods.

*****

Wed. 9 Sept. Dandy has come back! *[Graves' horse, Dandy, and Joel have a close relationship. See diary entries: June 8, September 5, and November 13, 1863, and January 9 and 25, 1864.]*

Thu. 10 Sept. Wrote to sister Sallie.

Fri. 11 Sept. Rec'd two letters from Kate Plotts, with her photograph. One from Kate Tirncrook.

Sat. 12 Sept. Wrote two letters to Kate B. *[Bull].* One to Brother James. Rec'd one from sister, Sallie.

[Joel's brother, James, was the second eldest child in the Edward-Rebecca Molyneux family. He was born in 1816, married Esther Tomlinson in 1845, died 1901. She died in 1897. They had eleven children, nine of which reached maturity. Their descendants go by the surnames of Molyneux, Hugo, McCarty, McCormick, Quail, Bennett, Whitely, Hottenstein, Higley, and Pardoe.]

Mon. 14 Sept. Wrote to Doc J. K. Bird. Rec'd a letter from David.

Tue. 15 Sept. Rec'd a letter from S.L. *[Seddie Locke]* Orders to harness and strike out. Leave Sulphur Springs at sundown. Move two mile.

[On September 15, 1863, President Lincoln suspended the writ of habeus corpus.]

Wed. 16 Sept. On the road early. Went to Beelton *[Bealton]* with an order and do not overtake the train this day. Cross the river above Rappahennoc St. *[Station]*. Camp with the supply train.

Thu. 17 Sept. Up and early. Join the train two mile ahead. The chickens suffer at a farm house here. Leave this place toward night, and move to near Cullpepper Courthouse. *[Is Joel telling us he is a chicken thief?]*

Fri. 18 Sept. Two letters: One from A. D. Pratt, one from H. Norton. The train moves to Cullpepper.

Sun. 20 Sept. Our regt. rec'd two months pay and clothing. Account settled. Rec'd $50.35. Expressed $50 home. Wrote to David.

[The Battle of Chickamauga, in Georgia, was fought September 19 and 20, 1863. In terms of casualties it was the second costliest battle of the Civil War. It was one of the few battles where Confederate troops outnumbered and had higher casualties than Union forces. There were 66,326 Confederates and 58,222 Northerners involved. Casualties: 34,624 (16,170 Union and 18,454 Confederates). Winner: Confederacy. General Braxton Bragg was the Confederate commander and Major General William S. Rosecrans was the Union commander.

[General William Rosecrans, like many Civil War generals, was a casual dresser. Someone once said of him, "He looked more like a third rate wagon master than a great general." Although credited with losing the Battle of Chickamauga, he won many other Civil War battles.]

Mon. 21 Sept. Fixed the pay rolls yesterday, but our company did not get their pay until today, and expressed the same today -- written by mistake yesterday.

Tue. 22 Sept. Wrote to S.M.L.

Wed. 23 Sept. Drew a pair of shoes and a pair of drawers.

Thu. 24 Sept. Was over to Culpeper. Also to Hd Qrs to help issue ordinance stores.

Fri. 25 Sept Wrote two letters: one to Martha Molyneux and one to E. Bedford. Fresh beef and onion soup for dinner, with soft bread.

Sat. 26 Sept. Rec'd letter from Kate stating the draft had taken place.

[Until this point in the war, the Union army had been largely dependent on volunteers. The United States Congress had passed and President Lincoln had signed the draft act March 3, 1863. The Confederate Congress had passed and President Davis signed the Confederacy Conscription Act, April 16, 1862. There were strong negative reactions to the draft in the North. On July 13-16, 1863, 50,000 rioters set fires and looted buildings in New York City. They were dispersed by Union veterans of the July Battle of Gettysburg.]

Sun. 27 Sept. Lieut. Charles Graves returned today. Was very glad to see him. He takes his old posish as ad't of First Brigade.

Mon. 28 Sept. Moved up to Brigade Hd Qrs. Shall take my old place again. Rumors of going to war!

Tue. 29 Sept.   Wrote to Thos. Pardoe.

[Thomas Pardoe, mentioned above, was Joel's uncle. He was married to Joel's elder sister, Margaret. Both were born in 1822. They parented eight children who reached maturity.

[Joel was related to the Pardoe family in several other ways. His sister, Mary, married Joseph Pardoe. He was born in 1813 and she in 1818. They were parents of seven children, six of which reached maturity. Their three sons, George, James, and Henry, served in the Union army. Joel was close to them.]

CHAPTER 15: OCTOBER 1863

Fri. 2 Oct. Rec'd a letter from sister Anna Vough. (Sister).

Sat. 3 Oct. Brigade moved quarters a 1/4 mile. Rec'd a letter from Jennie Molyneux. *[Joel had several relatives named Jennie Molyneux.]*

Sun. 4 Oct. Michael Farrell came over today from the Fifth Army Corps, Third Div., Fifth Pa. R. C.

Mon. 5 Oct. Wash day! Rec'd two letters: Jesse and Phide, for one, and George Molyneux for one. *[Joel's brother, George, born in 1824, died just after the Civil War, in 1866. His wife, Permilla (nee Travis), had died the previous year, in 1865. After the untimely death of the parents, Joel and Elvira raised two of their three orphaned children. Joel and Elvira also raised a former slave boy, Ned Jones, who had walked along home with the 141st Regiment, from somewhere in southern Virginia.]*

Tue. 6 Oct. Move 1/2 mile upon the other side of the pike. Billy Luke called to see me, Second Army Corps, Second Div, Second Brigade. Wrote to Kate Plotts.

Wed. 7 Oct. Wrote to Kate Bull. Will and Henry Bedford came back today to the company.

Thu. 8 Oct. C. Scott called. Wrote to Angeline Summers. Rec'd a letter from James Molyneux.

Fri. 9 Oct. Expecting an attack from the rebs. Orders to be ready at any moment.

Sat. 10 Oct. Strike tents and fall into line of battle. Saddled up an old one-eyed mare. Have not moved more than a mile. Cannon!

Sun. 11 Oct. Move! Hear cannon! Twelve doz. reb. cavalry came in sight upon our left. Soon after, meet some more upon our right, several hundred. Quite a skirmish with them. Cross Hazel and Rappahannoc *[Rivers]*.

Mon. 12 Oct. Saddled all night. Start early. Our brigade on picket at the ford. Report the rebs are crossing in force at Sulphur Spring. Hear cannon both right and left of us. Expecting to be attacked.

Tue. 13 Oct. Election day for Penn. *[Pennsylvania's gubernatorial election was usually for a two-year term, on even numbered years. But in 1860 it was changed to a three-year term. In both the 1860 and 1863 elections, Andrew G. Curtin won.]* Start by daylight. Have a small fight in the afternoon for our brigade is the only one in. Our regt. loses two men. Rebs soon run. We encamp at Greenwich.

Wed. 14 Oct. Start early and move rapidly with but short pauses. Pass Bristo Sta. *[Bristoe Station]*, Mannassas Junc., Bull Run, and go in camp at Centerville at four o'clock. Enemy has given hot chase all day.

Thu. 15 Oct. Move again. Pass Fairfield Station. *[Joel was mixed up in his place names for he was now near Fairfax Station. His previous day's entry shows the troops to be heading east through Bristoe Station, Manassas, and Centreville.]* Take dinner at a farm house. Potatoes, chicken, etc. disappear very quickly there, I notice. Had a very good dinner. Moved upon across the track and camped.

Fri. 16 Oct. Rainy and disagreeable and more so upon the account of the execution of one of the Five M. *[Fifth Maine]* for desertion. McPherson was shot before the whole div. War! War! War!

Sat. 17 Oct. Encamped. Wrote to sister Kate. Rec'd a letter from Will Rogers.

Sun. 18 Oct. We are laying still today. Wrote a letter to V.

Letter #41A

[The First Brigade, III Corps, of which Joel is a part, left White Sulphur Springs, Virginia (between Culpeper and Warrenton), and was marching in the Northern Virginia area. In September and early October of 1863, much of the war activity took place at Chattanooga and Chickamauga. Joel's main concern at this time, though, was not on important battles and campaigns, but rather that he has not heard from Vilie. Has she forsaken him? Did her papa forbid the relationship? Or, hopefully, is it just poor mail service?]

Oct. 18th *[1863]*
Hd Qrs, 1st Brigade, III Corps
[Fairfax Station, Virginia]

Dearest Vilie:

When last I wrote to you I then thought I would wait before writing again until I should receive an ans. from it. But I have waited until I can wait no longer. It must be you did not receive mine or yours has failed to reach me or else something more serious has occurred, which I trust has not been the case.

Since writing before, many changes has taken place, both with us here in this army and, as I also learn, with you that remains at home.

We left the Springs *[White Sulphur Springs, Virginia]*. I think the 15th of last mo., crossed the Rapahannoc River to Culpepper, and remained near that place until the tenth of the present mo. when we took a start back again, recrossed the river the 11th, and our brigade had a small fight the 13th, election day. Our regt. had two killed and 11 wounded. One wounded was in our co. The next day we came back by Mannesses and Bull Run to Centerville. We came to this place the next day, Fairfax Station. *[Fairfax Station, on the Orange and Alexandria Railroad, was several miles south of Fairfax Court House, now the city, Fairfax. Fairfax Courthouse had been vacated by Confederate troops early in the war.]*

Our old General Sickles takes command of this corps again tomorrow. He lost a leg at the Battle of Chancellorsville. I never before heard such hearty cheering as the boys gave him when he came back. While I write this I hear the band serenading him at Hd Qrs. We are all now in great hopes that our corps will remain near Washington for the future, and those go to the front who have been doing nothing for so long. Yet, we may be disappointed about this, but there are some things that look very favorable that it may be so.

[Generals Dan Sickles and Dan Butterfield were drinking buddies of General Joe Hooker. The three of them believed in living life to the fullest. They were liked by their troops, but came under condemnation of some other generals. General Meade described them to his wife as, "they are not the persons I should select as intimates." General Butterfield, formerly a New York businessman and an amateur musician, designed the bugle tune used for lights out, "Taps". First used in the Army of the Potomac, it later became used in all U.S. armies. Bruce Catton in The Glory Road *described its origins as follows, "Butterfield wanted a tune that, when played at the end of the day, would express the idea of a darkening campground with tired men snugging down to a peaceful sleep. The general whistled such a tune, and his bugler was able to play it on his instrument."]*

We are expecting to move in some direction tomorrow, as yet know not where. My health is very good now. Had a bad cold a few weeks ago, but that has taken leave of me, and it was quite welcome to do so. Once I heard that you had been very sick, but soon after I had a letter from Kate saying that you and Coz Martha had recently been there on a visit.

I hear Sallie's John and also your two brothers were drafted. I could hardly at first think it could be so, but since learn it is. I have not yet heard of what they intend doing if they pass inspection. You are beginning to realize in reality the dreadfulness of this cruel war.

[Sallie's husband, John, and Elvira's brothers were McCartys. McCartys were Quakers, thus pacifists. That is why Joel questions their intentions. The Union draft was just getting started and brought some problems with it, one of which was how to handle religious pacifists. Should they be drafted or not drafted, or allowed to pay an exemption? If drafted, could they be required to kill? These, and other knotty problems of how to handle religious pacificists, were not resolved during the Civil War.]

Will Rogers has been home on furlough. He wrote to me while there. My turn will come next, I guess, but do not think I can before winter.

In your last, you spoke of perhaps you might attend school at Westtown and asked my opinion. I would say if you should have such an opportunity you ought by all means improve it. I have often regretted that I have not made use of now lost opportunities for a more thorough education.

"My lieutenant," as I call him, has returned again and we are now at brigade Hd Qrs. I like my posish here right well. O! I must tell you, 'twas rather gloomy here last Friday. 'Twas cold and rainy and a man was shot before our whole div. for desertion. It was a sad sight to see him march behind his own coffin up to his grave, and then shot. 'Twas really dreadful to behold.

I am writing this by candle light. 'Tis Sabbath evening: the drums have just beat tattoo for roll call, and the call for lights to be put out has just sounded. So, my letter must soon close. It seems so very long since your last letter, but good night. I will write a line or two in the morning.

*****

Mon. 19 Oct.   We left our camp to retrace our steps again into Va. March back by Manassas Junction, and go into camp near Bristoe Station. The rebels are retreating.

Letter #41B

[Continuation of October 18 letter — written after a full day's march chasing Lee's Army of Northern Virginia. That evening, a concert by their army band made them homesick and warsick.]

Monday evening, October 19 *[1863]*
[Bristoe Station, Virginia]

Now if you will listen I will write another line or two. As I supposed, we have moved again today, but not toward Washington. We have marched some 15 mile today, and are in camp beyond Mannessas, near Bristow Station, on the railroad leading to Culpepper. Again the rebs are falling back, and we chasing.

Our band is playing again this evening. They have just finished the piece called "Departed Days". Now, they have struck up "Dixie Land". I cannot write while they play such pieces. Now, 'tis the piece sang to the words, "When this cruel war is over". I hardly know what we would do if it were not for our brass bands, two, and sometimes three or four, different bands play within hearing every fine evening. Yes, while they played the first piece I could but think of departed days, peaceful days spent far from here, far from all. Such painful scenes as we are now called to see, "Departed Days". Some of them were spent in that school house you know, and some of them were not spent till evening.

But "Dixieland" brings quite different thoughts. 'Tis of the very many who in Dixieland have took their stand and lived and died, etc—never to return again to their distant friends many of whom there are who they do not know, nor never can, even how they perished. "But when this cruel war is o'er,"— that brings hopes of brighter days. How often I think of that. When it is over and we can, if spared, all return home to our friends and enjoy their society. How much I wish that it was so I could talk with you this evening instead of writing, as I am.

My desk is an empty cigar box I picked up. My candle stick is the bottom of a tin cup, and my chair is my blanket folded up. Quite a fix, isn't it? I know you will excuse the appearance of my letter now, and please do so for not writing longer and more entertaining. After we get done marching about again I will try to do better. I have scarcely written a letter the past month. We have been on the move so much and so little chance for mailing.

Our mail came tonight. Almost everyone else rec'd a letter, save poor me. This will, perhaps, get mailed in the morning. Sometimes, I almost think your papa must have forbidden your corresponding with me entirely, but shall hope at least this is not the case. O! Do you think I dreamed only the other evening of talking with him, and just as I was going to speak to him with reference to our writing, I waked up. I know 'tis foolish to think or speak about dreams, but I would just been pleased to have learned, even by that manner, the real truth of the affair.

When you write, you will be candid with me, won't you? And speak of things as they are. 'Twill be the best way, for we can trust each other. Now, I must say good bye and good night. I will wish you a kiss, but they are not good cold, you know. I always thought so and please continue to except the love of your ever affectionate Joel.

P. S. Address: Hd Qrs., First Brigade, First Div., Third Corps, Washington, D.C.

*****

Tue. 20 Oct   Up at four and march before 'tis daylight. Pass Bristoe Station. The bridge is entirely destroyed, and much of the track. Near pass Greenwich a couple of mile and go into camp.

Wed. 21 Oct.   March at eight. Go six or eight miles on to the railroad near Catlet Station. Go into camp.

Thu. 22 Oct.   Move Hd Qrs a short distance. Rec'd two letters — one from sister Sallie, one from V.

Fri. 23 Oct.   Still in camp near Catlet. Troops are helping rebuild the railroad. Traded horses today. Gets to be rainy in the evening.

Sat. 24 Oct.   Rec'd two letters: David Molyneux and S.M.L. Moved across the railroad. Went on picket line to reinforce.

Sun. 25 Oct.   Are in the woods all so cosey *[cozy]*. Slept soundly. Duncan caught a rabbit. Ate him *[the rabbit]* for breakfast. Moved soon after to our picket line on the right and put up our tents.

Wed. 28 Oct.   Wrote to David Molyneux sending home the cheque for money expressed, etc.

Thu. 29 Oct.   Procured a pass and went down to Manassas Junction with Wm. Gilbert to find a sutler. Bought some tobacco, etc. Rode back after four o'clock, 12 mile. *[The tobacco he bought must have been for a friend, for Joel neither smoked nor chewed.]*

Fri. 30 Oct.   Moved today from Catlet. Passed Warrenton Junction a short distance, and go into camp.

Sat. 31 Oct.   The troops are mustered for pay today. George Pardoe and Michael Farrel came over today. Are in camp only one mile away. Windy evening.

CHAPTER 16: NOVEMBER 1863

Sun. 1 Nov.   Quite pleasant. Wrote to Edmund Bedford.

Mon. 2 Nov.   Rec'd a letter from Angeline Summers. Was very anxious to hear that John *[her brother in the army]* was safe. Wrote a letter for Stephen *[black servant, former slave]*.

Wed. 4 Nov.   A very pretty day. Geo. Pardoe was over again today. Rec'd a letter from V.

Thu. 5 Nov.   Ans'd V's letter. Cleaned up my saddle for review which did not take place the next day. Charley Scott called tomorrow. *[How's that again?]*

Fri. 6 Nov.   Expecting to march. Orders to be ready. Did not visit G.P. *[George Pardoe]* as I had hoped, for fear of moving. Are to leave at daylight.

Sat. 7 Nov.   Up till twelve, and again soon after two o'clock. I start at daylight for Kellys Ford. Arrive at Mt. Holly church soon after noon, and the fight has commenced. *[The Battle of Kelly's Ford, a slight Union victory, allowed Union troops to cross the Rappahannock River. The battle took place November 7 and 8, 1863.]*

Sun. 8 Nov.   Capt. Minard was killed. Yes *[yesterday]* we *[the Division]* also took 400 prisoners. *[The Army of the Potomac captured 1,629 Confederates.]* The rebs have retreated, and we are hard after them. Camp at Brandy Station, and sleep with our heads in a brush heap.

Mon. 9 Nov.   Capt. Sam Bryan, Second Div. close by. Move in the evening across the railroad, and camp near div. Hd Qrs. Nearly freeze in the night. The guards steal our coffee pot. Mountains white with snow.

Tue. 10 Nov.   Move a short distance today and put up our tent by one of the Johnny's chimneys, for we have routed them out of their snug winter quarters. *[It was a common practice for advancing soldiers to move into camps of the retreating army and use their vacated shebangs.]*

Wed. 11 Nov.   Hd Qrs First Brigade, First Div, Third Corps moves again today. Close by a clump of hardwood trees, has been reb Hd Qrs here. Pitch our tent on stony ground. Wrote to Sallie.

Thu. 12 Nov.   Lay still today. Are fixing up stabling, etc. Also winter quarters, kinder. I rec'd two letters: one from J. K. Bird, and one from David Molyneux; *[He]* has rec'd the money expressed.

Fri. 13 Nov.   Wrote to J. K. Bird. C. Scott called and lent me six stamps and *[I]* had Dandy *[Graves' horse]* shod all around. Owls are calling rain. *[The "owls" were probably mourning doves which coo with a lowing sound, similar to owls' hoots. "Shod all around" meant all four hooves of Dandy got new shoes.]*

Sat. 14 Nov.   Still laying around. Quite a heavy thunder shower in the evening.

Sun. 15 Nov.   Another *[shower]* this morning. Heavy firing to the left. Wrote a letter to S.M.L. Wm. Rogers joins our company after being absent for over a year.

Mon. 16 Nov.   A review today. Visiting with Wm. R. Wrote to A. D. Pratt. Learn the 68th are to go into the Third Brigade. Rec'd a letter from Kate Bull.

Tue. 17 Nov.   Are still at camp near Brandy Station. Wrote to Kate Bull.

Wed. 18 Nov.   Gen. Graham takes leave of his brigade to go to VC. Rec'd a letter from Edmund Bedford.

Thu. 19 Nov.   Lieutenants Bullare and Benson leave us to go with Graham. Wrote to E. *[Edmund]* Bedford.

[On November 19, 1863, President Abraham Lincoln helped dedicate the Gettysburg National Cemetery. Mrs. Lincoln tried to persuade the president to cancel the trip because their son, Tad, was ill. The keynote speaker, noted orator Edward Everett, made a magnificent speech that lasted two hours. President Lincoln made his five-minute speech to approximately 15,000 people. After it was delivered, Lincoln said of his own speech, "I failed, I failed, and that is about all that can be said about it!"

[Lincoln's Gettysburg words have been memorized by American school children ever since, and the address may be the most famous American speech ever delivered.]

Fourscore and seven years ago our fathers brought forth on this continent, a new nation, conceived in liberty, and dedicated to the proposition that all men are created equal. Now, we are engaged in a great civil war, testing whether that nation, or any other nation so conceived and so dedicated, can long endure. We are met on a great battlefield of that

war. We have come to dedicate a portion of that field as a final resting-place of those who here gave their lives that that nation might live. It is altogether fitting and proper that we should do this.

But in a larger sense we cannot dedicate, we cannot consecrate, we cannot hallow this ground. The brave men, living and dead, who struggled here have consecrated it far above our power to add or detract. The world will little note, nor long remember, what we say here, but it can never forget what they did here. It is for us, the living, rather to be dedicated here to the unfinished work they have thus far so nobly advanced. It is rather for us to be here dedicated to the great task remaining before us, that from these honoured dead we take increasing devotion to that cause for which they here gave the last full measure of devotion; that we here highly resolve that the dead shall not have died in vain, that this nation, under God, shall have a new birth of freedom; and that government of the people, by the people, and for the people, shall not perish from the earth.

Fri. 20 Nov.   Rec'd a letter from V. Wrote to John Summers.

Sun. 22 Nov.   Forwarded a letter to Edmund B. *[Bedford]*

Mon. 23 Nov.   Signed the pay rolls. Are preparing for to march in the morning. Moved into a new shebang.

Tue. 24 Nov.   Rainy day. The move is postponed. Wrote to Jesse and Phide.

Wed. 25 Nov.   Still in camp. Wrote for the Dushore Union. *[Weekly newspaper from back home in Dushore, Pennsylvania.]*

[In another theater of the war, the Battle of Missionary Ridge took place on November 25, 1863. This battle, in Tennessee, near Chattanooga, was the last battle in which Generals Grant and Sherman fought together. Soon afterward, General Sherman started on the Atlanta campaign, and on March 9, 1864, General Grant was commissioned lieutenant general in a reorganization that made him general-in-chief of all U.S. armies. His predecessor, General Henry Halleck, became the new chief of staff. General Halleck, an academy graduate, class of 1839, was third in his class of 31 graduates.]

Thu. 26 Nov.   We move today and reach the Rappadan tonight. Get lost from the div. Lieut. Graves goes to the div. as inspector gen., and I go with him.

Fri. 27 Nov.   Find out the div. *[We]* Ford the river and come up with the rebels and have an engagement. Our div. loses 200 or more. Camp close in front.

Sat. 28 Nov. Fall back and flank around to the left. Pass Robison Tavern on the pike, and come up with the Jonnys.

Sun. 29 Nov. Are momentarily looking for a fight, but the day passes with little more than picket firing. Camp close to picket line in range of shell.

Mon. 30 Nov. Awake early for me. Expect a battle today. Cannonading commences soon after sunrise, but subsides after a few volleys into occasion firing.

CHAPTER 17: DECEMBER 1863

Tue. 1 Dec.   Leave the front and go back with the train. Recross the Rappadan and go into camp. Retreating!

Wed. 2 Dec   Do not move till nearly night. Go a short distance, and get away from the staff. Get with the ammunition train and stay till morning.

Letter #42

[This letter to Joel is from his cousin, Martha Molyneux. She was the youngest sister of Samuel who had died July 2, 1863, at the Battle of Gettysburg. Born November 5, 1843, she had just turned 20 at the time she wrote this letter to Joel. She died February 15, 1867, unmarried. Her words, in referring to her brother, Samuel, expose the heartaches of families back home — heartaches brought about by having lost a father, husband, son, or in this case, a brother, in the conflict.]

Millview, Sullivan County, Pennsylvania
Dec. 2nd, 1863

My Dear Cousin:

This is the second time I have commenced an answer to your welcome letter. And I hope to finish this one. I am a very incompetent letter-writer, and know my letters are not interesting, so I delay writing as long as possible. But I like an answer to my letters very soon. I should have written sooner this time, but I could not find time to do so. Since I came from La Porte I have been busy all the time.

The first week we were getting ready for Will, Thomas, Eliza, and Jane to go to the consecration of the cemetery at Gettysburg. The second week, on Tuesday morning, they started leaving. Mother and I the only two remaining members of our family at home with two work hands and from Friday three drovers and the preacher till Sunday, the day that they came home. So, you may know that I must have been kept busy.

Last week was the wedding *[of David]* (of which I suppose you have had the description of 'ere this) and examination, two very important events, and this week Monday morning I commenced my school here and have twenty scholars. Our school ma'ams in this town are Misses Lee and Kelog from Albany, and Missus Warren, Rockwell, and Smiley from Canton. Miss Landon, Will Warb's *[Warburton's]* girl, is teaching the Fawcett school so he does not have her so near.

This fall I could but note the change that had taken place in our institution since the one here. There was but four that attended both places and our principal was changed. Also, in case it is the old and not the new, that I refer.

How I did wish that you were there for there was no one from this place but me, and gentlemen were scarce. I had a first best boarding place which was Mr. Mason's. You have been there so you know about it. Miss Ethlin was not at home, but going to school in Towanda, an event which I've very much regretted. But she was home once during my stay at her home.

Our school was better than I expected, but did not come up to Mr. Armstrong, according to my notion of things in general.

Weddings are all the go, now a days. I was really surprised when I had an invitation to David's. It was something that I did not expect at least so soon, but how frail our judgment is, especially on such matters. There is a talk of there being a double wedding at Warren's. At least they will not be far apart. Mr. Orland Haverly is frequently down to see Mrs. Hannah, and Mr. Frost is getting ready to build himself a new house. So, according to appearances *[it may]* not be long.

Our social circle is still diminishing, but I hope that we will be favored by your presence a while this winter. We had the pleasure of having W. R. home a while this fall. It seemed good to see him again. I hear that he has returned to his regt. now, so you have one more there but there is one *[brother Samuel]* that I fear will never be heard of more. We miss him more and more! Sometimes my heart almost sinks within me to think how our family has changed in two years. Before he left there was three and three, but now I am an odd one. Will, Thomas, Jennie, and Lizzie *[two brothers and two sisters]* visited the place where he *[Samuel]* did fall fighting the battle of freedom, and if it is ever in my power to do so, I mean to see that place.

The news has again reached us of another victory in the Southwest, and we hope to soon hear that all the rebels are whipped.

Our northern states have all gone Union in their elections this fall. Good for them, for it does the soldiers so much good to know those at home are with them yet, although the Copperheads did all in their power to elect Woodward in this state, but they did not come it, and we can rejoice over their defeat.

Forgive me, cousin, for not answering sooner. If it is so I can, I will do better in the future. All send their love and best wishes and you are never forgotten by your cousin, Martha.

P. S. Remember me to all inquiring friends, if I have any there.

*****

Thu. 3 Dec. Returned to our old camp at Brandy Station. Rec. three letters, two from Sallie and Kate. One from Abe McCarty. David is married.

Fri. 4 Dec. Hunter of Third Maine was shot today for desertion. He was a noble appearing man with full heavy beard. Marched behind his coffin, keeping step to music, the death march, as played by the band.

Sun. 6 Dec. Wrote a letter to my brother David -- congratulating him on the successful termination of bachelorhood.

Mon. 7 Dec. Am keeping house all alone. I admire the harmonious quiet of my domicil, but think alterations could be named that might prove equally pleasant.

Tue. 8 Dec. Wrote a letter for Stephen to his Ducky, Mary Ann Benson. *[Stephen, contraband servant of Lieutenant Graves, was the one whom Joel was teaching to read and write. See Joel's undated February 1863 letter.]*

Wed. 9 Dec. Rec'd a letter from S.M.L.

Thu. 10 Dec. Mailed a letter for sister, Sallie. Rec'd two letters: one from coz Martha, one from Doc J. K. Bird. Also, a paper from David.

Letter #43

[This letter to Vi is his last written to her in calendar year 1863. Having been in the army 16 months, he is due a furlough, which he received at the end of the month. It was his only furlough home in his 34 months of service.]

December 10th, 1863
[Brandy Station, Virginia]

My Dear Friend:

I'm all alone this evening, and shall occupy the time in answering your long since rec'd letter. Well! I am still well and have no complaints to make. I trust these lines may find you in health, and that 'ere this your brothers and mother may have recovered their health.

Since writing, this army has been across the Rapidan, and not being as successful as could have been wished; returned again and are now in our old camp again, near Brandy Station, in the vicinity of Culpepper. We had some fighting while away, but none of whom you were acquainted were hurt.

[Brandy Station, a small town on the railroad, is a few miles east of Culpeper, Virginia. The Rapidan River, which Joel's unit crosses and recrosses, starts in the mountains west of Culpeper and flows in a southeastern

direction to where it joins with the Rappahannock River, northwest of Fredericksburg.]

I will enclose a small keepsake I picked up near the rebel line in sight of the Jonnys, lost by some reb lover, a token of his true love. Two letters came for me today -- one from coz. Martha and one from coz. J. Bird. Had one from Kate and Sallie a few days ago. Kate was then visiting in Elkland. Said she was agoing to talk to you for me, did she?

So, my brother D. is married at last -- quite an event, to him at least. Did not see your name with those mentioned as being present. 'Twas from account of sickness at home, I presume. Well, I was not there either, at least they wrote of missing me (rather my nonsense, I guess.). I am not home yet on furlough, am I? But I have hopes yet that I may be this winter, but cannot tell when with any certainty. Will try to come the first of Jan. 1864.

[Brother David and Hannah Norton married November 25, 1863. The bridal couple wrote their own wedding invitations. David sent the following hand-written one to his sister, Sallie, and her husband, John McCarty:

Dear Brother & Sister, John and Sallie:

By request you are hereby envited to be at the House of Charles Norton on Wednesday the 25th of Nov. at one o'clock P.M., and if you could so arrange your affairs so as to come home here Thursday. Also, I would like it very much, and if you cannot come to both places, come where it suits you the best. Kate wishes me to ask you to bring with you your glass sause dishes, if you can do so conveniently.

Very respectfully,
Your brother,
D. Molyneux

I had a letter from Sister Abel last week. He is not married, it seems, yet. Someone wrote they thought it was Miss Lowe, and not Julia, he was courting.

I had to write this with carmine ink, for some scamp stole my black, so please excuse the use of it. The envelope is the style we have for our div. -- having the badge we wear. How do you like the appearance? This is the third letter I have written in the last month: One to D. *[brother David]* and *[one]* to Sallie. We had no chance of doing so while on the march. Wm. Rogers is now here with us; is well and cheerful.

I am at div. Hd Qrs again. Lieut. G. *[Graves]* was appointed upon Gen. Birney's staff again, and I am with him as before. I have his photograph, and if so fortunate as to see home this winter perhaps you will see he is noble looking as well as a first best fellow and brave soldier.

I live alone now since I came back here, but don't fancy the style a bit. I can manage the cooking part, but 'tis too lonesome. Have plenty to eat. I have just been looking into the closet or my cupboard or rather on a shelf to one side of my tent and for breakfast I can have, if I wish, fresh bread. Have on hand three loaves, 'tis for three days' rations. And then there is fresh beef and salt pork and seven large potatoes with plenty of salt, sugar, and coffee. Besides this I have a box of pepper and a lb. of butter. This I paid only 60 cts. for at a butter shop. O! I forgot, a hatful of dried apples, and two pints of white beans and a small basketful of hard tack. Haven't I lots to eat, don't you think?

I was patching and mending all last evening. Think I can make a patch look as neat as some I have seen some women do. But then you know I won't never patch nor cook nor darn stockings when I am out of the army. Not me!

Now I must close this for it just seems I could not think of anything interesting tonight. Trusting and hoping those dark times may soon pass away and brighter ones dawn. With my best wishes for your safety and happiness. Ever remember your absent and devoted friend – Joel.

P. S. Direct as formerly: Hd Qrs., First Div., Third Corps, Washington, D.C.

*****

Fri. 11 Dec.   Rewrote my letter for the Dushore Union, also mailed a letter to V. Wm. Rogers and J. Pennington took dinner with me. Wrote to Angie Summers.

Sat. 12 Dec.   Lieut made me a present of a V. *[letter from his Vi]* Took dinner with the boys in the co. Wrote to Geo. Pardoe.

Sun. 13 Dec.   Went with Mr. Cutter *[the sutler]* to carry him over to the Second Div. Rec'd letter from Edmund B.

Mon. 14 Dec.   Very windy today. A pr. of socks came for me by mail postage. Wrote to S.M.L.

Tue. 15 Dec.   Commenced to build a house for winter. Mr. Cutter, the sutler, gave me $1.95 for services rendered. Rumors of moving.

Wed. 16 Dec.   Wild as a lamb. Rec'd a letter from D. *[brother David]* and ans. it in the evening.

Thu. 17 Dec.   Rec. a letter from V. *[Elvira]* A muddy time, real disagreeable.

Fri. 18 Dec.   More rain and mud. Went with Lieut. G. *[Charles Graves]* and Capt. Markle to the station. Turns on cold and freezing.

Sat. 19 Dec. Ice in my tea kettle 1/2 inch thick. Rec'd a letter from Cousin Kate Tirncrook. Am ans. it.

Sun. 20 Dec. Rec. a paper from S.M.L and a letter from John H. Summers. *[Cousin]*.

Mon. 21 Dec. Lieut. made out my furlough today to go home for ten days. Hurah!!!!!

CHAPTER 18: JANUARY 1864

Fri. 1 Jan. 1864   Have been home on furlough of ten days. Start for to return and take the cars at Muncy in the evening.

Sat. 2 Jan.   Arrive at Washington by ten A. M. Visit the capitol and senate chamber, then go to the Sanitery Commission for to stay till the morning. 'Tis very cold.

[At the beginning of the Civil War, many civilian benevolent organizations helped Union soldiers. To impose some order on this chaos, the United States Sanitary Commission was established. Its purpose was to improve living conditions among the soldiers. One founder, George Templeton Strong, appalled by the filthy conditions of the soldiers, found: "Many soldiers went for months without taking a bath. Campsites were filthy, fetid, and poorly drained. They were ideal breeding grounds for dysentery, typhoid fever, and other diseases. Food was stale, moldy, and poorly cooked. At one camp, a sanitary inspector found hogs wallowing in the camp's water supply."

[The Sanitary Commission took on the needed job of improving sanitation conditions in camps, at railroad stations, in the field, etc. They provided hostel-type buildings, such as the one Joel visited in Washington, where soldiers en route could bathe, shave, change clothes, eat, relax, and sleep.

[The Commission constructively lobbied the federal government, particularly the inadequate U.S. Medical Corps, to improve sanitary practices of the armed forces. Under the leadership of Frederick Law Olmstead, the U.S. Sanitary Commission turned from a fledgling aid society to a much-needed national institution. It helped soldiers more than any other civilian organization. It was a predecessor to Salvation Army, formed in England after the war. The Salvation Army brought a Christian atmosphere; their motto: "Soup, soap, and salvation!"

[In 1862 Jonathon Letterman became medical director of the Army of the Potomac, and effectively reorganized that unit's medical system. His reforms were established throughout the other Union armies.]

Letter #44

[The following letter, from Washington, D.C., is Joel's first letter written since returning from his home furlough. He discusses his trip, and subsequent sightseeing in the capital, but the general tone gives the impression that all didn't go well back home. It may have had something to do with his relationship with S.M.L. with whom he was still corresponding.]

Washington, *[D.C.]*
Jan. 2nd, 1864

My Own Dearest Vilie:

I have reached this city safe and well. Am staying over night at the soldiers' home. I did not get here in time for to take the cars up to the front by the morning train, so I must lay over until tomorrow morning. But my furlough is good for one day longer than I expected so I am all right still.

I have been going the rounds of the city sight seeing what was to be seen. Was in and through the capitol, into the senate chamber, but congress was not sitting today. Visited the old capitol -- now a prison full of Jonny Rebs, 800 they said. And *[I]* had what is called a negative taken for some photographs. Will send you one when I get them, if they are good for anything.

[The U.S. capitol building was being built at the onset of the Civil War. President Lincoln ordered its completion during the war as a symbol to show that the nation would someday be reunited. Lincoln also ordered that the U.S. flag should keep the Southern stars for the same reason. The Washington monument, in Washington, was about one fourth erected at the beginning of the war, but work on it was suspended until after the war. Even today, one can see the difference in stone color between pre-war and post-war construction.]

I shall get to Hd Qrs by two o'clock P.M., if lucky, tomorrow. Doc J. K. Bird came with me as far as Northumberland; but wasn't New Years Day in the afternoon a cold one? As you say, I felt real chizeley *[chilly wet]* before we reached Muncy.

We did not go and see Kate. It was getting so late and was so cold I fear she will not like it, but she can't at least pull my ears for it. She must hurry and get to your side of the mountain, and next time I will call and see her.

I sent you once old Jeff's likeness and now I will send Uncle Abe's *[Postage stamps of Presidents Jefferson Davis and Abraham Lincoln]*. Sometime, you may have an album to keep photographs.

Doc and I had a New Year's eve dinner at Taylors, a roast goose, and I was more like eating a share of it than when at your home. Truly, I was almost the whole time while at home feeling just mean enough not for to enjoy my visit or hardly be sociable, though I must say everyone did their best to make my stay pleasant while with them. *[The above paragraph gives the impression that Joel had been ill during his furlough.]*

That likeness I let you see of Miss --- *[name unreadable]*, I gave to D., and shall neglect writing to her and some others for I intend, if possible, to have my letters to you longer and more regular. And also try to be more entertaining and worthy of your perusal, for though they are but friends I shall now consider it your right for to expect as much of me, even though you do not require it. What think you? *[Is the "Miss——" mentioned above, "S.M.L"?]*

Vilie, if I had not learned to respect you perhaps I should never have loved you as I do. I must say you have my fullest confidence and warmest love. And I have every reason to believe that it is fully returned. And I shall use my utmost efforts to retain the same, that you may never have cause to regret your preference. I fear that I shall now, more than ever, count the days that separate us.

Hoping that this reaches you, you may be in good health, and enjoying yourself. As to myself, I feel once more like I used to. Please do except my love and best wishes from your true friend – Joel to Vilie.

P. S. You must not be afraid to write confidentially of anything you may wish to speak, for you know 'Tis me and you, and nobody else now. Good bye V – from J.

*****

Sun. 3 Jan. Took the cars at 9:45 A.M., and arrived at Brandy Station at three P.M. Visited the boys at the company. Lieut Graves has reenlisted. and gone home on leave for 55 days. *[Brandy Station was on the Orange and Alexandria R.R, a few miles east of Culpeper, Virginia.]*

Mon. 4 Jan. Snow four inches deep. Am keeping old bachelors' hall. Storm! Stayed at home, in fact, how some ever, there is great quiet in the family.

Letter #45A

[January 4, 1864]
In Camp, *[Brandy Station, Virginia]*

Dear Brother: *[David]*

Having arrived all safe, I sit me down for to write a few lines hoping they may reach you soon and find you all still enjoying your usual good health. I did not reach camp until three o'clock Sunday, for since I came away different arrangements had been made at Washington about going up to the front. Only one train a day for passengers, that at 9:45, and I did not get there quite in time on Saturday for to take it. But it made no difference as my furlough lasted till Sunday, and my lieut. had gone home on a 55 day leave, having reenlisted for another three years. So, even if I had stayed another week it would not have killed anybody.

I found our boys in the same place. William Rogers is sick with a bad cold. Wm. Bedford is not as well as he might be near, and James Pardoe was complaining of feeling unwell. I must say this country agrees the best with me, for before I got back I felt like myself again, which I did not scarcely any of the time while at home. I thought Doc and I would freeze to death almost before we got to Muncy. *[J. K. Bird accompanied Joel on the return train as far as Northumberland. Northumberland is at the juncture of the West and North Branches of the Susquehanna River.]* We did not go to see Kate it got so late, and was so cold. S'pose she'll be mad, but at least she can't hurt me yet a while.

Part of the time, while away, it has been awful muddy here, but on New Year's it turned cold and froze all up tight making the roads very muddy.

This morning it commenced snowing, and now 'tis nearly four inches deep, and coming yet from the North East. You will have sleighing, I think, and we mud in a day or two. Furloughs are not being given upon account of so many Reg'ts going home that have reenlisted. So, if I had not got mine just when I did, should not have had it for some time maybe. Will Bedford rec'd his box day before New Years. I had mine and Will's express at Muncy. Mine cost $1.75. I shall look for it this week sometime. It cost me about $12.00 *[train fare]* both way while away, much less than I expected. I shall have nothing much to do for the time the lieut. is gone, but take care of the horses, but that will be enough in bad weather.

I had the honor of meeting Geo. D. Jackson at Muncy and *[had]* his company as far as Harrisburg. He says he is agoing to present a bill to have the State pay us ten dollars more a month, in addition to what the government gives us, but I shall sooner look for some thing the other way if he has the doing of it.

My letter must be short, and *[I shall]* write a few lines to Hannah on the other page. Give my love to father and mother. Tell them I am back safe and well, the same to the rest of the folks as you may have opportunity. With love I remain affectionate brother – Joel.

[We have no record of correspondence between Joel and his parents. He did send them messages, though, through his brothers and sisters, as above.]

*****

Letter #45B

[In camp, January 4, 1864]

For my sister Hannah: *[David's bride]*

It has truly been a long while since I ans. your letter, but you must please forgive the neglect of it or rather me, for so doing. I know you would if you could, but see how I am shedding tears while I write this!!!

My chimney smokes dreadfully somehow. I suppose Mrs. J. L. M. must be out of humor or something else the reason my fire won't burn.

[Joel makes reference to a country superstition: "If your lamp or fire doesn't burn well, someone is out of sorts with you."]

How I wish this snow now falling had been when I was at home, but then I was feeling so mean I should not have enjoyed it. I had not been so unwell while away when up there, but if I can have good health here why need I care. Perhaps someone might be persuaded, or be found, to live here in Dixie. Think I had better look out for a native here, and adopt this State in the future. *[Again, an oblique reference to his future bride, Elvira. It sounds as though Joel had suggested to Elvira that they move south after they married, but she refused.]*

I have had many letters to write now for a few days, and please excuse this for being so short and hurriedly written. Perhaps I can do better in the future. Please write some with brother's *[insert a note in with David's letter]* when he ans. this, and except many respects from your brother Joel to sister Hannah. Say to Jennie: "Her letter of Dec. 13 came tonight, Jan. fourth." One letter only was awaiting for me when I came back. Hd Qrs, First Div., Third Corps, Washington, D.C.

*****

Tue. 5 Jan.   The army is reenlisting. Sam Black was over to our corps today. Went to see Wm. Rogers as he was sick. Wrote letters.

Wed. 6 Jan.   Three more inches of snow. Traded horses with an orderly, gave $1.00 *[to boot]*.

Thu. 7 Jan.   Home. How sweet even the thought of home, with the hope that one day we may perchance once more thither return. Without this hope; how desolate the thought.

Fri. 8 Jan.   My express box came today, also the one I started for Wm. R. Will *[Rogers]* is still quite sick.

Sat. 9 Jan.   Lieut. Moore rides out upon Lieut. G's *[Graves']* horse and sprained his leg badly by falling with ——— *[unreadable because of ink blot]* horse was smooth shod.

Sun. 10 Jan.   Orders to move camp. Pack up it is, and off we go some three mile. Pass the notorious John Minor Botts' plantation. *[See entries January 13 and April 13, 1864.]* A woman drives *[by or past]* the div.

Mon. 11 Jan.   Locate Hd Qrs at a fellow's place by the name of Ricks. Help Corporal G. and sergt. build a tent. Get quite comfortably fixed up by night.

Tue. 12 Jan.   Finish our chimney and ride over to see Will R. *[Rogers]* Find him at the regt. hospital quite sick. Will have *[has]* a run of the fever from appearances. Trade horses with M.C.

Wed. 13 Jan.   Everything is lovely, etc. Preparations are being made for a carnival here at Hd Qrs. Old J. M. Botts and most of the officers in the div. are here in the evening and drunk.

["Old J. M. Botts" (John Minor Botts) had an interesting history. Born in 1802, he was sixty when his troubles began. He was a Virginia plantation owner, a lawyer, a Republican, and a politician. He practiced in Richmond, and had long-known, out-spoken Unionist views. Not only was he anti-secessionist, he was also anti-abolitionist. When Virginia joined the Confederacy, Botts left Richmond and retired to his plantation in Culpepper County, Virginia. When Richmond was declared under martial law (March 1, 1862), Botts was arrested and placed in jail for eight weeks. Then, he was released and he returned to Auburn Plantation to sit out the war.

[After the war, politician John Botts was presiding officer of the Republican Party in Virginia. He was considered for the position of congressman but declined because of age. He died in 1869. See Joel's diary entries January 10, 1864, and April 13, 1864, where Union troops were camping and reviewing on the Botts' Auburn plantation.]

Thu. 14 Jan.   Visit Will and arrange his bed by getting him some hay and a tick, etc. Spend the evening in the co. Write this after I get back. Knock down the table and spill ink over myself and book. *[A tick is a cloth case filled with cotton, feathers, straw, or other material to form a make-shift mattress. In the above case it was filled with hay.]*

Fri. 15 Jan.   Nothing special occurs. We have plenty to eat and to wear, and are generally in good health. The men seem disposed to be content.

Sat. 16 Jan.   Am washing today. Was over to the regt. Found Will *[Rogers]* on the mend. *[He]* Was asleep. Spent the evening in the company.

Sun. 17 Jan.   Writing letters all day. Went to church at the Christian Commission in the evening. Heard the first sermon for many months.

Letter #46A

Jan. 17, 1864
Camp near Culpepper, Va.

Dear Vilie:

Two weeks has at last passed by and Sabbath morning finds me employed as you were one week ago today. Your letter I rec'd on Thursday. It was the first I had heard from home since returning, and "pleased" was hardly a name for getting it. I do sincerely hope you may be at this time enjoying health and yourself. I am real well again and feel much different to what I did at home.

Am sorry to report our friend Will Rogers as being quite sick. *[He]* Has been unwell ever since I have been back. He has the symptoms of typhoid fever, but trust it can be broken before it goes much farther. Was over for to see him last evening, but found him asleep. He is at the hospital. The doctor thought him not dangerous.

You say the new church is to be dedicated today. I would indeed like to go with you there, for I should not only have the pleasure of attending it, but would like the sleigh ride, and more than all I should like your company. Just seems as if I could do anything if we could but visit together today. No, I did not know you were at school. Perhaps I would of called in if I had.

Guess I did sleep some late at Sallie's, but I did not care if I did, being at John's *[Sallie's home]*. Should not of slept so late if I had been somewhere else.

So, Vilie does not like the compositions. People I believe always did, and maybe always will, when they see an opportunity for teasing, especially those who only would too well like there might be something similar happen to themselves. You might tell Ellen the anecdote of the "anxious maid". When alone *[she]* prayed for a husband to come. The owl, you remember, hooted: "Who? Who?" When she thought her prayer was about to be ans., she said, "Most anybody, come!" Though I think the better way is not to notice such things, at least as little as possible and let them have it all their own way.

I had not heard *[the rumor]* of our being married, but at the time thought it possible such a story might get a start. I rode over with Sallie, but as it was storming people would not know but something was up or somebody else was with me. I am acquainted with a number of cases where the boys have really been married even upon as short furloughs as mine was, but I think circumstances should be far different from ours to make it a wise policy. For myself, I have no fears, but there is one that will remain true to me though she is litterally free (I am not afraid but that she will) at least so long as I am true to myself.

Vilie, you do not have any fear, do you -- that I may learn to gamble, drink, and swear? If you have, pray dismiss them, for I have had too good a mother to so easily forget her early training. If I were younger, possibly you might have more reason, but one must act from principle at my age, if ever. And not having formed such habits while young, 'twould certainly show indiscretion now to be led into them. I have just written this page wrong side up. Direct as formerly: Hd Qrs, First Div., Third Corps, Washington, D.C. – J.

*****

Letter #46B

[The following letter, written on odd scraps of paper, had no salutation, no return address, and no date. It's obvious from its content, though, that it was written to Vilie, and one sentence dates it 17 days after he has returned from furlough. Thus, it was written the same day as the previous letter.]

[At camp in Brandy Station, Virginia]
[January 17, 1864]

Abel is married without doubt. I suppose now you are glad and I am not displeased. I wish that I could think of him differently from what I do, but "forgive and forget past faults" is a good motto, if in the future we see that they are trying to live as they should. I am right glad you told him that you could not be his bridesmaid or waiter. Not that I could not be with you, but to have him know you were independent of him, and thought and acted for yourself and was your own keeper, if I can be allowed the expression. I wish him well, and truly hope Julia and he may live long and pleasantly together.

O! I said something of getting a likeness taken at Washington, but when they were sent up I so disliked them that I knew you would not want of such. I guess Sallie has one I sent her. Have you seen it?

I was at Washington when I wrote the last on my way back. Arrived the next day on Sunday. Found everything right. Only the Lieut. *[Graves]*, of whom I spoke, was gone home for 55 days. I hear that he is sworn in to serve three years more. If so, he will be here, 'tis likely, until after my time expires. For some reasons I am glad of it. I have two tent mates now, for we have just had to move our camp some three miles to where wood was more plenty. We have a comfortable shanty with a good chimney -- two bunks, one table, and three stools and a board floor. Quite housey-like, ain't it? We call it sometimes the "Wolf Den", as Wolf is the name of one that lives with me.

We have meetings here now every evening in the reg't by the Christian Commission, a society formed expressly for the benefit of soldiers. I shall go this evening, I think, and call and see Will *[Rogers]* also.

[The Christian Commission was an outgrowth of the New York City YMCA. Established in Washington after the First Battle of Bull Run by an artist named Colyer, its goal was to distribute Bibles, Christian tracts, and hymn books to soldiers. Commission men held services in camps, visited hospitals, and prayed with wounded soldiers in hospitals and on battlefields.]

We have pleasant weather here now. Have as many as five inches of snow since the first of the mo., but it has all nearly disappeared. 'Tis a pretty country about here. If the war was well over and peace fully restored, I should like to live in such a place. Did you really mean that some day you might consent for to cast your fortunes with mine in some other place than that of home, or vicinity, or even Pa.?

Oh! We will have time for talking of all such when I once am free again. Only 19 months at most, nearly half gone already. I used to think when school was more than half out it soon passed by the rest of the year. It seems almost as long, the 17 days since I saw you, as the 17 months before.

You must write very long letters, ever so much longer than mine. It will be your turn on Sunday next, but then you will not get this maybe by that time. Yours generally come in four days, while mine is oftener two weeks before reaching you. Write all about Abel's wedding, about the dedication, about the talk about us, and anything you think would be of interest. I shall have to ask pardon for the appearance of mine for using these scraps, but Vilie forgives, don't she?

Will say good bye, my love, with best wishes for your happiness, and remain you true friend, Joel L. M. Shall ever remember Vile M. Mc.

*****

Mon. 18 Jan.   Rains setting in which has caused us to sett *[set, stick?]* in the mud. Rumors of guerrillas inside of the picket line. Pickets posted, etc.

Tue. 19 Jan.   The rain goes away, but leaves the mud until night when it disappears. Went to Brandy Station. Changed cavalry jacket. Visited the Eighth Division.

Wed. 20 Jan.   Neglected for to write today, and now can't remember a thing excepting that I was at church at the chapel tent; Christian Commission in the evening.

Thu. 21 Jan.   Will Rogers is getting better!

Fri. 22 Jan. The mud dry. The roads are fast becoming good. Gregory and I rode over to the regiment.

Sat. 23 Jan. Was over to meeting again this evening. I saw Bishop Horton yesterday. He is back to the regiment again.

Sun. 24 Jan. Capt. Ford had lieut.'s horse out today. General inspection takes place. Was over to a bible class at C. C. Ez. Little rejoins the regt. *[Most Christian Commission services were held on Sunday afternoons, for Sunday mornings were taken up with "policing" the camp and inspection.]*

Mon. 25 Jan. Had Dandy *[Graves' horse]* over to Crocket. Fear he is spavined. *[A spavined horse has a bony enlargement of the hock associated with strain. This is the last mention Joel made of Dandy — presumably he was put to rest as a result of the foot problem.]* A great ball this evening at Gen. Carr's. $10 for a ticket. 100 couple present. Cost $4,000, supper $2,000.

Letter #47A

Jan. 25th, 1864
[In camp, Brandy Station, Virginia]

Dear Vilie:

It has not been two weeks yet, but I thought of writing some and finish it some other *[time]*, for I frequently forget to mention something when writing all at one time. Today is Monday and very fine. The sun shines warmly. The mud is nearly all dryed away, and the roads are getting quite passable.

We have been meeting every evening at the brigade only 1/2 mile from our Hd Qrs. A society called the Christian Commission. It is formed of different churches expressly for benefitting the army, and is the means of doing much good.

Will R. is getting much better but not able to be about or even sit up much yet. I see him nearly every day, and write letters to him occasionally. I wished to know if I should not write to his lady, but like his brother, it seems he has none. If I had no one to love me I hardly know what would become of me.

Oh! I must tell you of your last letter — how someone else opened it and thought it was his. The letters were given out in the evening, and his name was Holywood, and mistook the M for an H, not reading the whole of it. 'Twas given to him, but he saw the mistake as soon as he opened it and gave it to me. I did not care, as it was only a merry mistake, but wished it had been some of my other letters.

Last evening I had a letter from Geo. Pardoe, and one from David and Hannah, my new sister. She said that she had not seen you for a long time, so I take it you was not at the dedication of the new church. Also, *[she]* says that Abel was really married the day you spoke of, but mentioned no particulars.

I am agoing to guess that you wrote to me Sunday and think I will get it on Thursday. I will not mail this till perhaps after that. Say, did you ever see any more of that knife? Without thinking, I put it in my pocket. I left it with Sallie for you. I told her it was one I had stolen from you. So Tache sends love, does she? Ask her if she wished me to give it to James Pardoe. He frequently speaks of her. Maybe they write.

V: There is an old "cotton picker", at the plantation where we are -- 101 years old and real smart, too. I never saw such an old man before. I will go and talk with him some evening. I think if I was a slave I should not want to live that long a slave, at least.

But here comes a lot of secesh *[Secessionist]* women upon horseback. They want to get a safeguard to stay at their houses while our army is here. They are afraid of losing all their hens and chickens, etc. while we stay. Some of them *[the women, not their hens and chickens]* come almost every day, but no good looking ones.

There is to be a grand ball near here this evening for the officers. 'Tis said the fixings and everything are to cost $4,000. The table alone is to cost $2,000. The ladies are to come from Washington and elsewhere (big thing, ain't it?).

But just see, I have already wrote nearly a whole sheet, and did not think of writing but a little just to have commenced a letter. Maybe I can think clearer another day, and write more interesting, so this I will now put away in my portfolio and wait for more news and your letter. Good-bye – Joel.

*****

Tue. 26 Jan.   Was over to see Will R. *[Rogers]* Feel very much like having the spring fever. Disturbance on the picket line last evening, or rather this.

Wed. 27 Jan.   Much more like May than mid-winter. A great quantity of express boxes came for our div. today.

Thu. 28 Jan.   The boys of the guard are here, gay playing at ball and practicing with wooden short swords, fencing, beside pounding each other with boxing gloves. Attended meeting.

Fri. 29 Jan.   The day passes without incident. J. Rennington was over, and visited me. Had a decidedly good visit. Was out with Van Renslaer Morton horseback riding in the morning.

Sun. 31 Jan.   I was to see Will R. and thought to attend church but was too late.

Letter #47B

[January 31, 1864]
[In camp near Brandy Station, Virginia]

Dear V:

Now I think of finishing the letter begun nearly a week since. As I said before, I was going to look for your letter Thursday, but none came. I was some disappointed, to be sure, but life is full of such things.

I had a letter from sister, Sallie, this week and one from sister, Angie Summers. She is one of my bestest sisters. But she scolded me for not going out to see her when at home.

Will R. *[Rogers]* is able to sit up some, and hope to see him walking around in a few days. I have heard it said that the small pox was breaking out in the army. I have seen no cases of it yet. At Washington, I heard it was raging quite fearfully, but hope it may not be as bad as represented.

Curious, don't you think, that you never have good teachers for the school at your place. You said she was so pretty and not cross either. I thought maybe you would learn at least the first lesson -- you remember what that is?

I was going to say something about Randal, I hardly know why, but it just appears as though he could not be despised enough. If I was so as to talk with you maybe I could tell you of things that would lower him even in your estimation, if that was possible. I know many think him a good Dr. In my opinion, in some respects, he is, and in others he understands, drugs, etc. only too well and does not hesitate to use them when persons do not, just as he wishes, to have them. Vilie, you cannot shun him or despise him too much. *[It sounds as though Joel suspected Dr. Randall of over-prescribing drugs.]*

Today is Sunday and the last of the month. My enlistment will soon be half gone. At the close of next month I will be on the last half. Many have the opinion that we shall see the rebellion ended this coming summer. Hope it may be, for it can't end too soon. I will lay by my paper now and get my dinner, and go to my regt., to meeting, visit Will, and then write some more when I return.

I have been to see Will, but was too late for meeting. Will is much better. Had a letter from home, (Jesse). O! Do you remember what Phidie said, that

Kate told to Hannah similar to what you heard she said of you. It seems to have made hard feelings, from what I hear, between them. If I was at home I know I could not help teasing both of them for being "so foolish". Kate was much to blame for her part in the affair, but think it was not at all her intention to make a bad feeling. Kate was unthinkingly too honest. I have not heard from her for a long time, as I did not get to see her when at home. Maybe she is offended. Well, I must say I have been writing to you as I would not to any one else, but 'tis you and I, and we don't care, you know.

My letter is now quite long enough for this time. I can hardly think of what to say last; shall have only to repeat the same story in closing as before by acknowledging my sincere love for Miss E. M. McCarty, from Joel.

*****

CHAPTER 19: FEBRUARY 1864

Mon. 1 Feb. Another month has gone of wintery weather, but ending very fine weather. Is more like May than mid-winter.

Tue. 2 Feb. A great ball to go off here this evening. Three brass bands attend. Great ado! 300 candles! A rainy evening and a failure.

Wed. 3 Feb. Found a pocket book yesterday. No incidents of note. The guests that could not get away leave Hd Qrs this morning.

Sat. 6 Feb. The troops are under orders for marching and make a reconnaissance over the Rapid Ann *[Rapidan River]*. I hear artillery and musket until late in the evening.

Sun. 7 Feb. The trains and troops are returning from the reconnaissance to the Rapid Ann.

Letter #48

Feb. 7th, 1864
[In camp near Brandy Station, Virginia]

Dear Brother: *[Jesse and wife, Phide]*

Your letter came the 24th of Jan. I have delayed writing until today as there was not anything going off but the usual routine of camp life. I have my health as usual still and but few are sick in the regts. Will Rogers is now so as to help himself and move around without help. If he gains as fast for the next week, I think he will by that time be in his company again.

There has been a few cases of the scurvy or something very similar here among the boys, but nothing very serious. I also heard it said that the smallpox had broken out in the army, and was quite serious in Washington. How true, I cannot say. I have not seen any affected with it yet. The drs. have been vaccinating the troops all through the army by a general order. I had it tried upon my arm, and it is just about as sore now as there any use being.

Last Tuesday evening the officers had a grand hop, or rather ball, at our Hd Qrs, but it turned out to be quite rainy. It was almost a failure. Great preparations had been made to make a nice thing of it; a large floor several hundred feet in extent covered with canvas (wagon covers from the train), and lit up with four or five hundred candles, Chinese lanterns, etc. (colored paper). And nearly every flag in the division was brought and festooned around. 'Twas really quite a show and seemed too bad the weather spoiled their fun.

Our fellows, or the Jonnys, tried to get up some sort of fuss yesterday, I hardly know what. Our div. has gone out, one div. from each corp, 'tis said, (all went, I have since heard). In the afternoon we heard quite heavy firings of cannon and some musketry. Heard a body of rebs were on this side of the Rapid Ann *[Rapidan River]*, and had been driven back badly beaten. The camps are not broken up. Guards are left, also the guard at Hd Qrs remain, and as Lt. Graves is now home with his regt. I did not have occasion to go. Will and Henry Bedford, also W. Pennington, are on picket in another direction. The rest of our co. are to the front. This affair is what they surely call, I suppose, a reconnaissance in force to find out the enemy's position, etc. Perhaps before mailing this I may hear more. I have not heard from Edmund since I came back, only by others; that he was in the Invalid Corps. Geo. Pardoe was at Bull Run the last I heard from him.

The weather has for some weeks been remarkably fine. More like May than midwinter until the last three days or so. We have had some of nearly all kinds, thunder and lightning, showers, snow, sleet and rain and freezing.

We have not been paid since the first of Nov. The paymaster has been looked for a long time, but will not perhaps come now until four months are due. I was unlucky enough to find a pocket book one day last week, and no owner yet, but 'twas not half full, hardly $10.00.

O! What has become of the Dushore Union? I sent for it and only rec'd one no.*[issue]* yet. I do not think of anything more just now, and as this sheet is done for, I will get another and write a few lines to your wife, by permission.

The sheep fetched a little over what I estimated them to be worth. My love and best wishes to all. The same to yourself, from Joel.

*****

Mon. 8 Feb.   Moved down the street a few blocks and go to keeping house. Two of us, Gregory and I. Was over to Brandy St. *[Station]*. Seven traded jackets. Visited the 68th band, etc.

<u>Letter #49</u>

Feb. 8th, 1864
[In camp, near Brandy Station, Virginia]

My Friend V:

Am I not a naughty boy for addressing another letter to you whilst in Albany? *[Albany is a nearby township in Bradford County.]* Your letter arrived here the fifth day after mailing and eight from 23 leaves 15, and I do not think yours should be over three times as smart getting here as mine to you. But of course, you need not open it, if you do not choose after telling me not to write. Been home on a furlough, have you? Sister Anna Vough wrote me of seeing some at Sallie's, but left me to guess who. I wrote you the 27th, which by this time you may have received. I know just how glad you will be when your school closes, but perhaps you will teach the extra month spoken of.

Now, shall I tell you what we are at? Four days ago our corps *[Third]* and the Fifth *[Corps]* started upon an expedition to the left, toward the South Side RR. But I am not with them. A few of the guards were ordered to remain. I again happened to be one of the number. I think myself very fortunate upon account of it for the past two days has been stormy and cold, snowing and raining alternately, and then freezing everything thickly with ice. I have not heard but little yet from the troops that went, but they have been fighting considerable. I could hear the distant booming of the cannon yesterday during the storm.

O! How I pity the poor fellows that might get wounded –– perhaps remain through the night as they fall on the field. I earnestly hope that much may be accomplished, that all the suffering and hardships attending may not be of no avail.

There certain is a great change taking place with the people in our vicinity. My last letters state brother David and also that Cousin J. K. Bird are among the number seeking the "Right Way". I am glad such a change has taken place for I certainly never saw a community less effected by preaching than that has been for the past score of years.

Well, my chum says, "Hurry and get through writing." I s'pose he wants his dinner, which by the by will be neither roast turkey nor plum pudding. I have seen better fare than we get just at present, but I do not intend intentionally to complain, for I am much better situated than many. Going to Canada, be you? Certainly you are not afraid of being drafted? *[During the Civil War, as in following wars, some draft-dodgers evaded the draft by fleeing to Canada.]* I prefer volunteering. If you should, remember you have partly promised to join my regt. (Please excuse my nonsense!).

February 10th I will celebrate my birthday. You remember which one, I suppose? You ask me if I can read all your last letter. Yes, I guess. Did not miss any, I think, this time. Did I tell you that Abel's brother-in-law was in a regt. near me? I have not yet met with him. His name is Colter.

I am sorry that John P. *[John Pardoe McCarty, sister Sallie's husband]* should be drafted knowing that they *[Friends]* are so much against everything war-like. John, I think, is a fine fellow and sincere in his doings.

For fear this may not reach you before going home, I will not say much more. If I can, I will write to Eldredsville by the time you reach home, to welcome you back. You could lay me away a few days until you had had a good visit at home, and read me at your convenience. I trust these few feeble breathings will find you enjoying a full share of health and ever remember your true friend – Joel.

P. S. To Villie M.: My health is very good. I was glad to learn that you were succeeding with your school more pleasantly.

*****

Tue. 9 Feb. Built our chimney higher and fix up the house generally. The weather is fine and the 68th band is playing now at our Hd Qrs.

Wed. 10 Feb. My own birthday (29). I have lost a day and thought today was Tuesday, and file the above accordingly. Please to excuse the error.

Thu. 11 Feb. "Today I have been doing, thinking, and looking for nothing, and I have verily found it."

Fri. 12 Feb. Be still, sad heart! and cease repining
Behind the clouds is the sun still shining;
Thy fate is the common fate of all,
Into each life some rain must fall,
Some days must be dark and dreary.

[The last verse of Longfellow's, "The Rainy Day".

First two verses went:

The day is cold, and dark and dreary;
It rains and the wind is never weary;
The vine still clings to the mouldering wall,
But at every gust the dead leaves fall
And the day is dark and dreary.

My life is cold, and dark and dreary.
My thoughts still cling to the mouldering Past,
But the hopes of youth fall thick in the blast,
And the days are dark and dreary.]

Sat. 13 Feb. Then gently scan your brother man
Still gentler, sister, woman;
Though both may go a great way wrong
To step aside is human.

[From Robert Burns' Address to the Unco Guid.]

Sun. 14 Feb. Valentines Day at home. Here, 'tis merely the 14th of February. Rec'd some paper, *[from]* Kate Tirncrook.

Letter #50

Feb. 14th, 1864
[In camp near the Rapidan River, Virginia]

Dear Valentine:

Have you ever heard how it came that the 14th of this mo. was sett apart as Valentine's day? I do not remember the story correctly enough to relate it, though 'tis said the day was appointed by some of the ancient deities or goddesses, Venus, I think, for mortals "like you and I" to choose their mates. 'Tis also said that the birds choose theirs on certain days in the spring, but I have never yet heard there was more than one Mr. Robin or Blue Bird seeking the affections of some particular one of the gentler species. True love seems to run ever smoother with them.

Your very welcome letter I rec'd the eighth. I was so glad to hear from you again, as it was mailed in Hillsgrove I could not think who it might be from until I opened it, and you may scold me just a little after I tell you what became of it. I had just got me a new jacket, but it was too small so I rode over to the Station (three mile) to the post quartermaster for to change it, and do you think I never once thought that I had that letter in the pocket, until after coming back. But don't you scold! Is it because you said you loved me so that you would be pleased with anything that I did? I shall owe you two kisses for your confidence in me, Villie. No one will ever see that letter that ever heard of you, or I, so we won't care.

I do not now remember if I ever heard of what you mentioned to Charlie Herkamer. I am but little acquainted with him. S'pose he is like other folks — wants to love somebody and that somebody must be the best one he can find. So, he wishes to ask, like I, permission to love you.

Now, I will tell you I rec'd a letter a few days ago from a Miss Little that attended the Institute at Millview. I have never seen her since then, nor as much as thought of writing to her. I believe the girls are privileged to write first to soldiers, especially this year, 1864 (Leap Year). She did not write very sweet this time, s'pose that would be put in afterward, but I can't see ans. myself, somehow, could you?

I have heard Edmund Bedford was at home on furlough, also John Summers. Perhaps you may see them before they return, as they will be likely to visit at Sallie's.

Four days ago was my birthday, 29. I am much old, ain't I? Once I thought you 18; then you remember saying you was past 17. You do not get any older, do you?

We are having beautiful weather now. The roads are dry, everything pleasant. My health is good as anyone could wish. You are well I hope. Am sorry your brother is sick again. So, you will do as you said you wished to, shy you may if I ain't sick. Will that not do as well?

O! cousin Jenny, in writing the other day, asks if my watch is going yet. This makes me think it was stopped. If you had rather it was agoing and can read it by anyone that will not tease you that you can trust, send and get it fixed up, and if you say I may and not be offended, I will send something to pay it with.

My paper, as you can see, is nearly done, and you must pardon me for not writing more. Please write long letters and soon and ever remember that you have the best of wishes and sincere love of Joel to Vilie.

P. S. I did not have to leave camp when our army made the reconnaissance last week and over the Rapid Ann. I had a letter from Kate Bull yesterday. She is at home, and well, and not married. Will Rogers is write *[right]* smart again. He can walk about and will, I hope, soon be in the company again with the boys. Joel M.

*****

Mon. 15 Feb.   Draw a shirt and a pr. of drawers at my regt. *["Drawing shirt and drawers" meant being issued a shirt and long underwear from the supply sergeant. Joel drew many drawers during his 34 months in the army, for they wore out quickly since soldiers seldom took them off. Joel never mentioned taking a bath nor shaving while in the army. The standard Union soldier's uniform weighed about six pounds. It consisted of an all-wool blouse, trousers, and underwear (drawers).]* Snows in the P. M. -- ground white.

Tue. 16 Feb.   Went to the tailors at the regt. for my jacket. Been having it altered.

Wed. 17 Feb.   Skating ice in the brooks.

Thu. 18 Feb.   An almost innumerable cloud of crows keep around our camp cawing and staring us in the face like so many black imps.

Fri. 19 Feb.   Rode over to div. hosp. Saw Will R. *[Rogers]* and then went over to the Eighth P.V., and visited with the Capt. S. Bryan.

Sun. 21 Feb.   Walked over to the reg. and helped the Penningtons eat a chicken -- *[they]* having had a box from home.

Tue. 23 Feb.   Was talking with an old slave -- at 101 years of age. *[He]* Speaks of the great snow storm, and the Revolution, the War of 1812, and now says he can walk 20 mile a day. *[See February 23, 1864, letter for details of Joel's conversation with the former slave.]*

Letter #51A

[This letter was from Joel to his sister, Sallie, and her husband John. John Pardoe McCarty was born 1831 and died 1885. After his death, Sallie remarried Daniel Waters. No record of children in either union.]

Near Culpepper, Va.
February 23, 1864

Dear Sister and Brother:

At last I find myself ans. your letter rec'd some time ago. You have been look for this some two weeks, hain't you? But it didn't come for I have been too lazy (I s'pose that has been it) to start it.

Well, I am right well, as yet. The other boys are similar, unless it be Will Rogers. He has not recovered his usual strength, but still keeps on the mend, though. He is now at our div hospital. It is near Brandy Station, three mile of where we are encamped. I was over to see him a few days ago. He goes about some, and even has been doing light duty.

We are having very fine weather; the days are warm and pleasant, and the roads are dry -- a much pleasanter winter than last so far, but we may have stormy yet enough to make up for the past fine.

The reenlisted men are coming back now, quite fast. Lieut. Graves has not yet returned. I spoke of his being gone with his regt. when I returned. His regt., the 40th N.Y., are just back, and *[I]* shall look for him. Now, every day quite a number of reenlisted have taken the chance to a ----*[text obliterated]* rest.

My birthday, the tenth, passed, and I did not once think of it. Then came, what is called in your country, Valentines Day, but down here 'twas only the 14th of Feb., and yesterday was Washington's birthday. I am now past 29, real old. In three more days our time will be half out since being mustered into the United States Service, for if I do not forget, it was the 26th of August, 1862. I had a letter from Elvira M. not too long ago.

I hear Edmund Bedford has been home on furlough, but is not near well yet. He must have gone back this time if he did not get his time extended.

John Summers has reenlisted, and been at home, has he been out to see you? I did not think he would reenlist. I conclude when I serve out the three years that I am already in, for it will be my share of service, so at least I think at present. I have not heard of George Pardoe lately. The last I did he was with his company at Bull Run guarding the RR bridge. And Mike was one of the train guards going up and down with the trains from Brandy Station to Alexandria. I have not yet happened to be at the station when he was up.

Our mail has just come in and as I hear my name called I will go out and see what is for me. I find nothing for me but a Dushore Union of Feb. 18, and have just read the local news and Wash Pennington's article. Either he or the printer makes a mistake by saying we use oak and hemlock for fire wood. The truth is, I have not seen a hemlock yet in Va. He must have meant to say oak and hicory.

Cousin Kate Tirncrook wrote not long since. She wishes me to scold you for not writing to her. Her health is about the same. Kate Bull wrote not long ago. Do you think she will marry Will N. *[Norton]* Amelia B., I hear, is married, but not to a very promising fellow. Too bad! Villie has been very sick, I have heard.

There is a young man here at Hd Qrs, belonging to the band, by the name of Cornely. His parents belong to the Society of Friends *[Quakers],* and live in Philadelphia. They have lived there since the time of William Penn, and are quite a noted family. Ask John if he ever heard them speak of any folks there by that name? *[Brother-in-law, John, was a "Friend".]*

We have not been payed since the first of Nov., but are expecting the paymaster soon. I guess I told you of finding a pocket book with some ten dollars in it, or didn't I? But, no difference about that, only I could not think of anything else to write.

O! Did I ever tell you about jumping into a mill pond last fall? One dark night, when on the march, I went to hunt for some water for coffee and stepped in the edge of it in the mud, and thought it only a mud hole, and then jumped as far as I could to go over it, and lit in nearly middly deep, and then lit out as soon as I could. It was when we crossed Kelly's Ford on the Rappahanna. But 'tis getting late and will close. Goodbye, John, Sallie, and Georgia, with my best love and wishes, from Joel.

*****

Letter #51B

[near Culpeper, Virginia]
[February 23, 1864]

Evening -- I have been out visiting or rather making a call, and where do you suppose it was? Well, as you say, anything from down here is what you want, so listen a bit.

Our Hd Qrs is at the plantation of a man by the name of Ririe. He has some three slaves left with him, old ones. One old chap is 101 years old, and I have been having a talk with him of old times. He can remember of times before the Revolution. He lived then near the mouth of the Chesapeake Bay; says he remembers the big snow storm and that it was so deep that it covered up all the houses; that it began to snow of a Friday and snowed for a week; that they burned up everything in the houses for wood and then dug up on top and went on the crust and carried wood. The sheep and cattle died because they could not find them.

He heard the cannons when Lafayette came to this country to fight. I suppose it was at Yorktown, but he did not get to see Lafayette. He said that he was "right smart old" at the time of the War of 1812, and remembered a considerable of what happened then. He has had three different masters. One of his master's brothers, Morgan, married Millie Washington, General Washington's brother's daughter, he thought it was.

He says he has had three wives that had been sold and he could not tell how many children. He has all his faculties good yet. Is quite smart. Stands up straight. Says he can walk 20 miles in a day, easy. He never was whipped -- would fight first, run away, etc., then come back when he got ready and now intends to start north in a few days with his daughter and granddaughter. Joel.

*****

Wed. 24 Feb.   Lieut., now Capt., Graves came back last evening. A div. review today.

Thu. 25 Feb.   Sign the pay rolls and the reg. is paid two mos., Nov. and Dec., $26.

Fri. 26 Feb.   Maid of Athens, ere we part,
Give, oh give me back my heart!

[From Byron's Maid of Athens (1810)]

[The next lines of that verse:

>Or, since that has left my breast,
>Keep it now, and take the rest!
>Hear my vow before I go.

[The last verse in the five verse poem goes:

>Maid of Athens, I am gone:
>Think of me, sweet, when alone.
>Though I fly to Istambol
>Athens holds my heart and soul:
>Can I cease to love thee? No!]

Sat. 27 Feb.   Orders to march at six o'clock.

Sun. 28 Feb.   Our div. start upon a reconnaissance, pass through Culpepper and go beyond James City a short distance and encamp, perhaps ten mile.

Mon. 29 Feb.   Remain encamped through the day. The weather has a stormy look, and by night 'tis raining slightly.

CHAPTER 20: MARCH 1864

Tue. 1 March. Both rain and snow fell today. Ground is white. Some cannonading. The Sixth Corps is ahead at Madison C.H., and the cavalry are still farther.

Wed. 2 March. We start upon the return this morning. Our cavalry have been nearly to the Va. Central Railroad, destroyed. Blew up nine caissons and an artillery camp. *[Caissons were ammunition carriers for artillery.]*

Thu. 3 March. Captured 100 prisoners, little or no loss on our side. All quiet now and in camp.

Letter #52

March 4th, 1864
[In camp near Culpeper, Virginia]

My True Friend:

It now has been nearly three weeks in the stead of two as should have been since last writing. But when I explain that how we were upon the march last Sunday, starting out for a reconnaissance, and did not return for four days, you will pardon me. Our Division went as far as James City, a very small and mean looking village, some 13 mile of our present camp near Culpepper. The Sixth Army Corps went to Madison Court House and a body of cavalry went still farther, and nearly to the Va. Central Railroad -- some 80 mile distant from this point. The object appears to have been for to destroy a portion of it *[the railroad]* and find out the whereabouts of the Jonnys. I have not yet seen the correct account of the result, but hear a hundred prisoners were taken, and an artillery camp destroyed with a large amount of ammunition and clothing.

Your letter dated the 26th *[of February]* I received the second *[of March]*, and the one written previously, and at the time your throat was being so bad, I rec'd just before we started out on the little reconnoitre. Vilie, what you mention in your last in regard to poor health, etc., has pained me more than I can tell. I do not know as that I fairly understand you, and am sure I can not tell what to think. Is it that you wish to know my feelings and opinion upon that subject? Or has someone, as you say, told you as really coming from me? Such a thing! All that I can say is I have no remembrance of ever speaking to anyone upon the subject.

And know that I never have as regards to yourself, and as the subject has been introduced perhaps it would be well for me to express my thoughts upon it, which is simply this: That when a person forms an attachment to a lady and seeks her favor and declares his affection to her and she returns the same to him, and they are all to each other, that they could wish and by perchance one should lose his health, or otherwise be unfortunate, for the other to desert, forsake, or even to falter, upon the account of it, is not deserving to hear the sacred name of husband or wife. Anyone placed in that position would have great cause to be thankful for ascertaining how small-souled and despicable base was such a one, before their whole life was made miserable by being thrown inseparably together by marriage with them. I cannot even surmise any incident or circumstance that it could possibly have arisen from.

When you write I should like to know who the person was that told it and any other particulars if any. From the tone of your letter I shall not think you credited the report much. Vilie, you did not think such a thing of me, did you? I was truly sorry to hear of you being ill. I would do for you all in my power, which at present is that you except my love and sympathy. I am happy to know that you are better and I shall almost be inclined to think well of Dr. Randal for the future, if as you say, he has been the means of helping to restore you to health.

You ask, "Will I be home again in the spring?" I now do not think that I shall. It is not at all likely, so do not think of it. As a matter of course, Tache's turkey and pie and etc. are tempting, but although I be ever so much inclined to fall into such temptations, I cannot do as I may wish. Why did you think Jennie changed her mind when I was at home? Have you reference to the boy Isaac and myself for in some other way? Lizzie wrote me that many inquiries had been made of them respecting how I had spent my time while up on the Elklands and she said none were the wiser, from what they found out. We will have to give them credit for this.

So, John Summers and Eliza were quite agreeable? *[The "Eliza" mentioned may have been Sam Molyneux's younger sister, Eliza Ann. She was born in 1838, married Joseph Pardoe in 1871, and died 1882. No record of children from the union.]* I am pleased to hear so, but think there is no more than friendship, at least on his part, though they have been corresponding for some time past. Amelia B. married!!! Yes! And I have known those that were worse girls than she and not nigh as good looking, do the same. She has my wishes and not bad ones either.

The mail has just come in and I got a letter from Doc J. K. Bird, date 26. *[February 26]*. Yesterday, one from Cousin Martha Molyneux, the day your last came, I rec'd one from a girl that had never written to me before, you won't be jealous will you? If I say it was a very nice letter, but she is only eight years old and my niece, Sister Anna's eldest. She is pretty and well-behaved and smart. So say I! Can't I brag up my relations?

Cousin Angie is a very good girl. She has been like a sister to me. 'Twas too bad you could not be at the party at John's, but you have seen Angie, have you not, when she was at Sallie's in blackberry time?

I had understood from different sources that your neighborhood had seen considerable trouble of late. 'Tis much the better way to keep clear of all as much as possible, for there is quite enough that is unavoidable to be pleasant. Now, what shall I write to fill up the ballance of the page? I shall have also to think of the chamfor! There, that word is misspelled, "camphor." I guess I wish you could give me some tonight, not that I am sick in the least, but then I should be near you and could see and talk with you. I did not regret being almost strangled that time for it told me more than words could, your frightened look, that I was indeed truly and sincerely loved by Vilie.

Now, a letter is never finished until we close it, sign our name and etc. I can never end a letter scarcely. To suit me, it always seems rough and broken somehow, but then I can generally stop somewhere and somehow. So, with a verse I have just been reading, shall end this:

> When the flowers of peace shall brighten,
> Every trampled battle plain,
> And the cannons sound no more;
> When the battle flags are folded,
> On the sea and on the shore;
> With what rapture will we hasten,
> When the hour of victory cometh,
> To those we love – and home again.

[Source and author unknown.]

Affectionately yours, Joel to Vilie.

*****

Sat. 5 March. Rode with the capt. to the station. He is going to Washington. Fresh fish for dinner. Sergt. Scott and Horton take dinner and visit with me.

Sun. 6 March. Went to the station after the capt. Nothing else of importance.

Mon. 7 March. Fine weather. Capt. Graves expects to go and join Gen. Graham in North Carolina as Q A Gen.

Wed. 9 March. Gen. Birney returns from Washington. 141st goes out on picket.

[On March 9, 1864, General Ulysses S. Grant was commissioned lieutenant general which made him general-in-chief of the Union armies, the top rank in the Union army. Federal general ranks were: brigadier general (one star), major general (two stars), and lieutenant general (three stars).

[The Confederate army had one rank above lieutenant general called general (four star). In total, about 1,008 generals served in the Civil War, 425 Confederate and 583 Federal. Almost 40 percent of them had attended West Point Academy, and as a consequence many of them knew each other.

[During the war it was a common practice to "brevet" an officer. This meant that an officer was given a temporary rank, above his regular rank. For example, a colonel might be breveted to brigadier general. He would be called "general", and have the authority of a general, but would still receive the pay of a colonel. At a later time, he could be returned to "colonel", and lose his star, although he probably would still be called "General". Colonel Madill, of the 141st, was brevetted several ranks, then reduced in rank before being mustered out.]

Thu. 10 March.	A rainy day today. Keep closely housed.
Fri. 11 March.	Visited the regt. Saw Wash Pennington's father.
Sat. 12 March.	Nothing of any account. Spent the evening at the regt. hospital and at the company.
Sun. 13 March.	Review of the div. Fine day and nice time.
Mon. 14 March.	Liking and disliking:
	Ye who know the reason tell me How it is that instinct still Prompts the heart to like or like not At its own capricious will?
Tue. 15 March	Tell me by what magic Our impressions first are led Into liking or disliking Oft before a word is said?

[Source and author unknown.]

Letter #53

[This short business note to brother David had its envelope marked, Forwarded by the kindness of Ellis Bryan.]

Va., Mar. 15th, 1864

To David Molyneux, Esq.

Millview, Sullivan Co., Penn.

Enclosed I send $30.00 by Ellis Bryan as he will have a chance of getting it to you soon. I shall write to you and send by mail, which you will, 'Tis likely, rec. before getting this. No more at present. Your brother J. L. Molyneux.

P. S. Henry Bedford puts in $20.00, twenty dollars, with mine, to be handed over to Wm. Marsden when you may have the opportunity. Joel Molyneux.

*****

Wed. 16 March. "True happiness consists not in the multitude of friends, but in the worth and choice; Let them be good that love me, though few." *[Source and author unknown.]*

Thu. 17 March. Friendship has a power
To soothe affliction in its darkest hour.

[Source and author unknown.]

Fri. 18 March. I never nurs'd a dear gazelle
To glad me with its soft black eye
But when it came to know me well
And love me, it was sure to die.

[From Thomas Moore, <u>The Fire Worshippers</u>]

[The first lines of the above Moore verse go:

Oh, ever thus, from childhood's hour,
I've seen my fondest hopes decay;
I never loved a tree or flower
But 'twas the first to fade away.]

Sat. 19 March. Visited Co. K, and went to meeting in the evening at Christian Commission.

Sun. 20 March. Meeting at the theatre. Did not attend.

Mon. 21 March. *[The actors]* Commence to perform this evening at the theatre. Do not attend.

Tue. 22 March. Lent Billy Murphy one dollar yesterday, but as I find, he took it and got drunk. Am therefore resolved not to lend in the future to do the like.

[Joel, a member of the Wesleyan Methodist Church, agreed with their anti-alcohol drinking position. Prohibitionists were derisively nicknamed

"pump-suckers". Wesleyan Methodists had split from the main line Methodist denomination in 1843 over three issues: abolition (they were for), local church government (for), and secret societies (against). The splinter group was named the Wesleyan Methodist Connection (church) of America. In Joel's time it was The Wesleyan Methodist. It is now The Wesleyan Church.]

Wed. 23 March. Snowing some. Evening: Snowing much.

Thu. 24 March. Snow is nearly ten inches deep this morning. Johny *(horse)* died and was buried.

Fri. 25 March. Michael Farrel called. Has just returned a vet from a 35 day furlough.

Sat. 26 March. The day passed, as many others, with nothing of interest to engage the attention.

Sun. 27 March. Easter Sunday. Rode down to Culpepper with the Capt. Gen. Hayes at Hd Qrs, and is to command the Second Brigade.

Mon. 28 March. Past another day, but in the evening went to the theatre and got almost jammed to pieces. Saw three girls, an India rubber man, and a dwarf.

Tue. 29 March. The rain, rains, rain! A review was to take place for some cause. Does not – the rain, doubtless.

Wed. 30 March. Appearances indicate an awful struggle between the contending armies this season. May heaven aid the right.

Thu. 31 March. Orders for to change camp on the morrow. A disturbance in the guard; the effects of beer. Mrs. Birney goes home.

["Mrs. Birney" was General David Bell Birney's wife. Officers' wives visited army camps and stayed with their husbands. As provost guard at Division Headquarters, Joel was well acquainted with her since her husband was Commanding Officer of the Division. Seven months later General Birney died of malaria in Philadelphia.]

CHAPTER 21: APRIL 1864

Fri. 1 April. Moved with the Third Div. *[We]* Are now at the railroad near the St. *[Station]*, Brandy St. *[Brandy Station]*

Sat. 2 April. The First Div. is now in the Second Corps under Gen. Hancock.

Sun. 3 April. I always did intend, Single my life to spend
It much delighteth me, To live from woman free,
It's sure a happy life, To live without a wife.

Mon. 4 April. A female to my mind, I ne'er expect to find
A bachelor to live, my mind I freely give.

Wed. 6 April. To take to me a wife, Would grieve my very life
To think upon a bride, I can't be satisfied,
'Tis woman is the string, Such troubles on us bring.

Thu. 7 April. The joy I can't express
So great in singleness
I never could agree
A married man to be.

[Sources and authors unknown.]

[Joel may be seriously considering his marriage-bachelorhood options.]

Sat. 9 April. Heavy rain last night, high water and a number of railroad bridges carried away between us and Washington.

Sun. 10 April. I went up to the station with Charley Scott to visit Bish Horton.

Mon. 11 April. "A mountain of unhappiness out of a molehill of offense."

Wed. 13 April. Div. review in John Minor Botts' fields. *[See entry at January 13, 1864, for sketch of Botts.]* Reviewed by Gen. Hancock.

Sat. 16 April. The 141st Regt., Pa. V., received two months pay Jan. and Feb. – $26. Expressed $20 home. Forwarded to Isaac Rogers, care of Ellis Bryan.

Sun. 17 April. Theodore L. Wilkinson, Provisional Second H-Arty *[heavy artillery]* Ninth A. C., Battery E.

Fri. 22 April. The Second Army Corps was reviewed today by Gens. Grant, Meade, and Hancock in the vicinity of Stephensburgh.

Sat. 23 April. A queer sentence: "Sator are pote a et opera rotas." *[Joel has created, or repeated, a palindrome (word game made of a word, sentence, or paragraph that reads the same backwards as forwards). Joel's palindrome is indeed a queer sentence for it doesn't make sense.]*

Letter #54

Near Brandy Station, Va.,
April 24th, *[1864]*

Dear Brother: *[David]*

Your letter was rec'd in season, and now I shall try to ans. We are most of us still enjoying good health and are yet in camp. But the weather is fine and the roads are passable for a movement, and everything seems to indicate that we shall move soon.

Gen. Grant and Hancock, the latter commands the corps, our old corps. The Second, has been broken up and two divisions of it put into the Second Corps. The First, and Second, and Third Division was put into the Sixth Corps. Our Division is now the Third Division of the Second Corps. The div. is still commanded by Gen. Birney, as formerly. There is four divisions in the corps and it is estimated to be fifty thousand strong. In what manner operations will be conducted, we cannot tell. But 'tis evident the strength of both armies are concentrated for the coming struggle in this part of Virginia.

We received two more months pay the 16th, and we expressed to Isaac Rogers in care of Ellis Bryan, Muncy, etc. I sent twenty dollars, which with what I sent by Bryan when he was down here $30.00 will make fifty dollars from me. I wrote to Isaac sending him the receipt and with the amount from each and who for, etc.

I have received a letter from George and one from Sarah mailed the 18th. *[George and Sarah Molyneux were Joel's brother and sister. George, born in 1824, was seven years older than Joel. Sarah, born in 1837, was two years younger than Joel.]* It is rumored here that the mail will be stopped from the army for 60 days from the time the campaign opens, and I think it probably is true. If it should be so, you may not hear again from me for some time.

Many more have volunteered than I had any idea would in that vicinity. But I do not think Jonas is using his family just rightly by going. Wes. Rogers has written to Will since they came down, and they were then at Fort Ethan Allen, near Chain Bridge, and 'tis likely they will be brought up here to the front as he wrote they were drilling infantry drill, and I see a great many regiments of the heavy artillery are being brought out to serve as infantry for thirty days. I am not knowing to any that have reenlisted that can be accounted to your township, excepting Mike Farrel. He called to see me on his return, and said that he should be credited to Forks and said they told him an act had been passed prohibiting any from being accounted to any other place than to their place of residence. So, if this be the case all that have reenlisted belonging to the town. You can get credit of seeing to it, if such an act has been passed before they reenlisted.

I am still at headquarters and in the same situation as I was when at home. How long I may remain so is quite uncertain. Enclosed is two photographs. One of them is an old one that I brought away by mistake when I was at home. And the other I stopped at Washington and had a negative taken, and had the pictures sent to me, but they proved very poor ones.

Our regt. went on picket this morning to be gone three days. The picket line is about four mile from our camp. A man was shot yesterday on a picket post, to the right of the line where our div. picket. Our cavalry have a line of pickets in front of the infantry. Consequently, it must have been a guerilla between the lines.

The suttlers have all had to leave since the 16th. We have been minus of one considerable cause of trouble as they bring up such quantities of liquor — though they are not allowed to sell to privates. Yet, 'tis done on the sly and upon a large scale, as a bottle of whiskey, at most times here, commands a big price, often three dollars as anything.

We have a private now in the guard house that by some means had liquor sent to him, and had disposed of enough before getting detected to realize $1,500 (fifteen hundred dollars). He is now waiting his court-martial. At the time, he was on duty at an ammunition train. If by some means liquor could be kept entirely out of the army, from officers as well as privates, a vast lot of trouble and blunders would be prevented.

I saw Billy *[Luke]* a few days since. He is rugged. He, nor either of his brothers, have reenlisted. Capt. Sam Brien I see occasionally. His regt. lays less than a mile and in plain view of Washington. As I can think of nothing more of interest to write, I must close.

Give my love to father and mother. Tell Mary to be a good girl. My respects and best wishes to Hannah, and I remain your absent, but affectionate brother Joel. Address: Headquarters, Birney's Div., Second Corps, Washington, D.C.

*****

Tue. 26 April.   Our div. move out of their quarters and go in shelter tents upon the sod.

Wed. 27 April.   Mike Farrel called a few minutes. Says Will Norton is dead.

Letter #55A

[Brandy Station], Va.
April 27th, 1864

Dear Vilie:

This very warm day finds me writing and thinking of you. Trusting you are enjoying health and that your parents, brother and sister may have recovered their usual health 'ere this. I cannot do aught but wish you well and express my sympathy in these afflictions and anxiously as I look for your letters. I shall try not complain when I know that so much care and duty falls upon you.

My last was dated the tenth. If I remember, your last had just been rec'd. A week since, Sister Sallie wrote me. I had just written to her when I rec'd it. Hers is the latest I have from home.

Michael Farrel called to see me today. He is one of the train *[railroad]* guard from the station (Brandy St.) to Alexandria. He tells me that Wm. Norton died last Sunday, and that Samie Gilbert is dangerously sick, and that Jonas Bedford had been *[sick]* but was now better. "This cruel, cruel war!" How very many have lost dear friends, there is scarcely one but has lost one. Poor Kate, if she was sincerely attached to Will, how I pity her feelings. I have not heard from her for a long time, but I must not write this way or I may have the blues, or cause them.

Yesterday we bid good bye to our winter quarters and moved out into the open to try the simple shelter tent, and to sleep on the ground and cook out of doors. The fields are green again and the flowers all returning once more. Soon will come the dusty marches and another summer of toil and danger. We have the report that no mail will be permitted after once getting into a new wave. If it is for the best we must submit, but 'twill seem hard to be deprived of our almost only enjoyment. Who would suppose that I had a letter from our friend Isaac a few days ago? Did think maybe he would feel some like some other folks do, but to all appearances he has no other feelings than of friendship.

Vilie, I am so tired of hearing the drum, fife, and bugle -- seeing the white tents and white covered army wagons nearly as far as the eye can see on every side. 'Tis ever the same, how I wish for some quiet spot free from all such sights and sounds.

Oh!! You have the blues now? I think you will say, "No, not so!" but 'twould be such a pleasant change from this wandering uncivilized life to have a home, a pleasant place, quiet and peaceful. It would not need a mansion stately, but truly a home with love and you, and with the blessing of good health and our hands. We could live for each other and be happy.

*****

Letter #55B

[Written two days later, this letter is a continuation to Vilie.]

April 29, [1864]
[In camp, Brandy Station, Virginia]

I had the good fortune last evening to receive your letters of the 24th, and you can only imagine the pleasure it gave me. I was not looking for it quite so soon, was glad to hear your people were so much better, though I am sorry you have cut my fingers. Sharp knives will cut! But I will not scold this time, only to say that I should much rather have yours hurt than mine.

I shall guess. You were 19 that Wednesday the 20th, and that my letter was rather an indifferent present for a birthday gift. You say if I would only wait for you that you would soon be as old as me. Well, how long shall I wait? Until my three years are up? Then I shall be 30 and you 20. Maybe then we could change my "3" to a "2", or at least we could change us "two" to a "one". What think you?

I do not know what to think of Ike's request. He is certainly very good natured for to write to both of us. He is acting upon the principle that "Faint heart never won fair lady." You must do as your judgment seemeth best.

Sister wrote me that Lucy B *[Bothwell]* was soon to be married. People's taste differ. Widows or widowers are interesting to some if they are only sick. And some take their choice "almost anybody or none." It is too bad if Jobe has been jilted -- you mean by the Miss Williams, I suppose? My tentmate, formerly from Franklin, has just received a letter stating that Miss Mary Ann Varney was recently married to a Thomas Smiley. JOB can console himself in thinking that the Millview girls are yet left.

Vilie, I do not know when you will receive this letter. I have heard that no more letters can leave the army for the present, but will be stopped at Washington. 'Tis said letters can come but not go. I will send this and risk the chance, with he hope that it may reach you soon.

We broke camp one year ago today and started for Chancellorsville. We are now expecting to move any day, though as yet we know nothing of it. There, I believe I have written all my poor head can think of; the mail for today has just come, but none for me. Now I shall have to close and get supper ready. All the boys in our regt. from Sullivan are enjoying good health. Good bye – Affectionately yours. As ever, Joel to Vilie. Address: Hd Qrs, Birney's Div., Washington, D.C.

*****

Sat. 30 April.
I have sought for a friend that is loving
Kind, generous, gentle, and true
I have looked for a heart I could trust in
And found one, sweet Vilie, in you
O, what are the joys of a lifetime
If not shared by a friend that is true

Let friendship make firm now the reunion
May neither the bond ever rue;
In sorrow, misfortune, and gladness,
Let each to the other prove true.
O, the joys of a lifetime are blessings
When they're shared by a friend that is true.

[Author and source unknown. Possibly written by Joel.]

CHAPTER 22: MAY 1864

Tue. 3 May. Capt. Graves leaves. Report to the guard. Orders for marching. To move at half past 11 o'clock P.M.

Wed. 4 May. Started near midnight. Crossed the Repidan *[Rapidan River]* at Elys Ford, and marched to Chancellorsville. Arrived at three P.M. *[May 4 marked the first day of the Army of the Potomac's five week Rapidan Campaign. Major battles: Wildernesss, Spotsylvania Courthouse, North Anna River, and Cold Harbor. Campaign ended June 12, 1864.]* Distance three mile. Very tired. The road was lined with blankets and overcoats. *[It was common practice for Union soldiers on march to unburden themselves of their blankets and overcoats. These clothing items would be picked up by their following wagon train, and they could retrieve them at their next stop or that evening.]*

Thu. 5 May. Moved early and passed to the left of this place to Todds Tavern seven or ten mile and about faced; back again five mile to plank road from Chancellorsville. Found the rebs. Fought from four o'clock. Gen. Hays killed.

*[Union General Alexander Hays was commanding officer of the Second Brigade, Third Division, II Corps. He was in many battles of the Army of the Potomac and had been severely wounded at Second Bull Run. May 5, 1864, marked the first day of the three-day Battle of the Wilderness. The Army of the Potomac had had only minor skirmishes since Gettysburg, and General Grant pronounced it **"in splendid condition and feels like whipping somebody."***

A vicious battle was fought in tangled thickets of stunted pine, scrub oak, and sweet gum. This battlefield saw more destruction and horrors than any other battle of the war. In many cases, forest trees caught on fire and burned alive the wounded who could not escape. The Battles of the Wilderness marked the beginning of the end for the Army of Northern Virginia and for the Confederacy. The Federal army of 101,895 men was pitted against the Confederate army of 61,025. Union casualties tallied 17,666 and the Confederate toll at 7,750. Total casualties: 25,416 — making it the sixth costliest battle of the Civil War. Winner: Inconclusive. Loser: Both sides!]

Fri. 6 May. The battle opens early. Drive and are driven. 141st take colors. *[Colors the 141st captured were those of the 13th North Carolina Regiment.]* Both sides reinforced, *[by]* Long St. *[General Longstreet]* and Burnside, an awful charge upon Birney's Div. five and S *[?]* Div. are repulsed. Second Brigade break soon, reform, and resume position.

[On May 6, 1864, Confederate Lieutenant General James Longstreet, General Robert E. Lee's most able corps commander, was seriously wounded by his own men. General Longstreet recovered and fought in the final battles of the war. General Longstreet, graduating from West Point in the class of 1842, was 54th in a class of 56.

[It was ironic that two of Lee's best field generals were accidentally shot by their own troops, almost exactly a year apart, on almost the same battlefield. General Stonewall Jackson had been seriously wounded on May 2, 1863, at the Battle of Chancellorsville.]

Sat. 7 May.   Still fighting. 63rd charge and are badly cut up. Masked battery but little artillery used by either *[side]*. A strategic retreat of our Div and again return to positions. Train goes to Spottsylvania. Rebs supposed to be falling back.

Sun. 8 May.   Rebs reported gone. Army is changing position to follow Lieut. Bryan and Snell 12. Report at Todd's Tavern. Build fortifications. Expect an attack. Some shelling and smart musketry. Gen. Sedgewick killed.

[Union Army, VI Corps commander, Major General John Sedgwick, was shot in the head by a Confederate sharpshooter's bullet as he prowled the front lines, while placing his artillery. Ironically, he had just declared, "they couldn't hit an elephant at this distance!" He died almost immediately. Affectionately called "Uncle John" by his troops, he was the highest ranking Union general killed during the war. He was the third and last Army of the Potomac corps commander to be killed in action. Historians record General Sedgwick as being killed on May 9, 1864, but Joel's diary records it on May 8, 1864. (Possibly Joel made the May 8 entry the following day.) The identity of the sharpshooter is uncertain, but Sergeant Charles Grace, Doles-Cook Brigade, C.S.A., is a strong candidate as the marksman.

[General Sedgwick was a West Pointer, class of 1837. He ranked 24th in a class of 50 graduates, including Confederate General Braxton Bragg, Confederate General Jubal Early, and Union General Joe Hooker.]

Mon. 9 May.   Prepare for an attack. Gens. Grant and Meade ride by. rebs fall back, strike out again. Come up with them near the P. R. *[Po River]* Battery in position, shell and get shelled. Still fall back. Cross the P. *[Po River]*. Go into camp near Spottsylvania Court House.

Tue. 10 May.   Enemy on hand. Shell out a battery. Move to the left across the Po. Get awfully shelled. First Brigade charge the redoubts; get repulsed. Camp near the 141st. Both sides are strongly fortified.

[The Battles of Spotsylvania came shortly after the three-day Battles of the Wilderness. The Army of the Potomac's II Corps was at the center of the activity. The battle, raging from May 11 through May 19, 1864, involved 111,000 Union troops and 63,000 Southern troops. Casualties were 18,000 Union and 9,000 to 10,000 Confederates.]

Wed. 11 May. Skirmishing. Out patrolling. Hd Qrs shelled out. Deploy behind div. Start to rain on guard, get wet. At night we move; are shelled. Go to extreme left. An occasional minnie *[minie bullet]* relieves the monotony of the march.

Thu. 12 May. At daybreak, our corps charge the enemy, capture some 4,000 prisoners and 20 cannon, *[and]* shells. Our guard escort the gentlemen to near Fredericksburg, eight miles, very muddy. Stuart and Jonson among the prisoners. Heavy cannonading. Minnies for gnats at night. Wet!

[Confederate Major General JEB Stuart had not been taken prisoner, as Joel heard, but had been wounded the previous day at Yellow Tavern, Virginia. He was shot at short range through the abdomen by a sharpshooter of the 5th Michigan Cavalry. He was taken to the home of his brother-in-law, Dr. Chris Brewer, in Richmond, and there died of his wounds. At his death bed he asked attendees to sing his favorite hymn, "Rock of Ages."

[The first and last verses go:

> *Rock of Ages, cleft for me,*
> *Let me hide myself in Thee!*
> *Let the water and the blood,*
> *From the riven side which flowed,*
> *Be of sin, the double cure,*
> *Cleanse me from its guilt and power.*

> *While I draw this fleeting breath,*
> *When my eyestrings break in death,*
> *When I soar in tracts unknown,*
> *See Thee on Thy judgment-throne,*
> *Rock of Ages, cleft for me,*
> *Let me hide myself in Thee.*

His last words were: **"I am resigned; God's will be done."** *With his death, The Confederacy lost one of its most colorful, courageous, and gallant officers. His terse advice to his troops, while out on raids,* **"Behave like gentlemen!"** *General Stuart graduated from West Point, class of 1854. He was ranked 13th in a class of 46. Lee, learning of Stuart's death expressed his grief:* **"I can scarcely think of him without weeping."**]

Fri. 13 May. Skirmishing all day. No reply to our artillery. Learn that Wm. Rogers was killed yesterday. W. Pennington and Pierce missing. Ordered to report to Capt. Noble. A flank movement again to the left.

Letter #56

[In this letter to David, Joel discusses the Battles of the Wilderness.]

Battlefield, *[Spotsylvania Court House]*
[May 13, 1864]

Dear Brother:

I write a line to let you know I am yet in the land of the living. Our army moved on the second and have been fighting ever since the fifth. Losses have been heavy in killed and wounded. At The Battle of the Wilderness none of our company was killed, six or seven wounded, the most of them very slight. C. Webster and H. Bedford from our county but not bad. I have not heard from the regt. since yesterday's fight. We took some 7,000 prisoners yesterday with *[including]* Gen's. Ed Johnson and Stuart (not of the cavalry). The enemy has fallen back some again this morning.

[Confederate General Edward ("Allegheny") Johnson was captured at Spotsylvania's Bloody Angle. He was prisoner-exchanged a short time later and led his division in General Hood's invasion of Tennessee. He was captured again at Nashville.

[Joel mentioned a General "Stuart (not of the cavalry)" being captured. There was only one General Stuart in the Confederate army, the famous JEB Stuart. There was, however, a General Alexander Stewart in the Confederate army, but there is no record of his being in the Spotsylvania Court House battle, or being taken prisoner. Perhaps the officer captured was not a general or it may have been another unfounded rumor that Joel had heard.]

We have had a summer of gens. killed. Sedgwic *[John]*, a maj. gen, and Seymour, captain, Brig. Gen. Hays killed of our div. and some others that I do not now remember the ---*[text obliterated]*.

[Union General John Sedgwick was killed in this battle. He had commanded the VI Corps at Chancellorsville, Gettysburg, Rappahannock Station, Mine Run Operation, Wilderness, and at Spotsylvania where he was killed. His body was embalmed on the field and sent home for burial.

[Union Brigadier General Hays was commanding the 2nd Brigade, 3rd Division, II Corps, when he was killed in action at the Battles of the Wilderness. Union General Truman Seymour had been captured, not killed, as Joel heard.]

[Forty-seven Union and 77 Confederate generals were killed or mortally wounded during the war. That was eight percent of the Union generals and 18 percent of the Confederate generals who died of battle wounds.]

We are now near Spottsvillevania C.H. *[Spotsylvania Court House]*. Mail has just come in and will go out immediately so I have not time to write more. Perhaps it will not go through until I shall have an opportunity to write again. We are about tired out -- wet and rainy yesterday and today.

I have seen some 20 cannon that we captured. 'Tis said we have taken a much larger number. I went nearly to Fredericksburg to help guard the prisoners there yesterday. 'Tis some over 12 miles of *[from]* here.

Our supplies and c *[? probably was written "and etc."]* come from there now. I suppose there will be fighting again today. The sharp shooters have advanced and I *[hear]* them skirmishing already. Good bye. Love to all. Shall write soon. Joel.

*****

Sat. 14 May. Same place. Camped for the night in the pines to the rear of our works. Some skirmishing and artillery on our side. Burying the dead. Camp to the right in thick pines, moonlight. Fighting ten days.

Sun. 15 May. Move at daybreak to the left, leave the works taken from the rebs. Guards get lost from the div. Our divisions on to Gen. Burnsides. Shells come too close to Hd Qrs to be healthy. Camp and sleep undisturbed.

Mon. 16 May. Very little done today. Some skirmishing and an occasional discharge of a cannon. Hd Qrs move to the right. Camp and sleep undisturbed. Mail goes out.

Letter #57

[Near Spotsylvania Court House], Va.
May 16th, 1864

Dear V.

I have just time to write a line so you may know that I am still living and unhurt. The mail will go out in a few minutes, but do not know if it will reach you very soon. We have been marching and fighting for a week and you can perhaps judge our weariness.

I am very sad for I have to write of the death of William Rogers. He was killed upon the ----*[text obliterated]* where we charged the enemies' works. He fell dead. Henry Bedford and Charles Webster were wounded upon the sixth, but not dangerously. Our army has lost very heavy, but the enemy much more.

Our corps has captured near 6,000 prisoners. We are confident of success, and trust this campaign will end the war. We are now about ten mile of the city of Fredericksburg. Our men have it in possession; the wounded are sent there. We are close to Spottsville *[Spotsylvania]* Court House.

I think your last letter was dated the 25th of Apr. was rec'd the 28th. If this should reach you, say to sister Sallie I am all right yet. Please excuse this short letter and pencil, and except much love from Joel. Good bye, to Vilie.

*****

Tue. 17 May.   Still in the same place. Very little fighting done today. Second Div. guards sent back to regt.s. Also, some of our pickets driven in just at dark. Order to change posish postponed.

Wed. 18 May.   Expecting an attack or to attack. Guard deploys out. Hd Qrs move to an old former position. Sharp picket firing. Some cannonading. Draw fresh beef, get supper, go to bed, are routed out at 11 *[P.M.]* to move.

Thu. 19 May.   Up all night fiddling and marching. Take our posish some five mile south to the left at Andersons Villa. Our trains are attacked on the right. Div. is double-quicked to support smart engagement. Rebs fall back. Guard goes up in the evening.

Letter #58A

[First installment of a three-part letter to V.]

Virginia, May 19th, *[1864]*
[In camp near Chancellorsville]

Dearest Friend:

Again I pencil a few lines hoping this may find you well, etc. as I still can say that I also am. The weather is getting quite warm here; most like that of midsummer. We still occupy our old position where we came back to after the Battles of Chancellorsville. Have had no letter from you or home since we started to cross the river, I mean that was written since I wrote a short one to you as soon as we came back. Did you get it? Also one to Sallie.

I had a letter from G. Pardoe a few days since, he was then at Washington with his brother James who is there also in the hospital. *[He]* Went there previous to our move. Three Johnny Rebs were brought to our Hd Qrs this morning -- deserters from their army. *[They]* Came over to us and gave themselves up.

Appearances seem now to indicate as though we should remain here for some time. It seems lonesome now to go to my co., and so many not there. Nothing is yet heard of Wm. and Henry Bedford. Our Lieut. Watkins was not killed, as I first supposed, but only wounded and taken prisoner, but likely to get well and is paroled and sent home. I don't feel like writing a bit today. Feel dreadful lazy, somehow. But you have noticed that by my letter before this.

Now, I will tell you what I have been thinking of, that is if I keep my health till fall. I shall try to come home on furlough then. If I keep my present position, I think I can get one by asking, but maybe this war will be settled before then. I hope so for one it may be. A great many think there is a prospect. I have now been just five months since I saw you, five months last Sunday I think it is. What do you think?

*****

Fri. 20 May   At daybreak, our forces advance; catch the Johnnys asleep. Capture several hundred of their pickets. Our div. again resumes its posish on the left. Orders for marching at 11 P.M. Rumors of going to Peninsula. Mail goes out re *[via the]* river.

Letter #58B

May 20th, *[1864]*
[In camp near Chancellorsville, Virginia]

Good Morning V:

'Tis one beautiful morning. The sun shines so clear. Every one seems joyous, and our boys appear more than usually good natured.

Still my letter is not finished. I am getting careless, you may think. I thought certain of getting one letter today from you or Sallie, but none has come. I was to my regt. yesterday. Wm and Henry Bedford are heard from. They are at parole camp and not wounded. You may guess how glad we were to hear this news.

Your cousin Abel will soon have cause to think that I dislike letters as much as he. 'Tis too bad I have left both his and Jabe's so long unanswered, but really I have been writing so many that I have almost got to *[where]* I disliked the sight of a pen, but by and by I shall hope to get one on the way for them.

You say Leap Year you will agree to what I proposed. Well, this is Leap Year, I believe, and quite as soon as I could wish, even if I should get home this summer.

No, I have no dictionary down here and consequently have to guess at everything. So, I guessed you were pretty good at changing the meaning of what I wrote in a former letter. Well, never mind. If I am so favored as to return to you, we can talk this all over, can't we?

I am just wondering what you are doing four o'clock Friday afternoon, about the time for supper? Just place a plate for me, won't you? Right where I used to sit, but I am thinking you'll not let me know when it's ready ---*[text obliterated]*.

Well, I have had my supper: coffee, bread and molasses, but neither the bread or coffee was of your make, if I can remember how that used to taste at your house when I was there, days long since departed.

*****

Sat. 21 May. Upon the march to the left flank again. Pass Massaponax Church, Bowling Green, and Milford. Cross the Mattaponi River and camp. *[The Mattaponi River was made up of four small rivers, the Mat, the Ta, the Po, and the Ni.]* A hard march, very hot, reach here at five P.M.; 25 if not 30 mile.

Sun. 22 May. Building breastworks all day. Looking for old Bobby. Does not make his appearance. Move Hd Qrs, draw beef, coffee, and hards *[hard tack]*. Mail comes in. Rec. the first news letter since marching. Camp near the breastworks. Reb. gone.

["Old Bobby" is General Robert E. Lee and his elusive troops. The next day they located him, and the resulting Battle of North Anna River lasted three days, May 23-26. Union forces numbered 68,000 in this battle and Confederate forces 53,000. Casualties were 2,500 Army of Northern Virginia and 2,600 Army of the Potomac.]

Mon. 23 May. "On to Richmond" again soon after 'tis light. Fifth and Sixth Corps here. Find the Johns at Hannons. Birney's Div. charge and drive the rebs across the North Anna. Shelling us sharp. Getting used to them. Bivouc at a house. Find salt.

Letter #58C

Morning, 23rd, *[May 1864]*
[In camp in Virginia]

Good morning and also goodbye, for your letter is ready to go at last and the mail soon leaves. Hoping soon to hear from you, I close by enclosing my best wishes for your welfare and an abundance of love for yourself – Joel.

P. S. I would send a kiss, but I always like 'em warm!

*****

Tue. 24 May. Are aroused early by the rioting of shot and shell. 20 Ind. *[Indiana's 20th Regiment]* advance into the first line of redoubts patrolling. Busy. A corporal *[of]* Burnside's comes up. Johns shell the bridge savagely, guard cross the river, thunder showers. Bivouc and rest quietly.

Wed. 25 May. Nice morning. Find some beautiful magnolias in blossom. Rebs strongly entrenched near by. Picket firing, with now and then a cannon shot. Wash. Showers. Short of rations. Camp the same as the night previous, undisturbed.

Thu. 26 May. Showery. Visit the regt. Write letters. Mail goes out at three. Draw rations of hards *[hard tack]* and coffee. Pack up and hike out. Cross the river. Fool about till daylight. Some shelling and skirmishing done today.

Fri. 27 May. Very warm and on the march to the left flank again. Pass Concord Church. The road is strewn with dead horses. Halt an hour, and then march in the night. Stop in the vicinity of Hanover C.H. and the Parmunky *[the Pamunkey River]*. Fifteen or 20 mile.

Sat. 28 May. Upon the road again. Arrive at the Pamunky and cross on pontoons. Follow the R. road a mile and fortify ourselves at Pleasant Hill. On guard. Drew cornmeal. Rations short. Cherries ripe. Are early.

Sun. 29 May. All quiet this morning. Bands play. Go over to the regt. Gruel soup. Pack up our duds and move off. Pass the ground where the cavalry fought. Dead rebels! Bivouc close upon the enemy. Build breastworks.

Mon. 30 May. Sharp skirmishing and some artillery used. Mail. Rations come up and get five days issued. Picket line is advanced. Musketry, mortars, and cannon used freely.

Letter #59

Upon the Peninsula,
12 mile *[North East]* of Richmond
May 30th, *[1864]*

Dear Friend: *[Vi]*

Yours of May mailed the 13th was duly received and I was very glad to hear from you. That has been the only letter from or about home since starting on the campaign. I have written to you and Sallie previous to this which I trust you may have received. I, at present, enjoy good health and have so far escaped unhurt.

George Pardoe is said to be missing, thought to have been taken prisoner. I saw James Pardoe yesterday. He has not been so well as usual for the past week -- complains of sore throat. D. Bryan and W. Snell were all right a few days since.

We crossed the Pamunky River Saturday, the 28th, and are now between Hanover Court House and Atlees Station, about two miles of the Va. Central Railroad, and only 12 mile of the much spoken of Richmond. Battle fighting has been done the last few days, but we are now come up with them and find them quite strongly fortified. Some skirmishing and shelling has been going on today and still continues, but I do not think they will make much of a fight this side of the city.

None of our company have been killed *[during]* this campaign so far, with the exception of Will Rogers. Two are missing -- thought to be taken prisoner and some six or eight slightly wounded. The army is generally in good spirits, though sometimes we are short of rations.

Our train *[supply]* has just come up with a fresh supply from Port Royal, and there are many well pleased. 'Tis thought by nearly every one that Richmond will fall this time, and the rebellion will be ended, and no one can more heartily wish it may than your friend, J.

Now, I must hurry and close to hear of your enjoying so good health, and that your people had so much recovered. So Saidy T. has gone to Westown to school. 'Twill be so much to her benefit. I trust Joshua then continues to pay his respects to her; it seems but a short time since I first saw her a little girl at R. Bedfords.

You say that you should be so pleased could you but do something for me here if it were possible. You might help to pick some cherries if you was here. They are just now getting ripe. The beautiful magnolia is just in blossom. You might help to get them, but you are not here and I am glad that you are not. 'Tis no place for women. There is one woman that has been in our division since we have been out. The boys call her Gentle Anna. She is brave, and an excellent help with the wounded.

[During the Civil War, many female volunteers, like the woman Joel affectionately called "Gentle Anna", performed noble nursing services. An estimated 3,200 women served as nurses in the Union army, and an undetermined number served the Confederate forces. The American Red Cross had not yet come into existence.]

The mail came in today, and will go out again. I have penciled a letter home and this far to you. Tomorrow is the last of May; we now have less than 15 months *[out of his thirty-six-month enlistment period]* to stay.

I think that in my last I told you that I was doing provost guard duty at div. Hd Qrs again. I have been here since the first of the month. You will please excuse pencil, half sheet, mistakes, etc., and as I have little time or anything else at present, with the one exception of many kind regards and well wishes and love from Joel to Vilie.

P. S. Write soon

*****

Tue. 31 May. Sharpshooters advance and occupy the first line of rebel works. Guards deploy out close in the rear. Shells burst sufficiently plenty. Five Coham mortars pass to the front. Five guns quakered *[silenced, or put out of commission]*. Go in camp to be routed up and move back to yesterday's position. Canteen stole!

[The Battle of Cold Harbor, May 31 to June 12, 1864, was one more in the series of delaying actions by General Lee, and the attempts by General Grant to get south of the Confederate army to storm Richmond. At this battle, General Grant failed in his attempt to take Richmond by direct force, and he decided the key to capturing Richmond was to first take Petersburg. This battle was Lee's last great victory in the field. Combat strength of the Union army was 114,000 to 117,000, pitted against 59,000 to 60,000 Confederates. The Union army lost 10,000 to 13,000, and there were 4,000 to 5,000 Confederate casualties.]

CHAPTER 23: JUNE 1864

Wed. 1 June. Our troops fall back to our own rifle pits. Rebs advance, capture some of our pickets. Guards deployed, sharp picket firing. Pope of the guard wounded. Heavy fighting on the left. Orders to march. Straighten out during the night. The air is full of reports and rumors.

Thu. 2 June. On guard. Hot day. Fall in with D. Bryan, Sandy. Detail march ahead to pitch Hd Qrs. Heavy shower. Form line of battle and fortify. Hd Qrs near a swamp brook. An attack expected. Tired, wet, and sleepy -- care less of reb shot sent us.

Fri. 3 June. Some shell makes us an early call. Deployed out. Line to our right charge; take rifle pits, but are driven back. Many wounded pass us. div. moved to the right. Crazy man in a pen. Stack arms by the 141st. Shelled Hd Qrs. Rest back in cave. Rebs make a night charge.

[General Grant's massive frontal assault against General Lee's entrenched line at the Battle of Cold Harbor, on June 3, 1864, resulted in approximately 7,000 Union casualties and 1,500 Confederate casualties in under an hour, with 5,000 others on June 1 and 2. One participant there called it "the bloodiest eight minutes of the Civil War". A Civil War veteran reported later: "The dead covered more than five acres of ground about as thickly as they could be laid." This bloody Virginia battle was named for a nearby tavern.

[The prior four weeks involved some of the most vicious fighting of the whole Civil War. Joel's comment above, "Crazy man in a pen" underscores the tension, intense strain, and revulsion to which the soldiers were exposed. The next day his unit encamped by a "crazy house". In another place, he told of a soldier being tied to a tree.

[Many soldiers who deserted had broken mentally and emotionally under the pressures of battle, and thus many sick men were executed as traitors. If hit in the body by a mortar shell or Minie bullet, they were regarded as heroes, but if wounded emotionally they were court-martialed as cowards and shot. One factor contributing to the numerous emotional breakdowns during the Civil War was that some unstable candidates were not screened out before enlistment. Almost all volunteers were accepted "as is". More than that though, many well-balanced, even-keeled, men broke under the intense strain and physical hardships they were forced to endure. The miracle of the whole appalling situation was how many did survive.]

Sat. 4 June. Camp back of the crazy house. Mail! Sent out two letters. Knapsack wagon comes up. Go down on a tom fool's errand to supply train. Five mile for patrol. Back in the night. Rainy. Find Hd Qrs and div. gone. Burnside here instead.

Sun. 5 June. Unwell. Look up Hd Qrs. Find them near our posish of the night of June second. Another fool detail to *[visit the]* train. Hd Qrs fixed up to kill. Orders to move. March to the left. Evening pickets get to firing and shell to flying. Camp in the pines by a brook. Three days' rations.

Mon. 6 June. Move camp to the left by a mill pond. Ice. Band plays. Rebs try their hand to stop it. Purveyor comes up, sells out. Hd Qrs move back to the right of our line. Camp near an open lot and weather-worn old hut.

Tue. 7 June. Patrolling. Hd Qrs move back to near the mill pond. Cross the ravine. Some shells go a screaming over. Four days' ration; one day of pork.

Wed. 8 June. Still at the same place. Weather fine. Shells flying and one or two burst among us. None hurt! On guard. Mail! Letters from home!

Thu. 9 June. Fine and warm. Patrolling down to the train. Picket firing and some cannon to the right. 2 more days' rations issued – pork and beans.

Fri. 10 June. Same place. Sutler up. Wash clothes. Rumor of moving to Harrison A-Carze. Mill pond here. Balker's Mill on Elder Swamp tributery of the Chicohomony *[tributary of the Chickahominy River]*.

Sat. 11 June. Still in camp as before. Nothing of interest going on. Picket firing on the right of our div. Take charge of Capt. Noble's horses for a few days.

Sun. 12 June. By the mill pond, still. Sharp shooting some. Harkness calls. Orders for moving tonight. Get started at 11 P.M. Move to the left, toward James River. Up all night.

Mon. 13 June. The marching resumed in earnest. Make good time *[through]* Chicohomony Swamp. Cross the river in the afternoon; two branches. Four and two pontoons. James river country. Camp at sundown. Long march –– over 20 mile.

Tue. 14 June. Sleep undisturbed. Troops fortify. Last night saw Billy Luke. Move *[to]* James River. Cross in transports at Windmill Point. Hd Qrs at Willcox plantation or Flowery Hundred Row. Darkies fish. Gen. Birney.

Nice situation. Magnolia tree. See Capt. Graves and Gen. Graham and Lt. Bullard.

Wed. 15 June. Up and breakfast early. Pack up and march for Petersburg. Hot, hard, marching. Pass the 106th. See S. Black, L. Bryan, Fred Luke. Camp at night within two mile of Petersburg. U.S. colored *[troops]* are engaged. Guns captured.

[The Petersburg Campaign and Siege, starting June 15, 1864, lasted nine and a half months, to April 2, 1865. It was spread over 176 square miles, and involved six major battles, eleven engagements, forty-four skirmishes, and three expeditions. The Federal army suffered 42,000 casualties; the Confederate 28,000. Grant's forces averaged 109,000 men and Lee's 59,000. The Confederate defense line not only protected Petersburg, but also ran the distance of the Bermuda Hundred Peninsula on to Richmond, a front of about 35 miles.]

Thu. 16 June. Wake up and pack up, with shells to hurry us up. Move to the rear of a large wheat and oats field. Line is advanced toward evening. Two of our regt. killed and two wounded. Egan wounded. Guard deployed nearly all night. Fifth Corps come up. On guard.

Fri. 17 June. Mott commanding div. Hd Qrs move to the front of the line of redoubts. Draw rations. Visited by shells. Heavy skirmishing and artillery firing in the afternoon and nearly all night. Sleep beside a brook. Awake with one leg to soak.

Sat. 18 June. Up early. Breakfast. Guards deploy. Orders to advance Hd Qrs and *[then]* countermanded. Our div. charge the enemy and are badly repulsed. Lt. Col. Watkins killed! Drew one pr. of socks. Sergt. Scott wounded.

[Lieutenant Colonel Guy H. Watkins was one of the most courageous and well-liked men in the 141st Regiment. He had organized the regiment, in August of 1862, and frequently was its commanding officer when Colonel Henry Madill was not present. Prior to his army enlistment, Colonel Watkins had been an attorney in Towanda, Pennsylvania, and had served as district attorney in Bradford County. At the Battle of Fredericksburg, he became dangerously ill of fever, and was taken to a hospital in Washington where he recovered. He returned to the 141st Regiment at the "Mud March" at Fredericksburg where exposure prostrated him again. At the Battles of Chancellorsville he had his horse shot out from under him.

[On May 3, 1863, Watkins was shot through the right lung, captured by the enemy, released by the Confederates after a successful operation, and recovered. He was given an opportunity to retire with a surgeon's certificate,

but declined and tried to reach the 141st Regiment for the impending Battle of Gettysburg. He was unable to get through enemy lines to Pennsylvania, and returned to Washington. In May of 1864, Colonel Madill was injured, and Colonel Watkins assumed command of the 141st Regiment. Colonel Watkins was shot and killed, leading an attack in the Petersburg Campaign.

[In a regiment of heroes, Colonel Guy H. Watkins was a hero among heroes!]

Letter #60A

June 18th, 1864,
Near Petersburg, Va.

My Dear Friend:

At last I find myself penciling a few more lines in ans. to yours of the 26th of May, and that you may know I am yet safe and well.

We crossed the James River the 14th *[of June]* at Wind Mill Pond. Crossed on transport steamboats, and marched to this place the next day and have been fighting the rebs ever since, but mostly with artillery. I have not heard yet of anyone being hurt that was from our neighborhood. I saw Sam Black, Laws Bryan, and the Luke boys the 15th. They were well then. From them I learned that Wes Rogers had accidentally wounded himself in the hand — quite serious I do believe, but do not know how it happened.

Our lines are not more than a mile of the town, and our batteries have been shelling the place. Some say we may be in Petersburg tonight. I hope so, but *[think they]* may be mistaken.

*****

Sun. 19 June. Hd Qrs advance to Mineral Springs, but little active operation. Flag of truce sent in. Visit from Gen. Meade. Coehorn mortars taken front and shell during the evening. Heavy firing during the night on the left.

[The Coehorn mortar was a portable, smoothbore mortar invented by Baron Menno van Coehorn, a seventeenth-century Dutchman.]

Letter #60B

[In this continuation to Vi, Joel looks out his tent flap and gives us a kaleidoscopic view of what a Civil War battle camp looks and sounds like on a June Sunday evening.]

Sunday, June 19th *[1864]*
[In camp, near Petersburg, Virginia]

We are not yet in Petersburg, and but little nearer than we were yesterday. Our div charged the enemy in the afternoon (yesterday) and *[we]* were badly repulsed. Our div. lost very many –– several thousand from what I can find out. Our lieut. colonel was killed (Watkins from Towanda). I have not yet saw any of my company since the affair. Perhaps I may hear from them before mailing this.

I rec'd a letter from Sally the 11th, and one from Jennie Molyneux the 16th, written the eighth –– the latest news I have from home. I received in part the names of those who were drafted. Perhaps the next mail will bring me a full list. Nothing in the mail for me tonight. Last night I got a Dushore Union, June 9th. Say to Abel, if you think proper, that I will write him when we get situated so I have time. I can write to but a few while this campaign is in progress, and those few generally short pencilling.

I am happy to hear you are enjoying such good health. 'Tis one of heaven's blessings and hope you may always be so favored. *[Elvira had a congenital heart problem that stayed with her all her life. Although she was eleven years his junior, she died several years before he did.]*

You do perfectly right in serving Randal as you say, and if I am not very much mistaken some others will yet regret they formed an acquaintance with him. In my estimation, he is hardly deserving of common civility.

Of course, tease Josh, i.e. if he teases you, but would it not be politic to make a treaty of peace, considering both sides of the case?

I just wonder where you are and what you are doing this Sunday evening. What a contrast between what surrounds you and with what does me. To my left hand, on a little knoll, is a battery in position with their black mouths open toward the rebs. Behind them, in a hollow, caissons with ammunition. To my right is an ammunition train. A little front of this is our div. Hd Qrs. Then a line of rifle pits, and on a little further another line. Then a line of pickets. Now and then a cannon breaks out in its deep tones to remind us of actual war. A short distance to the rear I hear the musical tones of a band as it is playing. Close by me is a grave, marked with a pencil, a Sixth New Jersey Volunteer, killed June 16th.

O! There in the east is the moon. 'Tis full tonight! Surely this is at least the same as the one you see. Yes, there is the man picking his sticks! But 'tis dark now, and this is written by candle light. 'Tis time to try for sleep. Mail goes out early in the morning. I must send this so I close. Good bye. I shall try and write again in a few days. This has been written in such a hurry I have scarcely said any I wished to, so with much love, I remain your truly and affectionately, Joel to Vilie.

P. S. Enclosed is a magnolia. The flower is white, the size of a goose egg before it opens.

*****

Mon. 20 June. Near Petersburg. Brisk skirmishing. Corps to be relieved. Burnside with the Ninth take our place. In the evening we move back one and 1/2 mile and go to camp. Water scarce. Sleep on a mattress.

Letter #61

Front of Petersburg
June 20th, *[1864]*

Sister Hannah: *[new sister-in-law, David's bride]*

Your letter of May 31st I rec'd 8th of June & it was very welcome for it was the 1st I had rec'd from home since the opening of the campaign. Since then I have had one from Anna Wright, Sallie McCarty, and Jennie Molyneux. The latest written June 8th, rec'd the 16th giving partially the list of drafted *[men]* of our vicinity.

By the papers you may have learned by this time of our crossing the James River. Our transports crossed at Windmill Pt. or Williams Landing on the 14th. The next day we marched to near our present position. The rebels still hold the town. We have drove them from a line of redoubts and several line of rifle pits, but they yet have strong fortifications between us and the place.

The 18th, Saturday, our div. charged on their works, and were badly repulsed. I have not since had any opportunity of seeing the qrts. *[quarters]* of my company, but probably shall before mailing this.

Our lieutenant-colonel was killed and Charley Scott of Liberty Corners quite badly wounded. (Watkins from near Towanda was Lt. Col.) I saw Fred & Billy Duke, Sam Black & Dawson Bryan the 15th I have not seen any of the 112th H. Arty *[heavy artillery]* fellows since they came out. I hear Wesley Rogers accidentally wounded himself quite severely in the hand not so long since.

I hardly know what the prospect of taking the reb capitol at present is or even Petersburg. From appearances some move will be again made tonight -- perhaps another flanking operation. Grant will, in the end, I think, take Richmond, but he has not got it yet nor has Jeff Davis or his cabinet yet run away. And the stories of citizens keeping him under guard & ---*[text obliterated]* there is no credit given to such *[rumors]* here. Petersburg is 22 miles of Richmond. Our lines are about a mile from the town. The church spires can be seen. Our artillery have shelled and had it on fire several times. The rebel lines and ours are but little more than a stone cast apart (both in rifle pits, of course), and almost continual firing is kept up. I am still at div. Hd Qrts., and the minnies zip over and about us here quite to *[too]* familiar.

Gen. Mott is now in command of the div. (the 3rd). Gen. Birney has command of the corps (II). Gen. Hancock, at present, is unwell from the effects of an old wound, I hear. Our Colonel Madill has command of our brigade (the 1st) as Col. Egan who had the command for some time, the 16th, I think. The day we arrived here, the 15th, Butler's darkie troops made a good charge capturing some 6 guns (cannon). The corps took 16, and the next morning our brigade took a battery.

We get out supplies and mail now from City Point on the James 10 miles distant. We get plenty of grub now and mail near every day. This evening papers say we have Petersburg. I do not think it so but our guns are so they command it and the railroad also.

I came near forgetting to say that my health is good as usual, and so far escaped the bullets. I must now close this and get supper. Perhaps I may add another line before mailing. If not, goodbye, with my best wishes and my regards, and my love to Father and Mother. Tell David for to write soon & do so yourself. Say to Mary I will write soon as I can. Perhaps as she has plenty of time two letters to my one would not be remiss. Address: Hd Qrs 3rd Div, 2nd Corps. Your brother Joel. To H. N. Molyneux

P. S. Wheat is nearly fit to cut, and corn about tasselling out here – what is left.

*****

Tue. 21 June. Over to company. See D. Bryan, S. Black, and Joe Bedford. Order to move. March to the left three or more mile. Meet the Johns coming on a flank also. Form our line and commence to shoot. Hay issued.

[Providing horses with forage (hay, oats, etc.) was a problem for both armies, and was crucial for cavalry units.]

Letter #62A

[The following two letters were written at the siege of Petersburg. Joel and his buddies would be in this continuing battle for a long time. There are no

salutations, but the contents show the letters to a brother or sister — probably David, from the tone of it.]

Tuesday morning, June 21st *[1864]*
[In camp near Petersburg, Virginia]

Our corps was relieved last night by the Ninth, Burnside's — and we are now back a little from the front for to rest, but whether we lay here for a day or two or be moved to some other point, I cannot say. I saw our company this morning. One only has been wounded the past week. The boys from our vicinity are well. Our regt. has lost 20 or over since crossing the James. I saw Samuel Black of the 106th, David Bryan of the 84th, Joe Bedford of the 50th this morning. The 112th H. Arty. *[heavy artillery]* are now in front. Burnside's darkies relieved our div. Will Bedford has a recent letter from Elvira Molyneux giving the account of the drafted. *[Elvira Molyneux was Joel's cousin.]*

We are having dry warm weather. A shower or so visited us when upon the North Anna, 26th of May. None since. We have any amount of dust, and when troops are on the move it rises in such dense quantities that it can be seen for miles (but pack to move is the word again, so this must go back to my portfolio for the present).

*****

Wed. 22 June.   Water very scarce and poor. Our lines are advanced. Reb. drive the "Red Club" *[Army of the Potomac troops wore red badges sewn on their caps]* back in disorder. Our div. partly forced to fall back. Altogether a rough day. Gregory wounded. Our line is again advanced at Hd Qrs. Camp pine woods near yesterday. Odway shot accidently. Thueston wounded.

Letter #62B

[Written a day after the previous one, this letter continued on the same sheet of paper.]

Wednesday, June 22nd, *[1864]*
[In camp, four miles Southeast of Petersburg, Virginia]

We flanked around to the left of our line again yesterday, and are now some four miles left of Petersburg, or rather I should say south of it. And as near as I can tell a column of Johnnys were on the move at the same time to flank us, our advance has been skirmishing since late in the afternoon of yesterday quite briskly this morning.

I saw Sam Black last night. He had just been to the Ninth Corps. *[He]* Says Dan Fleming and Varguesson, also Ezra Rogers, are wounded but not dangerous -- that Ezra's is a flesh wound in the arm. This will be mailed this morning. I must now close. Hoping to hear from you all soon. Your brother, Jo

*****

Thu. 23 June. Remain in camp until quite late. Very hot! Then move Hd Qrs back to former position. Part of our corps brought back and build fortifications in the rear. Sharp firing when pickets relieved.

Fri. 24 June. Up early and breakfast. Div. back building rear breastworks. Heavy cannonading to the right, and some in our vicinity. John Farrel returns from hospital. Expecting momentarily to move. Has been very hot. Fifth Corps pass.

Sat. 25 June. Very quiet on the line and very hot early in the day. J. Pennington calls. Saw the 106th -- nearly all taken. The 22nd on guard. Row at sutlers. Ten at night picket firing and cannonading.

Sun. 26 June. Guarding ice house. Small show for showers. Wash shirt and drawers. Write to Martha Molyneux *[Samuel's sister]*.

Mon. 27 June. Day opens extremely hot. A slight shower in the afternoon. J. Pennington makes a call. Ride three mile to water a horse. Move Hd Qrs tents into the pines. Gen. Birney takes command of the div. again.

Tue. 28 June. Upon guard again. Mike Farrel makes a call. Fish pond. Dushore Union. Weather cooled by the shower. Seemingly nothing going on, only the occasional bam of a cannon.

Wed. 29 June. Very cool last night. Fighting off on the extreme left which proves to be Wilson's cavalry. Div. returning from a raid. Reported nearly all captured with their artillery and trains. Sixth Corps go to rescue. Noodle soup. *[A splotch on the paper had* "noodle soup" *written above it.]* False report, so said.

Thu. 30 June. Camped as usual. Ration of soft bread. Warm weather continued. Wrote to Jonathan Webster. Sent also a handkerchief to M. J. Black.

CHAPTER 24: JULY 1864

Fri. 1 July.   Camped as before. Dusty! Anyone can raise a dust now. Nothing important.

Sat. 2 July.   Very sultry, close and warm, shade our dwellings. A continued cannonading upon our right. Burnside Corps. Air full of report. Bob [Confederate] forts mined, etc. Tobacco, Sanita gifts, tomatoes, lemons.

Sun. 3 July.   Encamped as usual. The usual amount of firing, also. Warm weather continues. Appearances of rain. Dust in abundance. Conjectures of a ball tomorrow.

Mon. 4 July.   Another Fourth of July in Dixie. Firing increase and is kept up through the night, but the day is quiet as usual. Mike Farrel called a while. Gens. Mott and Crawford at Hd Qrs. Write letters, etc., thus passed the Fourth of 1864.

[Joel's comment "Another Fourth of July in Dixie" is not accurate for on July 4, 1863, he was at the Battle of Gettysburg in Pennsylvania.]

Letter #63

[The envelope and the top corner of this letter are missing, but its content shows it was written around July 4, 1864, to Elvira. His diary verifies he wrote letters that day.]

[Probably July 4, 1864]
[In camp near Petersburg, Virginia]

---- *[Paper torn. May have said, "My last letters to you"]* bear date of May 30th and June 19th possibly may have failed reaching you. We are having extremely warm days here now. The ground seems a pile of dust. Water is scarce and very poor quality, but *[I]* have enjoyed good health.

So far, those from our vicinity in our company that are left are usually well, except Wm. Bedford who has been troubled for some time with an ear ache. Henry B. is, I hear, well from his hurt, but not yet returned from hospital. Charles Webster died of his wounds the 21st of June at Alexandria, Va. Sam Black, Laws Bryan, and Fred Luke were taken prisoners the 22nd of June. George Pardoe, W. Snell, and D. Bryan are at home. I believe *[they are]* now mustered out of service. They are lucky boys, and hope they may always be as fortunate. I saw Joe Bedford a few days ago. I never had any acquaintance with him. Now, I will write a line or two of the war news and then the next will be something else.

Gen. Grant has not yet taken Richmond or Petersburg or the rebel army. Maybe he is going to wait until the Fourth of July, and make another Vicksburg affair out of it, but I do not think that he is situated so as to accomplish quite so much so soon.

—— *[paper torn]* paper I was trying to unfold for to write on the inside. It tore just as easy, and as my paper is not very plenty and not much time for rewriting, so I have sent it torn as it is and will apologize for doing so when I see you, if you wish.

The last letter I have rec'd was from Jennie M. -- written the eighth. I have the Dushore Union of the 23rd giving the *[names of those]* drafted of our County (JOB's turn this time and Thos. Pardoe). We have news too that King Glidewell and S. J. Bedford are married; all right if they are suited. I have not learned yet if Miss Lucy Bothwell has really married or not, but I suppose she has. I think she might have sent me some of her wedding cake, a nice box of cake and wedding dinner fixings would be so nice just now. That Tioga Sally I have not heard of since seeing you. Yes, I have too had a letter dated the 14th of Feb., but 'tis yet unanswered. *["Tioga Sally" was Miss Seddie Locke, teacher of Wellsboro, whom Joel frequently referred to in his diaries as "S.M.L.". Wellsboro was in Tioga County. His frequent correspondence with her, and their exchanging pictures may have been the cause of the friction between Joel and Elvira when he was home on furlough. This letter makes it clear he was discontinuing any romantic relationship.]*

I have not heard from Kate this summer, why I do not know. Poor Will N. *[Norton]* is dead, and now her other beau Mr. Taylor is killed. He belonged to the 58th P.V. *[Pennsylvania Volunteers]*. Do you ever get to hear from her? Kate had her odd ways, but for all I cannot help but think her better than many who make much greater pretense and show ——*[paper torn]* letter had been answered and this of course has to be all about something else, only I have just reread your last and do you remember what you said about "knowing how to keep house by the time the war is over"? Maybe I will keep that letter and then you cannot say, "Wait, wait until I'm 22 before I can leave Mama!!!"

I had a letter yesterday from cousin Angie Summers. She says that she had heard of you lately, and supposed I was familiar with the name. Oh, by the way, have you had the pleasure of a visit from D. B. since his return from Dixie? I'll guess he will say, "Elvira, did you get my letters? Did you ans.? etc., etc. Why not? etc., etc." But I'll not guess what you said or if you changed color; blushed any, you know. If you have paper room when you write, tell me how near I guessed.

I have not yet heard of George Pardoe getting home; stopped perhaps at Lewisburg visiting. I am so glad he is back safe or likely to be so. I wonder what lady will win his heart? He has written some to Angie Pratt, but she is old enough to be his aunt. (Do you know how old that is?) I used to think she thought so. Perhaps she was, but I thought some others were too. Was she a little mistaken or not? ----*[paper torn]* great many would come if they could get away. If they are seen deserting they are shot down then.

Part of the time I have been writing this and part of the time doing duty. And part, yes a big part, too, cooking for me. I have all sorts of dishes that can be made out of such as we have to make from. Now, 'tis dark, and I write by firelight so a line and this will be closed. I think Michael Farrel came to see me today -- one from our place of the Pa. reserves that reenlisted. He has lately been promoted to a sergt.

Well, Vilie, now where have you been today and have you had a good time? But I shall have to wait a few days for an ans. Perhaps your letter will come tomorrow -- the one I have been waiting for. This will reach you about the 12th perhaps, or maybe not till the 15th. Now, I must say good-bye and wish you good health and that you still except the love of your friend – Joel to Vilie.

*****

Tue. 5 July. Letters from home. Geo. Pardoe writes that his term *[at Lewisburg College]* has at last expired, and is once more at home and a citizen. Nothing worthy of special note today.

Wed. 6 July. Reports of Ewell and Breckenridge being at Martinsburg with a corps making a raid toward Pa. Some interest taken in regard to what they may accomplish.

Thu. 7 July. Upon guard. Alabama reported sunk by our gunboat Kearsarge upon the 19th of June. Continuous mortar and picket firing through the night tonight.

[During a 21-month global cruise, the Confederate ship, CSS Alabama, captured, burned, or sank 69 Union vessels worth almost $6 million. Union sloop, USS Kearsage, caught up with her off the coast of France, engaged, and sank her. That sea battle was one of the famous naval actions of the war. The sinking of the Alabama prompted the message sent by her flag officer, Samuel Barron: "It is true we have lost our ship, but we have lost no honor!" Most of the Alabama crew were captured by the USS Kearsage, although some were picked up by a British yacht, and thus escaped to England. The CSS Alabama had been built in Liverpool, England and launched as a Confederate ship July 29, 1862.]

Fri. 8 July. A heavy cannonading abruptly commenced lasting only a few minutes. Was over to the ambulance train forge.

Sat. 9 July. Relieved of taking care of horses at last. Am on police. Draw rations of cabbage, beans, sugar, coffee, salt and hard bread, pork, fresh beef, salt and soap, candles, and potatoes.

Sun. 10 July. On guard. Three Johnie Rebs came in during the night. Sixth Corps gone after the Pa. raiders. Some of ours take up their position, rebs thought us skedadling.

Mon. 11 July. Washed jacket, etc. Gen. Birney makes a diner. Maj. Gens. Burnside and Hancock present with some 1/2 dozen brigadiers *[brigadier generals]*. Orders to pack for moving.

Tue. 12 July. Move at day break a mile or more to the left and rear; then lay over for the day and night. Troops lay in the hot sun and dust. Tearing down breastworks. Rumor all sort see life.

Wed. 13 July. Move again this morning back to the right — opposite of Petersburg. Awful dust. Camp in burnt woods. Our corps, said to be detached from the army, are now carrying in reserve.

Thu. 14 July. Arrange our tents with shades. Hd Qrs drunk. Rebel raid still in progress. Brigade goes out on fatigue, destroying old reb. redouts. Contracting our lines.

Fri. 15 July. Our lines are strongly fortified. The troops are inactive during the hot weather, but still on the alert for any hasty movement. Gabions and facines are being made in large quantities and conveyed front.

[Gabions were large, cylindrical, wicker baskets with top ends open. When set upright they served to hide artillery pieces and screen defensive positions. They were filled with stones, earth, brush, or snow. They were several feet in diameter and five or six feet high.

[Fascines were bundles of sticks, tied together, probably 12 to 18 inches in diameter, and six or more feet long. Sometimes they were stood upright between the gabions to fill in the chinks. Or they were used to fill in ditches or make revetments for riverbanks. Fascines comes from the Latin, "fascina" which is also the root word of the Italian Fascist political party, The words gabion and fascine have almost disappeared from our English language. Sometimes, though, on our coins and emblems, we see pictures of fascines (bundles of sticks tied together to signify strength in unity).]

Sat. 16 July. The rebellion has now raged over three years and the end cannot be foreseen yet. O! The world of misery that has been endured and heaven only knows what is to come.

Sun. 17 July. 'Tis the Sabbath, but how few of us realize it and even very many know not the day from any of the rest. Will a just heaven grant success to our cause while we violate this sacred day?

Tue. 19 July. Rains today, two or three nice showers, which lays the dust nicely. On guard.

Wed. 20 July. Capt. Brayman takes the posish of provost marshall. Called out to suppress a riot or something else. Playing chequers *[checkers]*.

Letter #64A

Va., July 21st, 1864
[In camp, in front of Petersburg]

Dear Friend:

Yours of the third I rec'd the seventh. My last to you previous to this was written the fourth. I sincerely hope you still enjoy health and yourself. As for me, I am doing the best I can at both, which is full as good as I generally average.

Well, did you go to Hillsgrove upon the Fourth? I heard there was quite a nice time there. I, as you supposed, concluded not to go myself. Should not wonder if I had been at home, but we would have gone. I think you should have went if you had the opportunity. "All work and no play makes, etc., and etc." You know the old saying, and two sober people wouldn't ans. no how.

So, you think Geo. Pardoe's cousin very pretty. If you really thought it was true that I would fall deeply in love if I could but see her. Me thinks you make a very bad investment when you gave me yours; for my love would be a poor exchange if a pretty face would steal it from you. Now, Vilie, don't you wish you had yours back again?

You said that you would have me kill the mosquitoes if I were present at the oak tree when you was writing. We have plenty of them here, but they are very pious insects. I tell you they come together every favorable evening and they will sing over us and prey over us like good fellows!

We had a nice rain here the 19th which lay the dust and cooled the air also. Since I wrote before, our corps has changed position back to the front of Petersburg where we are in camp at present. We are in reserve, ready for to be moved to any point Gen. Grant send us. Nothing important has been done since writing before, pickets keep firing at each other and a few shells are sent over by both sides night and day. How long it will remain so is uncertain. Some think not very long.

I presume the rebel raid into Pa. scared some up there and perhaps pleased some, too. Our last news was that they had been driven back into Va., and then we heard they took another start for Pa. again, but I don't like them enough to write about them anymore this time. *[The Confederate raid Joel refers to was ordered by Confederate General Jubal A. Early, and led by McCausland.]*

I had a letter from Sallie the 16th -- the last I have had. I generally get your letter the next day after I write to you, so I will look for an ans. to my last tomorrow or next day. I am sorry if Lyb is disappointed in Corn. I never had any acquaintance with him, perhaps the attentions of Dr.---- *[space left blank by Joel. Randall ?]* displeased him.

I presume Joshua and Sallie A. harmonize still. You can give my best wishes to them, to him, you know he can forward her part on to her. I wonder if she will think that I send it first to you if he does? So, you sometimes wish you had taken the opportunity and gone to school with her? Vilie, if you have a chance for to attend a good school a term or so, I do not think you ever would regret that you had done so.

I see some good-natured, "look-pleased" boys today. A regt. the 20th Ind, three years out today, start for home tomorrow. Thirteen months more and if I, should live to see that come, may do the same. There are only about 80 left of the regt. -- some having reenlisted! Guess I will not reenlist, would you?

O! I am ever so much obliged for the paper and envelope, but 'tis not necessary to send, thinking I cannot get them here. We have a suttler store only four rods from our house with a plenty of sich things. I will not be afraid to say so if I need anything in that line. Night is near. The mail leaves soon, and this must close my short letter. I will write sooner upon account soon at least as I hear from your letter that is on the way. Good Bye, with much love to Vilie from Joel.

*****

Fri. 22 July. On guard. No a. *[no activity]*. Mott takes command of div. Birney goes to 10th Army Corps. Guns inspected by lt.

Letter #64B

July 22nd, *[1864]*
[In camp, in front of Petersburg, Virginia]

The mail went out sooner than I supposed last evening, so my letter does not leave till today. I am upon guard today and have but little time for anything else. I suppose you would laugh if you could see me walking back and forth in front of Maj. Gen. Birney's tent. Again, good bye. Yours truly, Joel.

*****

Sat. 23 July.   Washed pants today. Another inspection. Farrel goes to his regt.

Sun. 24 July.   Went to Ninth Corps, H. Arty. *[heavy artillery]* Visited Hank B. and others. Saw Petersburg reb's seven sisters and Petersburg Express. *[trains?]* 50th P.V., Capt. Brayman, inspects us.

Mon. 25 July.   On guard no. one. Stood two tricks. Ambulances on the move. Second Corps under orders for marching.

Tue. 26 July.   Still another inspection. Two guards punished for untidiness. Orders for to march at four. Start just before dark; cross the Appomattoc at Point of Rocks, 7 PM. Rest an hour at daybreak at Turkey Run on the James. Very tired.

Wed. 27 July.   Cross the James on pontoons. Gun boat, also a Monitor here. Rebs in vicinity. Form line of battle, advance. Barlow captures picket line and four 20 lbers. *[pounders]* Gun P. *[placements]* throw tea kettles, they send a few solid shot and retire. Grant, Sheridan, and Ingalls *[Generals Ulysses S. Grant, Philip Sheridan, and Rufus Ingalls]* pass by us.

Thu. 28 July.   Lay in camp during the night in rear of the rebel works along the road. Our men about face the road works, then get orders to move. March soon after dark.

Fri. 29 July.   Marched all night. Crossed the James and Appomattoc again and returned to the front of Petersburg. Arrived soon after daybreak. A hard march for the boys. Reb forts and ours. In night, witness an artillery duel.

Sat. 30 July.   Moved again last night nearer front. Are at 18th Corps. Reb. ft. blown up. Heavy cannonading all along the line. Burnside made an advance, but think nothing has been gained. Shells fly in every direction. Move back.

[In Joel's succinct statement, above, "Reb. Ft. blown up.", he is referring to an elaborate plan by the Union troops (48th Pennsylvania, from the coal mining area) to dig a 500-foot tunnel under the formidable fort at Petersburg, place four tons of black powder there, and blow a hole in the fort's defenses. (They used black powder, for dynamite was not invented until 1866, in Sweden, by Nobel.) The explosion created a crater 170 feet long, 30 feet deep, and 60 to 80 feet wide. Unfortunately, Union troops were unable to take advantage of the situation and the assault turned into a debacle. In the three hours of fighting

over 4,000 Federal troops were killed or wounded, out of the 20,000 engaged. Confederate losses were 1,500 out of 11,000 engaged.

[On July 30, 1864, 2,600 Confederate troopers moved north on a foray and captured the city of Chambersburg, Pennsylvania. They gave an ultimatum to be met in three and one half hours, "Give us $100,000 in gold or $500,000 in greenbacks or we'll burn your city." The city fathers couldn't raise the total amount of ransom money so the Confederates took what money that had been raised, then looted, and burned 266 houses and other buildings worth about $1.6 million. The attack was in retaliation for Union troops burning the towns of Staunton and Lexington, in the Shenandoah Valley of Virginia. Colonel William Peters of the 21st Virginia Cavalry was ordered to set fire to the town, but refused. Peters was temporarily arrested for disobeying, and other officers were ordered to burn the town. This "city-burning" was a prelude to what was to happen later to Atlanta, and various towns and cities in Georgia, South Carolina, and North Carolina.]

Letter #65A

July 30th, 1864
Near Petersburg, Va.

Ever Dear Friend:

Yours of July third was rec'd the seventh and ans'd the 19th, and your last of July 25th came yesterday, and this morning finds me penciling an ans. to you. Upon these hints you sent me for a longer letter. Well, Vile, if I comply with your request, and if it should not all prove interesting, you must be willing for to pardon my failing to make it so. And mark it down as being too large an undertaking for so little a boy and you must also pardon a considerable of war news and for my using a pencil, and maybe shall not finish either today.

Let me see! Today is Saturday. Last Sunday the 25th, when you were writing to me, I was to the heavy artillery regt. visiting, but I found only four of the 14 that left Elkland and Forks a few months since. These were Henry Black and Henry Baldwin, James Norton, and Henry Hunsinger. They were well then, and camped a mile and a half from us.

Upon the 26th, we rec'd orders for marching, and packed up and started just before night. We crossed the Appomattox River at Point of Rocks; then proceeded to the James River and crossed it at Jones Neck on pontoon bridges just by daybreak. Here lay the gunboat "Hunchback" and a large monitor. The rebs had been making advances upon our forces there, so our corps was sent there to drive them back. We found them a half mile from the river and fortifying themselves. Our corps made an advance upon them, captured four large guns and two or three hundred prisoners. We lay there that night and next day. Then, in the night our corps marched back to our old position, or nearly, in front of Petersburg. I do not know the exact distance, but should think much as twelve mile. We were some tired, you may guess, when we got back, as well as sleepy.

Last night we packed up again and moved out to the front as an attack was to be made in the morning (this morning). A few shells in the night, by way of compliments to us, came screeching over us from the rebel fort "Clifton" across the Appomattox. Our Hd Qrs are close by that of the 18th Army Corps. We breakfasted early and anxiously awaited the "ball" to open. It commenced on our left, in front of the Fifth Corps by our men blowing up two forts our fellows had undermined. This was the signal for us to commence here in front of Petersburg and ever since it has been the "Rockets red glare and bombs bursting in air", etc., etc.

We are in a good position for seeing what is going on in front of us. I can see a part of Petersburg at a distance of less than two mile. It lies on the banks of the river, mostly on this side or the right bank, I believe. The city has been on fire already a time or two from our shells. Some two mile below the town and nearer than that to us, but upon the other side of the river is the rebel fort Clifton and in plain view as many *[as]* 1/2 dozen more of their forts are in sight. I just saw the dust raise from a 200 pound shell dropped into Clifton by our men. The mortar that threw it was near three mile from the fort.

*****

Letter #65B

Afternoon of July 30, *[1864]*
[At siege of Petersburg, Virginia]

At this time the cannonading has nearly ceased. What has been effected by the bombardment thus far I have not learned. We could hear quite heavy fighting upon our extreme left, and a report came in that we had driven the enemy five mile, but do not know as to its truth. 'Tis very warm now and this is likely why we remain quiet. Without doubt toward night it will be recommenced. Yes, they are starting up now and quite brisk. I can hardly count the different reports of the artillery.

Gen. Mott *[Major General Gershom Mott]* has the command of our div now. Gen. Birney has been placed in command of the 10th Army Corps. Now I will close this for the present and write upon the other sheet about something else if I can think of anything.

*****

Sun. 31 July. Came last evening to our old camp before going over the James. Wash up and get rested. Upon guard. Soldiers tied up for firing off their guns.

Letter #65C

July 31st *[1864]*
[At siege of Petersburg, Virginia]

Well V, I find one sheet is filled full, if it ain't so smart, and maybe shall have the same luck with this.

So, you and Lizzie have been playing "staying up with a fellow". I suppose beaux are rather scarce now. Lizzie's never had a very large string of them either for a good girl. We generally have been upon good terms with each other and think her quite trust worthy; but when you say her brother Will never thinks otherwise than friendship, there is more room to be mistaken. At least I do not know why he should not. He is able and quite willing to support a woman of his own. Perhaps he may not in regard to you think of aught else than friendship. 'Tis most likely he does, at least he is a respectable honest fellow, and you will go with such whenever you see fit.

I hope you may have a pleasant visit. So Birt is playing the agreeable to Miss Minnie V. I could not say about his being good enough, at least he is smart enough.

*****

Letter #65D

July 31st, *[1864]*
[At siege of Petersburg, Virginia]

The firing last evening did not last long, and everything remained quiet. The result of yesterday's fighting now appears to be one rebel fort of 16 guns and 300 men blown up. Two lines of fortifications taken, but one was again retaken. Our men lost a good many. We are now encamped as we were before any movement over James River. We have orders for moving again at eight o'clock this afternoon. J.L.M.

*****

CHAPTER 25: AUGUST 1864

Mon. 1 Aug. Another month put in. Discouraging news from all parts. Write letters. Play chequers, and listen to rumors.

Letter #65E

August 1st, *[1864]*
[At siege of Petersburg, Virginia]

With my letter still unfinished you will soon be of the opinion that this is as funny a letter as Ike's, if I do not get it done soon. I think that he has written three letters in all since being down here. It is hard for him to write letters.

I had a letter from Kate a few days since. She is living near Hughesville. She spoke of Will N.'s death and I think she has felt badly about it. She thinks her friends, upon your side of the mountain, have forgotten her. I am sorry for JOB *[Joel's brother-in-law]* if he has to come down here against his will, and of course he don't want to. Some girl will feel bad upon his account and she will be not alone. *[The "girl to feel bad" was JOB's wife, Lydia. Jonas and Lydia had ten children at the time he entered the army.]*

Torment the flies! I wish you could but see how thick they are down here. They keep a person busy brushing them off his head and face. I think them equal to mosquitoes. It would be handy to have someone to mind them away. So, I'll wish I was away from them and was *[home]* so this letter did not need to be written.

I think 'tis likely you will be bothered some in reading all this pencil letter. Let me know in your next if you could make it all out. If you cannot, lay it by until I am there and I will help to, but I *[have]* some doubt if we should care anything about old letters for a while at least. For I should want to hear those funny stories you dare not write. Won't you write just one? You say you can confide in me?

O! V., if this should reach you before you see Lizzie, I was going to tell her that I received the word sent me by way of D.B., but that would be "telling tales out of school". So, it is as you see best or not. Lizzie used to say there was, she thought, no such thing as abiding affection. Do you think there is any danger of her getting you *[to be]* of the same opinion? If there is, I shall be afraid to have you confidential with her. But I shall sooner think her mind has changed from what report says of certain letters that pass between her and a certain cousin of mine. Anyhow, I think he could quite easily persuade her out of that belief. Does she ever speak of him? But I must say good-bye to Lizzie for this time and soon to you also for the present.

If it was August first, 1865, instead of '64, I should soon think of seeing you and visiting as we pleased. But if another year rolls as safely by then, O! then the world will go well with us, then. I have not told you that I am well, as I remember, but am glad I can, with the exception of a slight cold. And I hope you may, upon the receipt of this, be in the enjoyment of perfect health. Now, Vilie, good-bye. Except much love from your ever true friend. Joel to Vilie. Address: Hd Qrs, Third Div., Second Army Corps.

*****

Tue. 2 Aug.   Wars and rumors of wars. Who says Sherman is licked? Still encamped the same.

Wed. 3 Aug.   Upon guard at No. 1st and paymaster troops are being paid off.

Thu. 4 Aug.   Visited at the regt. and 84th. Saw Dave B. and Geo. Newman Vohle. Our sutler up with goods. Took dinner with Will Bedford and J. Rennington.

Fri. 5 Aug.   Michael Farrel and Johnny called today. Visited and took dinner. Went with as far as regt. Heard Black, Chet King, A. Baldwin, and W. Beyles were dead.

Letter #66

Camp near Petersburg, Va.
Aug. 5th, 1864

My Dear Sister: *[Identity of the sister unknown, but likely Angie or Sallie. Joel had six sisters: Mary, Lydia, Margaret, Esther Ellen, Ann, and Sarah (Sallie), plus cousin, Angie. His five living brothers were: John, James, George, David, and Jesse. This letter had many paper holes, making it difficult to read.]*

Once more I find myself penning to you a few lines. Your last was rec'd the 16th. I did not intend to have delayed so long, but time passes, "waiting for no man". I have my usual good health, excepting a cold taken *[during]* our last expedition. I saw James and the rest of our camp yesterday; found them all well.

From the papers you will have seen that our army has been moving and fighting ----*[paper torn]*. *[Our]* Corps made a reconnaissance over the river ----*[paper torn]* the 27th, had ----*[paper torn]* fight and a hard ----*[paper torn]* four guns, a few prisoners and then came back to Petersburg again. And *[on]* Saturday the 30th an assault was made to take the rebel work and the town, but failed. It was begun by blowing up a rebel fort in front of Burnside's Corps. His men was then charged through and carried two lines of their works, but could not, at least they did not, hold them. Our side lost, 'tis said, 3,000. I do not know where the blame rests for the failure.

The cannonading that day was awful. Our Hd Qrs was situated so we had quite a good view of Petersburg and the line in front of the 18th Army Corps and a number of rebel forts, but was not so as to determine anything that transpired in front of Burnside's, but could hear the musketry, the fort as it went up, etc. We are encamped now as we were before going over the James.

The troops are getting paid off, four months pay, $58. Our regt. has not been paid yet, but *[is]* to be in a day or so. *[Joel's pay, as a private, was four months for $58.00 (probably $13, plus three months at $15). In February 1864 pay had been $13 per month. The following October, a private was receiving $15.00 per month. In February 1865, Union privates received $16.00 per month. Confederate privates had somewhat lower pay levels, but their paper money, particularly toward the end of the war, was devalued.]*

I had a letter from Eliza *[probably Eliza Snell, mentioned below]* since her visit with you, and one from Mary mailed the eighth. Mary begins to write quite a good letter, and as every letter speaks very favorable of the new minister, 'tis to be hoped that he is the right kind of a man. That circuit has had too many of the ——*[paper torn]*.

From what I hear, JOB is bound for Dixie. The others near you, I believe, are given clear *[discharged from the service]*.

In about another year, if I should live so long, I will be about clear too. Geo. Pardoe writes that it agrees with him to be a citizen. He will be apt to marry early, won't he think? I was talking to James about what you spoke. I think he had made up his mind to something of the kind before. I guess he will express to George.

Eliza Snell *[cousin]* says that she can get the likeness. She thinks —— *[paper torn]* has not killed anyone, has he? But, from the stories I hear, the women will club together after while and ——*[paper torn]*.

Yesterday, the president appointed ——*[paper torn]*. Our ration meat was *[a]* cod fish apiece. The Sanitary Commission has been issuing considerable to us lately – such as canned tomatoes, pickled onions and raw ones, potatoes, and turnips. They help to make up quite good fare.

Afternoon: Mike Farrel was here for dinner. His regt. is 1 1/2 miles of us. He is well. I went back with him as far as our regt. James is not very well today. Our suttler has just come up with a stock of goods. This is perhaps the reason he told me his folks wrote to him that Lem Black was dead. Some of the boys said they hear also that Chet King, Henry Baldwin, Dan Vargueson, and Will Boyles (Charles' son) were all dead. I do not know how they heard or if it be true.

I was at the regt. Jones belonged to, a week ago last Sunday. Baldwin, Hank Black, Jim Norton, and Aaron Hunsinger were there and well then. I suppose they were in this last fight. We have not yet come across the 58th regt., the one Geo. Glidewell and those others are in. I do not know for certain what corps it is in, some say the 18th, and some the 10th. Gen. Birney has now command of the 10th Corps. Gen. North commands our div. Our regt. is in the Second Brigade, and our col. *[Madill]* commands it now, and I must either look up another piece of paper or close. Guess I'll find a small piece.

*****

Sat. 6 Aug. Fighting yesterday on the right. One of our forts said to have been blowed up. Rebs charge and badly repulsed. Lieut. V. to Lieut. Gerrald.

Sun. 7 Aug. Will Bedford called with Thomas Warburton of the 36 Wis. Walked over with them to his regt. in the Second Div., First Brig., Second. Also went to the 187th to see James Warburton, First Div., Fifth Corps.

Mon. 8 Aug. Thomas and James Warburton called. Stayed till after dinner. Was to corps Hd Qrs with turned in animals *[probably horses and mules]*.

Tue. 9 Aug. Upon guard today. About ten o'clock an awful explosion was heard. Have since proved an ammunition boat at City Pt. A large number of lives lost.

Fri. 12 Aug. Orders for moving. Upon the road by three o'clock toward City Pt. Very hot. Men fall out fast and many men struck *[sun stroke]*. Reach City Pt soon after dark.

Sat. 13 Aug. Our corps all came up during the night. We lay in the sun all day and just at dark go aboard the transport John A. Warner. Great conjectures as to where we are agoing. At ten o'clock we start up the James. Band plays and *[we]* go to sleep.

Sun. 14 Aug. At midnight, or thereabouts, we were awakened. The vessel had made landing at Deep Bottom, near the pontoon bridge. Div. does not get ashore till after daylight. "reb dispatches." Boat ride, etc. Camp near our posish of July 27th. Rain. Saw Gen. Grant today.

Mon. 15 Aug.   Hd Qrs out of humor. Gen. Hancock and Maj. Hancock. Rebs occupy their old line. We move up and mass in their front, concealed, firing and fighting at intervals. Gunboats shell the rebs. Reb. capt. taken. Some stray "potash kettle".

Tues. 16 Aug.   Camped in view of the enemy's lines. Second Brigade charged on their works last night, also this morning. A reb. gen. killed (Chalimass). Col. Craig of the 105th P.V. killed. Our co.: one killed, one wounded, one missing.

Letter #67A

Deep Bottom, *[Virginia]*
Aug. 16, 1864

Dear Brother: *[David]*

I shall today try and ans. your letter rec'd a week ago, which was gladly opened and read. I still have good health. The rest, from that vicinity of whom you are acquainted, are well also. I rec'd a letter from Jesse and one from Dr. Bird today, stating that Theodore was home on furlough, etc. I have not heard anything very straight from his regt. very late. Mike Farrel I saw the fifth of this month.

We are now upon expedition across the James. We started from the front of Petersburg the 12th, marched to City Point, and went aboard some transports in the afternoon of the 13th, and were taken to Deep Bottom some ten mile up the James from that place, and by soon after day light we were ashore upon the opposite or northern side of the river. The expedition consists of our corps (the Second) and the Tenth, both under the command of Maj. Gen. Hancock and quite a heavy force of cavalry. (While I write a dead rebel, brigadier gen., is being taken past in an ambulance -- killed this morning.)

We landed at the same place we crossed the 26th of last month, and made the point. Before attacking Petersburg, we found the rebs nearly as we left them, excepting the picket lines, but little was done the day we landed or yesterday, besides getting into position.

Several gunboats are in the river along by us, and are at work whenever they can sight the enemy. Our div. has been lying massed in the woods in close artillery range of the rebs' earthworks -- unbeknown to them, I suppose, as no fires are allowed, and the boys kept out of sight.

Gen. Birney has now command of the Tenth Corps. He formerly commanded our div., 'til within a few weeks. He is upon our right and today there has been quite heavy firing in that direction. I have just heard he had captured a line of their works with 200 prisoners. The dead gen. reb., Sumner I think his name, is the one I mentioned as being carried past. I suppose *[he]* came from that part of the line.

I hope this move may prove a success. I do not know as I shall have a chance to mail this today or for several days. If not, perhaps I can report further progress of operations before sending this to you. Our regt. has not been paid since leaving Culpepper in the spring, nearly six months is now due us. Part of our div. has been paid lately.

Did you get the thirty dollars *[I]* sent up by Ellis Bryan about the middle of March? Also $20.00, twenty, more that I expressed the middle of April to Isaac Rogers, your account? But it would not make much difference with my few pounds, but taking the whole together would sum up a few dollars. That U.S. bond, I think, is exchangeable for six percent gold bearing interest bonds from what I see in the different papers. You can find out and do as you think best.

*****

Letter #67B

[Continuation of August 16 letter to David.]

Afternoon, August 16, *[1864]*
[Deep Bottom, Virginia, at siege of Petersburg]

Instead of Sumner, the reb. gen.'s name is Chaulmness, or some such thing. *[Army records show C.S.A. Brigadier General John Randolph Chambliss, Jr., was killed August 16, 1864, at Deep Bottom. General Chambliss was in the 1853 class at West Point — the same class as U.S. Major General Sheridan and four star Confederate General Hood.]*

There has been considerable fighting on different parts of the line today. Our brigade, the Second, as our regt. has been transferred to that lately, is upon the right of the line and not massed here with the rest of the div., as I had thought. Then the Tenth Corps, then our other two brigades on the left next to the river.

Col. Craig of the 105th P.V. had command of our brigade. He was killed in a charge made today. Also Gen. Gregg was killed today, commander of one of our cavalry div. Our brigade has charged twice and the loss is considerable, but they drove the enemy and hold their ground. I have not heard anything from our regt.

A charge is intended to be made this evening here on the left. Quite heavy firing is going on in the direction of Petersburg, but suppose it is a diversion in favor of our movements here. Fort Darling is said to be less than five mile of this point.

The weather is quite warm, but showers visit us occasionally which keep down the dust. Two of our Sullivan boys that were slightly wounded at the Wilderness *[Battle]* returned to the co. just before crossing the river: D. Sperry and Peter Miller, *[and]* H. Bedford had not reported, but 'tis getting dusk and I must close for this evening.

*****

Wed. 17 Aug. The Jonnys came with a flag truce to get the gen.'s body. Some prisoners taken say that they were conscripted at church last Sunday. Heavy cannonading last night toward Petersburg. Midnight rations.

Letter #67C

August 17, *[1864]*
[At siege of Petersburg, Virginia]

The mail goes out this morning and this with it. Nothing of importance has transpired since last evening. Give my love to all at home. Write soon – Good-bye, Joel. Address: Hd Qrs., Third Div., Second Army Corps, Washington, D.C.

*****

Thu. 18 Aug. Visited the regt. Sergt. Sinclair is gone. Saw D. Brian. Rebs charge nearly the whole line in the evening. They get repulsed. Our div. pack up and recross the James and night march it back to the left of Petersburg.

Fri. 19 Aug. Learn the Fifth Corps have taken the Weldon RR and hold it. Our div. take their old posish in front near the Norfolk and P. RR. A dirty camp and rainy afternoon.

Sat. 20 Aug. A full police day at Hd Qrs. Bishop Horton calls as he returns to his co. from convalescent and French F. *[French furlough]* Suttler up. Shelled smartley last night. Two hundred rebs went by *[probably Confederate prisoners]*.

Sun. 21 Aug. Upon guard. Inspection. Shells sent freely by the rebs last night and several previous ones. Fine day. Rebs try to retake the railroad. See three hundred prisoners go by, and 'tis reported we have taken 1,500.

Mon. 22 Aug. Reb deserters report their case as being nearly hopeless. Picket line. Doz. messengers.

Tue. 23 Aug. When musing on companions gone,
We doubly feel ourselves alone.

Wed. 24 Aug. Upon guard today over the prisoners. Mortar shelling in the evening. Fine sight -- 1/2 dozen at a time in the air.

Thu. 25 Aug. Cavalry fighting on our left. They get driven back. Also, two div. of our corps lose five pieces of artillery. Fifth Corps still hold the Weldon RR. Guards taken out to reinforce.

Fri. 26 Aug. Police day *[Clean up day]* Went with some convalescents to Third Brigade. Was given two new overcoats. Hancock reports our loss yesterday at 1,200, and that the enemy lost much greater.

Sat. 27 Aug Two years today since I was mustered into the U.S. Service. Great changes have taken place since then. What the coming year may disclose we can only hope and trust. A fine view of mortar shelling.

Sun. 28 Aug. Upon Friday night a Fifth Corps suttler shot one of our soldiers, of the 73rd N.Y., that had been trying to make a raid on his tent. Sharp skirmishing on the right.

Letter #68

Hd Qrs., Third Div., Second Corps
Aug 28, 1864
[South of Petersburg, Virginia]

My True Friend, Vilie:

This Sabbath morning I seat myself down to ans. your last two letters of Aug. fourth and 20th, and I see by turning to my diary that my last to you was August first. I hardly know how to apologize for this long delay. True, much of the time we have been quite busy tramping from one place to another.

Upon the 12th, our corps went upon an expedition over the James River and did not get back for a week. You saw the account of that by the papers. We had a fine ride up the river upon a transport, but as it was in the night we did not see as much as if it had been day.

While we were away, the Fifth Corps took possession of the Weston Railroad, and on the 25th *[of August]* the rebels attempted to drive our men off the road. *[Above railroad was probably the Weldon RR.]* Our div. was not engaged, the other two had a severe engagement, and their loss is estimated at 1,200, but the rebs did not get the road back besides losing a much larger number than our men. If you have a map, and wish to know where our camp is, and if you can find the Petersburg and Norfolk RR, then just upon the south side of the road and two mile of Petersburg is where I am scribbling this letter.

My health since writing before has been good. The other boys of your acquaintance are well as far as I know. I saw Gen. Grant and Mede [*Major General George G. Meade, class of 1835 at West Point, and commander of the Union army at Gettysburg*] yesterday, and last night we had a splendid view of mortar shelling. Both sides threw shells for three hours along the line from here to James River. Sometimes 1/2 dozen would be in the air at one time, but one could not help but shudder to think what desolation perhaps they were causing. Fortunately, none were thrown near where I was, or perhaps I would not of thought they looked so nice.

O! Do you think yesterday finished my two years, so now every day helps to wear off the last year? I cannot help but think of the many changes over those two eventful years have made, and what the next may bring. But we can only hope and trust for the best.

So, you have visited Millview? I had a letter from Phidie yesterday stating that you had been there. She and I have always been good friends, but you must not tell her anything that you not would care for others to know. I really do not think Kate intentionally meant the harm that was caused by her imprudence. I should hope not at least. She did not consider far enough ahead I think is where she failed.

So, you have a chance for to visit Canada if your uncle meant it, and you can possibly. Of course, I should go if in your place, and you say, "What if I never come back?" If you did not, I presume it would be upon account of — well because you did not want to and of course I should not come after you, only when I came home perhaps I should be appraised of being drafted again, and go there just to get clear of that, you know.

I feel sorry for JOB. I do not think that he will like soldiering. When you know his address you must send it to me. The next draft takes place the fifth of Sept., about the time this will reach you. I suppose that will catch up some poor fellows.

Then, you think you are getting schooled in saying the "Good bye." For my part, I prefer the "How do you do." But good byes will necessarily come, and 'Tis best to receive them as best we can. Already I discover one awaiting me at the close of this page. I will try and write soon again as I shall not be able to make this a very long one.

Now, dearest friend, good bye. My sincerest wish is for you, that health and happiness may be yours. Affectionately, Joel to Vilie.

*****

Mon. 29 Aug. Police day. Was out fixing up house for court martial. Raided: sieve, flower pot, etc. Mortar shelling continued.

Tue. 30 Aug. Upon guard. Ulysses Grant and his two sons ride by.

Wed. 31 Aug. Went to court martial with two prisoners, Fulton and Hannin. Fort Morgan ours.

[Fort Morgan, in Alabama's Mobile Bay, was one of the best fortified points in the Confederacy. At the time of its capture, the fort was commanded by highly regarded Confederate Brigadier General Richard L. Page. He was taken prisoner, and was not released until September 1865. He had originally lived in Norfolk, Virginia, and spent his later years there, part of the time as superintendent of the city's public schools.]

CHAPTER 26: SEPTEMBER 1864

Thu. 1 Sept.   Brisk cannonading on our right; cause not known. Wash day. Pleasant day and first day of fall or autumn months.

Fri. 2 Sept.   Battery man shot to death with musketry at nine o'clock for deserting to the enemy. *[He]* belonged to the First Div., Second Army Corps. Citizen from Smithfield here.

[On September 2, 1864, the city of Knoxville, Tennessee, was captured and occupied by troops under Union General Ambrose E. Burnside. Eastern Tennessee had strong Union loyalties; so the capture of Knoxville was pleasing to President Lincoln.]

Sat. 3 Sept.   The Johnnies report Atlanta taken by Sherman. *[Union Major General William Tecumseh Sherman was sixth in his 1840 class at the Academy.]* Four and five *[Confederate deserters]* come in every night.

Sun. 4 Sept.   J. Howe returns to duty. Visited regt. Draw clothing: one pr. pants, one pr. drawers. Atlanta officially announced as taken.

Mon. 5 Sept.   Midnight: Last night our artillery opened a heavy fire along the whole line on account of the fall of Atlanta. Johnnies return compliments. *[Confederate artillery guns return the fire.]* Great cheering Johnies.

Tue. 6 Sept.   The railroad from City Pt. Road to the Weldon was commenced on Sunday in this vicinity. Tonight a train passed over the road. A bridge here 40 rods long, 14 ft. high at this point -- (Norfolk RR).

Wed. 7 Sept.   Very cool weather, especially the night. Jas. Fulton and E. Hamins sent to government works for selling whiskey. *[See entry August 31, 1864.]* Jas. Pardoe called. Turned in a Springfield rifle. *[In the Union army whiskey was called "tangle foot" or "oil of gladness".]*

[The "Springfield rifle" was the principal rifle of both armies. More than 1 1/2 million were manufactured. The Springfield armory, at Springfield, Massachusetts, was able to produce about 250,000 rifles per year.]

Thu. 8 Sept.   Reports of the capture of Mobile. The news is favorable from all quarters. Four and five deserters come in every night.

Fri. 9 Sept.   Wm. Bedford called in the morning. Packed overcoat in knapsack wagon. Went down to regt. Shell came quite close. The weather pleasant. Four Johns *[came in]* last night.

Sat. 10 Sept.   Picket line advanced in front of Ft. Stephens. Captured over one hundred prisoners. *[We]* Lost one col., one lt. wounded, and toward daylight the Johns returned the favor by taking 30 or more of our pickets. Artillery!

Sun. 11 Sept.   Our and reb pickets keep a continued sharpshooting now, day and night. Looking for to move Hd Qrs. Nights getting to be chilly. Construction Corps going away.

Mon. 12 Sept.   Contributer to the Phil. Inq. *[newspaper, Philadelphia Inquirer]* looking for facts respecting our Friday night affair. Gen. Mott and Staff move to the new qrs. Jerry Rilter. Police whiskey ration missing.

[The "Friday night affair" was probably execution of the First Division battery man for desertion that took place on Friday, September 2, 1864.]

Tue. 13 Sept.   Guard moves to new camp. Busy building tents and working about Hd Qrs. Continued sharpshooting. Minnies *[rifle bullets]* drop in about us frequently during the night. Tenth Corps Hd.

Wed. 14 Sept.   The new RR was completed last Sunday to the W. RR. It was commenced and done in 11 days. Rebs shell the ensign daily.

[See entry August 19, 1864. The Weldon Railroad, connecting Petersburg with the South, was a main supply route for the Petersburg fortress. Twenty miles of it, though, from Petersburg south, had been disrupted by Union forces, and the Confederates had been forced to "wagon" their supplies for that distance.]

Thu. 15 Sept.   Continual sharpshooting. Our pickets fire 100 rounds daily. One hundred fifty recruits for the Sixth New Jersey. Rumors of rebels on our flank.

<u>Letter #69A</u>

Hd Qrs, Third Div, Second Corps
Sept. 15th, 1864
[At the siege of Petersburg, Virginia]

My Dear Friend:

Yours of Aug. 21st was rec'd the 25th and ans. the 29th. I have again the privilege of making you a paper visit, and shall endeavor to be as agreeable as I can make. I suppose that if I do the best I can, you will pardon the failure. There is not anything important transpiring at present to tell.

Our div. captured one hundred prisoners on Friday night last, by advancing our picket ----*[paper torn]* a short distance; the rebs in turn captured 30 more of our men soon after. Since that ----*[paper torn]* and ours have not been as good friends as before. Previous to this they often met between the lines to trade papers, tobacco for coffee, etc. Now, they shoot each other every chance they get. Hardly a day passes without someone getting hit by their sharpshooters. Our camp, or rather Hd Qrs, is 3/4 of a mile away from the reb line so you see we are not so much exposed to danger as many others are. Only now and then a stray ball or shell visits us.

A new railroad has now been built running close to our camp. If you have a map of Virginia you can tell near where it is and where we are referring to. The new RR commences at the City Point RR leading to Petersburg, one mile from that place running south; crossing the Norfolk and Petersburg RR two miles from the town and just by where we are at present and thence on in the same direction to the Weldon RR. The distance is some ten miles or a trifle over. It was commenced the first of the month and finished in ten days.

Vilie, I have not reenlisted yet, and I guess we will not have the chance to do so, and if they should give us that privilege you need have no fear of my turning Vett, for three years in the service is enough for me at one time. One month of the last year has already nearly passed by. I trust the war will end up this winter. Sometimes I think it will, but we cannot tell. Certainly, with the fall of Atlanta and to all likeliness also Mobile, with a number of their officers ----*[paper torn]* now the report of Gen. Har ----*[paper torn. It may have been Confederate Major General Hardee.]* and Moseby too as being killed, we can at least hope for the best and that our skies may soon be clear and bright as ever over our once happy land.

[In the above paragraph Joel repeated a rumor that Mosby had been killed. Captain John Singleton Mosby was not killed. Mosby was one of the South's most colorful, and successful, cavalry officers. Twenty-eight years old, he and his Rangers, performed the stunt of capturing a Union general. A Union colonel had made a statement that "Mosby was nothing but a horse thief." Mosby heard that the colonel was staying in the town of Fairfax Court House, Virginia and devised a plan to capture him. With a small cavalry unit of 29 men, they stealthily moved into the town but instead of capturing the name-calling colonel, caught General Edwin H. Stoughton, two other officers, 30 men, and 58 horses. They performed that daring feat without firing a shot.

[Shelby Foote, noted Civil War historian, amusingly describes the Fairfax incident in <u>The Civil War</u>: "Mosby ... entered the general's headquarters, stole upstairs in the darkness and found the general asleep in bed. Turning down the covers, he lifted the tail of the sleeper's nightshirt and gave him a spank on the behind. "General," he said, "did you ever hear of Mosby?" "Yes", Stoughton replied, flustered and half awake; "have you caught him?" "He has caught

you," Mosby said! The above incident took place two years earlier, in March 1863, and thereby established Mosby's reputation."

[When General Lee surrendered the Army of Northern Virginia at Appomattox Court House, in April of 1865, Colonel John Singleton Mosby and his famous Rangers (43rd Battalion of Virginia Cavalry) did not surrender. Instead, they disbanded. Colonel John Mosby was not pardoned until 1866. After the war, he became prominent in politics and ably served his country for many years. He became the United States Consul in Hong Kong and was assistant attorney in the U.S. Department of Justice.]

I do wonder what for letter I am writing this time. I shall not dare look over it for fear it would not pass and I should burn it and you not get a letter at all. Sallie wrote to me the second of Sept. stating JOB *[Jonas O. Bedford]* had a hard time getting started and thought perhaps he would get a situation in some hospital in Phila. I hope he will succeed. *[Later, 43-year-old Jonas did become a hospital orderly.]* The draft has been postponed, I hear, for a few days, until today the 15th, *[if]* I heard correctly.

Some boys from my regt. have just made a call, so your letter has lain aside to chat awhile with them. They tell me one of our regt. has been killed and one wounded by the rebs since Friday. Jas. Pardoe is well. He is the only one you are acquainted with, I believe, unless it be you know me, do you?

I hear your cousin, Lydia, is intending upon going to school during the winter at Muncy, I think I heard it was, and also that of attending the Institute in the Fall at Millview. She, perhaps, intends upon teaching. I will wish her success. I shall most certainly ---*[paper torn]* for to be assistant superintendent or school director or something of that style when you and her both get to teaching.

I suppose Dr. Randal's praises are yet sung by them and maybe you received warning to be very careful of certain ---*[paper torn]*.

*****

Fri. 16 Sept   Butler is said to have the James River. *[General Benjamin Butler was considered one of the poorest Union generals.]* Canal done. No unusual occurrences. Dutch Gap.

[Dutch Gap was a canal dug by Union troops and manual laborers. The James River made a long loop, and much of the loop was under control of Confederate artillery. Thus, Union boats could not go up the river. Dutch Gap cut across 174 yards of land and involved a lot of earth moving for it went through a hill. It connected two parts of the river and saved transversing five miles of Confederate-dominated territory. The canal was not used during the war, but was used thereafter for commercial traffic.]

Letter #69B

Sept. 16, *[1864]*
[At siege of Petersburg, Virginia]
[In camp near railroad]

Your letter still not finished. I was interrupted in my writing so often that it grew dark and *[the letter]* had to be lain aside. And what do you think I received last night? 'Twas something that pleased me very much and was nothing less than your letter of the 11th. I was really glad ----*[paper torn]* I know how it makes us imagine many ----*[paper torn]* of the suspense caused by not receiving letters when we expect to get them. If you had scolded just a little, I would not have blamed you.

But, I thought I did not have any chance to write. But I think a short one might have been wrote. Forgive me, Vilie, if the neglect caused you uneasiness. I shall endeavor to not let so much time pass again without hearing something from me. I shall be happy to get a photograph when you have them taken. I think I will get an album to keep photos in. Don't you think them rather nice? At least a nice one with nice pictures in.

You spoke of the likeliness of Jennie M. and Geo. Luke being married soon. I have not heard of his getting home yet. The probabilities are that they may get married I think. My acquaintance with him is limited, but I know nothing to the disadvantage of him. Go, or not to go to Hillsgrove with D.B. you ask. You must suit yourself, Vilie. Do as you would be done by. You understand the case better than I, and the likeliness of being any remarks made that would be *[deemed]* unpleasant by others.

I hope you will succeed in attending the institute. You would enjoy it much, I think, and have an excellent opportunity for improvement. I will not be there this time to cause you to be ----*[paper torn]* attend. Did you know that I was very much disappointed that you did not attend the other?

I have read and reread your letter, but as it lays beside me as I write I discovered four little words I had not noticed before, as they were underlined, do you remember them? "Much love to you!" How we love to be told of this by those we much love, one would think that after being fully assured of the fact that our affections were returned or rather reciprocal, (is that too big a word?) we could easily remember so important an event. I think love lives upon love and actions and little deeds that express it. Really, 'tis a curious thing, love is. And I believe 'tis very good to take! A person has to be some careful though, that is not used to it.

My scribbling is getting about to an end for this time. I will try and have you hear from me soon again. I hope you are enjoying health and have disposed of those blues you mentioned; they are bad companions. I am enjoying usual health. Once more, good bye for awhile, and with much love for you. Believe me sincerely, your admirer, Joel to Villie.

P. S. "Absent yet awhile." A few short months, though short they must be long without your society; but yet we must endure it, and our love will be the sweeter when we meet. JLM.

*****

Sat. 17 Sept.   Construction Corps men sinking the new railroad tracks so as to protect it from reb. batteries. *["sinking the tracks" probably meant building embankments.]* Volunteers coming in freely.

Sun. 18 Sept.   Visited regt. Sergt. Scott calls. Send stamps to Harkness.

Mon. 19 Sept.   J. Pennington made a call. Roast beef for dinner. Was to corps Hd Qrs for express goods in the evening.

Tue. 20 Sept.   Telegraph news of a victory over the reb. in the Shenandoah Valley. 3,000 prisoners taken. Three more wounded, and in our hands four gen. and some artillery. Great cheering.

Wed. 21 Sept.   Heavy cannonading early this morning. Supposed to be on account of good news. Flat-nosed prisoner escaped from guard house.

Thu. 22 Sept.   "Flat-nose" recaptured. Third Brigade paymaster here, Maj. Webb.

Fri. 23 Sept.   Good news again from the Shenandoah Valley. Sheridan capture 3,000 prisoners and 16 piece artillery. Driving early, 20 mile.

Sat. 24 Sept.   Morning. Early a salute is fired in honor of our late successes. A report comes that Killpatric *[Union Major General Judson Kilpatrick, May 1861 class at West Point]* has reached Augusta, Ga. and set 3,500 of our men at liberty. Another heavy salute is fired.

Sun. 25 Sept.   Expecting to move Hd Qrs to the Jones house, but the Ninth Corps Hd Qrs occupy it. Our corps Hd Qrs move to the house formerly occupied *[by the]* First and Second Div. Relieve the Tenth Corps. Heavy fighting in the right.

Mon. 26 Sept.   Heavy fighting on the right reported yesterday; the particulars not yet learned. Our Brigade, the Second, is relieved.

Tue. 27 Sept.   Petersburg is reported as being evacuated. Albert Burchard *[probably Brushard]*, Co. K, 141st, was killed while on picket by rebel sharpshooters. Paymasters, but no pay!

Wed. 28 Sept.   Orders to pack up and be ready for moving by four o'clock.

Thu. 29 Sept.   A dispatch came that the Tenth and 18th Corps were across the James and had taken Chapman's Bluffs and the New Market Road. We are still packed up, but not moved.

Letter #70

[This letter, and ones for several months following, find Joel still at the long drawn-out siege of Petersburg, Virginia. Although unnamed, the letter probably was to David, since political matters, draft, assessments, and voting were topics of interest to him.]

Hd Qrs, Third Div., Second Corps
Sept. 29, 1864
[At siege of Petersburg, Virginia]

Dear Brother: *[probably David]*

Your letter was duly rec'd and this morning I shall try and write a few lines in ans. My health is good; so is that of the rest of the boys. One of the Bradford boys of our company was killed on Tuesday, the 27th, while on picket. The news from Sheridan in the Shenandoah *[Valley]* has good effect here, and suppose will with you and on the result of the coming election.

[General U. S. Grant relieved General David Hunter of his command, and appointed Major General Philip Sheridan in his place. General Hunter was one of the poorest Union generals. Sheridan's activities were largely in the Shenandoah Valley. Sheridan stood 34th in his 1853 class at the Academy.]

A movement will be made here soon. Petersburg is reported as being evacuated by the rebs. A deserter came in this morning stating that it was true. Nearly all the troops on this line have orders for to move at a moment's notice. We expect to move tonight sure, but whether to the left or right, we cannot tell. Our regt. does not get paid yet, but expect to be soon. But as we are likely to move, 'tis uncertain when we will be now.

I suppose it will be necessary for me to be assessed and some tax payed to give me a right to vote. I wish you would see to it, if I have not been *[assessed]*. I do not know whether George has given my cow in as mine or his to the assessor. For me to vote here 'twill be necessary for a receipt from the collector to be sent to me. It will be too late, I suppose, for the first election unless already done. But I should like to have things right for the Presidential. You had better also see that the rest of our boys from the vicinity are properly assessed and provided with receipts that their tax is paid.

[A morale problem in the Union army was slowness in monetary payment. Joel and his buddies had not been paid for about seven months, yet they had current expenses. In Joel's case, he gave up one of his cows to the county assessor to be able to vote.]

I have not had any chance of finding out about Michael Farrel. I heard he was taken prisoner, but do not know it from any straight source. I shall look up Theodore's regt. to the first opportunity. I have never visited it but once.

I came across Jerry Ritter, the chap that used to live at Lyons, and was often up with cattle to Huckells. He is in the Construction Corps. They recently built a new railroad from City Point to the Weldon *[Rail]* Road and just in the rear of our defenses. 'Twas built eleven mile in eleven days. They *[the construction crew workers]* went away last Saturday for Strasburg up in the Shenandoah. *[Strasburg is west of Front Royal, and south of Winchester, Virginia.]*

Recruits have been coming in fast lately; our company has had eleven. One was Babb's son from Gelany Mills and another was a brother of Jake Lorah. The draft, I suppose, went off the 19th, and those that are enrolled know their fate. 'Twill bear pretty hard on Elklands.

[Joel's 1st Division, III Corps, was transferred to the 3rd Division of the II Corps in an attempt to refill the depleted ranks of the famous II. The II Corps, according to Civil War historian, Bruce Catton, in <u>A Stillness at Appomattox</u> "had been fought out and used up. It had been the most famous corps in the army. It had stormed Bloody Lane at Antietam; it had taken 4,000 casualties at Fredericksburg. Without flinching it had beaten back Pickett's charge at Gettysburg; and it had broken the Bloody Angle at Spotsylvania. But now it was all shot to pieces, and instead of being the army's strongest fighting unit, was the weakest."]

Your sowing so large a piece to wheat will keep you busy, as hands must be scarce. The weather is quite moderate here now. Very little rain has fallen lately.

What has become of the Dushore Union? I do not get a paper a month. I heard Lathrop had one *[sent]* to the army, but do not know as 'tis true. I noticed in the last number that Frank Warren was up for County Commissioner. I suppose there is little chance of getting a Union ticket elected in that county. I do not think of anything further now, and as I have not much time, I will close this with my best wishes for all of you at home. Write soon. From your brother, Joel.

*****

Fri. 30 Sept.   Recruits and convalescents in large numbers are forwarded to the front. Heavy fighting on the left. The Fifth and Ninth Corps engaged. Three line of works taken, and a few pieces of ordinance. Heavy mortar shelling.

Letter #71

Camp near Petersburg, Va.
Sept. 30, *[1864]*
Hd Qrs, Third Div., Second Corps

My Dear Friend:

Yours of the 25th was rec'd last evening and this morning finds me engaged in writing a short letter in ans. It must be a short one for we are packed up for moving and have been now for two days and nights. But I can perhaps write a few lines. My health is good and *[I]* have no complaints to make.

We are expecting busy times now soon. Two of our army corps have gone over the James River again (10th and 18th) and last night a dispatch came that they were driving the rebels in every direction; that they had *[taken]* Chapman's Bluffs and also the New Market road, leading to Richmond. Before this reaches you, doubtless there will have been eventful times here and about the rebel capitol.

You say, "Please do not reenlist!" Vilie, I do not think of doing so. Three years in the service is long enough for me at one time. Besides, our regt. has not ever had the chance to do so and maybe will not have. I hope at least 'twill not ever be required for I trust the war will be ended 'ere our enlistment expires.

With your letter I also rec'd one from Cousin Eliza J. Snell with the sad news of her brother Frank's death. This cruel war! We scarce can realize the depth of meaning to those words. George Pardoe, I learn, is at Lewisburg attending school. *[Lewisburg College, on the West Branch of the Susquehanna River, was probably the closest college to George's home area. It is now Bucknell University.]* You quite agreeably surprised me with saying that Hettie H. had won his favor and that he had actually visited with her already. But what does she think of his attention? Is she pleased or will he prove a disappointed youth? I must say of Hettie, that to my eye and way of thinking, she is a worthy young lady and will bear acquaintance well. *[George Pardoe did not marry "Hettie H." Instead, he married Mary Simpson.]*

So, you are expecting to attend the institute? I still wish you a pleasant time and that it may be highly instructive. I would enjoy one week there if I could only be present, I do believe that I should laugh right out in school, I do. I have met with Mr. Dobson once or twice, but my acquaintance with him is quite limited. His sister, I have never seen, but do you really think her capable of carrying me away?

Now, I must tell you what I found this morning. I thought last evening I had read all of your letter, but somehow in reading the underlining and that written upon the edges I failed to read the last page. It was only the more pleasant this morning. 'Twas like finding a ripe peach long after thinking them gone from the tree.

I could not say that I will come home on furlough this winter. I may not get the chance but if one is possible, I may. I scarcely think you will get homesick at Millview. I cannot say that I have been truly so for the past two years, though there is some difference, this, or Institute, here we make up our minds that we have to stay and to make the best of it.

My cousin, Doc Bird, often writes that he will be a substitute in my place while I am away if I wished, etc. and would wait upon them, i.e., my girls and stay with them if I only would say who. Perhaps you may see him at evening services, etc. You may think him *[in]* some ways like Ike, a little odd. You may, if you see him, tell him what your opinion is of him. *[Joel is suggesting Doc Bird escort her to social functions so she will be able to attend and won't need to go alone. See October 17, 1864, letter for her negative reaction to that dumb idea.]*

I suppose Cousin Martha M. will attend. You will see Eliza, 'tis likely, quite often. If anything should occur that might make it necessary perhaps her opinion would be of as much service as any one I could recommend excepting of course ones own judgement which must be always exercised. Now, I must close. Good-bye, as ever your true friend and admirer – Joel.

P. S. Much love and many good wishes, from J. L. M.

*****

CHAPTER 27: OCTOBER 1864

Sat. 1 Oct   Morning opens with a rebel charge to retake their works. Ninth Corps is driven out of one line. Our div. ordered to the left. Take the cars in the afternoon. Ride to the Weldon Road *[railroad]*, and march to the Yellow House, thence to the Half-way House.

Sun. 2 Oct.   Div. ordered to advance. Left flank charge and retake lost works. But little resistance. Guards dep *[deploy]*. Follow up the rebs. Find them. Charge, and get repulsed. 141st: One killed and eight wounded. Camp Half-way House.

Mon. 3 Oct.   Div. engaged in building fortifications. 150 Jersey recruits come up. Hear the cars run upon the South Side or Lynchburg Road, two 1/2 miles *[from here]*.

Letter #72

[At siege of Petersburg, Virginia]
Camp in the field
Oct. Third, 1864

Dear Brother: *[probably David]*

Having opportunity, I thought I would write a few more lines. Our div. broke camp on Saturday the first, and took the cars and landed at the Weldon *[Rail]* Road; then marched to the extreme left of our lines where the Fifth and Ninth Corps have been making advances toward the South Side *[Railroad]* or Lynchburg RR. Saturday was a very wet, rainy day and the trip was none too pleasant. Our forces had advanced near three mile, taken two or three line of works, a few prisoners, and a piece or two or artillery with very small loss on our side.

Yesterday, our div. went out on a reconnaissance to feel of *[out]* the rebs, to find there *[their]* whereabouts, etc. We flanked to the left and advanced over a mile skirmishing nearly all the way. At length, we came up to them and found them strongly entrenched and, as we had no artillery with us, did not make much of an attempt to dislodge them more than to find out their strength, etc.

Our regt. lost one killed and seven wounded -- none of our co. Today and last night our men have been engaged in building forts and fortying *[fortifying them]*. I heard the cars running upon the Lynchburg road last night, some three mile away. I think 'twill be useless for the Johns to try to drive us from this point as it is a very good position to hold. How soon we shall try again for the road, I do not know. The 10th and 18th Corps are north of the James *[River]*, and from accounts have been very successful, so far as heard from.

I had a letter from E. Bedford yesterday. He is getting along fine. Jones is with the regt. now, up here in front he writes, but I have not run across it since he and Theodore returned. Since I wrote before, I have heard that our officers had made arrangements for having those entitled to a vote, assessed, etc., according to some order issued by the War Department. So, if this be true we shall be all right as far as voting is concerned.

Our regt. will miss getting paid, I suppose, this time again upon account of this movement. Seven months is now due our regt. The greater part of the troop have been paid. The First and Second Div. of our corps remained back in front of Petersburg to hold our lines there and 'tis likely we may go back after a few days unless another advance is made at this point.

The weather does not show as favorable for camping the last few days as it had been along back. Doc. Simmons, of our co., returned today. He was wounded in the first part of the campaign.

The institute is about commencing now, from the latest news I have from home. I suppose it will not be as largely attended as when at Millview before. I suppose all of you within reach will have chances of taking boarders.

Eliza Snell writes that Franklin died of his wounds and that Luther had enlisted. I have not seen a list of drafted men yet from our county. I expect it must have taken place as I hear it has in other places. I have just seen our lieut. and he says that "our names were merely sent home for assessment," so, 'twill be necessary to have it arranged as spoken of before I suppose. I do not think of anything more, so as the mail leaves soon, I will close. My best wishes for you all. Joel L. Molyneux.

*****

Tue. 4 Oct.   Div. still remains at the Half-way house. Slashing and fortifying. Ninth Army Corps Hd Qrs. Gen. Parks pitched along side ours. Gen. Warren of the Fifth Army Corps. returned to the yellow house.

[Union officer Brigadier General Gouverneur Warren was commander of the V Corps, and had participated in many battles of the Army of the Potomac. He had been wounded at Gaines Mill and there is a monument to him on Little

Round Top, in the Gettysburg Cemetery, where he had distinguished himself. Later, he was relieved from his command by General Sheridan and charged with being slow in getting his troops ready. That military stigma hung over him, and ruined his career in the army. In 1879, a court of inquiry exonerated him. An engineer, he was in the Academy class of 1850, and was second in his class of 44.]

Wed. 5 Oct.   Gen. Farrie, Third Div., Ninth Army Corps. relieves our div., and soon after dark we rejoin our corps near Petersburg. Div. Hd Qrs pitch at the Jones house.

[In March 1864, the Confederate ship C.S.S. Florida began a career as a raider. By October 5, 1864, the C.S.S. Florida, having captured 37 vessels, arrived at the port of Bahia, Brazil. In the Bahia harbor she was rammed and captured by the U.S.S. Wachusett. The Brazilians protested and fired shots at the Wachusett, but to no avail. The Union warship steamed out of the harbor with her prize, but on the way north the C.S.S. Florida had a collision with an army transport and sank, November 28, 1864.]

Thu. 6 Oct.   Are busy all day fixing up and clearing away and ransacking old camps for boards, etc. Get a good supper. Build our shanty. *[The used boards were utilized to build their shanty.]*

Fri. 7 Oct.   Busily occupied in the spare time not on other duty, and get quite nicely fixed.

Sat. 8 Oct.   Sign the pay rolls and receive six months pay, $90 -- $35.50 for clothing money not drawn -- total $125.50. Maj. Assen, Paymaster.

Sun. 9 Oct.   Expressed home to David Molyneux $100, also $75 for James Pardoe, and $75 for William Bedford. -- Total $250.

Mon. 10 Oct.   The money was taken to City Point today by Barbes, the Chaplain, and expressed. Very cool night and a white frost this morning.

Tue. 11 Oct.   Was to the regt. this morning to attend state election. Voted congressman, assembly men, and county officers. Rec'd receipt for money expressed.

Wed. 12 Oct.   News came yesterday that Sheridan had again been successful in defeating the rebels in the *[Shenandoah]* Valley capturing ten guns and several hundred prisoners.

Thu. 13 Oct.   Private A. Lawrence sentenced to be hung. Was read his sentence, also a reprieve from the president.

Fri. 14 Oct.   Heavy guns heard toward the James *[River]*.

Sat. 15 Oct.   Visited the 141st. D. Sperry called in afternoon. Getting ready for inspect. Young lady dies, belonging to the family at Jones house.

Sun. 16 Oct.   On police. Burying horses and oxen. Go to City Point on the cars to make an arrest, but do not find our man. A Conn. Copp. *[Connecticut Copperhead]* arrested and put into guard house.

Letter #73

Oct. 17th, 1864
[In camp, at siege of Petersburg, Virginia]

My Dear Friend:

Your ever welcome words mailed the 13th I rec'd the 16th or last evening, and as I feel in an agreeable humor just now I am going to imagine myself sitting by you for the purpose of having a social talk.

Maybe you are at school and 'tis quite possible for the day is Monday, and 11 o'clock A.M. If you think the others will notice me talking with you, and make remarks, you can hide me perhaps or send me away. As you do not say anything, I shall take it as permission for me to remain by you and talk. Who knows but I can persuade you to let me find you a way to go home on Saturday and visit with you till Monday morning. I know you are really homesick, Vilie, from the way you have been talking to me lately, for you did not mention what you were studying or who was the best scholar or how many attended, how many boys, who they were, who the young ladies were, and where they boarded, etc., or even what seat you occupy and who sits at the desk I used to do. No one ever mentions my name in your hearing, I presume, do they?

I freely pardon you for not writing more when you had the headache. I never was troubled by it much, but enough to know that I would not want for to write letters while under the influence of it.

You do not fancy Mr. Bird, you say. Why should I care? Only to be as friends? I almost knew you wouldn't like him, for I have never scarcely saw a young lady that did. Why it is so, I cannot tell. Some folks, you know, have a way of laughing that is displeasing. And some we cannot tell hardly what does ail them, and perhaps there is nothing, only that they are not attractive and are without good points to recommend them.

Since my last talk with you, our div. has been upon a reconnaissance to the left of the Weldon RR. We were gone five days. We had quite a heavy skirmish fight one day, but none of our co. were hurt. We are now near the position we have occupied the past two months.

Hd Qrs is at what is called the "Jones House". A family lives there by that name -- an old gentleman and three or four women, his daughters and grandchildren. One young lady, aged 15, was buried this morning. She had been sick for several weeks of typhoid fever. 'Twas sad to witness the lone few that followed her to her grave. But while I could not help but sympathize with them under their existing circumstances, yet I also thought of the many Northern mothers and sisters for whom I could more sincerely feel sympathy who have, and are being daily called, to mourn.

Yesterday, I visited City Point, had a ride upon the cars there and back. The distance is 12 mile, I believe. James River is a fine sight with its many swift, moving craft of all kinds.

[City Point, advantageously located at the juncture of the Appomattox and James Rivers, made a good supply depot. Ocean-going vessels came to this landing point and unloaded supplies for the Army of the Potomac. Light railroads, supplemented by animal-drawn wagons, carried food, clothing, equipment, pontoon bridges, guns, and ammunition to the troops entrenched opposite the Confederate lines at Petersburg.]

So, you have been having some photos taken? And do you know that pleases me for maybe if I am real good you will send me one? You board at Millview and you can scarce help but have lively times with them. Thomas, no doubt, frequently remembers me to you, perhaps more than is pleasant. You can hardly help but like Aunt Matty. Jennie, you will find, is the girl at home, and you I think will cease to wonder why I recommended her so favorably to Abel. *["Aunt Matty" was Joel's elder sister, Margaret. Fifth child in the family, she was 13 years older than Joel. In 1846, she had married Thomas Pardoe. He died of pneumonia in 1866, and she passed away in 1870. Eight children resulted from the union, four of whom reached maturity.]*

How pleased she must be to have Geo. L. come home safe and well. I will write to her soon. May I ask if they judged who my letter was from? At least they could not tell by the address, I think. I see my paper is nearly written over and but a sorry letter written, I fear. You must write soon as convenient and as long as possible. Now, I must take leave of you with my best wishes, sincere respect, and much true love. Adieu, my dear Vilie, from Joel.

P. S. Vilie, I begin to think if ever I get well away from Va.; I shall never want to return again. In ten months I hope to bid it good-bye forever. Where is our friend, Jabe? If you have heard from him send his address, if you know it.

*****

Mon. 17 Oct. The usual routine of guard duties, etc. Funeral of Miss Jones! *[Funeral was for the 15-year-old daughter Joel mentioned in his October 17 letter.]*

Tue. 18 Oct Procure an order on the C. S., and buy potatoes and cornmeal at three 1/2 cts lb. each. Oscar Frost here. We have mush and milk for supper. *["Oscar" must have been a country cousin of Jack Frost. Mush is a dish made of boiled corn meal. It is eaten like a hot breakfast cereal, with milk and sugar or molasses. When cooked, and solidified, it may be sliced, fried, and served with hot maple syrup.]*

Wed. 19 Oct. Maj. Gen. *[David B.]* Birney is dead. Died this morning at Phila. The loss to our army is a serious one. He formerly commanded the Third Div., Second Army Corps., but lately the Tenth Army Corps.

[General David Birney contacted malaria and died October 18, 1864. He was brother of Federal General William Birney. They were sons of James Gillespie Birney, a strong anti-slavery leader, who unsuccessfully ran for president in 1840 and 1844. The brothers were born in Huntsville, Alabama. At the Battle of Gettysburg, General David Birney had taken command of the III Corps, after General Daniel Sickles had been wounded in the leg at the Peach Orchard.]

Thu. 20 Oct. Guard mounting this morning and drill in the afternoon. Mortar shell plenty in evening. Sheridan again victorious.

[On October 20, 1864, President Abraham Lincoln issued a proclamation setting aside the last Thursday of November **"as a day of thanksgiving and praise to Almighty God, the beneficent Creator and Ruler of the Universe."** *Actually, many of our presidents, starting with George Washington in 1789, have proclaimed thanksgiving as a national holiday. It is now the fourth Thursday in November.]*

Fri. 21 Oct. A dispatch from Gen. Sheridan states that he captured 43 cannon and 1,600 prisoners. The Pennsylvania state election has gone Union by 3,000 maj. *[majority]*

Sat. 22 Oct. A disgraceful drunken row in the guard. Bates, the clerk, and Gibson Leyte in guard house. Whiskey!

Sun. 23 Oct Wild geese flying south!

Mon. 24 Oct. Appearance of moving camp. Rumors rife, but we do not go.

Tue. 25 Oct.   Are packed ready for an expedition, and yet do not get away.

Wed. 26 Oct.   Today we get under way. Start soon after noon, the Second and Third Div. of the Second Corps move to the left, go in camp at a small farm house with orders to move at two A.M. of tomorrow.

Thu. 27 Oct.   Upon guard in the night. Do not move till four A.M. Find the Johnies soon, but only light skirmishing till afternoon. Get advanced a long way without much hindrance. Are attacked desperately. Lose cannon and some prisoners. Retake the whole, with some 1,500 of the Johnies.

Fri. 28 Oct.   Evening we fall back and make a connection with the Fifth Army Corps, and today return to our former position. Hd Qrs at the Jones house.

Sat. 29 Oct.   In the action of the 27th, our co. had one killed and two wounded. In regt., two killed and ----[text obliterated] wounded. Densmore of the guard wounded in the hand. D. Ryan, of the 84th, leg broken.

Letter #74

October 29th, 1864
[In camp, at siege of Petersburg, Virginia]

Dearest Friend:

This evening finds me busy writing letters, one of which I shall dedicate to Vile, thinking that after the news of another battle she would look for news from me.

Yes, we have had one more terrible battle, and for the men engaged as hard a fought one as any during the campaign. On Wednesday the 26th, two div. of our corps started upon an expedition toward the Lynchburg RR. Early Thursday morning we found the rebel outposts and drove them nearly ten mile and almost to the Lynchburg Road. Here they had a large force prepared to meet us, and attacked us upon three sides almost at the same time, and an awful battle raged from three o'clock P.M. till night. That night our two div. fell back and joined the rest of our army again. We captured some 1,500 prisoners.

I do not know the loss our men have met with, but 'tis quite considerable. I think the enemy lost three to one, at least. Our company had one killed and two wounded. D. Bryan of the 84th P.V., cousin of the other David, was shot through one ankle. The balls flew the thickest I ever found them yet, but I was favored to escape untouched. We are now encamped the same as before the move as when I last wrote to you.

O, do you think that I have just had a letter from JOB, dated the 26th. He is in the First Div. of our corps, but that was not in the fight. I shall try and look the boy up tomorrow if he can be found. Tonight, I heard from my brother David, dated 26th. Two days ago I had a letter from my cousin, Bird *[probably Doc, although it may have been his brother, George Copeland Bird]*. He writes that the institute has broken up from Coperheadism.

It is past eleven o'clock while I write this. I have had to stand guard two hours from nine till eleven, and your letter not being quite finished has to be by candle light, for the mail leaves at daylight in the morning. Inform my sister, Sallie, that her brother still lives, if you see her. I have written to her only a few days since.

I am sorry the school terminated so unpleasant. The one previous passed off so satisfactory to all. You would hardly get acquainted and possibly regret attending. I am anxiously watching for your letter with photo. I have a small album nearly full of home pictures, and just want a few to sett it off. I have kept the best place for yours, do you think?

Well, Vilie, 'tis now less than ten mo. then I shall perhaps have the pleasure of looking at the original. That will to me be, if permitted, a happy day. You will excuse, I know, this short letter for at three o'clock I shall have to be out again for two hours, and if I do not get some sleep, I will be feeling nearly the same as some mornings, you know when. I will close with a good night, a good bye, a kiss, and much love from Joel to Vilie.

*****

Sun. 30 Oct.   Went to the right of Petersburg to visit Jeb McCarty, but found he had been discharged one week ago. Picket line attacked in evening and a score of First Div. captured.

Mon. 31 Oct.   Police day. Employed in making brooms. Wash. Reg. mustered for two mo. pay, Sept. and Oct. These *[two months]* I bid adieu, not to be met with in service again. *[It was unusual to have "police day" on a Monday. Generally, they were scheduled Sunday mornings.]*

CHAPTER 28: NOVEMBER 1864

Wed. 2 Nov.　　　Frank Stone over from our regt. today. Make some fresh soup dumplings out of graham flour.

Thu. 3 Nov.　　　Brick mining; strike a good vein; get enough for chimney, and wheel them into position. *[The "good vein" he mentions was a vein of clay. The clay was formed into rude bricks to dry in the sun.]*

Fri. 4 Nov.　　　Busy building chimney in shanty and doubling up our bed. Draw a cavalry jacket and haversack. Cold winds. *[Keeping warm was a major winter activity for armies on both sides.]*

Sat. 5 Nov.　　　Lawrence, the deserter, is sent away today. He was a poor, miserable, and mean man.

Sun. 6 Nov.　　　Mud puddle frozen over, but a very fine day. 41 Johnnies brought to Hd Qrs; captured last night while attacking our picket line. Attack made at eleven P.M. Much artillery and musketry used. Johnies badly repulsed -- our loss, 20.

Mon. 7 Nov.　　　Soft and rainy with mud plenty. On guard.

Tue. 8 Nov.　　　Election day for president and vice president. It all passes off quietly. The 141st voted 195 for Abraham Lincoln and five for McClellan.

[In the November 8, 1864, presidential election, General George B. McClellan (D) ran against incumbent President Abraham Lincoln (R). McClellan's running mate was George H. Pendleton of Ohio. Andrew Johnson, a Democrat, was nominated as vice president by the Republicans and elected, with Lincoln, on the National Union ticket. Senator Hanibal Hamlin, Maine, had been Lincoln's 1st vice president. When President Lincoln was assassinated, in April 1865, Vice President Johnson became president. Candidate McClellan had been commander of the Army of the Potomac, until fired by President Lincoln. He was second in his 1846 class at the Academy.]

Wed. 9 Nov.　　　Lively mortar shelling in the evening. Went to corps Hd Qrs with a John deserter.

[In November 1864, and thereafter, much of the Civil War fighting was in Georgia and the Carolinas. General Sherman's policy of devastation of the South was largely unknown in the North, for he was out of touch much of the time. Sherman was 6th in his 1840 class at the Academy.]

Thu. 10 Nov.   Telegrams of the news of election coming in. Hunsinger court-martialed. Heavy dumps *[dumplings]* for dinner. O. Frost with us visiting.

Fri. 11 Nov.   Weather moderate and troop in half winter quarters.

Letter #75A

Evening of the Eleventh of Nov., 1864
[In camp, at siege of Petersburg, Virginia]

My Dearest Vilie:

Your more than welcome letter mailed the seventh, I received last evening with the photograph enclosed. So, you conclude I would not like the picture. Why, V., 'tis just what you promised me? Do you not remember? I being so much the oldest, that you would hasten to catch up, and now if it is a true likeness (but I don't think it is) I shall not be afraid of your claiming to be the "bestest-looking", as I used to be.

O! Now I must tell you that I rec'd a letter from Geo. P., and he writes that Ellen M. says you have been keeping her awake, etc. -- suppose it is to keep in practice. Geo. L. and Jennie will, 'tis likely, match soon. My opinion on the sitting question is, everyone, or rather every two, to their own notion.

I think that I should be quite contrary to Frankie. If I had been there and proposed a kiss if you would not go, then we would take that watch and sett the hands at a little past nine, and have a long, long talk. You can do as you like about getting it to going again. If you remain at home and not teach, 'tis likely it would not pay you for the trouble. I wrote to you the 30th of Oct. which you will have rec'd before this date. My letters seem to be much the longest in making the journey. Yours mostly arrive here the fourth day after mailing, while mine are two weeks, if not longer.

I heard D.B. has purchased *[the]* Mason D. Bedford farm. It is quite a nice situation, and D. will now certainly *[want to get married]*. His case will be like that you say of Ike. He will want a wife, and perhaps he will not be quite so particular as formerly, either. If he, like Ike, thinks you are out of the number to be thought of. 'Tis too bad that somethings happen as they do, and such good fellows, too.

Did Lizzie guess who was the writer of the letter she remailed to you? As it would be postmarked at Washington, I presume she would.

*****

Sat. 12 Nov.   Visited the bombproofs near Fort Davis.

Letter #75B

November 12th, *[1864]*
[In camp, at siege of Petersburg]

Your letter did not get finished last evening, so this evening finds me scribbling. I rec'd one letter tonight. 'Twas from my cousin Angie S. Her soldier has returned, I understand, but she does not speak much of him. I wonder if he is a weekly visitor?

I fear you will have cause to think this the poorest letter of all you ever received. I have been trying to finish before my candle burned out, and 'tis not more than one inch long now. I always want time to think, and when I hurry *[I]* can scarcely think of anything. Well, I own up. Beat in a fair race. The light will soon be a light no more and away I go to the suttler store for another. Candles are cheap, only 15 cts apiece. Everything they keep for sale almost tastes of money.

You ask, will I "come home this winter"? I really cannot tell. I shall if a furlough of a longer time than ten day can be had. I will at least come home next summer if my life is spared till then. You may expect me about the first of Sept. Then, do you suppose people will talk about us? If I should say once a week to Jennie, she might say twice a week to me, you know last winter.

I always knew that it was difficult for me to get a good likeness taken, but I did not know that you were so. Maybe it is because -- I won't say. But maybe the both of us could if we were to sit for one. The last I had taken were the worst I ever had.

My sheet is nearly over. I began to think your letter would never arrive. 'Twas nearly four weeks from the time I rec'd your previous one. I read it over enough times to make up for it. I know that I have more spare time than you, when we are not upon the move. Affectionately yours, Joel. Now, I will once again say, good bye. All my love is yours, if you will accept and keep it, and I believe you can keep it good a long while, it will only need to be carefully kept in a warm place in your affections.

*****

Sun. 13 Nov. Write a letter or two, and spend some time at reading. The band plays church music.

[A great morale booster of both armies was their use of army bands. Church music, as mentioned above, was popular, as was sentimental music. The most popular song, "When This Cruel War Is Over", by Charles Carroll Sawyer, went:

> When we last did meet
> Dearest love, do you remember,
> How you told me that you loved me,
> Kneeling at my feet
> Oh, how proud you stood before me
> In your suit of blue,
> When you vowed to me and country
> Ever to be true.

[And the chorus:

> Weeping, sad, and lonely,
> Hopes and fears how vain!
> Yet praying, when this cruel war is over,
> Praying that we meet again.

[Grown combat veterans would sing that song and weep unashamedly. It expressed deep, inner feelings of those who had gone to war so blithely in an age when no one would speak the truth about the tragic reality of war. Joel frequently used the expression "when this cruel war is over", and probably his verbal expression of wistful longing came from the title and chorus of the above song.

[Next in popularity, "Tenting Tonight on the Old Camp Ground" stated feelings of loneliness, homesickness, and dejection — common in both armies. Its words:

> We're tenting tonight on the old camp ground,
> Give us a song to cheer.
> Our weary hearts, a song of home,
> And friends we love so dear.

[The chorus yearns:

> Many are the hearts that are weary tonight,
> Wishing for the war to cease;
> Many are the hearts that are looking for the right,
> To see the dawn of peace.

[Both North and South armies liked Stephen Foster's songs, "My Old Kentucky Home", "Old Folks at Home", "Old Black Joe", "Carry Me Back to Old Virginny", "Way Down upon the Suwannee River", and "Nellie Gray". Stephen Foster, although a Northerner from Pittsburgh, Pennsylvania, wrote many songs about the South. He had attended Towanda Academy where Joel and Colonel Madill had gone to school. Soldiers also liked the old favorites, "Drink To Me Only With Thine Eyes", "Auld Lang Syne", and "Home Sweet Home". "Battle Hymn of the Republic" took the Union armies by storm. Music was written by Wm. Steffe and the words were by Julia Ward Howe.

>Mine eyes have seen the glory
>Of the coming of the Lord;
>He is trampling out the vintage
>Where the grapes of wrath are stored;
>He hath loosed the fateful lightning
>Of His terrible swift sword:
>His truth is marching on.

[The chorus:

>Glory, Glory, hallelujah
>Glory, glory, hallelujah!
>His truth is marching on.

[Second verse:

>I have seen Him in the watch fires
>Of a hundred circling camps.
>They have builded him an altar
>In the evening dews and damps;
>I can read his righteous sentence
>By the dim and flaring lamps;
>His day is marching on.

[Fifth verse:

>In the beauty of the lilies
>Christ was born across the sea,
>With a glory in His bosom
>That transfigures you and me;
>As He died to make men holy,
>Let us die to make men free,
>While God is marching on.

[An unknown Confederate soldier, hearing Union soldiers sing the above song, complained: "How can we win the war when the opposing army has a song like that?"]

[Other popular Civil War songs were "Tramp, Tramp, Tramp", "Just Before the Battle, Mother", "Tenting on the Old Campground", "Shoe Fly Pie", and "Pop Goes the Weasel".]

Mon. 14 Nov.   All the guard out for guard mounting. Skirmish drilling in afternoon.

Tue. 15 Nov.   Went to Mede's station for express boxes. Away nearly all day. Gen. Egan started for home, being wounded slightly a few days ago on picket.

[Major General Thomas Egan, in command of the 1st Brigade, 2nd Division, II Corps, was wounded November 14, 1864. He had also been wounded two months earlier at Petersburg. He later returned to the service, and was in the Shenandoah Valley at the end of the war. Mustered out in 1866, he was a customs official for 15 years.]

Wed. 16 Nov.   On guard mount and guard. Rec'd an unexpected letter.

Thu. 17 Nov.   Rebs toss many shells over. Wrote to sister, Sallie, enclosing five dollars for shirts. Appearance of a move.

Letter #76

[This letter to Jesse discusses political and business matters back home.]

November 17, 1864
Hd Qrs, Third Div., Second Corps
[In camp, at siege of Petersburg, Virginia]

Dear Brother:

I have been puzzling my head for a long time to decide whether I have ans. your last letter to me or not. And without coming to any conclusion, have concluded to write again. This date finds me still in health, also the others here of your acquaintance. Weather is now quite moderate; have had but little rain yet; have had some cold nights -- sometimes freezing up the water holes.

Since the last *[letter to you we did]* move to the left and fight. On the 27th of Oct. our portion of the army has lain nearly quiet, excepting the picket passes and sharp shooting.

Election passed off quietly here. Our regt. voted 195 Lincoln and five for Mac. Lincoln, by the day's papers, state Mac as getting three states: Kentucky, Del., and N. Y.

Rumors are quite plenty here at present. Sherman is said to be on the way past Charleston. I suppose 'twill kill or cure. I suppose some movement will be made here yet before settling down for the winter.

I have not heard anything of Jonas since he rejoined his regt. It is now in the 18th Corps and on the other side of the river. I have heard nothing of Michael, but what has been written from home. I have been on the lookout for his regt., but as it is five or six mile further to the left than us, I do not get the chance of making inquiries as I intend to the first opportunity.

I think that in reference to what you spoke of, the old cow, I wrote you saying that you might make the best of her as you saw fit, and allow me what you could afford. I have agreed to let David Molyneux have a ewe lamb for some other things I have got of them. You can let them take one of those at your place or if the Rinebolds have more than they care to keep, 'twill make no difference to me. I suppose you are all busy fencing, etc. as no hands are to be hired. David must have work enough with all his new ground.

Tell Abram's folks I will write soon as I can. Their letter was rec'd all right, but as 'tis late in the evening I will close with my best wishes to you all. Write when convenient. Your brother, Joel.

*****

Fri. 18 Nov.   Drill deploy as skirmishes, etc. Burning old letters – "Joys that I've tasted, the letters I've burned, words of affection, with hopes of return."

Sat. 19 Nov.   Autumnal rains setting in. Crosby, the A. C. G. clerk, in guard house. Sent six dollars to E.S. Gregory. Jo Pennington calls.

Sun. 20 Nov.   Provost badges arrived. Buy one of Gregory, intended for Frank Stone. Price $2.00.

Mon. 21 Nov.   No abatement of rain. Wet day for police. Virginia flat –– a fact.

*[On November 21, 1864, President Abraham Lincoln wrote his famous consolation letter to Mrs. Lydia Bixby upon hearing of the death in battle of her five soldier sons. President Lincoln's eloquence was misplaced, for only two of the five sons had been killed. Nevertheless, the letter stands as a benchmark for demonstrating Lincoln's compassion and concern for families of soldiers who died for their country "...**of five sons who have died gloriously***

on the field of battle." *His poignant letter continued:* "I feel how weak and fruitless must be any words of mine which should attempt to beguile you from the grief of a loss so overwhelming. But I cannot refrain from tendering to you the consolation that may be found in the thanks of the Republic they died to serve. I pray that our Heavenly Father may assuage the anguish of your bereavement and leave you only the cherished memory of the loved and lost, and the solemn pride that must be your to have laid so costly sacrifice upon the altar of freedom."*]*

Tue. 22 Nov.   Another man in chains, First Mass., H. Arty. The weather catching a cold. *["man in chains" meant one of their own soldiers had lost his contact with reality, and had to be forcibly restrained. He was suffering an emotional breakdown.]*

Wed. 23 Nov.   The coldest morning of the season. Cold fingers! Upon guard mount. Over to regt. Saw E.S. Little. 'Tis said we are to have roast turkeys for Thanksgiving dinner.

Thu. 24 Nov.   Hoora for Thanksgiving Day! No turkey as yet, only those of the buzzard type. A trip to Third Brigade, also to corps Hd Qrs. in the night. Turkeys have arrived!

[As a means of introducing variety and interest into Union soldiers' rations, the Sanitary Commission recommended companies set aside money to be used for butter, milk, vegetables, condiments, cooking utensils, etc. The program was called "The Company Fund". Their abundant 1864 Thanksgiving day meal may have been part of that plan.]

Fri. 25 Nov.   Thanksgiving dinner consisting of turkeys and chickens roasted, cakes and cookies, mince pies, and plumb *[plum]* pudding, frosted cake, canned peaches, tobacco, apples, potatoes, and other things too numerous for to mention, ice cream.

Sat. 26 Nov.   Unwell from recent high diet, but hope to recover. *[Perhaps the reason he got sick on his furlough, a year earlier, was rich diet.]*

Sun. 27 Nov.   Went to the Eighth Jersey, three mile. Mortar shelling today quite brisk on both sides. Cause unknown.

Letter #77

[Vilie now had a teaching job. Joel again brought up the political dispute that broke up the institute meeting in Millview. Earlier, it was mentioned as being Copperheadism. The issue, whatever it was, vexed Joel.]

Hd Qrs, Third Div., Second Corps
Nov. 27, 1864
[In camp, at siege of Petersburg, Virginia]

Dear Vilie:

This will, perhaps, find you in the school room and surrounded by a group of very affectionate urchins. You are so interested in your new duties that, as a matter of course, I shall not suppose you the least mite homesick or hardly *[having]* time to listen while I bother you with my ink and pen conversation.

One mile of the turnpike? You say I used to know all the schoolhouses upon the main road leading there, but maybe the one I am thinking of is not the place. Does the house stand upon the left hand as you go, above the road in a cluster of sumac, painted white and high from the ground? When you write I will expect a general description of all your adventures, etc., and how Lyb is situated and if her school is not the one known as the Dodge school, nearby Mr. Kellogg's. *["Lyb", Samuel's widow, was Elvira's cousin.]*

Now I will talk of what we are at here, etc. As for me, my health is good. We are in the same place as when writing before. The weather is quite fine now. A few days ago we had a three days rain which supplied us with mud a plenty. Perhaps we may stay where we are for the winter, but 'tis not certain yet.

Last Thursday was Thanksgiving Day, and what do you think we had sent to us as presents and for our dinner? You will scarcely believe me when I say that we had roasted turkeys and chickens and plumb *[plum]* pudding, a dozen different kinds of cake and as many more of pickle, potatoes, apples, canned peaches, and even ice cream, tobacco, etc., etc. I do not mean we had as much of all this as we wished, but nearly all had something, and a great many had a little of everything. It reminded us of home and friends, and that they had not forgotten the soldiers in the field.

I have not yet made an application for a furlough and 'tis quite uncertain if I will be able to get one. I intend for to try; but may be disappointed. I think your *[negative]* opinion of political disputes being introduced into the Institute is quite right. It was really ridiculous!

Cousin Eliza *[Snell]* has written me not long since. She is some of a politician. I am just now wondering if you agree with her upon the question of friendship and love. She used to advocate there was no such thing as undying love – 'twas only a strong friendship, she would say. Perhaps you may have heard her express herself upon the subject. If so, do you agree with her? Or do I agree with you? When I say from experience, observation, etc., I conclude there is such an article as abiding affection. Eliza would have you think my losing sleep made me ill, when home last winter? I am afraid if that was the case I should be sick all the time for every third night here I have to be up half of the night, and often more upon guard, etc. I would risk it again, I think, if instead of my being here in Va. this Sunday evening was at your comfortable home in Elkland -- sitting by you upon that lounge, for instance.

But what a short letter, you say. I think to myself, but I have been busy all day and have just written a letter to my brother-in-law, Jonas Bedford, and we have to blow out the lights at nine, and 'tis nearly that now. So, good bye, dearest and best friend, Vilie. May the choicest of blessings be yours is the wish of JOEL.

P. S. Please pardon my using a yellow envelope.

*****

Letter #78

Hd Qrs, Third Div., Second Army Corps
Nov. 29th 1864
[In camp, at siege of Petersburg, Virginia]

Dear Brother: *[David]*

Your letter was rec'd last evening, and permit me here to wish you joy in your happy presentation of an heir, and the new social position in which you are placed. I was much surprised upon hearing of the event or not *[having heard]* the remotest whisper of probabilities had the winged winds born hitherward.

[David and Hannah had been married just one year; the new arrival in their family was named William Manley. When grown, he married Effie Jane Northrup, and they had three children.]

My health is yet fine. James Pardoe and Wm. Bedford are well. The weather is very moderate now -- not even frosty at night. A week back we had a three day rain, and previous to that the nights were cold. Last Thursday, Thanksgiving Day, we were presented with a dinner consisting of roast turkey and chicken, mince pie, plumb pudding, various kinds of cake, cheese, butter, and even ice cream, tobacco, apples, potatoes, canned peaches, etc. and so on. All, I believe, got something, but of course not in very large quantities. The turkey and chicken was enough for one good meal, after it was distributed. I had my share, if not more!

We are now anxious to hear the result of Sherman's movement through Georgia. The last we heard of him, he was reported to be at Macon and Augusta, and had met scarcely any opposition. I hope he may meet with success. Our corps is moving further to the left. I think our div. will be to the left of the Weldon *[Rail]* road tomorrow, the Ninth Corps relieves us.

[On November 16, 1864, Union General William T. Sherman departed Atlanta, Georgia, and launched his famous "March to the Sea". He left Atlanta a smoking city, its economy in ruins. His objective seems to have been not just to crush the rebellion, but to crush the South. Several times, Joel commented negatively about the harsh and ruthless conduct of Sherman's troops.]

It seems tough to leave good shanties and strike out, but anything so it helps to end up this curs't war. I think we shall be quieted down by the time that box can reach here. It would be kept back at Washington, anyhow, if we should be on the move.

The money I had reference to was what I had sent home previous to that which you mention. But, it makes no particular difference. Some of the boys here spend all their wages and more too. And some save everything they can and, as I am often asked what amount I had sent home, was the reason for the inquiry.

I have just had a letter from Uncle Joel Bennet in ans. to one written to him. They are well. *["Uncle Joel Bennett" was married to Joel's aunt Sarah. In his August 28, 1862, letter, Joel told of visiting them in Sonestown, Pennsylvania.]*

As we are to start from here at daybreak, I must close this as 'tis now late in the evening. With love to all. Good bye – Joel.

*****

Wed. 30 Nov. Our division gets relieved by the Ninth Corps troops, and we are ordered to the extreme left, left of the Weldon RR. Hd Qrs are pitched at the site of the Poplar Grove Church.

CHAPTER 29: DECEMBER 1864

Thu. 1 Dec. Was upon guard last night at the station, and am upon guard today by the regular turn of system post. Jno. Dickinson deserted.

Fri. 2 Dec. Clearing away old rubbish, all hands, for Hd Qrs have at last decided to make Hd Qrs at the site of the Poplar Grove Church.

Sat. 3 Dec. On police and busy all day policing up the battery grounds. The squad system is broken up and regular detail made.

Mon. 5 Dec. Signs of another movement. Orders to be ready, etc.

Tue. 6 Dec. Expecting to move in the morning. Out on patrol. About among the safe guards and to the picket line. Refugees Claypoles going to Jersey.

[See diary entry February 8, 1865, where, two months later, the Union army was still using the Claypole house. It was common for both armies to move into houses where they were stationed. Many of these houses had been vacated, but it was unusual for a Southern family to move to the North, as the Claypoles did.]

Wed. 7 Dec. Our detail to remain in camp. Division gone to the left.

Thu. 8 Dec. Returned stragglers state that our div. was across the Blackwater at midnight. Their destination appears to be N. C. *[North Carolina]* -- Noteway, Wilmington.

Fri. 9 Dec. The First Div. moved to the left, and is reported to have engaged the Johnies. Reb cars rattling all night.

Sat. 10 Dec. First Div. forced back. Third Div., Sixth Corps, move out and engage the Johns, but do not stand fire.

Letter #79

Dec. 10th, 1864
[At siege of Petersburg, Virginia]

My Dear Friend:

By this time you are fairly initiated into your new position and have decided about how pleasant a situation and school you have. I never was into that neighborhood, and have but slight acquaintance with any who live in that vicinity, but if I were at home now I do not know but that I should be there 'ere long, especially if the sleighing was good. I believe you and I never went sleigh riding, but the once, "the Watch Night". Yes! and the time Lyb would go with us, when I was going to drive over with you home. I supposed then she did that because she thought I, or we, rather she wouldn't. Did she ever tell you of going back how I took 'vantage by taking a kiss? School was out then, and I did not care much what I done.

Our first snow fell here last night, about two inches of sleet. At present, rain is slowly falling. Since writing before, we have changed our position and moved to the left farther, and to the south of that Weldon RR, you often hear spoken of, and last Wednesday, the seventh, our div., along with the Fifth Corps, went on an expedition, but as yet I do not know where. Some say they have gone to Wilmington, N. C., though I hardly think that is the case; more likely it is to destroy the Danville Railroad.

I can hear cannon, while writing, away off in the direction they went and suppose they have found some Johnies. Now, you are guessing why I am not with them. Well, the reason is that I was with a few others ordered to remain to guard some deserters and other prisoners until the division returned. While the rest are away we are up every night from four to six hours. If Eliza's opinion was correct, ain't you afraid 'twill make me sick?

So Aunt Eliza Warren is agoing to have you married to cousin Will M.? It is nothing strange for her. She gets many a couple married before they know anything of it themselves. It answers a very good purpose, I think. You see, it gets a person kind of broke in and when the real affair takes place, it will not seem so terrible.

It will soon be a year since I saw you, and only a few months more and I hope to see you again. Then you think I must take part of the teasing that you get? Well, we will see. Maybe we can dodge some of it. I have dodged a good many cannon balls down here, and think 'tis the better way not to be hit, if we can help it.

George Pardoe, no doubt, will have a splendid time during vacation with his Henrietta. She will be just a gay little niece, you know. There is nothing like having smart relations. I always forget, you being a school ma'am, and *[I]* write at random. I always seem to think that you are just the same laughing girl as when I was so busily employed teaching you that first lesson. Did you then think that that was the lesson I tried the hardest to have you learn? And most wished for to hear you recite? Well, it was and I was studying in the same book. But, then I guess I had the start of you, for I had at least looked over the lesson before school began.

Evening: My letter is nearly done, but not quite. I have just come in from standing guard two hours. It is now nine o'clock. I find a letter in my tent that came this evening from my cousin Kate Plotts. She is attending school at the seminary at Lewisburg, nearby the college where Geo. is. *[The "seminary" was Lewisburg Seminary. Lewisburg is on the West Branch of the Susquehanna River.]*

Oh! I must tell you that we had roast turkey for Thanksgiving dinner, or did I speak of it in my last? Goodbye Vilie. I wish you the best of success in your school, and that you may not get the least bit homesick, and that I may soon receive a very long letter with full particulars from my true friend. Affectionately – Joel.

*****

Mon. 12 Dec. The div. returned today from the raid down the Weldon RR. The farthest point reached was Bellfield. They destroyed 15 mile of the RR.

Tue. 13 Dec. Found but few rebs, but plenty of guerrillas and found a doz. of our men murdered for which orders were to burn every building within reach. Sussex C.H., etc. burned.

Wed. 14 Dec. Relieved from guard. Have been upon guard seven days and nights while the div. was away. Hd Qrs select a new site. Commence clearing away and fixing up, etc.

Thu. 15 Dec. Work near the picket line cutting poles, etc. for the new Hd Qrs. Two load of express boxes for the div. I got one that was shipped the 28th from Muncy.

Fri. 16 Dec. Guard over prisoners at work upon new Hd Qrs.

Sat. 17 Dec. At work building a new shanty at the new Hd Qrs. News, good news, again from Gen. Thomas. Also, a report of the capture of Savannah. *[General George Henry Thomas was a Virginian loyal to the Union. His Army of the Cumberland had succeeded in taking Nashville (December 15-16, 1864). There, 55,000 Union troops had 3,061 casualties. General Hood's C.S.A. Army of the Tennessee, about 30,000, had about 1,500 casualties and 4,500 captured.]*

Mon. 19 Dec. Move from the old camp to the new – almost a family quarrel. House building goes on bravely.

Tue. 20 Dec. The guard ordered to fall in. Twelve men selected for to shoot the deserter Dixon on Friday. Twelve more as escort. I am one of the latter. Built a wooden chimney today.

Wed. 21 Dec. Supernumerary. *[Some "supernumeraries" were used for supplying the places of such as might fall in action or for better management of the rear ranks when front ranks were advancing or engaged. Others were extra men who had not yet been assigned a regiment or division. In his diary entry of February 1, 1865, Joel mentioned another supernumerary.]* The day 3/4 rainy. Revise the doorway to our shanty. Dixon, the deserter, manacled.

[On December 21, 1864, General Sherman captured Savannah, Georgia and on December 22, 1864, sent his famous message to President Lincoln: **"I beg to present you, as a Christmas present, the city of Savannah with 150 heavy guns and plenty of ammunition, and also about 25,000 bales of cotton."** *]*

Fri. 23 Dec. The day for Dixon's execution: The div. is formed by the W. RR *[Weldon Railroad]* and the detailed guard for that purpose with the prisoner march the entire circle in the rear of his coffin. At 12 A.M. he is shot.

Sat. 24 Dec. Jacob Lorah calls today *[for]* a few minutes.

Sun. 25 Dec. Merry Christmas. dinner: Apple dumplings, coffee, bread, and butter. Visitors: E.S. Little, Wm. Bedford, and Dent Stahl.

Mon. 26 Dec. Get a pass started for to visit the 18th Army Corps. Upon guard no. one. Squads of convalescents, Thurston, etc.

Tue. 27 Dec. Writing letters.

Letter #80

Evening, Dec. 27, *[1864]*
[At siege of Petersburg, Virginia]

My True Friend:

I am behind time a few days with this letter to have rec'd one of later date from you. 'Ere ans., yours of the 11th was rec'd the 17th. I also wrote to you the 11th. I sincerely hope this will find you well and situated more pleasantly than you at first of the school anticipated. But, really Vile, I fear you are in for an unpleasant time. You will find it necessary to have at *[your]* command a large amount of patience, and all the judgment that generally falls to one person.

At this time, I will suppose you are at home, from what you stated in your last. One year ago last evening! Do your remember? I was with you there, too. I hope those teeth may have quit troubling you. (Should have been in the P. S. part.) You have thought of me, 'tis likely expected me home this time, but furloughs are not being granted except upon extreme cases. I do not now think there will be much prospect of getting one at all, till August, then dear Filie, if a kind Providence permits, we can enjoy each other's society once more.

I have heard you were having a good snow for sleighing. Here the weather is moderate and a little rainy. We have been quite busy changing camp since our div. returned from the raid I spoke of in my last. They were gone six days and 'tis likely you may have seen the account of what they done.

We are having very good news from the armies south. Sherman has taken Savannah, and Wilmington, N. C. is the next place on the list. I think surely, with the fall of these places, the rebs will be forced to sue for peace. I said I did not expect a furlough, but I do *[receive]* one for two days. I have just heard from Jonas Bedford, by way of a letter, he is some ten mile of us, and I think of trying to find him tomorrow, as there are a number more with him of my acquaintance. His regt. is near Point-of-Rocks, by the Appomattox, seven mile above City Point. *[Joel visited several Point of Rocks. Another Point of Rocks, mentioned during the Gettysburg Campaign, is a secluded village on the Maryland side of the Potomac, between Leesburg, and Frederick.]*

You ask if I remember the sawmill? Where the road turns toward your school? Yes! But 'tis more than ten rods from the tavern, unless the hard times since I have travelled it have very much shortened the distance. I think that 'tis just 80, and there is a watering trough by the turning place, and it turns three ways for Sunday too. Am I right?

While I think of it, does Bonaparte Roberts' family live near your school? I think he did formerly, if not now. I ask because he is here in my regiment. My health is usually good. I trust you had a pleasant time on Christmas and will wish you a happy New Year!! Good bye. I wish to mail this tonight, and to do so must close now – with much love, I remain yours, JOEL.

*****

Wed. 28 Dec.   Pole raising, etc. Pass for forty-eight (48) hours returned, approved at the regt., in evening.

Thu. 29 Dec.   Address: Edmund Bedford, U.S. General Hospital, Anapolis, Md. "This page is all that's left me now. The end is drawing near."

Sat. 31 Dec.   Are expecting to make Jonas a visit in the morning. Adieu.

[Jonas Bedford entered the Union army even though he was 43, and had a wife and ten kids. A photograph of him, at the time, shows a middle-aged hospital orderly holding a broom at attention.]

CHAPTER 30: JANUARY 1865

Sun. 1 Jan. Visited Jonas Bedford, Henry Black, H. Baldwin, E. Rogers, and T. P. Wilkinson at the 18th Army Corps, Second Penna. Volunteers, Heavy Artillery, in company with Wm. Bedford. Found them on the Lookout St., Point of Rocks, on the banks of the Appomatox.

[At the beginning of the new year, 1865, peace was in the air. One question in the North seemed leading. "When peace comes, how will the returning states be treated?" In addition, the North was concerned about constitutional abolition of slavery. A third concern was how to handle reconstruction of the South. Actually, some reconstruction of the South had already started in Louisiana, and the proposed 13th Amendment was about to come up again, after an earlier defeat.]

Mon. 2 Jan. In the afternoon returned to camp 15 miles, situated one mile south and west of the Weldon RR at the place known as Yellow House.

Sat. 7 Jan. "Say, who knocks there?" says I
"Who there then?" says I.
"Then", says she
"Here am I"

[On January 7, 1865, President Lincoln relieved incompetent General Benjamin Butler of his command of the Department of Virginia and North Carolina. A "political general", he was one of the poorest generals in the Union army. He was disliked by Northerners and Southerners alike. He was influential politically, though, and President Lincoln was reluctant to relieve him until after the 1864 election.]

Sun. 8 Jan. I would if I could
If I couldn't, how could I?
I couldn't without I could,
Could I? Could You?

Sat. 14 Jan. Capt. W. W. Braman, Pro Mas of Third Div, Second Army Corps, takes leave of the guard. He leaves the army tomorrow having been mustered out of service. Capt. Morrow takes his place, Seventh Jersey.

Sun. 15 Jan. Fort Fisher was taken by storm today by Com. Porter of the navy and Gen. Terry of the army. 'Tis situated at the mouth of Cape Fear River, N. C.

Tue. 17 Jan.   The div. is reviewed today, by brigades, by Maj. Gen Humphreys and Brev. Maj. Gen. Mott.

Letter #81

[The purpose of the following letter to Vilie was not only to keep in touch, but question her spirituality, and to state his own position. During his several years in the army, he has contemplated his own spiritual values. He proffers some views on how his community back home should be acting.]

19 Jan. 1865
[In camp near the Appomattox River, Virginia]

My Friend:

Will think this letter just a little behind time, for time has fled away so fast that I had a little suspected that the two weeks had lengthened into three. My last from you came the fourth of Jan. – dated Dec. 11th. I continue in good health and trust you are permitted to enjoy a full share of the same.

Upon New Year's Day, instead of being home on furlough, I was visiting Jonas Bedford and some others of my acquaintance. His regt. is 15 mile away from ours, so I stayed with him one night, and had a very pleasant time. I have not heard from home very lately. Last evening I rec'd a letter from Geo. Pardoe stating he spent a vacation and the holidays at home. *[He]* Says you did not get to visit home then, as was expected. He saw Lyb and had a nice time generally, especially while at Hillsgrove. Cousin Eliza Snell writes that he *[George]* visited Hettie and that rumor is inclined to say she was destined to be my niece. *[George did not marry Hettie.]*

The protracted meeting at the church at Forksville continues. My cousins at Millview are numbered with those that are endeavoring to live better. That vicinity has long been a hard spot *[in which]* to awaken a religious feeling. And I should be glad to hear that all the people of that place had become reformed, for Vilie, I sincerely believe that is the way we all should live *[as]* a Christian, although as such I have never professed to be. Yet it is very easy to observe that those who do, and live up to their privilege are the happier. I do not remember as we have ever spoken to each other upon this subject, and *[we]* are in that respect entirely unacquainted. Every person, at least a thinking one, forms opinions. Some always think as their parents do, no matter what that is. And others are just what the good fellow is that talks to them. I like to meet occasionally with a person with a mind of their own –- deciding their course from the knowledge they can acquire, and the experience of others. And when they feel sure of being right, let nothing turn them from it.

Perhaps at some future time we may be better acquainted in this and many other respects. Not that I think people should all think and act alike, for I do not, yet there are some points upon which they should agree -- especially if their paths through life are together. Well, I guess you will think something has happened -- writing as I have. Ain't you afraid my face has grown long as when I was teaching.

O! Wouldn't I like to reverse the operation and go to school to you! But, my paper and candle warn me to soon have done with what I have to say, which by the by is that you find no serious trouble, I trust, with your school, and upon receiving this you will write a long letter to your truly affectionate friend, Joel.

P. S. It is after nine o'clock, and I have been sitting up writing home and to you. I thought maybe I should get one from you tonight, but for some reason the mail has not come in. We have been getting good news from the South. Wilmington, 'tis said, is captured.

O! I hope this war is near to an end. Everything appears to *[have]* taken an early finishing stroke. There has been quite enough blood spilt and homes desolated.

Good bye, and motto this time is "Hope on, hope forever." Joel.

*****

Sat. 21 Jan.   Purchased this diary this day of the First Brigade purveyor, for thirty-five cents.

Mon. 23 Jan.   Heavy guns were heard last evening and all through the night in direction of Dutch Gap.

Tue. 24 Jan.   A large amount of express boxes came for the div. today. Certainly, I think ten wagon loads.

Wed. 25 Jan.   The firing on the evening of the 22nd was from the rebel iron clads from Richmond. Their attack proved a failure.

Letter #82A

Evening, Jan. 25th, 1865
[Encamped near Warrenton, Virginia]

My Dear Friend:

Your letter dated the 18th and mailed the 20th I received this evening, and I need not say how glad was I to hear from you. I have just written you, but when you say, "Please do write" how do you suppose I can help but take my pen and scribble away? I said 'twas evening and 'tis past nine o'clock. With your permission, I propose keeping you company until eleven. Then, I must keep company with Miss Minnie for two hours *[doing guard duty]*. You will not be jealous will you? But maybe you would like to know her full name, so I'll introduce her to you as Minnie Rifle. My love for her is not very serious, and I think in seven months more I will bid her farewell and not cry either.

Tomorrow, I will visit some of my friends in other regt.s. if I can get leave, for I have recently heard of a number from Sullivan that I am acquainted with. One is Willie Snell; then there is Collins and his son Alph, and Mars Levering and Julia Black's brother-in-law Colter, and some others you are unacquainted with.

There is no snow here, and the weather is much milder than with you so you must not think we are enduring the hardships of such a winter as visits old Sullivan by any means. True, when we are on duty and *[it]* is storming it is anything but pleasant. But our cabins are comfortable, generally, and we are not always on duty.

I have lately rec'd a letter from Geo. Pardoe, and *[it arrived]* since his visit home New Years. He mentioned your not being there but that he saw Lyb. I also heard that he visited Miss Hettie. There is, I begin to think, quite a prospect for a niece there.

There has been a wedding in that vicinity also: Henry Campbell and Kate Norton. Cousin Jennie M. writes and asks me if I am an intending to do likewise when I return. Henry has very lately returned from the army. What shall I tell Jennie? *[Is this a proposal of marriage? Or are they already engaged?]*

So, you are in trouble and hardly know which way to turn, but Vilie will not think of giving up, I trust, unless there is no chance of succeeding. Remember, "If you find your task is hard", etc. Albany is not the worst place in this world.

I have heard you women, that thought themselves "Ladies" swear. You are right, it does look bad, seemingly much worse than for a man. Yet, 'tis equally as much sin in the man. I am ashamed to confess that here nearly five out of six men swear, but I can honestly say that I am not guilty of that sin. I wish that 'twas so I could visit your school and boarding place -- how I should tease you and pay up for old times. Now, I'll put this by and will write another sheet tomorrow. Goodnight. My candle is out, Vilie.

*****

Thu. 26 Jan.   Visited the 207th Pennsylvania Volunteers in company with Wm. Bedford. Had a pleasant time. Also, was at the 208th Zone Brigade, Third Div., Ninth Army Corps.

Letter #82B

Evening, Jan. 26th, *[1865]*
[In camp, near Warren Station, Virginia]

Now, for another sociable talk. Shall I tell your about the visit? Just listen then. Wm. Bedford and I started at eight A.M.; walked one mile to Warren Station; stepped onto the cars; rode three mile; then walked 1/2 mile; and we were at the 207th. *[We]* Visited with friends there until dark; took the cars; and have just arrived back to camp; eaten supper; and am now telling to you my adventures.

I fear that my promise to write the extra sheet was rather rashly made, for now I find myself face to face with it. My ideas seem very few and uninteresting (what a long word). You will have been home 'ere this reaches you.

It really seems about as difficult for you to get a furlough as I. You surely have not played the school ma'am to perfection or your opportunities of getting transportation would surely not have been so few. School keeping is like the fine arts. There are many parts to be learned, and that is one of the fine points. You know, of course, I have dealt some in that line, and naturally have made some observations and one is this: That a real school ma'm is careful to have some attentive friend of the opposite side of the house, and she is still more careful that said friend drives nice horses and sleighs.

And many other things they do, of which I will tell you when I write my book about school ma'ams. It will doubtless be a splendid book, and I think of having plenty of pictures in it too. You will buy one, I suppose? You remember, don't you, the Molyneux's Dictionary that was to be? They will both be published at the same time.

This time I am writing a wild goose letter, or at least my pen is made of a wild goose quill, and it squeaks every time I make a letter. I try to have it write sober and precise epistle to you, but 'tis no use. Away it goes about some nonsense almost before I know it.

Well, what do you think? I have just reread your letter and found one whole page that I had not read. I was very much surprised to find it 'twas the last page on the first sheet. Suppose I was in too much of a hurry. Mail came in very late, and today *[I]* was away visiting.

O! But what fun I will have with George Pardoe, and how he will wonder how I hear such things. But he will never, never know; that was the way to have a falling out. I like such, but no other kinds are excusable. I do think that 'ere long you may become quite a school ma'am for you have at least had the offer of a way getting home. David B. sure thinks the old adage true, "Faint heart never won fair lady", and perseverance will win eventually. What a pity it is W. C.'s son is not at home. 'Twill perhaps be a life-long regret for both son and father.

I do not expect to visit home this winter. Only a few furloughs are given, and those to persons having friends dangerously sick or urgent business that requires their presence. Possibly, with the present bright prospects of our armies, we may not be held our full time. But I little think I shall get home until August; seven months only, but they appear long thinking of them all at once – most as long as your seven weeks in Albany. I do say here is my two sheets almost filled, and the quill continues to squeak as if it would like to blacken another, but not this time.

With my earnest wishes that you may be enjoying a full share of health, and that your pupils have become well behaved and attentive, I remain truly yours. With much love to Villie, from Joel.

*****

Sat. 28 Jan. Yesterday and last night was quite cold. Think 'twas the coldest of the season. Froze skating ice in wash basins, water pail, etc.

Sun. 29 Jan. Received a visit from Alph Collins, E.S. Little, and Wm. Bedford.

Mon. 30 Jan. Visited the 61st Regt., Pennsylvania Volunteers, in company with E.S. Little. Saw Wm. Snell and Dan Haverly, Jr.

Tue. 31 Jan. A pleasant day. Jan. ends fine. Great interest throughout the army and country; rumors of every kind are afloat. One is that Vice President Stephens of the Rebel congress came into our lines last evening. Great hurrahing along the lines in consequence. Peace, how earnestly that boon, is desired by AMERICA'S SONS! May February be the month forever made memorable by the satisfactorily settlement of this cruel war. Yours truly, Joel L. Molyneux.

[President Davis recommended to the Confederacy Senate the appointment of General Robert E. Lee as general-in-chief of the Confederate armies. The measure came too late to have any effect, and General Lee continued primarily as commander of the Army of Northern Virginia.]

CHAPTER 31: FEBRUARY 1865

Wed. 1 Feb. Am upon guard today from eleven A.M. till one P.M. On post No. Four, special guard seven, till nine P.M. Supernumerary Hoffler, deserter, attempts to escape while unhandcuffed. Brought him back after wounding him. *[He] Is [of the] 124th N.Y.*

[Joel's oral account of the above incident, to his son, Robert, many years later, was as follows: **"The prisoner, Hoffler, ran for it. Being on guard and not wanting to alert the enemy to our position, I decided not to shoot him. Rather, I chased him, and as he was climbing up over an embankment, I threw my rifle, bayonet attached like a spear, and impaled the deserter in the leg."**

[Hoffler was returned to prisoner status, and executed several weeks later. See diary entry February 17, 1865.]

Thu. 2 Feb. Rumors without number. Indications of a move. Vice President Stephens and others surely in our lines.

Fri. 3 Feb. Jan. 31st: an act was passed by the house of representatives forever prohibiting slavery in the United States or territories. Yeas 119, Noes 56. Bully, boys!!

[On January 31, 1865, the U.S. House of Representatives passed the 13th amendment — abolishing slavery. The bill went to the individual states for ratification, and by December 18, 1865, two thirds of the states had given their approval.]

Sat. 4 Feb. Orders for marching. I am to remain for camp and ring guard.

Sun. 5 Feb. Div. on the move toward the left. The Ninth, Fifth, and Second Corps form the expedition. Musketry and artillery heard in direction of Hatchers Creek. Rumors.

[The Battle of Hatcher's Run, as it was later called, lasted until February 7, 1865. It was part of the Petersburg Campaign. About 35,000 Federals were at least partially engaged, with about 1,512 casualties. About 14,000 Confederates were involved. Their casualties are unknown.]

Mon. 6 Feb. The Fifth Corps get driven back. Our Third Brigade are attacked but repulse the enemy.

[On February 6, 1865, General Robert E. Lee assumed command of all armies of the Confederacy. He said he didn't want the job, and didn't have the time nor ability to do it.]

Wed. 8 Feb. Div. remain near Hatchers Run, building breast work and forts. Hd Qrs join to fix up at the Claypole house. *[See December 6, 1864, entry in reference to the Claypole family.]*

Thu. 9 Feb. Riley of the 11th Mass. condemned to be executed tomorrow. Got his sentence postponed.

Fri. 10 Feb. My thirtieth birthday and the third one celebrated in the army. Upon guard. Still at the old Hd Qrs.

Sat. 11 Feb. "'Tis sweet to know that there is an eye that watches for our coming, and will grow brighter when we come."

Sun. 12 Feb. Have moved to near Hd Qrs at the Claypole house. 'Tis a sandy, piney country.

[On February 12, 1865, the United States presidential electoral votes were counted. The incumbent, President Lincoln, received 212 votes and General McClellan 21.]

Wed. 15 Feb. Are busy building a stockade shanty.

Thu. 16 Feb. Move into our new quarters -- four of us in together: Messrs Goheen and Riggs of the 57th Pennsylvania Volunteers and E.S. Gregory and myself of the 141st P.V.

Fri. 17 Feb. Hoffler of the 124th New York was executed today for desertion; a sad affair! I helped in carrying his coffin when marched through the div. Eleven Johns came over.

[On February 17, 1865, Federal troops, under General Sherman, captured Columbia, South Carolina, capital of that state. That night, the city burned, although it wasn't determined who set the fires. It may have been invading Federal troops, resident Negroes, drunken soldiers, or Federal prisoners released from Confederate prisons. Quite likely it was departing Confederate soldiers who where destroying anything that might prove useful to the North, such as cotton.]

Sat. 18 Feb. Working upon quarters. Detailed as asst. com. in guard. Went to the 110th *[in the]* evening.

Mon. 20 Feb. The weather continues favorable and very favorable reports arrive that Charleston and Collumbia *[South Carolina]* are ours. Five Johnnies come tonight.

Tue. 21 Feb. One hundred guns fired in honor of the fall of Charleston and Collunbia. Twelve Jonnies come in. H. Bedford returns to regt.

Wed. 22 Feb. Washington's birthday. One hundred guns fired in honor upon square. Rumors of an attack from the enemy is expected.

Thu. 23 Feb. Lowery *[gloomy]* weather. Visited the regiment.

Fri. 24 Feb. Wilmington *[North Carolina]* officially stated as having capitulated. Rumors of the evacuation of Petersburg. On the right, heavy cannonading.

Mon. 27 Feb. Signed the pay rolls, and rec'd four month's pay. Sixty-four ($64) dollars. Maj. Assen, paymaster. Regt. paid up to Jan. 1st, '65.

Tue. 28 Feb. Another month gone. Mustered out for two more mo. pay, and out the same.

CHAPTER 32: MARCH 1865

Letter #83A

Hd Qrs, Third Div. Second Army Corps
March First, 1865
[In camp, near Hatches Creek, Virginia]

My Dear Friend:

At last gets *[written]* the letter purposed to be at your home awaiting your arrival after the closing of your school. But lo and behold, the first of March finds me commencing to write it. My last was written the eighth of Feb., 20 days since. Soon after that we moved to another position, and having fresh quarters to put up and considerable of other duties also. Our time has been taken up so you certainly will pardon me, will you not?

I yet enjoy my usual good health. Others of your acquaintance here are also enjoying the same. You, and I will suppose, *[are]* now at home and enjoying your self once more with friends and home comforts. Sleighing you are not having, from my last advises. O, how I should like to be in that vicinity and enjoy a few good sleigh rides. Perhaps you would help to enjoy them with me?

Our friend Randal is married, I am informed, to Miss Kate G. What will the rest of his admirers do, think you?

Cousin J. Bird has lately written to me and he professes to have chosen the Good Way *[accepted the Lord]*. The reformation in that neighborhood has been quite general. I am rejoiced to hear of it, and hope they may all continue in well-doing. Cousin Eliza Snell writes that Miss Hettie H. has a Bryan friend, sueing for her favor. You and her are some alike, or should I say, George and I?

What good news of late has been coming from Gen. Sherman and others in the South? Savannah and Charleston, Collumbia, and Wilmington have fallen into our possession. The war must certainly come to an end shortly. If only it could be settled without any more fighting, what a mercy 'twould be. I hope sincerely such another campaign as last spring's may not be in store for us. Deserters come from the enemy to us quite numerous. From six to a dozen every night arrive at our Hd Qrs alone. At City Point the number is estimated to be one hundred per day.

Four months pay has lately been given the troops, and some of the boys are having high times for there is hard cases here as well as in Albany. Did you ever see a drunken man? I hope, if not, you may never witness the sight.

*****

Thu. 2 March. Sent by J. Pennington to City Point, fifty dollars ($50). James Pardoe sent fifty dollars and William Bedford sent thirty five, in all $135. expressed to David Molyneux, care of Ellis Bryan.

Fri. 3 March. Visited the Sixth Corps, Ninth N. Y., and 61st P.V. Was at Patric Station, etc.

[On March 3, 1865, the U.S. Congress passed the act setting up the Freedman's Bureau which was to have overall supervisory powers over those in the South dislocated, or needing temporary assistance.]

Letter #83B

March third, Evening
[In camp, near Hatches Creek, Virginia]

Letter still unfinished. Almost constant duty. Besides rainy, bad weather has kept me from writing. I do not think that I will dare to specify any time for writing again, for something is about certain to prevent my doing as I propose. I had hoped a letter from you 'ere mailing this. Perhaps one will come this evening. We get mail every evening and it goes away every morning.

I called to see one or two of my friends today. Wm. Snell for one; two others were cousins from N.Y. that I had not seen before being in the army.

O! Do you like to read old letters? I have some almost too good for to burn. You must not be surprised I should put one in some time to be called for in a few days less than six mo., but this sheet is filled, and I must interline or close. *["Interline" means to turn the letter upside down and write between the previously written lines.]* No mail tonight, I hear called out so I will close this, seal it, and carry it to the office. Good bye once more, and except my best wishes for your health and happiness. Also, much love from Joel.

P. S. My tent mate has just received an express box from home, and we are faring, in consequence, very good. At present. I am expecting to receive one in a few days. A very large number of deserters came in last night.

*****

Sat. 4 March. A heavy wind and rainstorm. The day for the inauguration of President Lincoln to his second term of office.

[President Lincoln's Second Inaugural Address set a tone of reconciliation with the Confederacy, at this the winding down of the war. He pronounced these firm words of inspiration, hope, and understanding:]

> *Neither party expected for the war, the magnitude, or the duration, which it has already attained. Neither anticipated that the cause of the conflict might cease with, or even before, the conflict itself should cease. Each looked for an easier triumph, and a result less fundamental and astounding. Both read the same Bible, and pray to the same God; and each invokes His aid against the other. The prayers of both could not be answered — that of neither has been answered fully. Fondly do we hope, fervently do we pray, that this mighty scourge of war speedily pass away.*

With an eye to the future, President Lincoln gave his view of a proper peace:

> *With malice toward none; with charity for all; with firmness in the right, as God gives us to see the right, let us strive to finish the work we are in; to bind up the Nation's wounds; to care for him who shall have borne the battle, and for his widow and his orphan, to do all which may achieve and cherish a just and a lasting peace, among ourselves, and with all nations.*

Tue. 7 March. Wm. Snell was here at Hd Qrs to see me. After dinner I went with him to the regt. Am on guard today.

Wed. 8 March. Good news from Sheridan. Deserters report early and command as being captured by Gen. Sheridan.

Thu. 9 March. Rumored that our div. was to go into the *[Shenandoah]* Valley. Moses Joseph made lt. in the guard house.

Fri. 10 March. Rains continued. Guards are in quite good spirits. Every one is getting drinks that can lead to the unlucky.

Sat. 11 March. Corps reviewed by Gen. Grant. My express box arrived that was started the 16th of Feb. Everything all right. Probabilities of a move.

[On March 11, 1865, President Lincoln issued a proclamation giving Federal deserters a free pardon if they turned themselves in within 60 days. Failure to do so would result in loss of citizenship. Confederate General Robert E. Lee made a similar proposal to Confederate troops who had deserted.]

Letter #84

Near Hatches Creek, Va.
Evening, March 11th, 1865

Dear Sister: *[Sallie]*

This evening finds me answering your letter that should have been done before this. The present finds me quite well, and the same may be said of all the others of your acquaintance here.

A few days ago, I visited the Ninth N.Y. in the Sixth A. C. *[Army Corps]* and found Charley Groesbeck and Alfred Sloan. I did not know *[recognize]* them nor they me. Charley's health is not first rate. He was busy at that time, and *[I]* did not make but a short visit. I expect them to make me a call soon. I saw Will Snell, too. His regt. lies near their's -- about a mile of where we are. I hardly know when I wrote my last letter. The move made by this part of the army. the fifth of Feb. caused us to change camp and build new quarters some two miles further to the left and front. I think I wrote you about that time.

O! My box came all right. The shirts will suit, I think, to a T, though I have not been in them yet. I have a lot of the berries and apples stewing while I write this. The box was nearly a month on the way and *[I]* am thinking that I shall not have time to consume the many things sent. Wm. B. has been here and taken his portion. James will be here to get his, I guess, this evening. I will enclose three dollars to help finish paying for the shirts, and I will endeavor to repay you for the trouble I have made, etc. some time hereafter, besides being many times obliged, also.

I have rec'd but one letter this month, that was from Geo. Pardoe a few days since. He writes that he will go to Poughkeepsie to attend a Commercial College there. He must intend being a mercantile man. I wish him success. His present term *[at Lewisburg College]* closes this month.

We rec'd four month's pay the last of Feb. James and I expressed $100 to David.

Today our corps was reviewed by Gen. Grant. He is getting things in shape for an early campaign. The news of late has been very good. Sheridan is again victorious in the *[Shenandoah]* Valley I hope that everything may continue in our favor, and in a few months I think surely this war must end. Their troops are hopeless of success and desert at every opportunity. Nearly from one to two hundred of them have been rec'd at army Hd Qrs daily for some time past.

The schools are supposed *[to be]* all closed and the school ma'ams have gone, and come home. The sleighing must by this time be melting away, and the sugar season commencing. Some such things I would like to have a hand in, but the five months and a few *[days]* stand between, but "while there is life there is hope".

Oh! The weddings: Randal and Kate G., and D. Potter with Lib Wilkerson. I have nothing to say, but some things are queer, and queer things do take place, you know.

I was glad to hear that such good had been accomplished at that protracted meeting. I would have liked to attended, but we are situated quite differently, instead of enjoying such privileges. Doc Bird writes me a very good letter saying that he has commenced a New Life. I hope they may all continue right. The package of letters have all been ans., excepting Rebecca's, and that must be soon, or I will be crossed off her list.

Write soon, as convenient. Excuse a short letter, having but little time to spare this evening as we have an inspection early in the morning. Tell John he was lucky for being drafted when he was. I have not learned yet if the draft has taken place. Except my love, and the same to John. With respect to all who may enquire, from your brother, Joel.

*****

Sun. 12 March.   Roads fast drying and even getting dusty in places.

Mon. 13 March.   Fine March continued. Nice and moonlight. Rumors and expectations of moving soon. Cheering along the lines, and considerable of musketry upon account of deserters coming in.

[The South had been debating the advisability of using Negro slaves as soldiers. On March 13, 1865, the Confederate Congress approved their use. Owners were asked to volunteer their slaves and it was understood that slaves who served would be set free. The action came too late in the war to be of any value to the South, and few blacks served in the Confederate army. Many Southern blacks, however, served in Union forces.]

Tue. 14 March.   Eighteen deserters came in last night.

Wed. 15 March.   Snow, rain, rainy night. Some deserters last night, but did not learn how many.

Thu. 16 March.   High winds and showery. Eighteen deserters last night came in to our div. guards drafted for the firing party for an execution on the 18th.

Fri. 17 March. Winds continued. Nine Jonnies *[came in to surrender]* last night. The movement is postponed.

Sat. 18 March. John Smith, Eighth Jersey, executed for desertion to the enemy. Shot to death by musketry. Cannonading upon the right in evening.

Sun. 19 March. Band plays church music, etc. Write letter.

Letter #85

Near Hatches Creek, Va.
19th Mar., 1865

Dear Friend:

This pleasant Sabbath morning finds me commencing a few more lines to you. The last I have heard from you bears date of Jan. 31st, and I have written, when this is done, three letters since. Perhaps the deep snows of Sullivan may have blocked the roads so that since your return home the mail has been delayed. In fact, no letters have reached me this month from S. *[Sallie]*, so I conclude that to be the case. My health remains quite good. *[I]* Have no cause to complain whatever.

We are yet in camp, but have been expecting a move for some days. The weather is fine and spring like. The roads are quite good and dusty in places. We will certainly have something to do 'ere long, and how I hope we may be successful and terminate this cruel war. Furloughs have been stopped so that I shall not think of seeing you until Aug. Only four whole months! They will soon pass by, and then these three long years will be ended. Vilie, you can scarcely imagine how very long they seemed to me when we first parted. A month did not appear to make the number less.

Are you busy in making maple sugar now? After such a winter I shall suppose there might be a good season for it. I always enjoyed a visit to the sugar bush, especially when the kettles were about to be swung off full of the foaming sweet – just ready to be molded into great cakes. If I were in Elkland now, and should happen along just at the right time, would you not give me just a little piece?

[A sugar bush is a grove of sugar maple trees used to produce maple sap. In early spring, farmers tapped their maple trees, collected the sap in little buckets, and carried the sap to their evaporator. There, syrup was made by the simple process of evaporating off most of the water. Further evaporation of the syrup yielded cakes of maple sugar. It took 30 to 50 gallons of maple sap to yield one gallon of syrup. Syrup was used in the home as a sweetener on

breakfast pancakes, corn bread, waffles, toast, hot mush, etc. Maple sugar cakes served as candy and as sugar.]

O! I must tell you about Geo. Pardoe. I asked him about a certain upsett, etc. He does not know what to think of it. He does not, for once, imagine how I hear. I will enclose his letter, but be careful that Hettie does not find out that you ever mentioned anything to me. He is welcome to get ahead of me if he can. I shall also enclose a portion of the envelope *[which]* upon the outside he writes an ans. to a couplet sent him. Also, upon the outside I was out of stamps then and the army not paid since the first of Aug. Since, we have been paid for four months, but about the letter or superscription, as he calls it, was this: "Soldier's letter. Shove it through. Nary red, but six months due." I am quite proud to know we have such a poetical young man for a relative.

Do you know who this old man is that he refers to? Write the particulars of them, but be careful, and I will also, that they do not get the start of us. I suppose he corresponds with her, and it is likely Miss Hettie will help him what she can.

Cousin Eliza Snell writes me frequently of what is going on around Hillsgrove. Eliza *[Samuel's widow]* is a good cousin, and writes the best of letters. Her brother, Will, is near here in the Sixth A. C. I see him occasionally. Lybie Mc. and all other teachers, I presume, *[are]* now at home. You are fully resolved to not teach again, I suppose? I have forgotten most of the little I ever knew, so that I shall not think of teaching again.

Is the draft scaring the people up there, or are they getting used to such things? Not thinking of anything further, I will wait for the arrival of your letter. You cannot tell how I wish to hear from you. Will you not please to write very soon after getting this? Except my truest love and ever remember me with affection. Joel. Please excuse the yellow envelope.

*****

Mon. 20 March.   Sister, Sallie's, birthday; she being 28 years old. No letter yet this month from home.

Letter #86

[This letter to Joel is from former teacher, C. R. Coburn, Towanda Academy. At this time, Professor Coburn was stationed in Harrisburg, Pennsylvania's state capital, as State Superintendent of Schools.]

Pennsylvania Department of Common Schools
Harrisburg, *[Pennsylvania]*, March 20, 1865

Dear Friend:

You may be assured that I was happy to receive your kind letter. It is pleasant to be remembered by pupils. I am glad to learn of your good health. Many of those who went out with you have died in one way or other. You should be thankful to God you have been spared. Ah, I hope "this cruel war" will soon be over and our friend will again be with us.

Give my best regards to James Coburn *[his nephew]*. Tell him that I think he could write to me more frequently. Say also to him that I have sold my house in Towanda, and expect to start tomorrow morning to go up and move down my things and family on a raft to go to Middletown, nine miles below here. The river *[Susquehanna]* here has been higher than it was ever known before. The whole county along its branches and the main stream has been swept clean. Yours, with respects, C. R. Coburn

[The move Superintendent Coburn planned was from Towanda to Middletown, a distance of 200 or more miles via the Susquehanna Canal. Imagine putting your household goods and family on a raft trip of that length.]

*****

Tue. 21 March.   Hear Mary M. is dead. Appearance of rain and at night get at it quite considerable. Still in camp, and no letters.

Wed. 22 March.   Jonas Bedford visits us and *[he and]* I visit at regt. most of the day. Stays all night, three in bed, etc.

Thu. 23 March.   Winds and hurricane. Corps reviewed. Visited by sand storm. Trees twisted off and torn up. Men and animals killed. High winds again in the night.

Fri. 24 March.   Play chess and checkers and write letters. *[Joel carried his chess pieces all during his service. I learned to play on that set, and still own it.]*

Sat. 25 March.   Awakened by artillery. Reb charge upon the right, and we upon the left. They take Fort Steadman, only to get repulsed. Altogether, we take 3,000 prisoners.

Sun. 26 March.   Sunday! All quiet today, but an occasional shot on the picket line. One man wounded yesterday.

Mon. 27 March. Great rumors afloat of another move. Sheridan is reported as being here, and that his cavalry *[is]* with the Fifth, Sixth, and Second Corps.

[Many Confederate soldiers were being captured and deserting at this latter stage of the war. Word was out that they would be treated reasonably. On March 27, 1865, Lincoln met with Generals Grant and Sherman, plus Admiral Porter, aboard the <u>River Queen</u> ship at City Point, Virginia. There, the president proposed they grant U.S. citizenship to rebels who laid down their arms. This conciliatory attitude on the part of the president laid the groundwork for favorable terms of the peace that came the following month.]

Tue. 28 March. Will move to the left. The 24th Corps is also reported here. We are to move in the morning. All packed up. Peach trees in blossom.

Wed. 29 March. Start upon our spring campaign. The Fifth Corps and Sheridan with his cavalry go to our left. We also move to the left meeting with no opposition, and build works, and go in to camp near our old battlefield of Oct. 27th, 1864.

[This Siege of Petersburg was the beginning of the Union Army of the Potomac's final offensive against the Confederate Army of Northern Virginia. There, 125,000 Union soldiers were pitted against 50,000 Confederates. Grant's plan was to keep General Lee and the Army of Northern Virginia separated from General Joseph Johnston in the South. Union General Sherman, also in the South, provided a pincer against which Generals Lee and Johnston, even if united, would be ineffective.]

Thu. 30 March. The Fifth Corps and cavalry have a fight! Our lines are advanced. Rebs fall back out of the works. *[We]* build fresh works, and camp in hard wood and hard rain.

Fri. 31 March. Our div. moves left and takes the old battlefield for its position. Reb. fort in front makes it a villious *[villainous]* place. We are deployed and get shelled. Gen. Grant rides along the lines and he gets shelled. Fifth Corps gets driven back. Our First Div. gets engaged and checks the enemy's advance. Our men are now close under the reb. fort, and the S. S. *[sharp shooters]* keep them from working their guns. Our lines are being straightened and strengthened.

CHAPTER 33: APRIL 1865

Sat. 1 April. Our lines remain nearly quiet. Hear cannonading on the left and also on the right. In the evening John Henrys cheer lustily. Pickets keep up a continual firing. Rebs seem to be trying our lines. Artillery opens on our right.

Sun. 2 April. This morning *[opened]* with a tremendous roar. Something is up. Sixth Corps has broken through near Petersburg, and carrying everything before them. Our men advance up on the fort, take it and on we go for Petersburg. Arrive before dark. Johns still hold the town. A. P. Hill killed!

[General Ambrose Powell Hill, a valiant commander and one of the best generals in the Army of Northern Virginia, fought with distinction in many battles. In the above-mentioned engagement, one Union corps forced a breakthrough that isolated a section of the Confederate army at Hatcher's Run. General Hill rode forward to close the breach and was killed by a band of Federal stragglers.

[On April 2, 1865, General Robert E. Lee gave up the city of Richmond and pulled his troops out of the fort of Petersburg, one step ahead of his foes. Confederacy President Jefferson Davis and his cabinet also left Richmond, and the Confederate States of America became a government on the run. President Davis and some members of his cabinet went to Danville, Virginia. They stayed there a week and then moved on south to North Carolina and finally to Georgia where they were captured at Irwinville.]

Mon. 3 April. John Henrys evacuate during the night. Richmond also gives up. The army retreat; we after them, cross the S. S. *[South Side]* RR. Cannon and caissons are abandoned. March till midnight. Prisoners brought in: 218.

[Richmond officially surrendered to Union troops at 8:15 A.M. on Monday, April 3, 1865. Union troops occupied both Richmond and Petersburg. Rioting followed and much of Richmond was looted and burned.]

Tue. 4 April. Up early and march at eight A.M. A Gen. and large lot of prisoners brought in. Also a band of M. *[mercenaries]*. Bad roads and have to corduroy. Go into camp before night. A pleasant situation: The country is romantic; ground rolling ridges. Machine shop burned today.

[On April 4, 1865, President Lincoln visited the recently vacated Confederate capital Richmond.]

Wed. 5 April.   Routed up at three. Move at daylight. Go two mile and then draw rations. Go ten more and we come up with the Fifth Corps and the cavalry on the Danville RR. Cavalry heavy had a brush here and have captured quite a number of prisoners and several stands of colors.

Thu. 6 April.   Up early. Cavalry go to the left. Our corps to the right. Pass Roanoke St. or Petersville. Skirmishing commences. Gen. Mott gets wounded. Sight their train. They make a stand. Charge them out of it.

[Some historians called this several days' engagement "The Battle of Sailors Creek". Actually, it was the "The Battle of Sayler's Creek" which was, and still is, the name of the creek. Union forces of 36,500, opposed 16,900 Confederates. The Union had 1,180 casualties and Confederates 7,700. Union forces captured about 8,000 Confederate prisoners.]

Fri. 7 April.   Capture some 300 prisoners, quantities of ammunition, destroyed cannons. Caissons and bake ovens abandoned. At night we capture part of their train – some 300 wagons, with horses, mules, etc. This morning we move and soon find more Rebs, wagons, etc. Strike the Lynchburg R R at High Bridge -- 21 span, 110 ft. long, 100 ft high -- four spans burned. Here is a branch of the Appomatox in Amelia County. Eighteen pieces of artillery spiked *[temporarily disabled by driving a spike into the vent]* and left. Negro soldiers of the Ninth Corps. J. H.'s make a stand and we get a brisk fight. We are near Farmersville *[Farmville]*.

[The minor Battle of High Bridge was the last fighting of the war for the 141st Regiment.]

Sat. 8 April .   Rebs retreat in the night. Strike a pike road, coal mines, pick up lots of John H. stragglers. Cannonading ahead. Flag of truce. Pass New Store. Draw 3/4 rations: hard bread, no coffee or sugar. Men grumble; nightmare. Go in camp between three and four A.M. with prospect good for tomorrow.

Sun. 9 April.   More cannon heard this morning. Move six mile with no opposition. Another flag of truce. Three hour armistice. F. H. officers and Southern Express wagons pass. Great excitement!! Gen. Mede comes and announces that Lee has surrendered. Tremendous excitement and cheering.

[From a practical point of view, Lee's surrender of the Army of Northern Virginia, Palm Sunday, April 9, 1865, Appomattox Court House, marked the end of the Civil War. Some other Southern armies, though, continued fighting for the next several months. Other Confederate units disbanded without surrendering.]

Mon. 10 April. Remain in camp. Orders to stop foraging *[stealing food and feed from local residents]*. Lee's forces estimated at near 25,000 — opened the campaign with near 80,000, all gone. Rumors that Johnson *[Confederate General Joseph E. Johnston]* had surrendered. *[General Johnston surrendered April 26, 1865. See diary for that day.]* Peace prospects and home meditations.

[After his surrender to General Ulysses S. Grant, commander of the Union armies, Confederate General Robert E. Lee, commander of the Confederate armies, addressed his troops in the Army of Northern Virginia:]

> *After four years of arduous service, marked by unsurpassed courage and fortitude, the Army of Northern Virginia has been compelled to yield to overwhelming numbers and resources. I need not tell the survivor of so many hard fought battles who have remained steadfast to the last, that I have consented to this result from no distrust of them, but feeling that valor and devotion could accomplish nothing that could compensate for the loss that would have attended the continuation of the contest. I have to avoid the useless sacrifice of those whose past services have endeared them to their countrymen.*
>
> *By the terms of the agreement, officers and men can return to their homes and remain there until exchanged. You will take with you the satisfaction that proceeds from the consciousness of duty faithfully performed, and I earnestly pray that a merciful God will extend to you his blessing and protection.*
>
> *With an increasing admiration of your constancy and devotion to your country, and a grateful remembrance of your kind and generous consideration of myself, I bid you an affectionate farewell.*

Tue. 11 April. We march back to New Store. Twelve mile muddy marching, but no straggling now. The Johns are paroled, or are to be soon.

[On April 11, 1865, President Abraham Lincoln addressed a crowd gathered at the White House. He defended the newly-created state government of Louisiana, and told his audience that reconstruction plans must remain flexible. It was his last public address.]

Wed. 12 April. March to Farmersville *[Farmville]* 20 mile. Pass Willis Mountain and Buckingham Court House. Hard day's march. Farmersville is a pretty little town of some 2,000 inhabitants.

Thu. 13 April. March in the mud, very bad game, more slow, pass High Bridge. Stream up; have to wade, boys holler. Trains and artillery get behind. Go in camp near Burkeville. Fifteen mile today. Draw rations of pork and get a mail.

Fri. 14 April. Good Friday. Remain in camp till near night. Hd Qrs then move a short distance and fix for resting a few days. The captured rebs have been paroled. Guerrillas report, etc.

[There were many bands of roving guerrillas, most of whom were former Confederate soldiers who had deserted. Their actions were governed by greed, but had some overtones of patriotism. Outlaw-bushwhacker, William Clarke Quantrill, and his raiders, caused great devastation in Kansas, Missouri, and Kentucky. He was captured by a group of Federal stragglers in Kentucky.

[On April 14, 1865, the United States flag was again raised over Fort Sumter, South Carolina — four years to the day it was forced down. General Robert Anderson, directing the flag-raising, was the same officer who had surrendered the fort four years earlier.

[On the night of April 14, 1865, President and Mrs. Abraham Lincoln attended a play at Ford's Theater in Washington. At the theater, about ten that evening, John Wilkes Booth shot the president through the head. He died the next day.]

Letter #87

[This is the letter Joel has been aching to write for months. It announces the Confederate Army of Northern Virginia has surrendered to the Union Army of the Potomac. After the famous surrender, most regiments within the Army of the Potomac stayed together and started the long walk back to the Washington area where they were to be mustered out. Southern troops were allowed to retain all their possessions, except their guns, and go home.]

Near Burkesville, Va.
April 14th, 1865

My Dear Friend:

Your letter of March 16th has just been received, and a spare moment today is improved in ans. it. By this you will see I am yet spared life, and I can also enjoy good health.

Since writing previous, our army has been marching and fighting, and also wonderfully successfully. We started upon our campaign the 29th *[of March]*, the day your letter was written. Upon the second of April, the enemy's lines were broken, and we took possession of Petersburg and Richmond. Lee's army retreating towards Lynchburg, and almost without halting we followed after him fighting more or less every day.

Upon the ninth, our forces surrounded him and he was forced to surrender with the remainder of his army, some 25,000 men with all his trains, etc. We had captured, previous to this, near 40,000 from him. Lee *[was]* within 30 mile of Lynchburg when he surrendered, and in Buckingham Co.

We are now marching back toward Richmond or Washington, have marched 50 mile the last three days. We now think the war is near its end. Do you not think we have been wonderfully successful? And our losses have been very light considering what has been successful. Our regt. has had none killed, one slightly wounded. Our div. General, Mott, was wounded but not dangerous. Our former Colonel, Madill, was wounded, and has since died. He was made a Gen. last winter. *[General Henry J. Madill was indeed wounded, but did not die, as Joel had heard. General Gershom Mott, former New Jersey business man, had an unstable army career. After the war General Mott became a railroad employee.]*

I have time to write little more as the mail leaves soon. I rec'd a letter from Sister Sallie same time as yours. The mail had not reached us before now, since the first of April, so you may guess how glad I was to hear from you. I was happy to know that you had "chosen the good part, that cannot be taken away", and I know that you will not forget your friend that is yet out of that Ark of Safety.

Vilie, I hope soon to come home now. I think our services will no longer be needed. The only thing that makes me feel sad is that there are so many that came out here with us that will not return.

I will write again when we get through our march, and have time for such things. This place is 50 mile of Richmond. I do not know if we are to have transportation or not. Except my kindest regards and ever remember me with affection, as ever yours, Joel. To Vilie:

P. S. Excuse haste. J. L. M.

*****

Sat. 15 April.   Gen. Anderson was to raise the stars and stripes upon Ft. Sumter yesterday. We still remain in camp, as usual. A telegram -- "Lincoln dies this morning at 22 minutes past seven o'clock!"

Sun. 16 April.   Dispatch comes that: "President Lincoln has been assassinated and that Secretary Seward and son murdered." The feelings of the army is excited to a high degree. We are still near Burkeville.

Mon. 17 April.   Second dispatch: "Lincoln is dead. Sect. Seward not dead, is likely to recover. Lincoln's assassin is not taken yet." He is said to be J. Wilkes Booth. Hd Qrs changes position.

[On the night of April 14, 1865, John Wilkes Booth shot and killed President Abraham Lincoln. That same night, another assassin, Lewis Payne, tried unsuccessfully to kill Secretary of State Seward. Seward was at home, in bed, recuperating from a carriage accident he had been involved in a week earlier. Seward's son and a male nurse saved the secretary's life.]

Tue. 18 April.   Resign my position as Assistant Comm. McCarron goes to his reg. Co. H. goes home. Still have warm fine days.

Wed. 19 April.   The day appointed for the president's funeral. All unnecessary work suspended. 21 minute guns fired. Mobile *[Alabama]* reported taken officially.

[On April 19, 1865, President Abraham Lincoln's funeral was held in the East Room of the White House. Lincoln's funeral sermon was delivered by Phineas Gurley, pastor of the New York Avenue Presbyterian Church, which President Lincoln attended, in Washington, D.C. The president's body was then taken by train to Illinois for burial.]

Letter #88

Near Burksville, Va.
April 19, 1865

Dear Brother: *[David]*

Was glad to hear you all were well. I had just written a short letter to you the morning I rec'd yours in the evening. Our corps is yet in camp near the place the junction of the Danville and Lynchburg RR. The weather is now quite warm and the mud caused by recent rains dried up. Woods are nearly in full leaf, perhaps some ahead of those in Sullivan. 'Ere this you have the full particulars of our short and most successful campaign. Lee's army has been paroled, all under a Col. What disposition is to be made of the officers I could not say.

Right in the footsteps of our rejoicing comes the doleful tidings of the assassination of President Lincoln and Secretary Seward. Our last dispatch states that Seward may recover, but that the president died the morning of the 15th, and will be buried today. The 21 guns fired for the occasion has just ceased. 'Tis sad to think that just as the great work of crushing the rebellion is accomplished that the hand of a vile traitor should end his life. Indignation against the perpetrators runs very high here. 'Tis said the assassin has been caught, and he is an actor named Booth, but I need not write particulars as you will have them 'ere this reaches you.

We are hoping that part of the army will be mustered out, and that the '62 men will be the ones, but nothing reliable is yet received what will be done.

I have just rec'd a letter from J. H. Summers *[Cousin John]*. 'Twas written the 29th. He was well then. Had the command of his company, they were expecting a movement & that they would join General Thomas *[General George Henry Thomas]*.

I have not heard from Jonas since the move. I think I wrote of his visiting me after his visit home.

It was fortunate that Michael got home before he was taken down sick. I was glad to hear that he had got released. I trust 'ere this he has so far recovered his health as to be around again. In regard to his inquiries about Johny, I can only say that he returned to duty in his reg. sometime last summer, and the last time we crossed the James River at Deep Bottom, and had an engagement, he was wounded in the ankle, how serious I never could learn. He has never returned from the hospital, but has been transferred to the Invalid Corps. I do not know his address. If Michael wishes I do not know that I can find out by inquiries of his company officers.

I was very sorry to hear that D. G. Huskell *[hard to decipher, question on spelling]* has again been taken again with the crazyness. It must cause so much sorrow for his friends. From what I hear of Randal *[Dr. Randall]* I would like to help tar him.

I was quite surprised when I rec'd Martin Price's letter. It had been so long hearing from him. He must of joined the army nearly at the time I did.

The money I sent I was glad to hear you rec'd without causing you much trouble. I do not suppose we will get payed again before being mustered out.

You are doubtless into your farm work now -- hands being scarce will make work plenty during the planting season. If a few of us boys that are lying idle here could put in a day or two it would help some, especially if they would take hold like they do when after rails for cooking coffee. I have seen farms large as yours striped of their rails in 15 minutes, coffee cooked, and the head of the columns moving out again. It looked tough in the first, but nothing after one gets used to it.

[When troops were on the march and stopped for a rest break, the first ones to arrive would build fires on which they would start heating water for coffee. If available, they would use wood rails from farmers' rail fences. At that time, most farm fences were zigzag rail fences made with split logs eight to

twelve feet long. They made good firewood since they were dry and the right diameter to ignite easily. Instead of a round bonfire, they would have a long fire with many rails burning at the same time and heating a line of tin coffee pots. The last troops to arrive would have their coffee water already heated and the first ones would be off again.

[Armies of both sides would march 20 to 23 miles per day over good terrain. Occasionally, they would walk 25 to 30 miles per day. There were instances of their walking 35 or 36 miles per day. Confederate troops had the reputation of being able to walk faster and farther than Union troops. One reason for this was that they didn't carry so much. Southern troops jestingly referred to Union soldiers as dray horses and themselves as race horses.]

I do not think of anything more to write so will close, hoping these lines may find you all enjoying health, with my love & well wishes to all, I remain, as ever, your absent brother, Joel

*****

Thu. 20 April   Jo Johnson officially reported as having surrendered.

[Actually Confederate General Joseph E. Johnston surrendered later, on April 26, 1865. Generals Johnston and Lee graduated in the same class (1829) at the Academy. General Lee was 2nd, and General Johnston was 13th in the class of 46 members.]

Fri. 21 April.   Feel somewhat indisposed. Headache and boil upon my chin. Short cake for dinner. Yet encamped near Burksville.

[On April 21, 1865, Colonel John Mosby, the famed "Gray Ghost" disbanded his famous troops. Most of them went to Federal outposts and applied for parole.]

Sat. 22 April.   Convalescent bill of fare: boiled flour dumplings in addition to our usual rations.

Sun. 23 April.   Sixth Corps said to have started for Danville. Moses Joseph brought back. Draw trousers.

Mon. 24 April.   Indications of our corps moving.

Tue. 25 April.   Nation's fast day. All serene. No move for us. The president is lain in his last resting place, Illinois. 13 guns fired at four A.M. and one every 1/2 hour after till eight P.M., then close with 13. *[Written on the side of the paper, "An error."]*

Wed. 26 April.   Nothing out of the usual routine of camp life, save sensation rumors of '62 *[enlistees of 1862]* men to be called in, etc.

[On April 26, 1865, Confederate General Joseph E. Johnston surrendered his Army of the Tennessee to Union General William T. Sherman, Durham Station, North Carolina.]

Thu. 27 April.   J. Wilkes Booth, the assassin of the president, is announced taken. Detective Baker found him and an accomplice at Front Royal. He was killed.

[Assassin John Wilkes Booth and accomplice, David E. Herold, were found not at Front Royal, but near Port Royal, Caroline County, Virginia. That was south of the Rappahannock River at the farm of Richard Garrett. Company L, of the New York 16th Cavalry, surrounded the barn and called upon the two men to surrender. Herold came out and surrendered. Booth refused to surrender. The barn was set on fire, and Booth shot and killed himself.]

Fri. 28 April.   Visited reg. Officially announced that Jo Johnson had surrendered. Great cheering and the wood is illuminated. Bottles and guns fired muchly.

Sat. 29 April.   Blue today. Toothache! Days seem long now we have nothing to do.

Sun. 30 April.   Church music by the band. Upon guard.

Letter #89A

[The following letter to Vi showed that although the "cruel war" was still very much on his mind, the tone of his writing was distinctly different. Now, he knew for sure he was coming home again, and it wouldn't be a matter of whether he was one of the lucky survivors. The men of the 141st Regiment, and other regiments of the Army of the Potomac, had a long walk ahead of them back to Washington, D.C. But that didn't dim their spirits.]

Near Burkesville, Va.
April 30, 1865

Dear Friend:

This Sabbath afternoon finds me penning a few more lines for your perusal. With the exception of a slight headache, I still enjoy my usual health. We are yet encamped at the same point as when last writing to you upon the 14th. How much longer we are to remain here is quite uncertain. I have rec'd but one letter from you yet since your school closed. That *[one]* bears the date of March 29th. I have *[had]* no letters from home later than the 20th Apr.

I will suppose that all the people *[of the]* North are very glad the war is at an end. Yes! The cruel war is over at last, and we are in hopes that within a month we shall be upon our way home. I can but feel glad at the prospect of returning once again to home and friends, our government saved, and the blessing of peace ours.

Yet, feelings of sadness will come when the thought of those others that left home with me that they, many of them, will never return to their friends. Of the 12 that came out at that time from our place, six are sleeping in a soldier's grave. *[Of the twelve boys from the Elkland area who had enlisted with him in Company K, six of them had been killed.]*

A very sad affair was the murder of the president. His loss was felt deeply by the army. Lincoln was a good man, and the nation could ill spare him at this time. But his murderer has already met his fate. On the night of the 25th, Booth and one of his accomplices was captured, but of this you will have heard, 'ere this reaches you. They had already escaped into Virginia. Booth was killed before he was taken.

[Joel identified with President Lincoln, and thought of him as a personal friend. Probably many people thought of President Lincoln in that way. Both men were compassionate and forgiving, and had deep religious feelings. Both wanted to save the Union.]

A wedding, I have heard, was to take place at Millview some time soon, my last letter stated. Jenny has, I presume, 'ere this, bid adieu to single life. Jennie certainly is a fine girl, and I hope George is worthy of her. I have concluded not to finish the letter today. I do not feel like writing, and the mail does not go out till tomorrow, so adieu for the present.

*****

CHAPTER 34: MAY and JUNE 1865

Mon. 1 May.   All day preparations are being made for a march back to Richmond. Distance 55 mi. by rail, three mile further by the dirt road. We lay two 1/2 mile from junc.

Letter #89B

[Continuation letter to Elvira]

May 1st, *[1865]*
[Encamped near Burkesville, Virginia]

Quite early I have taken my pen to finish the letter. Mail has just come in, but no letters for poor me. Our boys are all talking of going to Washington. The impression is quite general that we start in a day or so. Last night we were visited by heavy thunder showers. The clouds, like a spoiled child, seemed inclined to sudden fits of weeping. This morning the air is damp and cool, and my headache is all gone, so when the sun comes out you and I may go a Maying. In fancy's dreams last night I was at home, and I thought I made a promise to call your way today. Well, I have pretty good hopes of this proving real 'ere long.

Say, Villie, have you grown any older while I have been away? Are you yet only 17? The wheel of time has continued to roll me around placing a vast distance between the once disappointed youth and the poor old soldier I now see myself.

I hear your Aunt Chloe has passed meeting and premeditates matrimony. And Sallie writes that my niece Rebecca has such notions also. She *[Rebecca]* needed both age and discretion when I came away, in my opinion. I hope you are enjoying good health and that I may hear from you soon. Please to except my best regards and much love from your absent friend, Joel to Villie.

[Joel mentions, "Aunt Chloe has passed meeting". Among Friends, important matters, as betrothals, were brought before the assembled church for finding the will of the Lord. Chloe's having "passed meeting" indicates the church body approved of her intended betrothal. The "niece Rebecca", mentioned above, was Rebecca Sarah Pardoe, daughter of Joel's sister, Mary. Sister Mary and husband Joseph Pardoe had six children who reached maturity. Rebecca was born in 1847 and died in 1927. She married Henry Norton, October 6, 1866. They had nine children.]

*****

Letter #90

[Although Joel corresponded frequently with his cousin, this is the only letter we have from Joel to J. K. It adds a touch of nostalgic sadness at war's end.]

Mr. J. K. Bird
Millview, Sullivan County, Pa.

Burkesville, Va.
May 1st, '65

Dear Friend Doc:

I embrace a few minutes this afternoon to ans. your letter, which was duly rec. We of your acquaintance here are enjoying a full share of health. We came to this point the 13 Apr. after the surrender of Lee, and have since lain still, encamped.

Today appearances indicate that we will be upon the move soon. I think by to morrow we will be on the march. The impression is that we are to march from here to Richmond, thence to Alexandria. If so, twill take us near two weeks, as the distance must be near two hundred miles.

Well, Doc, the "cruel war" at last comes to an end, with the surrender of Joe Johnson, I think the fighting ends. I feel sorry that Gen. Sherman, after accomplishing so much, should lose all his well-earned fame by one false step. The assassin of the president has already met his fate; he was captured the evening of the 25th -- the account you 'ere thus will have seen.

Last night we had heavy thunder showers here, leaving the air quite cool today. Last spring at this time we had not yet broken camp. What important events have transpired during the past month, the one almost crowding upon the other. Dock, I cannot write a long letter this time. I hope to see you by the 4th, if not sooner. Then we can dispense with pens and papers, and I can but feel glad at the prospect of soon going home to meet my friends. Our Government maintained, the rebellion crushed, and peace once more spreading its fair wings over our land. Yet there comes a sadness with the thought of returning, when I think of the little band that left Elkland and Forks in company *[in Company K]*. Of the twelve, six now sleep in the soldiers' grave. To them, there is no returning from the war, and with their friends there is no reunion in this world.

Trusting these few feeble breathings find you enjoying health and your self, and that you kindly remember me to your mother and the rest of your folks I will subscribe myself. Your friend, as of old, J. L. Molyneux. Hd Qrs, 3rd Div., 2nd Corps, Washington.

*****

  Tue. 2 May.   Are to march at one P.M. and move accordingly. March by the junction Burkesville and follow the Richmond RR to where we struck it and encamped April fifth, 14 mile.

  Wed. 3 May.   Column move at six A.M. Pass Geetersville *[Jeterville]*, Five Points, 30 ton of rebel ammunition, one acre of caissons, Amelia Court House. Cross the Appomattox and camp. A hard march. Div. red.

  Thu. 4 May.   Div. center. Marched with regt. in afternoon. Go in camp within nine mile of Richmond. Windy and rains during the night. Are to start early in the morning.

  [On May 4, 1865, Confederate General Richard Taylor surrendered the 12,000 troops of the Department of Alabama, Mississippi, and East Louisiana — thereby ending all organized Confederate resistance east of the Mississippi River. General Taylor was son of former U.S. President Zachary Taylor, and brother-in-law of Confederate President Jefferson Davis.

  [On May 4, 1865, President Lincoln was buried in Springfield, Illinois.]

  Fri. 5 May.   Continues to rain and gets quite muddy, but we are on to Richmond. Pass the outer works. The city looms in sight. Encamp near Manchester. 58 *[58th Regiment]* close by us. See: G. W. G., G. B., and G. Potter. Richmond at last!

  Sat. 6 May.   Afternoon march through Manchester. Cross the James and we are in Richmond. Pass Castle Thunder and the Libby prisons. See Gen. Mede *[Major General George G. Meade]* and Hallec *[General H. W. Halleck]* . Pass the monument and C. S. Capitol.

  Sun. 7 May.   Very hot and many get sunstroke. March us inhumanely. March five mile out of the city and encamp. Fine country. Black Snake, and French, cookery march today. By six A.M. cross the Chicahominy, pass Hanover Court House out of R *[Richmond]* -- 20 miles. Cross the Pamunky on pontoon and encamp. 18 miles today. High Div. led ill and pine tips.

  Mon. 8 May.   March early, pass Concord C.H. Leave the telegraph road to the right, and Bolling Green *[Bowling Green]*. Encamp a distance from the road. Rains during the night. Are 30 mile of Fredericksburg.

  Tue. 9 May.   Are in the rear of the corps today. Cross the Mattox or Matte River, and the Po. Have gone 18 mile. Camp upon the right of the road in an orchard of bamboo.

Wed. 10 May. Twelve miles to Fredericksburg. Rains during the night. Pass Massaponax Church after crossing the Ny River. Reach the heights of St. Mary. Take dinner. March through the city, cross the Rappahannoc on pontoons. Go through Falmouth *[Bellaire]* five mile out and encamp. P. and S. fight. Milk and have cake.

[Officially, the Civil War ended May 10, 1865. U.S. President Andrew Johnson issued a proclamation declaring armed resistance to be at an end.]

Thu. 11 May. Bad roads, corduroy them. Very hot! Many are *[overcome with]* sunstroke. Thunder shower and hail storm. Cold! Wet through. Feel bad. Long night on rails. Marched ten mile, I learn. Two horses killed by lightning.

Fri. 12 May. Move at 11 A.M. Really not as bad as expected. Go in camp before sundown. Capt. Brady has two men tied up. Passed Dumfree *[Dumfries]* on our right and Wolf Run Shoals.

Sat. 13 May. Up at four A.M. and resume our march on by-roads. Cross the Oquicon *[Occoquan]* Creek on pontoons. Outer defenses of W. *[Washington]*. Strike O. and A. RR *[Orange and Alexandria Railroad]* at Burkes Station. Cross the Acatink *[Accotink]* Creek by wading. Hd Qrs at Mt. Heaths. Eight mile *[south]* of Alexandria. Supper: biscuits.

Sun. 14 May. Sabbath. Do not move today. Citizens numerous. Hear of the capture of Jeff Davis at Irvinville, Geo., the 11th. Sleep in the barn. Milk breakfast.

[C.S.A. President Jefferson Davis, his wife, and a few senior Confederate leaders were captured in Irwinville, Georgia, on May 10, 1865, by the Fourth Michigan Cavalry and the First Wisconsin Cavalry. President Davis was held in prison for two years, but never brought to trial.]

Mon. 15 May. Move today some three mile to Bailey's Cross *[Roads]*. Hd Qrs established a good spring and pleasant site. Visit the regt.

Tue. 16 May. Put up summer quarters. Rations of soft bread, etc. Upon guard. Boys anxious to be mustered out.

Letter #91

Near Washington
May 17th, 1865

My Dear Friend:

Here comes another letter. Now, don't be scared when I say maybe it is the last you will receive from me. Yours of Apr. 26th rec'd the fifth inst. *[instance]*, and 'twas a very welcome letter. My last to you was written just as we were about to start from Burkesville for Washington.

Our march was commenced on the second. We marched through Richmond on the sixth and through Fredericksburg on the tenth, and arrived within a few miles of here the 13th. We are five mile of Washington at a place called Bailey's Crossroads. The distance we have traveled in coming from Burkesville is two hundred miles; which was quite a walk you may well believe.

I said maybe this might be my last letter for we are hoping to be discharged soon and then you know 'twill not be necessary to write letters. I suppose we are to have a grand review, and then be mustered out. How long a time will be required for the purpose 'twould be impossible to say -- perhaps one week from this may see us upon our way home and yet with such a large army possibly a month might elapse before this long hoped-for event takes place. So, after you get this I shall not ask you to write for in all probabilities I should not get it. If anything contrary should occur and we are likely to be retained longer, I will write and inform you.

Today, the weather is very warm and I even sweat just writing. The hot sun is tanning us boys brown as Indians. I'm thinking my appearance will maybe cause you to think otherwise of my good looks spoken of in your last, in connection with the new schoolhouse.

Jennie M.'s wedding was quite an important event at Millview. I rec'd a letter from her just previous to yours. She is quite pleased with her George; in fact, is her "beau ideal" of a husband. I am glad of it. I shall call probably and see them on my return, through Baltimore.

Won't I have lots of places to visit when I am back. Perhaps I may call to see you one of them days for Jennie will not be on hand to continue a plan to get you to come and see me at Sallie's.

I have often thought of that joke. If sister, Sallie, does not get a letter at the time you receive this you can tell her I am well; also the rest of the crowd. I wrote to her directly upon receiving her last, or rather I had mailed it just as I rec'd it, I think.

I am now nicely rested after our long march and ready to go again. The prospect is that we shall have to march to Baltimore. 'Twill not take us long as we are going toward home. The distance is 40 mile from W. *[Washington, D.C.]*

For want of time before the mail leaves I must soon end my writing. I trust you are in the enjoyment of health and yourself. And it is with much pleasure that I look forward to the time when I may be permitted to once more enjoy your society, for truly I can say the days seem longer now that intervene since the prospect of meeting with you has become more certain and the time less distant.

Once more adieu with my heart's best wishes and the affection of ever yours. Joel to Miss E. M. McCarty.

*****

Thu. 18 May.   Plenty of rain with lightning and thunder. Review next week, 23rd and 24th.

Fri. 19 May.   Plenty of rumors about who gets mustered out. Laurel in bloom.

Sat. 20 May.   On guard. Wm. B. visits and says we are to start for home before the review.

Letter #92

Baileys Cross Roads, *[Virginia]*
May 20th, '65

Dear Sister: *[Sallie]*

I am seated for the purpose of writing just a line to you as it has been some time since my last was written which I think was about the center of April, and by the by your last was rec'd at that same time.

Well, we are once more back again to Washington, or within eight mile or less. Our return march was quite a long and tiresome; being over 200 miles, and the weather hot. We passed through Richmond on the sixth and through Fredericksburg on the tenth and arrived in this vicinity or the 13th. We, of our acquaintance here, are all in usual good health and of course good spirits for we are soon expecting to be discharged.

The muster-out papers are underway. We expect to start by Monday the 22nd. Perhaps we may be detained a few days at Harrisburg, etc. before our final clearance is given us. I am yet at Hd Qrs, but will join the regt. tonight or tomorrow.

A grand review is to go off here on Tuesday and Wednesday. Our army on Tuesday and Sherman's Wednesday. I should like to have witnessed it, but don't care. 'Tis raining and my papers begin to dampen so I can hardly write. I have just rec'd a letter from Sister Anna, and another from Geo. P. *[Pardoe]*

If I can, I will stop and see Cousin Jennie Lake at Baltimore, and George at Lewisburg, but *[may]* not be able.

I do not know yet if our regt. will retain its organization until we reach Towanda or not. If so, we will go with it there. Perhaps I may get home 'ere this reaches you. If I do, you need not open it, as the woman said. I shall not have time for any more so, goodby till I am home once more with good wishes, I remain as ever – Brother Joel.

*****

Mon. 22 May.   Getting ready for the review; are to be in our best rig and look our best -- to wear white gloves, etc.

Tue. 23 May.   Our army is reviewed today by President Johnson and Grant, Sherman, etc. in Washington. Cross the Potomac on Long Bridge and return by the Pontoon --- *[text obliterated, probably "Bridge"]* below the Aquaduct Bridge. Everything pleasant and was a grand affair.

[For two days, May 23 and 24, 1865, more than 200,000 Union soldiers marched through the streets of Washington, from the Capitol to the White House, in a final military parade. The Army of the Potomac paraded May 23, followed the next day by Sherman's Army. For more than six hours per day, victorious soldiers passed through cheering crowds. For the first time, since April 14, 1861 (fall of Fort Sumter), the flag at the White House was flown at full staff. The VI Army Corps missed the big review, but had its own parade on June 8.]

Wed. 24 May.   Fair day for review of Sherman's army. *[I]* was not present but hear everything was satisfactorily accomplished.

Thu. 25 May.   J. Lorah visited us. His regt., 208th, lays upon the other side of Fairfax Seminary. His brother, Wm., and Thos. Dent also called.

Fri. 26 May.   Opens rainy and rains nearly the whole day. Air is quite chilly. Am not relieved yet from Hd Qrs, though 17 Maine men have been.

[On May 27, 1865, President Johnson ordered most persons imprisoned by military authorities to be discharged.]

Mon. 29 May.   Up early, and go to my regt. unrelieved. Expect to start for Washington, but do not today. First night with the regt. for two years and six months. Eddie B. joins in, looking finely. Been away *[detached from his regiment]* 22 months.

[On May 29, 1865, President Johnson granted amnesty and pardon to all persons who directly or indirectly participated in the existing rebellion, with a few exceptions. All property rights were restored, except as to slaves, and in some special cases.]

Tue. 30 May. Reveille at dawn and the 141st takes up the line of march for Washington. Arrive at eight A.M. The 200th *[Regiment]* and we take passage for Baltimore, at two P.M. Visit Jennie L.*[Lake]* and take the X.

Wed. 31 May Arrived at Harrisburg soon after one o'clock A.M. Stop at the soldiers' R. *[? Retreat, hostel]* Breakfast there in the morning, then take a stroll through the market. Meet the reg. March through the town, thence to Camp Curtin. Have wedge tents and cooked rations. Turn in knapsacks, haversacks, canteens, etc. Also our gun and equipage. 142nd Regt. arrives.

[The "wedge tent" was a moderate-sized, canvas tent, with an opening that resembled a "wedge" or an "A". To Joel, sleeping in one of these spacious tents and having "cooked rations" were luxuries.]

Fri. 2 June. 207th and 210th Regt.s. arrive. Our pay rolls are here and expect pay tomorrow. Visit the insane asylum and the Harrisburg cemetery. Return through the town. Walk down town in the evening. *[It is interesting to note that of the sights to see in Harrisburg, Joel visited the insane asylum and cemetery.]*

[On June 2, 1865, Confederate General Edmund Kirby Smith surrendered the 43,000 troops of the Trans-Mississippi Department to Union General Edward Canby at Galveston, Texas — officially disbanding the last Confederate army. Not all Confederate troops went home. Some formed roving bands of guerrillas, many headed for the far west. Some became mercenaries and hired out to Mexico and various other countries.]

Sat. 3 June. Take knapsack to Union Hotel. Hoffman *[and I]* then visited the Statehouse. Visited Traff Coburn. *[James Coburn was former fellow student from Towanda Academy, and the one whom Joel's former teacher, C. R. Coburn, inquired about in his letter to Joel (March 20, 1865). James Coburn, in his own personal Civil War diary, mentioned visiting his uncle in Middletown on this date. (A copy of the Coburn diary is on file at the Library, Archives Building, Army War College, Carlisle, Pennsylvania.)]*

Sun. 4 June. Pay master at last. Receive one hundred and eighty three dollars and 25 cents ($183.25) and my discharge. Home now is the word.

Mon. 5 June. Leave Harrisburg at daybreak for home. Arrive at Muncy at eight A.M. Take breakfast, then start for home in hired conveyance. Reach Millview at dusk.

Are home at last, safe and sound, and my own man again!

CHAPTER 35: AFTERTHOUGHTS

AFTER THE WAR

Private Joel Molyneux's Civil Wartime writings ended June 5, 1865. Then he was out of the army, back home, and reunited with his family and friends. He returned to his parents' home farm, near Millview, Pennsylvania. He and Elvira McCarty married December 27, 1865. Joel gave up teaching and became a full-time farmer. His father, Edward, died in 1872. His mother, Rebecca, moved in with Joel and Elvira after her husband died. Rebecca departed from this realm ten years later, in 1882.

Joel built a new house in which he and Vi raised a family and lived there the rest of their lives. Farmer Joel became active in community affairs. He accepted the Lord, and the couple helped establish a new church (Warburton Hill) in their home neighborhood. Joel and Elvira parented six children who reached maturity: Mary, Rosa, Robert, Silas, Wardner, and Winifred. Joel and Elvira were blessed with 15 grandchildren who reached maturity, seven of whom are still living at this time (December 1995).

One of the grandchildren, Roberta Grange, tells of visiting the Joel-Elvira home sometime around 1910-1912. She was surprised at finding a furnace in the house. There was also a bathroom and kitchen sink, although there was no indoor running water at that time.

Roberta related in her journal: *"Grandfather was in charge of butter-making. His technique was to separate the cream by means of a hand-turned separator, store the cream in a cool place in the house basement, and when it was sour, to churn the butter. But first grandfather had to catch the dog, collar him, and set him up on a sloping-upward treadmill, attached to the churn. The dog walked forward on the inclined plane to maintain his position, and the treadmill turned the churn to make the butter. Then, when churned, grandfather 'worked it' (kneaded it with a wooden ladle to squeeze out the buttermilk, and mix in salt). Lastly, he packed the butter in firkins to store until taken to town and sold."*

Roberta's journal continued: *"The farm itself had rich soil and could grow almost anything. There were all kinds of fruits trees in the orchard, including apples, cherries, peaches, and pears. Grape vines were trained on arbors that led from the backdoor of the house to the outhouse. Grandfather kept hives of bees, and they produced buckwheat honey for family use."* (Buckwheat is a grain crop grown in northern Pennsylvania.) *"Some of grandfather's wheat won first prize at the Columbia Exposition (Chicago, 1898). He had a medal and certificate to attest to the award."*

Roberta went on with her memories of her grandparents' farm home: *"On Sunday mornings, Grandmother would call, **'Joel, get ready for breakfast.'** That was the signal for the whole family to gather around the table. Grandfather read a selection from the Bible. Then all knelt by their chairs while Grandfather prayed — quietly and simply! There was self-respect, dignity, and a respect for others in all phases of life in that home."*

Elvira died in 1913. Joel died in 1915 -- two years after he had attended the famed 50th Gettysburg Survivors Reunion (July 1, 2, 3, 1913) in Gettysburg at the National Cemetery. Joel's name, along with all other Pennsylvania soldiers who fought in that famed battle, is on the Pennsylvania Monument in that beautiful cemetery. Joel and Elvira were buried in the Molyneux cemetery at Millview. Joel continued writing letters throughout his life.

SOME UNANSWERED QUESTIONS

I have several questions I would like to discuss with Joel if he were here.

Why was he not promoted above his private status?

Brigadier General John H. McLain, Army of the United States, Retired, Sarasota, Florida, discusses the specific question of why Joel was not an officer, did not aspire to be one, and was not offered a promotion, even though he was a dedicated, hard-working, intelligent, and loyal soldier.

"Joel was in a position that made him virtually unpromotable. Although officially on the rolls of the 141st Regiment, Joel was on detached service with the provost guard of the division headquarters. His promotion would have had to come from his own regiment, but his regiment understandably gave their promotions to men present in their own ranks.

Joel's leadership qualities were belatedly recognized (February 17, 1865) when he was detailed assistant commander of the guard, but with no increase in rank. He resigned that position on April 18th, 1865 -- perhaps to clear up any obstacle to his discharge, i.e. being too early for early release."

I concur with General McLain's reasoning. He himself came up through the army ranks from private to general, and quite naturally understands the army's promotional system. As a former teacher, General McLain has a keen understanding of the teacher-turned-soldier, Joel.

I also feel that Joel did not strongly aspire to be an officer. By staying as an enlisted man in the provost guard he was under the direct command of Charles Graves, and Joel mentioned several times how much he admired and liked working for him.

By being in the provost guard, Joel had a horse. He liked to ride and liked taking care of horses. And, since he had a bad ankle, probably the long marches would have incapacitated him. Throughout the war, his ankle gave him little trouble. The long walk from Appomattox Court House back to Washington was tough.

Who was the mysterious S.M.L. with whom Joel frequently corresponded? Why the secrecy? I'm convinced S.M.L. was Miss Seddie Locke, teacher in Wellsboro, Pennsylvania. I think their correspondence and exchange of photographs was the cause of the problem Joel and Elvira had when he went home on furlough, Christmas 1863.

What was the nature of the problem Joel had with Dr. Randall? What caused Joel's strong feelings of antagonism?

Did Joel write letters to his parents? He doesn't mention writing any, and if they had been written I'm reasonably sure they would have been saved. Nor is there any indication that Joel's parents wrote him. Why? It's possible both parents were functional illiterates, although I have seen a copy of Edward's handwritten will (1873).

A more plausible answer is that since both parents were quite old during the term of Joel's service they may have been content to hear read aloud his letters written to their children, Joel's siblings. If the parents had personal messages to Joel they could have asked one of the regular correspondents to slip it in their letters. Joel did send them messages, e.g. asking his mother to make him a vest with pockets, a pair of woolen mittens, a warm hat, to keep out the rain, and little bags for sugar, salt, and pepper, and asking to have a pair of shoes made for him.

Why was Joel's cousin, J. K. Bird, nicknamed "Doc"?

Why was Abel, Joel's friend back home, nicknamed "Sister Abel"? What was his last name? Was Abel effeminate, sickly, homosexual?

What happened to Samuel Molyneux at the Battle of Gettysburg? Joel could not locate him and became convinced he had been killed. The most reliable report was by a Company K soldier, T. Phillips. Joel learned from Phillips that Samuel had been hit and fell. (See August 11, 1863, letter.) Official records of the Union army show Samuel as being killed on July 2, 1863, at the Battle of Gettysburg. Officially, there were no effects.

On December 2, 1863, Sam's sister, Martha, wrote Joel that she and the family were persuaded Samuel had been killed at Gettysburg. Her family (including widow, Elizabeth) had gone to the dedication of the Gettysburg National Cemetery, on November 19, 1863. They were in the crowd that heard the famous Lincoln Gettysburg address. While there, they searched for some evidence of him, but found none.

Veteran pension records show a pension was paid to Samuel's widow, Elizabeth (d. 1885) and to three children, Geary, Elizabeth, and Edward until September 26, 1914. Pension checks were first sent to Pennsylvania, and then later to Iowa.

We'll probably never know why Sam's body and effects were never found. We need to keep in mind, though, that Civil War soldiers did not have identification dog tags. I believe Sam died on the Gettysburg battlefield, and his body buried in an unmarked, mass grave at the Peach Orchard. Sam was a legitimate war hero who gave his life for his country! I'm proud to own him as a great-uncle!

JOEL'S MESSAGE

With regard to the letters and diaries included here, the reader may be left with an uncertain feeling as to what he has read. This collection of Civil War writings is not the usual war account, for it's not centered around actual battles and fighting. That is not the central theme of what Joel put into words. What, then, was the message of Private Joel Molyneux? And what is he saying to us today?

I asked some friends and Joel descendants to review this book in manuscript form, and to relate their reactions as to what Joel was saying. Look beneath the surface and tell who the man Joel was and what he stood for.

*****

- ♦ Gilbert Ward, Sarasota, Florida, spent his life in the armed services (U.S. Air Force), and thus stands as a solid sounding board for personal reactions to what has been presented here.

"Private Molyneux's letters and diaries yield some assessments of Joel the man. His thoughts centered on keeping contact with his acquaintances, friends, family members, and girlfriend, Elvira. He was a loyal, effective, and knowledgeable soldier, more interested in people than war.

His feelings and doubts about his own side in the conflict never colored his actions of duty. His compassion and humaneness toward the Confederate soldiers never caused him to lose sight of the terrible fact they were the enemy. The awfulness of war comes through as he writes of friends getting killed, wounded, captured, deserting, or becoming sick. It emerges as he writes of participating in executions of Union army deserters, and impaling a run-away deserter with his bayonet. That personal account is spell-binding! He did what he had to do!

Joel adequately portrays the mundane and humdrum routine of a soldier's life which brings into contrast the absurdity of some fairy-tale accounts of war as being romantic and exciting. His camp activity centered around keeping warm, taking care of the camp and horses, scrounging for food, and visiting his old regiment and friends. Those activities bring into contrast the duty, excitement, fear, and stupidity of war itself. His main concern was with life's true values, i.e. thinking of the needs of others, keeping his family together, and reconciliation of man with God. As an example, some of his comrades could not read and write, but that did not prevent Joel from writing letters home for them and for former slave, Stephe. Additionally, he taught Stephe to read and write.

His roots were deeply bound in the teachings of Jesus when it came to relationship with his fellow man. After returning home he accepted the Lord, and became a 'born-again Christian'. Joel was a role model to the younger soldiers and makes a role model to the youth of our country today. He was a good, considerate man and his writings tell us how to get along with one another, even though he himself was thrust into the terrible duty of killing his fellow kind. Joel brings to us, a generation several times removed, a viable voice from battles fought by our ancestors. In a true sense, Joel is ancestor of all of us — not just his few blood descendants.

Joel's writings show how one man participated in the moving events of the times, coped with his circumstances, and left something of value to those who have an ear to hear."

*****

- Dr. Ronald Erchul, professor and writer, Virginia Military Institute, Lexington, Virginia, spent his career in the armed services (U.S. Navy). He provides cogent insights on Joel's writing ability and communication skills.

"Joel's love of writing was his therapy. In a world turned upside down it provided some order as he recorded the disorder and confusion around him. Writing has the ability to stabilize an individual, and is also a good way to ensure a memory will not be lost.

Joel, the letter writer, was a real communicator! It is possible to look at his poor spelling and believe otherwise, but spelling and grammar are only writing techniques. Communication is where skill is involved and true genius shines. Writing communication is the ability to pluck some thoughts from your mind, put them on paper so the reader can read them, and thus discern your thoughts. It is quite possible, and often happens, that a person can be a wonderful communicator, and yet be a poor speller. That was Joel! And conversely, being a good speller doesn't make a good communicator.

In the group of letters presented, by far the worst spelling of all was the one of January 12, 1863, to Joel from his minister, Reverend Sniffin. That lovely letter is the most powerful one in the whole group. It communicated right from the heart! In that forceful letter we read these intense questions: *'You have been taught to respect and receive the gospell that offers life to all, but as we were not quite sure that the child of such rare privilege, the young man of an amiable character, has he improved his gracious opportunity? Has he found the Savior of Sinners? Has he given his heart to God, as he has given his body to his country?'*

*****

- Hunter Barrett, boyhood friend from Wellsville, Pennsylvania, was also a former member of our armed services. An artillery officer, he participated in the World War II invasion of Normandy:

"I found the manuscript most insightful. One gains an impression of the Civil War through the eyes of a private soldier, day to day, year in, year out, that proves to me that wars don't change, only the tools. In historical perspective it may be one of the few books on the Civil War that outlines the war from the perspective of the troops, a history written at the time it was happening and not at some later date, when an individual's thoughts are naturally compromised and altered. This account should be of real interest to many military and social historians of the period."

*****

- A fourth reviewer, cousin Charles Kehler, Ithaca, New York, comments:

"The letters and diaries are worth preserving! They are worth reading! It is too bad Joel did not include more details of the war itself, but since the folks back home were getting newspaper accounts of the various battles he probably thought that was enough for them to know. Obviously, he did not want to record the horror of the slaughter of some of those battles, and, reading between the lines, it seemed that he had often been in more personal jeopardy than he cared to worry his family and sweetheart with.

In the diary section, I got out maps to follow their progress, and was fascinated by the markedly zigzag advance/retreat pattern of the 141st Regiment. I knew where many of the big battles had taken place, but had long since lost track of their exact sequence or who had participated in which ones."

*****

- A great-nephew of Joel's, Dr. Kenneth Wright, former army officer, medical doctor, and author, Syracuse, New York, says:

"I have been intrigued in reading of Joel's Civil War tenure. As a former military man myself, I was especially interested in how he, a private, associated with men of rank, but was able to remain humble. He endured the sights, sounds, smells, and evils of war with equanimity. That is a major point reflected in his correspondence. His associations with the important men were not temporal. Colonel Graves and Governor Curtin, for example, remained lifelong friends of ex-private Joel.

Joel's letter of April 14, 1865, to his future bride, Elvira, reveals a desire to share in the spiritual growth manifested in religious services back home, as well as in the army where he was. These words struck me: **'You may guess how glad I am to know that you had chosen the good part that cannot be taken away. I know that you will not forget your friend that is yet out of the ark of safety.'**

Joel's letters show insight into his inner character. Kipling's verses fit Joel.

> *If you can talk with crowds and keep your virtue*
> *Or walk with kings – nor lose the common touch*
> *If neither foes nor loving friends can hurt you,*
> *If all men count with you, but none too much*
> *If you can fill the unforgiving minute*
> *With sixty seconds' worth of distance run,*
> *Yours is the Earth and everything that's in it,*
> *And, which is more, you'll be a man, my son*

<u>*If*</u> *by Rudyard Kipling.*

> *So walked he from his birth,*
> *In simpleness, and gentleness,*
> *and honor, and clean mirth.*

<u>*Barrack Room Ballads*</u> *by Rudyard Kipling."*

*****

♦ Joan Clippinger, author and historian, Wellsville, Pennsylvania, discusses the intrinsic essence of Joel Molyneux.

"My initial impression of Joel was that he was a sensitive, caring person! His letters reflected a certain maturity with which he was able to express his concern and love for those at home while he himself faced awesome tribulations of war. Although his letters and diaries conveyed information about some of his experiences in the army, his main concern and interest were the activities and welfare of those back home. That sensitivity, along with his literary quality, caused me to fall in love with Joel Molyneux.

Joel was an intelligent man who truly loved and respected his family and prioritized them above everything else in his life, including himself. His correspondence home, and reciprocal letters from loved ones, were vital to his sanity, as he faced the insanity of war. That sensitivity was expressed over and over — not only to his brothers, sisters, brother-and sisters-in law, and cousins, Doc and Angie, but also and most especially to his beloved Elvira.

He inquired constantly about familial activities occurring among family and friends at home. Many of his letters recounted the incoming stories and informations as he expressed his opinions and concern for what was happening at home. Perhaps he was repeating and reliving these experiences, through his correspondences, as he focused and pictured them in his mind. He may have used this technique to reassure himself that everything was still stable at home, and his loved ones were not being adversely affected by the war.

He shared a few adventures and private thoughts about his experiences in the army, but never complained. He expressed his impressions of the war matter-of-factly, rather than emotionally. One has to read between the lines to understand the emotional impact his military service had upon him. It wasn't until after the Union's victory that Joel mentioned any personal health problems, and at that time complained about the long march back to Washington from Appomattox Court House. His lack of complaining eased the concern of his loved ones for him. At this time, he felt free to express personal thoughts and tell of his problems, for now he was on his way home, and no one need worry about him any longer.

His camaraderie with friends and family members who were mustered into the army and served with him was a mixed blessing. Friendships, of course, eased the loneliness and homesickness, but they accented and magnified his grief as these friends and relatives died. At the end of the war, Joel expressed exhilaration at knowing he would be returning home soon. At the same time, he expressed heartfelt despair as he recounted those who '*were sleeping in a soldier's grave and would never return home again.*'

Joel closed his March 22, 1863, letter to sweetheart, Elvira, with the heartfelt words: '*My love to you, Joel.*' I liked that! I'll end this letter with the same words, '*My love to you, Joel.*'"

*****

♦   John C. Hamrick, Christian speaker, Powder Springs, Georgia, looks into the heart of Joel:

"*Reading the diary and letters of Private Joel Molyneux is stimulating and informative. Three things stood out about Joel: his humaneness, his lack of hatred of the enemy, and his lack of desire to be an officer. I discuss them in that order:*

I was impressed by the innate humaneness of Joel. He was a compassionate man! He searched for and brought wounded friends and acquaintances off the battlefield. He visited wounded and sick in hospitals. He wrote letters for those who needed help. He taught a former slave Negro, Stephe, to read and write. He talked with understanding to a 101-year-old slave.

He mourned for the 15-year-old Confederate girl, named Jones, who died of typhoid fever, near where they were encamped. He regretted so few attended her funeral: ''Twas sad to witness the lone few that followed her to her grave.' That sentence in his October 17, 1864, letter tells of Joel's compassion.

As an amateur student of the War Between the States, I have studied numbers and tactics, interspersed with descriptions of specific events by eyewitnesses. Joel seemed delightfully in touch with the true nature of what was going on around him. He was able to show me what the world was really like in the midst of the carnage. His May 19, 1865, diary entry spoke volumes: '**Plenty of rumors about who gets mustered out. Laurel in bloom!**' *Two and a half years of experiencing fighting, woundings, deaths, sickness, and privation, and now even the excitement of going home, have not dulled his senses to the blooming of laurel. He mentioned the beauty of magnolia blossoms four or five times, and even sent one home to his Elvira. There's a man who maintained his balance! That balance helped keep him alive and well during his 34 months of service.*

Joel's lack of hatred for the men who had been trying to kill him, appears to have been inborn. He had the courage of his convictions, and thus was able to allow his opponents in battle the same right and respect. He would have sorrowed just as much looking into the dead eyes of a fifteen-year-old reb, as for one of his own. If he had been in a position of responsibility in the post-war reconstruction, things would have gone better. My state of Georgia needed some Joels around then.

My third impression of Joel was that he was so "laid-back" that he didn't want the responsibility of being an officer. Certainly, he was officer material! Now, on reflection, I feel I judged hastily as I read the first part of the book. By the time I had finished the manuscript, I concurred Joel was in an unpromotable situation, and he uncomplainingly resigned himself to his private status. We read in the Bible that the humble shall inherit the earth. That verse fit Private Joel Molyneux.

I would have liked to have known Joel personally. Now, after reading his letters and diaries, I feel as though I do know him!"

*****

- Ms. Marion Barnette, Mobile, Alabama, discusses Joel's use of letter-writing to maintain his mental and emotional balance:

"In the 1861-1865 period, our country experienced a form of national insanity. How else can we explain what went on then? Many soldiers, on both sides, experienced emotional and mental breakdowns. Although no accurate statistics tally their numbers, Joel mentioned fellow-soldiers being: **'tied to a tree, locked up in a crazy house, crazy man in a pen, another man in chains,'** etc. Drinking was a common form of release for some. Others used aggression — picking fights with fellow soldiers, burning houses, even cities, killing innocent civilians, and so on. Some committed suicide! Many deserted!

Joel used letter-writing as a balancing umbrella to maintain his grip on the tight rope of his sanity. The important things in his life: home, family, friends, sleigh riding, making maple syrup, and church activities represented the commonplace normality of life back home. He kept in touch with those life-saving, basic activities and values by writing and receiving letters. He set up a regular cycle of existence that clung to those important aspects of living. The remarkable thing about the situation was that he was able to do it at all while experiencing the rough camp life, terror of battle, threat of being wounded or killed, or of being taken prisoner. He was able to endure the sights, sounds, and yes even the smells of wounded men, the contact with diseases of many varieties, and the constant loneliness of a soldier's life. His own letters were constant reminders to himself and to others that he would someday be returning to the real world of home.

What did Joel mostly write about? He discussed his own common, humdrum, day-to-day activities — building a chimney or doorway for his shanty; scrounging writing paper for letters; catching crayfish and chubs;

gathering wild berries, chickapins, and grapes; taking a horse to get him shod; going for the mail; getting ready for a review; guarding a prisoner; attending Sunday afternoon church service; mending socks; drawing shirts and drawers from the supply sergeant; and of course, writing letters.

He was involved in some important activities, and did see important men of the time, and was in the middle of crucial battles and campaigns of the Army of the Potomac. Yet, it was meaningful to him to record his own daily routine activities — no matter how dull they may have appeared.

So, as I wondered about Joel's insistence on concentrating on the mundane aspects of his life, I concluded his writing about these activities was the very thing that kept him alive and fit in that crazy world. He used his commonplace activities and wrote letters about them as a prescription to maintaining his wellness."

*****

♦ Jack Love, Bryan, Texas, found himself reliving the Civil War:

"Although I have a Southern heritage, as I scanned the Quill of the Wild Goose *manuscript I found myself in the Union Army of the Potomac. It was a strange feeling! The young soldier, Joel, made the century-old silent sounds come alive in my mind.*

As I read on, I found myself being drawn to those distant camps. In my mind, I could almost hear the camp sounds. I myself served in the army, and can still recall my own reservoir of sounds — banter of troops, mail call, chow time, and the lonely nights I spent nights writing letters to 'my Elvira', my young wife at home. At night, as Joel wrote to 'his Elvira', I was there with him. I sat beside him in the doorway of his little shebang. I shared a corner of his knapsack, and held his candle so he and his quill pen could write. I joined him in writing his letters and hoping to return home — not just wistfully hoping, but solemnly promising to return.

Reading these singular letters late at night, I could sometimes close my eyes and picture his surroundings. Several times I went to sleep, and dreamed I was there. In his September 8, 1862, letter to his sister, Sallie, I felt as though I wasn't dreaming — that I was actually there, and viewed this Potomac River scene with Joel: **'We have a very fine view from our camp. We can see nearly all of the city of Washington and Alexandria with the Potomac River stretching out nearly as far as the eye can reach, with schooners, sloops, gunboats, etc. To look at them in the distance they resemble a lot of dead trees in an old swamp'.** *The realism of that 133-year-old scene whisked me there! That's what good writing is all about!"*

*****

- One of Joel and Elvira's grandchildren, Dr. Evan Molyneux, has been a practicing physician in La Grange, Georgia, for the past half century. Evan has always liked horses, as have others of the Joel grandchildren. I presume they inherited this love of horses from Joel. Dr. Evan recalls his grandparents as follows:

"I recall one special thing about grandmother, Elvira — her eyes! They became sharp when she was angry! One time, about 1910 or thereabouts, when we were visiting them, I was playing on the floor of her farm house kitchen. I had a hammer and accidentally broke the oven thermometer gauge of her kitchen range. Her sharp eyes pierced me then, and I haven't taken a hammer to a kitchen stove oven thermometer since that occasion.

I remember Grandfather Joel well, especially his Scripture reading and prayer. Before each meal, we all kneeled around the table in the old dining room. Reverence filled the room on those occasions!

As a young kid of six or seven, I also recall grandfather, Joel, visiting our farm home near Houghton, in Upstate New York. That was just after Elvira died in 1913. Memories take me back over the eight decades so I can still see him walking, stately erect, about the farm. His right arm is behind him, holding the small of his back. While there on that visit, he whittled wooden willow whistles for us kids.

I loved both grandparents very much!"

*****

- Carol Bird Tomkins, Bryan, Texas. a granddaughter of Joel and Elvira, relates:

"From reading Joel's letters and diaries a character trait impressing me was his care. It showed itself in many ways. He retrieved wounded soldiers after a battle — not just once, but after each military engagement. Then, he saw to it that they got to a field hospital. His compassion in these battle situations was apparent. Note this paragraph in his February 8, 1864, letter to Elvira: **'O! How I pity the poor fellows that might get wounded — perhaps remain through the night as they fall on the field. I earnestly hope that much may be accomplished, that all the suffering and hardships attending may not be of no avail.'** *"*

He visited sick and wounded comrades in the various hospitals. If they died, on the field of battle or in a hospital, he wrote letters to their families, explaining the circumstances of their death. The letters to the Samuel Molyneux, Charles Grange, and Little families must have been heartrending to write, for the soldiers-sons and their families were close friends.

Joel's consideration of others stayed with him throughout his life. As an example, after Joel and Elvira married, they adopted Joel's two nephews who had been orphaned. Joel and Elvira also took in and raised a former slave boy, Ned Jones, who at war's end, had walked north with the 141st Regiment.

Mother said Joel and Elvira's rural Sullivan County farmhouse, where she grew up, was a haven of rest for some who wanted to get away and relax. That was true of Charles Graves, who, after the war, became an ambassador.

Mother also commented on Joel's love of words. As a teenager, she and her dad had a little game they played. She would get out the dictionary and try to find a word to stump him as to its meaning. She was rarely successful for Joel had a wide vocabulary. He also liked games, and almost always beat her at chess.

Elvira, too, had a ministry of tenderness and mercy. As a practical nurse, she helped neighbors with sicknesses and childbirths. I proudly acknowledge Joel and Elvira Molyneux as grandparents."

*****

- Joel and Elvira had 15 grandchildren, another one of whom is Rosemary Molyneux May, housewife, Horseheads, New York. She reflects:

"Although grandfather, Joel, passed away many years before I was born, his spirit lived on in the house that he built and where I grew up. My father was Wardner, Joel and Elvira's youngest son. Portraits of Joel and Elvira hung on our parlor wall, so I looked at them every day for many years.

Joel was a kind and compassionate person! He possessed a goodness, not to be mistaken for naivete. His standards, rooted in Christianity, were ones he chose to live by.

Now, concerning the letters he wrote during the Civil War: Joel acted as a communication liaison between the young men at the front and the folks back home. In some instances, his letters were the only communication available.

He was widely acquainted. He knew many soldiers from surrounding counties, but how he knew them is a mystery since in those rural areas the only transportation was by horseback or buggy. The sheer number of people he knew, as mentioned in his letters, is incredible — given the remoteness of his farm home in Sullivan County.

Joel's writings show he maintained close contact with God, with family, and with friends. Those intimate contacts counteracted the war horrors he faced. I am proud to be the youngest grandchild of Private Joel Molyneux. His Civil War writings constitute a lasting gift."

*****

- Joel has a great-grandson named Joel. That Joel Molyneux, naturalist and teacher, living in Winnebago, Minnesota, reflects on his ancestor, Joel:

"Great-grandfather, Joel, had a vision for America. The world he lived in then was one of atheism, materialism, and corruption covered over with a layer of complacency. Joel lived in that world, but was not caught up in it. Even as an ordinary private in a large army, he acted as a light — not only to other soldiers surrounding him, but also to the people back home. In the army, he probably stuck out like a sore thumb with his old-fashioned stands on honesty, devotion to duty, teetotaling, and non-swearing. But I'm sure that didn't bother him.

As I read his writings, now a century later, I am impressed he saw his duty as being an upright man, and not just as being a good soldier. I learned a lot from my ancestor, Joel. Not just about him, but my own personal obligation for me to be a standard to the folks surrounding me."

*****

- Joel's descendant, Calvin Seetin, age 12, student in Alexandria, Virginia, comments on the *Quill of the Wild Goose* manuscript:

"Joel Molyneux, the soldier, was my great-great-great-grandfather, so obviously I never met him. His diary and letters, though, told me a lot about him — about who he was and his personality. It seems to me that Joel liked to write because he constantly wrote long letters and entries in his diary. I wonder if I'll ever have as much to write about or enjoy writing as much as he did.

Last year, when my 6th grade class took a trip to Gettysburg, I took along Joel's diary as a guide. Most of the kids were interested. One of my friends even used the diary for his report. In the Gettysburg Cemetery, we stopped at the Pennsylvania Monument and we found Joel's name listed there, with the 141st Regiment, Company K. We also found Samuel Molyneux's name as being killed at that battle. We took a picture of me standing in front of the monument.

It is interesting to know that someone in my own family took part in the making of history."

*****

- Many of Joel's letters were written to his brother, David. David's great-granddaughter, Louise Molyneux Woodhead, discusses Civil War food as described by Joel in his writings:

"As a country storekeeper, in Joel's village of Millview, I was interested in Joel's many references to food. My attention was first drawn to the paucity

of food, and its lack of variety and quality. Its nutritional level was grievous. In that first year of Joel's enlistment it was lamentable.

We learn from Joel's letters and diaries that Union Army food did improve in quality as the war wore on. Joel's December 10, 1863, letter reported: **'Have on hand three loaves, 'tis for three days rations. And then there is fresh beef and salt pork and seven large potatoes with plenty of salt, sugar, and coffee. Besides this I have a box of pepper and a lb. of butter. This I paid only 60 cts. for at a butter shop. O! I forgot, a hatful of dried apples, and two pints of white beans and a small basketful of hard tack. Haven't I lots to eat, don't you think?'**

In a letter written February 5, 1863, Joel said: **'Day before yesterday near 200 boxes came ... right in to where I am. The marshall has them all opened and searched for liquor. If it is found, it is taken. ...nearly 2/3rds of the eatables was spoiled upon account of delays.'** *In his February 8, 1864, letter he wrote to Villie:* **'I have seen better fare than we get just at present, but I do not intend intentionally to complain, for I am much better situated than many.'**

Joel and his buddies made some attempts at living off the land. One place he wrote: **'A wild turkey was chased through our camp and caught.'** *To sister, Sallie, October 18, 1862, he related:* **'We bought a fish line yesterday, and last night we took turns watching for rebs on the other side, and fished. When it was my turn, I caught a nice eel, one fine bullhead, and a chub. There are five of us at one post: Sam M. myself, Sperry and Gower from Davidson, and N. Brown (Lyman's brother). Altogether, we had in the morning one eel, four bullheads, and the chub which made a good meal for the whole of us. We get but little besides hard crackers, hard tac, when on picket or on a march.'**

On September 29, 1862, he wrote Elvira: **'We have just had our breakfast of bread, crackers, and meat. Our daily bread here does not have any butter upon it. The red spot on the corner of this sheet is not blood, but merely grape juice. I have been picking some for we have some sweet with the bitter. Grapes are quite plenty, and some of them are very good and then there is a lot of chestnuts. They call [them] chickapins. They grow upon little bushes from two to four feet high in little burrs like chestnuts, and they taste much the same. There's plenty of them. I saw yesterday for the first time persimmons — with its fruit which are about the size of Siberian crabs, [crab apples, about the size of a marble] and taste worse while green than anything you ever thought of.'**

Soldiers also supplemented their diets by buying food from sutlers. On December 26, 1862, Joel wrote home: **'I have managed to live on my rations** so far, and had my health. Everything I have bought since I left home has not exceeded $5.00. Suttlers here sell butter for 60 cts. a lb., cheese for 30, a loaf of bread like one of mother's big biscuits is 15 cents or two shillings. I'll stick to my hard bread, meat, and coffee before I'll patronize such thieves.'

On July 8, 1863, they marched all day and their supply wagon didn't catch up with them. The last sentence for that diary entry was one word: 'Supperless!'

In a letter dated December 24, 1862, Joel said: 'While writing I was called out to help unload quartermaster goods which took us till nearly midnight. Some 40 wagon loads ... for our div.' Joel was in for a surprise the next day. Here is his account of Christmas Day, 1862: 'I wish you a merry Christmas, Phidie. What do you think I had for dinner? Roast turkey, chicken, mutton, potatoes, green cellery, all kinds of wines, etc.? I saw Gen. Birney and staff at 'em, and had hard work to keep from making a charge upon the whole pile of officers and all, but at last made a masterly retreat and dined upon coffee and hard tac. Why, Fide, I'm getting fat down here on such high living.'

I'll say this for those Civil War soldiers, the ones who made it through the war were survivors!"

*****

- J. K. Bird played a prominent role in Joel's life. The cousins corresponded frequently. J. K.'s great-granddaughter, Grace Ann DeLong, genealogist, Lebanon, Pennsylvania, adds this information about the relationship of the two cousins:

"John King Bird, mentioned so often in the Quill manuscript, is my great grandfather. J. K. and Joel were first cousins. J. K. was son of George Bird, and Joel was son of Rebecca, George's youngest sister. My mother, Florence Rohe Toothaker, remembers her grandfather, J. K., but has no clue as to why he was nicknamed "Doc".

J. K. was born 1837 and died 1923. Wife, Carolyn (nicknamed Carrie), was born, 1844 and died 1907. They lived their whole lives on the Bird homestead farm along the Little Loyalsock, and were buried in the Bird Family Cemetery, on their farm.

I enjoyed learning about Joel Molyneux through his Civil War writings. I am grateful the Molyneux family saved the letters and diaries, for they make delightful reading. I'm also pleased I was able to contribute the letter from Joel to J. K., dated May 1, 1865. That letter has been in our family for 130 years. Exactly one month after that letter was written, on June 1, 1865, J. K. married his girlfriend, Carolyn Yonkin. Joel was unable to attend the wedding, *for on that day he was in Harrisburg, Pennsylvania, turning in his equipage. He arrived back in Millview four days later, on June 5, 1865. Following the war, J. K. and Joel were neighbors their whole lives — living on farms about a mile apart.*

I'm proud to be part of the Molyneux-Bird heritage!"

*****

♦ At the termination of the Civil War, Colonel Henry J. Madill resumed his law practice in Towanda, Pennsylvania. Many of his descendants still live in that area. Here is a letter from William B. Madill, Monroeton, Pennsylvania.

"Colonel Henry J. Madill, commanding officer of the 141st Regiment, is my great-great-uncle. He left a detailed diary of the Civil War which is on file in the Archives Library, Army War College, Carlisle, Pennsylvania. I was especially interested in reading Joel's diary, and being able to compare it with the colonel's.

One sentence in Joel's September 29, 1862, letter caught my eye: 'Goodie, here comes our Col. Madill. We all like him, and will do anything for him.' Another sentence, dated October 19, 1862, stated: '... but our Colonel Madill is a noble fellow, a warrior, and a man to boot. **He is down against drinking, swearing, card playing and spending money at the suttlers. Our boys all like him, though 2/3 of them are guilty of the above-named vices.**' I feel sure Colonel Madill had the same warmth of feelings toward Private Joel.

The daily journal and Joel's letters to girlfriend, Elvira, made fascinating reading. I could not put the manuscript down until I had completed it."

*****

SUPPLEMENTARY INFORMATION

Children of Edward and Rebecca Molyneux

	Born	Married	Died
John Molyneux	1815	1843	1896
James Molyneux	1816	1845	1901
Mary Molyneux	1818	1840	1850
Lydia Molyneux	1820	1843	1912
Margaret Molyneux	1822	1846	1870
George Molyneux	1824	1853	1866
David Molyneux	1826	1863, '79, '97	1920
Jesse Molyneux	1829	1852	1910
Esther Ellen Molyneux	1831	1854	1881
Ann (Anna) Molyneux	1832	1853	1916
Joel L. Molyneux	**1835**	**1865**	**1915**
Sarah (Sallie) Molyneux	1837	1859	1914

Children of Joel L. and Elvira Molyneux

	Born	Married	Died
Mary M. Osthaus	1869	1899	1949
Rosa M. Grange	1871	1898	1958
Robert Molyneux	1873	1897	1947
Silas Molyneux	1878	1917	1951
Wardner Molyneux	1881	1912	1969
Winifred M. Bird	1883	1915	1969

BLACKS in the CIVIL WAR

At the beginning of the war, blacks were not used by the Union as soldiers, although they were used as civilian laborers by the military. Towards the end of the conflict, black troops were used freely in the North and to a limited degree in the South. All over the North, blacks organized military units and offered their services to the Union. In July 1862, just a month before Joel enlisted, Congress provided for the use of black troops. The successes of these black troops in combat created a positive attitude toward their use by the Union.

Almost 180,000 blacks served officially in the Union army, and many others served as scouts, spies, and laborers building fortifications. Joel spoke of Dutch Gap several times. Black Union troops and black laborers dug most of that canal.

Joel mentioned the great explosion at the Petersburg fort. Originally, in the overall plan of attack, black troops had been trained to enter the crater, after the explosion, and probably would have been successful in that skirmish. At the last moment, however, a decision was made to use untrained white troops instead and thus the Union fiasco there. Meade issued the order for the change, and Grant approved it. They were fearful of racial repercussions if the black troops had incurred high fatality rates during the battle.

Black troops made up less than 10 percent of the Union army, but their casualties were disproportionately high. Their combat role was made more severe since many Confederate units executed captured black prisoners and their white officers. One white officer of black soldiers became famous in the North when he was killed leading an unsuccessful assault on Battery Wagner, near Charleston, July 18, 1863. When buried in a mass grave with his black soldiers, he became a hero of Northern abolitionists. Of the 180,000 blacks serving in the Union army, about 30,000 died. After New Orleans was captured by the Union, a regiment of free blacks was mustered there on September 27, 1862, as Union soldiers.

Few blacks, slaves or free, were used as troops by the Confederacy, although some were involved toward the end of the conflict when the South was running short on manpower. Most blacks who did serve were blacks who had "passed." Their roles, use, numbers, and casualty rates are not readily available. It is notable that at least two Union majors and 29 captains were African American. Fourteen black Union soldiers won the Congressional Medal of Honor, the country's highest military decoration.

An estimated 20,000 black sailors served in the United States navy during the war. No estimates are available for black sailors in the Confederate navy --

probably there were very few. Two black naval heroes emerged from the war: Robert Smalls, a slave, escaped from Charleston by hijacking a ship. He was later enrolled as a master in the Union navy. William Tillman, another slave, was on board a captured schooner, the *S. J. Waring*. He single-handedly recaptured the ship from the Confederate prize crew, and later was awarded a prize of $6,000.

WOMEN in the CIVIL WAR

While on the subject of minorities in the war, we might mention the role women played. There were at least 400 women, detected, who enlisted in the Confederate and Union armies disguised as men. Probably there were many others who served their terms undetected. One woman warrior, Sarah Wakeman, has had a book, *The Uncommon Soldier* by Lauren Cook Burgess, written about her -- based on letters she wrote home. One reason these women could get by, undetected, was that in both armies there were young boys serving -- with no facial hair and high voices. Also, physical entrance exams were cursory, at best.

One girl, Emily from Brooklyn, was a drummer "boy". Harriet Tubman, abolitionist, helped in planning a raid in South Carolina. Madam Turchin, spouse of Colonel Ivan Turchin, led his 16th Illinois one day in Tennessee after her husband was wounded. In the Confederate army, Sally Tompkins, was commissioned as a captain of cavalry by C.S.A. President Jefferson Davis, September 9, 1861. After First Bull Run, nurse Tompkins established a hospital that proved to have a remarkable recovery rate. She was the only woman, in either army, to hold a regular commission during the war. Two women, Doctors Clapp and Walker, were surgeons in the U.S. army. One woman was a chaplain. Of course, there were also many female nurses and helpers of all sorts who did yeoman service in both armies. Joel spoke highly of the kindly and courageous lady he knew, "Gentle Anna".

An estimated 3,200 women served as nurses in the Union army. A smaller, undetermined number served Confederate forces. Dorthea Dix was superintendent of nurses for the U.S. government during the war. She insisted that army nurses be at least 30 years of age and "plain in appearance." Her strict views earned her the nickname, "Dragon Dix." Louisa May Alcott, author of *Little Women* was a civil war nurse.

HORSES in the CIVIL WAR

Some Civil War horses, especially those ridden by generals, became famous. Union General McClellan's favorite horse was Daniel Webster. He also rode Burns, but only in the mornings. Horse Burns had a habit of bolting for the stable around supper-time -- with or without his rider. General George Meade's favorite horse, Baldy, was wounded four times. He nevertheless lived and walked in his general's funeral procession in 1878.

General Grant had several horses, but the one that became well-known was Cincinnati. Grant also had Jack, Fox, Kangaroo, and Jeff Davis. Grant, noted for his skills as an equestrian, liked large, powerful horses. General Ben Butler rode Almond Eye; General Thomas rode Billie. General Joe Hooker rode Lookout. General Kearney's horse, Decatur, was killed at Seven Pines. At the time of Kearney's death, the general was riding Bayard.

General Sheridan's favorite horse was called Rienzi. After the horse died, Rienzi was stuffed and exhibited in the Smithsonian. General Sherman's horse, Sam, was wounded several times, but always recovered. Sherman lost three other horses in battle and rode Lexington when he entered Atlanta, and in the Grand Review in Washington at war's end.

Confederate General Robert E. Lee's famous horse was Traveller, a big gray. But the general also rode Lucy Long, Richmond, Ajax, and a roan. After the war General Lee became president of Washington College, in Lexington, Virginia. He took Traveller with him there and was frequently seen riding the big gray across the campus.

General Fitzhugh Lee's horse was Nellie Gray. General Ewell's favorite mount was Rifle, a flea-bitten gray.

"Stonewall" Jackson's favorite mount was a little mare, Sorrel, and this was the horse he was riding when he was wounded at Chancellorsville. General JEB Stuart's favorite mount was a wonderful, thoroughbred mare, Virginia. This was the horse which carried him across the 15-foot ditch near Hanover, in York County, Pennsylvania. The general also rode Highfly. General Nathan Bedford Forrest lost 29 horses in combat, but King Phillip managed to survive the war. General Albert Johnston was riding Fire-Eater, a thoroughbred, when he was killed at Shiloh. General Patrick Cleburne lost his horse, Dixie, at Perryville.

Joel mentioned several of his army horses by name, but one he became attached to was not his but Colonel Graves' horse, Dandy.

PETS in the CIVIL WAR

There were other domestic animals in the Civil War armies, including dogs, cats, birds, et cetera, but little is mentioned of them. General Robert E.

Lee, for example, kept a chicken in a cage under his cot. Supposedly, it laid a fresh egg for him every morning that became a part of his breakfast.

Many units carried mascots with them. One famous mascot, "Old Abe" was an eagle with the 8th Wisconsin. The 12th Wisconsin Infantry had a young bear. Many regiments had dogs and others had kittens and goats.

The 9th Connecticut Infantry had a trained pig named "Jeff Davis". He stood on his hind legs, held a pipe, and put on a good show. The 34th Massachusetts Infantry had a whole army of dogs. They would bay at the moon, chase rabbits, and upon occasion chase a reb or one of their own men.

One Civil War dog had a book written about him: *The War Dog: A True Story* by John D. Lippy, Jr. The 11th Pennsylvania Regiment had a dog named Sallie, and her story has become famous. A cast bronze replica of Sallie stands at the base of the granite monument of the 11th Pennsylvania at the Gettysburg Cemetery.

TENTS in the CIVIL WAR

At the beginning of the war the Sibley tent was commonly used. It was round, and resembled an Indian teepee, with a fire in the middle, and a smoke escape hole in top center. It accommodated a dozen men sleeping with their feet towards the fire. If one had to get up, most of the others awoke, and it may have been the device that taught more Civil War soldiers to curse than any other Civil War contrivance.

The wedge tent was a moderate-sized canvas tent, with an opening that resembled a wedge or an "A." Designed to hold four men, it often had five or six men sleeping in one. When six got in, the men were forced to "spoon." If one turned over all had to turn the same way. To erect, it was stretched over a six-foot pole, rope, or fence rail. Covering about 50 square feet it was too big and heavy for field use. Thus, its use was limited to camps, rendezvous depots, or for troops stationed permanently. To Joel, it was a luxury to sleep in one, comparable to the "cooked rations" that he also mentioned in his diary.

Hospital or wall tents were 14 feet by 14 feet and held eight patients. They had vertical walls and were high enough you could stand erect.

Soldiers in the field used "dog," "pup," or shelter tents. Each soldier carried a half-tent. At the end of a day's march, two soldiers would button their two half-tents together. They would drape it over a horizontal pole or rope, support the rail with their guns, stuck vertically in the ground, with bayonets down. Two assembled "tent d'abris," as the French called them, measured 5 foot 2 inches by 4 foot 8 inches (in 1864 it was enlarged to 5 foot 6 inches square). These shelter tents proved useful as roofs over shanties and shebangs, or as shade in the summer. In the first year of the war, the Union army issued about 40,000 "dog" tents. In 1864, they issued about one and a half million. Confederate soldiers in the field used fewer tents, and many of those used were obtained from Federal troops.

APPENDIX: THE 141st REGIMENT

THE UNION ARMY, VOLUME I. (1908)

Colonel Henry J. Madill; Lieutenant Colonels Guy H. Watkins, Casper W. Tyler, Joseph H. Horton; Majors Israel P. Spaulding, Casper W. Taylor, Joseph H. Horton, Charles Mercur. This regiment was composed of recruits from the counties of Bradford, Susquehanna, Sullivan, and Wayne. It rendezvoused at Camp Curtin, Harrisburg, where it was mustered into the U.S. service in the latter part of August 1862 for three years. It was barely organized when it was hurried to Washington, arriving on August 30 during the progress of the second battle of Bull Run. It was a raw, inexperienced regiment and the privations and exposure of the first few weeks told heavily on the health of the men, 300 being in hospital at one time and 500 being reported unfit for duty.

It was assigned to the 1st Brigade (General Robinson), Birney's Division, III Corps. It remained at Washington, engaged in perfecting itself in drill and discipline, until the close of the Maryland campaign, and was then posted at Poolesville for a time, engaged in picket duty. It went into winter quarters at Falmouth on November 25, and was in reserve during most of the battle of Fredericksburg, losing but one killed and four wounded. At the battle of Chancellorsville the 141st was heavily engaged. It sustained its chief loss in a desperate charge on the morning of the third day of the battle, where it fought with great courage and lost 235 killed, wounded, and missing out of 419 in action. Lieutenant Colonel Watkins was severely wounded and was taken prisoner.

The Regiment reached the field of Gettysburg on the evening of July 1, 1863, after a most fatiguing march. On the next day it went into position at the angle of Sickles' line, on the right of the Peach Orchard, which was the most exposed part of the whole field. Its action was most heroic throughout the day, during which it sustained fearful losses. It went into action that morning with 198 men, and lost during the battle 136 killed, wounded and missing, or nearly 70 percent of its numbers. Its total loss during the two days was 149.

In the ensuing campaigns in Virginia it was engaged at Kelly's Ford, Locust Grove, and several minor actions. Winter quarters were established at Brandy Station. While there many convalescents returned to the ranks. Its strength was further augmented by the transfer of many men from the 105th, 99th, and 110th Pennsylvania Regiments.

It entered the spring campaign of 1864 as part of the 4th Division, II Corps. In a single charge at the Wilderness the 141st Regiment captured 50 prisoners and the colors of the 13th North Carolina. It was fiercely engaged at the Po River and a few days later at the "bloody angle." In front of the regiment, in the latter engagement, stood the great tree cut in two by bullets and whose trunk is now one of the treasured memorials of the war at Washington. Around this tree the enemy's slain were strewn by the hundreds. The losses of the regiment amounted to nine killed, 98 wounded, and 21 missing. It was first regiment to plant its colors on the enemy's works in a gallant charge at the North Anna River.

More severe fighting followed at Cold Harbor, and on June 14, 1864, it crossed the James. Lieutenant Colonel Watkins was killed while leading his men in the charge on the works of Petersburg on June 18, 1864. Major Tyler now assumed command and was promoted to lieutenant colonel. On July 1, the regiment numbered only 170, and it had only seven of its original 30 officers.

During the balance of the year it shared in all the fighting of its corps, being engaged at Deep Bottom, Strawberry Plains, on the Weldon Railroad in October and again in December. It was stationed during the winter near Fort Hell, and on March 27, 1865, began its final campaign, taking part in the final assaults on Petersburg and maintaining its reputation for gallantry in the bloody engagement of Sailor's *[Sayler's]* Creek.

At the surrender of Lee it was in line of battle, prepared to continue the bloody fighting if necessary. On May 28, 1865, it was mustered out at Washington, D.C., with the exception of the recruits, which were transferred to the 57th Pennsylvania.

Few regiments achieved a more honorable record for gallantry and efficient service. The number on the regimental rolls was 1,036, and its losses were 156 killed or died of wounds, 404 wounded, and 75 captured or missing.

MAJOR BATTLES of the 141st REGIMENT

Battle of Fredericksburg – Dec. 12-15, 1862
Battle of Chancellorsville – May 1-3, 1863

Gettysburg Campaign – June 11 –July 24, 1863
Battle of Gettysburg – July 1-3, 1863

Bristoe Campaign – Oct. 9-22, 1863
Battle of Kelly's Ford – Nov. 7-8, 1863

Mine Run Campaign – Nov. 26 –Dec. 2, 1863
Battle of Po River – May 1, 1864

Rapidan Campaign – May 4 –June 12, 1864
Battle of The Wilderness – May 5-7, 1864
Battle of Spottsylvania Court House – May 11-20, 1864
Battle of North Anna River – May 23-26, 1864
Battle of Cold Harbor – May 31 – June 12, 1864

Siege of Petersburg – June 16, 1864 –April 2, 1865
Before Petersburg – June 16 –18, 1864
Battles of Weldon Railroad – August, October, December, 1864
Battle of Deep Bottom – July 27-29, 1864
Battle of Strawberry Plains – August 14-18, 1864

Appomattox Campaign – March 28-April 9, 1865
Battle of Sayler's Creek – April 5-6, 1865
Battle of High Bridge – April 7, 1865
Appomattox Court House Surrender – April 9, 1865

ACKNOWLEDGMENTS

This book is the joint effort of many persons!

Joel: Thank you for writing the letters and diaries. Vi: You were farsighted to collect and retain Joel's Civil War letters and diaries for the first 50 years they were saved. I thank you for your reader-friends who will read this book and recognize your husband's writings as being special. Mother, Winifred Molyneux Bird: thank you for your heartfelt conviction and vision that your dad's Civil War letters and diaries should one day be assembled in book-form and available to the public.

Various other Molyneux family members preserved the bundles of Joel's hand-written letters and diaries for the past 130 years. Temporary custodians included Cora Molyneux; family of Uncle David Molyneux; my sister, Carol Bird Tomkins; and cousins Dr. Max Molyneux, and Colonel Silas Molyneaux, Lockport, New York. Cousin Myrtle Molyneux Clark, Idaho Falls, Idaho, first typed the hand-written letters and diaries.

Many others helped with this book. As an act of love the following friends reviewed and edited this book: Professors Cyclone Covey of Wake Forest University and Ronald Erchul of the Virginia Military Institute; cousins Dr. Kenneth Wright, Syracuse, New York; Charles Kehler, Ithaca, New York; Phoebe Molyneux, Winnebago, Minnesota; Gilbert Ward of Sarasota, Florida; Hunter Barrett of Wellsville, Pennsylvania; and Lois Brennan of Burke, Virginia. For a scholarly job of editing, I thank Louisa Brown of Plano, Texas, and General John H. McLain, Sarasota, Florida.

Editor Joan Clippinger, of Wellsville, Pennsylvania, read the manuscript several times and offered excellent suggestions. She will always have a warm spot in my heart for her hours of dedication to the book. Cousin Louise Molyneux Woodhead, family genealogist, Millview, Pennsylvania, provided much of the family and Sullivan and Bradford County information. Civil War historian and archivist, Dr. Richard Sommers, Army War College, Carlisle, Pennsylvania, provided direction and Civil War information.

I thank Kenneth Robertson, Blacksburg, Virginia, and son Kim. The photos came from Carol Tomkins, Carl Molyneux, Jeff Kowalis, Will Flumen, Wes Small, Ronn Palm, Ruth Harvey, Grace Ann Delong, and the Photo Lab, Army War College, Carlisle, Pennsylvania. Wife, Phylis, did the maps.

Finally, I thank the Lord for allowing me to help with the book. – K.M.B.

INDEX

141st Regiment, 1, 2, 3, 16, 18, 19, 28, 29, 33, 51, 62, 71, 75, 89, 98, 105, 109

—A—

Accotink Creek, 8, 289
Alexander, Edward, 57
Alexandria, 3, 28, 29, 31, 32, 34, 125, 151, 169, 181, 204, 287, 289, 305, 308
Alexandria-Georgetown Canal, 28, 29
Andersonville Prison, 9, 25
Antietam, 19, 35, 36, 50, 113, 220, 231
Appomattox Court House, 3, 227, 277, 297, 302
Appomattox River, 211
Aqueduct Bridge, 28
Aquia Creek, 85
Arlington Cemetery, 40
Arlington House, 42
Army of the Potomac, 1, 3, 4, 16, 30, 32, 34, 43, 45, 49, 51, 52, 54, 55, 56, 57, 58, 63, 66, 68, 75, 84, 85, 90, 100, 108, 128, 135, 139, 149, 184, 185, 191, 202, 235, 238, 242, 279, 284, 292, 305
Army War College, Carlisle, 19, 20, 293, 311, 322, 328, 330
Atlees Station, 193

—B—

Bailey's Cross Roads, 289, 291
Baines, Lucy, 89, 93
Barnette, Marion, 304
Barrett, Hunter, 300
Bates, Samuel P., 19, 31, 99

Battle of Chancellorsville, 108, 135, 189
Battle of Cold Harbor, 194, 195
Battle of Gettysburg, 16, 108, 118
Battle of Hatcher's Run, 264
Battle of Sayler's Creek, 277
Battles of The Wilderness, 3, 184, 186, 187
Bedford, Edmund, Will, Henry, 77, 84, 98, 100, 101, 102, 105, 110, 118, 126, 129, 140, 152
Bedford, Jonas O., 45, 113, 181, 241, 251, 257, 258, 259, 274
Bedford, Tillman, 110
Bedford, William, 152, 202, 215, 217 224, 236, 251, 256, 258, 262, 263, 268
Bennett, Uncle Joel, 252
Berry, General Hiram G., 78, 95
Bird, George Copeland, 21, 77
Bird, J. K. ('Doc' or John King), 64, 77, 79, 88, 104, 105, 120, 127, 130, 140, 145, 146, 150, 152, 164, 173, 218, 233, 287, 297, 310
Bird, Lydia (nee Hannant), 4
Bird, Powell, 4, 24, 41
Birney, General, 4, 53, 55, 174, 179, 196, 201, 203, 207, 212, 217, 218, 310
Birney, General David Bell, 87
Bixby, Mrs. Lydia, 248
Black, Sam, 51, 153, 197, 198, 200, 202, 204,
Blacks in the Civil War, 313
Bloodgood, J. D., 19, 99
Bloody Angle, 187
body guards, 58
Boonsboro, 111, 113
Booth, John Wilkes, 279, 281, 284
Botts, John Minor, 154, 178
bounty jumpers, 35
Bowling Green, 191
Bragg, General Braxton, 131, 185
Brandy Station, 139, 140, 145, 151, 156, 157, 158, 160, 162, 163, 168, 169, 178, 179, 181, 182, 318

Bristoe Station, 105, 134, 136, 138
Bryan, D., 193, 195, 201, 204
Bryan, Ellis, 175, 176, 178, 179, 219, 268
Bryan, Laws, 198, 204
Bryan, Sam, 42
Bucknell University, 232
Bull, Kate, 140
Bull Run, 27, 30, 31, 32, 42, 75, 106, 134, 135, 157, 163, 169, 184, 314, 318
Burgess, Lauren Cook, 314
Burkes Station, 289
Burnside, General, 4, 52, 54, 66, 75, 85, 96, 207
Butler, General Benjamin, 258
Butterfield, General Dan, 135

—C—

C & O Canal, 28
C.S.S. *Alabama*, 206
C.S.S. *Florida*, 236
Camp Curtin, 3, 24, 26, 293, 318
Camp Whipple, 32, 36
Campbell, Henry, 261
Catlet, 138
Catlet Station, 105
Catton, Author Bruce, 100, 135, 231
Centreville (Centerville), 106, 113, 142, 143
Chambliss, General, 219
Chancellorsville, 184
Chancellorsville, Battle of, 95, 97, 98, 185, 197, 320
Charles Town, 46
Charleston, 46
chickapins, 38
Christian Commission, 79, 91, 155, 157, 158, 176
City Point, 231
City Point RR, 226
Clippinger, Joan, 302
Coburn, C. R., 20, 273, 274, 293
Coburn, James (Traff), 47, 274, 293
Cold Harbor, 3, 184
Company K, 16, 22, 108

Concord C. H., 288
copperheads, 89
Craft, David, 19
Culpepper, 135, 136, 145, 154, 155, 168, 171, 172, 177, 219
Curtin, Governor Andrew G., 3, 4, 24, 26, 33, 80, 83, 85, 97, 117
Custis, George Washington Parke, 49
Custis, Martha , 46

—D—

Dandy (horse), 102, 110, 120, 136, 138, 140, 149, 168, 322
Davis, C. S. A. President Jefferson, 53, 89, 120, 150, 276, 288, 289, 314
Deep Bottom, 282
DeLong, Grace Ann, 310
Dennison, Lottie, 21, 57
Diefenbach, John, 48
Duke, George, 105
Dunham, Lieutenant, 59
Dushore Union, 141, 147, 163, 169, 199, 203, 205, 231
Dutch Gap, 227, 260, 313

—E—

Early, General Jubal, 209
Egan, General Thomas, 247
Emancipation Proclamation, 11, 13, 36
Emmitsburg, 107
Erchul, Dr. Ronald, 299
Everett, Edward, 140

—F—

Fairfax Station, 134
Falmouth, 85
Falmouth Station, 103
Farrel, Michael, 78, 85, 133, 138, 177, 180, 181, 203, 204, 206, 215, 216, 218, 231
Farrie, General, 236

323

Foote, Author Shelby, 226
Forksville, village of, 4, 22, 37, 38, 61, 84, 259
Fort Davis, 243
Fort Steadman, 274
Foster, Stephen, 34, 246
Frederick City, 107, 111, 113, 118
Fredericksburg, Battle of, 14, 15, 51, 54, 75
Freedman's Bureau, 95, 268

—G—

Gaines Mill, 235
Gentle Anna, 194, 314
Gettysburg, Battle of, 3, 7, 15, 16, 19, 21, 24, 25, 106, 108, 112, 118, 120, 128, 131, 143, 198, 204, 239, 297, 320
Graham, General, 4, 94, 140, 174, 197
Graham, Mrs., 94
Grange, Charley, 21, 22, 109, 110
Grange, Harold (Red), 38
Grange, Joseph, 107
Grange, Roberta, 295
Grant, General Ulysses S., 4, 10, 75, 78, 101, 141, 175, 179, 184, 194, 205, 208, 210, 217, 222, 269, 270, 275, 278
Graves, Charles, 41, 46, 74, 78, 79, 82, 83, 85, 90, 96, 103, 106, 108, 110, 115, 118, 128, 131, 141, 145, 146, 151, 156, 163, 168, 170, 174, 184, 197, 296, 301, 307
Gum Springs, 106

—H—

Half-way House, 234
Halleck, General H. W., 288
Hamrick, John C., 303
Hancock, General, 4, 178, 179, 201, 207, 218, 221
Hancock, Major, 218
Hanover (city), 193, 315
Hanover C. H., 192

Harpers Ferry, 33, 41, 42, 113, 114, 115, 116
Hatchers Run, 265
Haverly, Dan Jr., 263
Hays, General Alexander, 177, 184, 187
Hazel River, 133
hemophilia, 41
Herold, David E., 284
High Bridge, 3, 4, 277, 279, 320
Hill, General Ambrose Powell, 4, 8, 45, 88, 276
Holt (tent-mate), 76, 78, 88
Hood, General, 219
Hooker, General Joe, 4, 52, 66, 75, 76, 87, 89, 95, 128, 135, 185
Horses in the Civil War, 314
Horton, Bishop, 158, 220
Howard, General Oliver Otis, 95
Howard University, 95
Humphreys, General, 259

—I—

Ingalls, General Rufus, 210
Irvinville, Ga., 289

—J—

Jabe, 56, 64, 79, 83
Jackson, General 'Stonewall', 4, 26, 27, 30, 32, 43, 52, 95, 97, 99
Jacobs, Professor, 109
James River, 198, 211, 227
Johnson, General Ed., 187
Johnson, Vice President Andrew, 4, 242
Johnston, General Joseph E., 278, 283, 284
Jones House, 238
Jones, Ned (slave), 133

—K—

Kehler, Charles, 300
Kelly's Ford, 3, 139, 169, 318
Kennedy, 'Jackie', 47

Kennedy, President John F., 47
Kipling, Rudyard, 301

—L—

Lake, Jennie, 292
Lee, General Robert E., 3, 4, 30, 47, 51, 99, 108, 120, 128, 191, 263, 265, 269, 276, 278, 316
Libby Prison, 288
Lincoln, President Abraham, 4, 36, 84, 85, 140, 239, 242, 248, 278, 281
Lippy, John D., Jr., 316
Little, Ezra, 21, 87, 99, 158, 249, 256, 263
Littlestown, 109
Locke, Seddie M. (SML), 21, 52, 64, 84, 93, 97, 101, 106, 130, 131, 138, 140, 145, 147, 149, 205, 297
Longstreet, General James, 52, 110, 131, 185
Love, Jack, 305
Luke, Billy, 59
Lynchburg RR, 234, 240, 277

—M—

Madill, Colonel Henry J., 19, 33, 39, 280, 311, 318
Madill, William B., 311
Manassas, 13, 22, 28, 29, 30, 117, 134, 138
Manassas Junction, 136, 138
Manchester, 288
Markle, Captain, 147
Marye's Heights, 57
Mason Rogers, 38
Massaponax Church, 191
Mattaponi River, 191
May, Rosemary Molyneux, 307
McCarty, Elvira, 5, 14, 26, 28, 295
McCarty, John Pardoe, 31
McCarty, Silas, 40
McClellan, General, 4, 32, 34, 35, 49, 50, 52, 55, 75, 99, 242
McDowell, General, 4, 25, 32, 42, 75
McLain, General John H., xiii, 296,

Meade, General George G., 4, 75, 108, 128, 198, 222, 288
Milford, 191
Millview, Village of, 61
Mine Run Operation, 187
Molyneux, David, 138, 140, 176, 236, 248, 268, 312
Molyneux, Dr. Evan, 306
Molyneux, Edward, 4
Molyneux, Eliza, 21
Molyneux, Jennie, 111
Molyneux, Martha, 20, 78, 83, 89, 90, 118, 127, 131
Molyneux, Rebecca (nee Bird), 4, 77
Molyneux, Samuel, 3, 21, 26, 27, 31, 32, 34, 43, 65, 71, 78, 79, 96, 98, 102, 104, 110, 112, 115, 122, 127, 143, 144, 203, 250, 273, 297, 298, 306, 308
Molyneux, William, 4
Monocacy River, 22, 106
Mosby, John, 14, 226, 283
Mott, General Gershom, 201, 212, 225, 259, 277, 280
Mt. Heaths, 289

—N—

National Emergency Training Center, Emmitsburg, 111
New Store, 278
Noble, Captain, 187
Norfolk and Petersburg RR, 220, 226
North Anna River, 3, 184
Northregg, General, 4
Norton, Ester, 65
Norton, Hannah, 59, 73, 125
Norton, Kate, 261
Norton, Will, 181

—O—

Olmstead, Frederick Law, 149
Orange and Alexandria RR, 135, 289

—P—

Pardoe, George, 31, 38, 42, 51, 54, 63, 68, 77, 83, 85, 92, 98, 106, 108, 113, 118, 124, 128, 129, 132, 138, 139, 147, 159, 163, 169, 193, 204, 205, 206, 216, 232, 254, 259, 261, 263, 270, 273, 292
Pardoe, James, 31, 37, 46, 51, 54, 91, 115, 118, 121, 126, 152, 159, 193, 236, 251, 268
Pardoe, Thomas, 42, 132, 238
Parmunky, 192
Pemberton, General John C., 101
Penn, William, 169
persimmons, 38
Peters, Colonel William, 211
Petersburg, 1, 3, 33, 34, 194, 197, 198, 199, 200, 201, 202, 204, 205, 207, 208, 209, 210, 211, 212, 213, 214, 215, 216, 218, 219, 220, 221, 222, 225, 226, 228, 229, 230, 232, 234, 235, 236, 237, 238, 240, 241, 243, 244, 247, 250, 251, 253, 256, 264, 266, 275, 276, 279, 319, 320
Petersburg and Norfolk RR, 222
Petersburg Campaign, 197
Pets in the Civil War, 315
Pleasant Hill, 192
Point of Rocks, 106, 210, 211, 257, 258
Pope, General John, 4, 30, 75
Poplar Grove Church, 252, 253
Porter, Admiral, 275
Porter, General, 52
Potomac Creek Station, 103
Pratt, A. D., 130
Priestley, Joseph, 4

—R—

Randall, Dr., 160, 173, 199, 209, 227, 267, 271, 282, 297
Rapidan River, 22, 119, 123, 145, 162, 163, 166, 184
Rappahannock River, 3, 51, 139, 146, 284
Rappahannock Station, 187
Richmond, 3, 36, 40, 42, 63, 81, 98, 154, 186, 191, 193, 194, 197, 200, 201, 205, 232, 260, 276, 279, 280, 286, 287, 288, 290, 291
Robison, General, 44
Rogers, Isaac, 178, 179, 219
Rogers, Will, 21, 29, 32, 37, 44, 46, 49, 51, 69, 87, 105, 118, 134, 136, 155, 157, 162, 167, 168, 193
Rosecrans, General William S., 131

—S—

Sallie (dog), 316
Sallie (sister), 139, 189
Sanitary Commission, 149
Sedgwick, General John, 185, 187
Seetin, Calvin, 308
Seymour, General Truman, 187
Sharpsburg Pike, 111
Sheridan, General, 4
Sherman, General William T., 4, 8, 252, 284
Siberian crabs, 38
Sickles, General Dan, 4, 90, 135
Sister Abel, 56, 65, 146
Smith, General Edmund Kirby, 293
Snell, Charles, 42, 46
Snell, Eliza, 21, 80, 216, 235, 259, 267, 273
Snell, William, 193, 204, 263, 268, 269
Snickers Gap, 106
Sniffin, Reverend B. D. G.S., 20, 61, 62, 88, 129, 300
South Side RR, 164, 234, 276
Spotsylvania, Battle of, 186, 187, 231
Spotsylvania Court House, 3, 19, 45, 184, 187, 188, 189
Springfield rifle, 224
St. Joseph's Academy, 108, 111
Stafford Courthouse, 86
Stahl, Dent, 256
Stephe (former slave), 74, 139, 145, 299, 303
Strong, George Templeton, 149

Stuart, General JEB, 4, 7, 14, 82, 93, 186, 187
Sugar Loaf Mountain, 106
Summers, Angie (cousin), 20, 37, 68, 72, 83, 88, 98, 124, 127, 133, 139
Summers, John N. (cousin), 2, 93, 126, 141, 148, 166, 169, 173, 282
Susquehanna River, 152
Sussex C. H, 8, 255

—T—

Taylor, General Richard, 4, 81, 111, 288
Taylor, Miss, 64
Tents in the Civil War, 17, 20, 29, 32, 181, 316, 317
Thomas, General George Henry, 117, 247, 255, 282, 315
Tirncrook, Kate, 111
Todds Tavern, 184
Tomkins, Carol Bird, 306
Tomlinson, Esther, 130
Tompkins, Sally, 314
Travis, Warren, 78, 86

—U—

Uncle Joel, 24, 252
U.S.S. *Kearsage*, 206

—V—

Vallandigham, Congressman, 96
Va. Central RR, 172, 193
Vice President Stephens, 264
Vough, Abram, 93
Vough, Anna, 78, 133, 164

—W—

Warburton, James, 217
Warburton, Thomas, 217
Ward, Gilbert, 298
Warren, General, 4, 34, 78, 96, 99
Warren, General Gouverneur, 235
Warren Station, 262

Warrenton, 105, 118, 119, 123, 134, 138, 260
Washington, President George, 10, 47
Watkins, Lieutenant Colonel Guy H., 99, 197, 198, 318, 319
Webster, C., 84
Weldon RR, 220, 221, 225, 226, 234
Wells, Aunt Ellie, 7
Wellsville, 7, 300, 302
Whipple, General Amiel Weeks, 95
White Sulphur Springs (in Virginia), 3, 118, 120, 121, 124, 128
Wilderness, Battles of the, 184, 187
Wind Mill Pond, 198
Women in the Civil War, 314
Wood, Governor, 122
Woodhead, Louise Molyneux, 308
Wright, Dr. Kenneth, 301

—Y—

Yellow House, 234